RESERVATIONS, REMOVAL, AND REFORM

RESERVATIONS REMOVAL AND REFORM

The Mission Indian Agents of Southern California 1878–1903

VALERIE SHERER MATHES and PHIL BRIGANDI

UNIVERSITY OF OKLAHOMA PRESS : NORMAN

Also by Valerie Sherer Mathes and Phil Brigandi
A Call for Reform: The Southern California Indian Writings of Helen Hunt Jackson (Norman, Okla., 2015)

Also by Valerie Sherer Mathes
Helen Hunt Jackson and Her Indian Reform Legacy (Norman, Okla., 2015)
(ed.) *The Indian Reform Letters of Helen Hunt Jackson, 1879–1885* (Norman, Okla, 1998)

Publication of this book is made possible through the generosity of Edith Kinney Gaylord.

Library of Congress Cataloging-in-Publication Data

Names: Mathes, Valerie Sherer, 1941– author. | Brigandi, Phil, 1959– author.
Title: Reservations, removal, and reform : the mission Indian agents of southern California, 1878–1903 / Valerie Sherer Mathes and Phil Brigandi.
Description: Norman : University of Oklahoma Press [2018] | Includes bibliographical references and index.
Identifiers: LCCN 2017050784 | ISBN 978-0-8061-5999-7 (hardcover : alk. paper)
Subjects: LCSH: Indian agents—California, Southern—History—19th century. | Indians of North America—California, Southern—Government relations—1869–1934. | Indians of North America—California, Southern—Social conditions—19th century.
Classification: LCC E78.C15 M38 2018 | DDC 323.11970794/9—dc23
LC record available at https://lccn.loc.gov/2017050784

The paper in this book meets the guidelines for permanence and durability of the Committee on Production Guidelines for Book Longevity of the Council on Library Resources, Inc. ∞

1 2 3 4 5 6 7 8 9 10

CONTENTS

▼ ▼ ▼

ILLUSTRATIONS

Figures

Map

Table

PREFACE

This study grew out of our interest in the history of the American Indians of Southern California and early efforts to help them retain their homes and their livelihood. The story is complicated, influenced by many factors and individuals, both Indian and non-Indian. Often overlooked in other studies has been the role played by government Indian agents appointed to investigate, assist, and protect the Indians and their interests. While policy was set in Washington, the attitudes and actions of these agents had a significant influence on how those policies played out in California.

Rather than write a detailed study of a single village or tribe, we have chosen the Mission Indian agents as a lens with which to view a broader selection of the various issues and events all too common in Southern California in the second half of the nineteenth century. Land tenure, water rights, education, law enforcement, health care, and other issues enter into the story. Along the way we also met prominent tribal leaders, Indian rights advocates, Mexican settlers, and American pioneers, both sympathetic and self-serving; their stories embellish the history of these Mission agents, who remain the central focus.[1]

We begin with an overview of the ten government officials who served Southern California from 1850 to 1877. Most were special agents, appointed to investigate the condition of the Mission Indians. These officials repeatedly recommended the establishment of reservations and the appointment of a regular government agent. The first two reservations were established in 1870, but both were quickly cancelled. More new reservations were established in 1876–77. Not until 1878 was the Mission Indian Agency permanently established, headquartered in San Bernardino and later in nearby Colton. In August 1887 it became the Mission-Tule River Consolidated Agency with the addition of Tule River and Yuma Reservations and a single village near Santa Ynez in Santa Barbara County. The Hoopa and Klamath reservations in Northern California were also briefly attached to the agency. In 1895 agency offices were moved from Colton to San Jacinto, where they remained until 1903, when the agency was dissolved and control of the reservations was divided between officials stationed on various reservations.

At its peak, the Mission-Tule River Consolidated Agency spread over the entire length and breadth of California. As such, it presented both a contrast to the centralized government reservation typical in other parts of the country and a special challenge to federal policy-makers and California agents. This study focuses on San Diego and Riverside counties, where the greatest concentration of Mission Indian reservations was located.

After examining the special agents, this book follows the tenures of the seven regular agents, with each chapter devoted to a single agent. The chapters vary in length, depending on the agent's length of service and the events of the time. Some stories, such as that of securing the Morongo Reservation, stretch through the terms of several agents. In other instances, such as the Warner Ranch Removal, our attention focuses on one example of a type of event that took place repeatedly.

The Mission Indian agents were a mixed lot. Some were dedicated, some mere placeholders, and a few border on being scoundrels. Samuel S. Lawson (1878–1883) was zealous in his efforts to assist the Indians. John G. McCallum (1883–1885) and Horatio N. Rust (1889–1893) found ways to personally profit from their service. John S. Ward (1885–1887) believed the Indians had to be forced to change their ways, while Joseph W. Preston (1887–1889) used force against white usurpers, albeit reluctantly. Francisco Estudillo (1893–1897) found that sympathy for the Indians was not enough, while Lucius A. Wright (1897–1903) saw his best efforts thwarted by some of the same problems the Indians had faced for generations. All of these men were political appointees, beneficiaries of a "spoils" system and beholden to the elected officials who appointed them. In every case their reports and official correspondence provide valuable first-hand information about the life and status of Southern California's Native people.

In the past, the Mission Indian agents have been studied only in a piecemeal fashion. Only one, John McCallum, has received a full-length biography (more a hagiography, if truth be told), and two others have been the subject of journal articles.[2] Others are mentioned now and then as part of a larger story, but little effort has been made to compare and contrast their tenures. We have relied primarily on their own reports and correspondence, and when appropriate we quote them to convey their beliefs, sentiments, attitudes, and expressions of failure and accomplishment. Our intent is not to condemn or praise them but to present their stories in a fair manner. Their writings are balanced by other contemporary sources, including newspapers and court records, and the work of modern scholars. Especially useful were George Harwood Phillips, *Chiefs and Challengers: Indian Resistance and Cooperation in Southern California, 1769–1906* (2014), and Richard L. Carrico, *Strangers in a Stolen Land: Indians of San Diego County from Prehistory to the New Deal* (2008), which cover much of the same ground but from a different perspective.

Along the way we have received help and encouragement from many other scholars and scholarly institutions. George Phillips, Albert Hurtado, Brian Dillon, Bob Chandler, and an anonymous reviewer all read and commented on earlier versions of this manuscript. The agency records in the National Archives (both in Southern California and in Washington, D.C.) have been invaluable, as were the collections of the San Diego Historical Society, the Honnold Library at the Claremont Colleges, the Seaver Center at the Los Angeles County Museum of Natural History, the Southwest Museum's Braun Library (now part of the Autry National Center), the Bancroft Library, the Huntington Library, and other intuitions. Annual reports of the Women's National Indian Association, the Indian Rights Association, and the Lake Mohonk Conference of the Friends of the Indian have provided additional material.

Our goal is simply to present a summary of the careers of the men who served as Mission Indian agents, both special and regular, set against the events of the times. In the end, we hope this book will provide some new insights into the problems the Southern California Indians faced and a better understanding of the efforts made to help them (or too often, hinder them) in their struggles to survive.

RESERVATIONS, REMOVAL, AND REFORM

Map by G. W. Ward. Copyright © 2018, University of Oklahoma Press.

CHAPTER 1

▼ ▼ ▼

SUPERINTENDENTS AND SPECIAL AGENTS, 1850–1877

> In accordance with instructions received, I have visited those portions of California in which these Indians live; have observed their present mode of life as compared with the past; have investigated carefully conflicts which have arisen between them and the whites respecting settlements on the public lands, and on private land-grants; . . . have consulted white citizens whose contact in life with these Indians renders their experience valuable in attempting to devise plans for the benefit of the Indians, as well as also of the whites, . . . and have, I trust, devised some plans by which, if approved and carried into effect, both the Indian and the white communities will be materially advanced, morally and physically, in their several and relative conditions.
>
> —*Charles A. Wetmore, Report (1875)*

Beginning in the 1850s a steady stream of government special agents visited Southern California, all trying to answer the same question—what should be done about the Mission Indians? Charles A. Wetmore was one of the last, and like his predecessors he found mostly farmers and laborers, many living in adobe houses, and often practicing Catholics—a legacy of Franciscan missionary work dating back more than a century. Yet these peaceful people lived in fear. Their population was in decline, and their lands were continually subjected to encroachment by unscrupulous white settlers. What they needed, Wetmore and the other special agents reported back to Washington, were reservations to secure their homes and a regular government agent to look after their needs.[1]

This chapter provides a brief overview of these early special agents—their tours of inspection, their interaction with various Indian leaders, and their recommendations, which ultimately led to the creation of the Mission Indian Agency and a reservation system for Southern California. It was a long, slow process, in part because the federal government's attention was often focused on more warlike tribes in the Southwest and on the Plains.

California passed from Mexican to American control with the signing of the Treaty of Guadalupe Hidalgo in 1848, ending the Mexican-American War and marking a change in status for the region's Indians. While the Spanish and Mexican governments had viewed them as citizens, recognizing at least a possessory right to their lands, the new American government would deny them citizenship for generations, with little regard for their land rights. "[T]he location of an Indian family or families on land upon which a white man desires to settle is, in law, no more a bar to such settlement than would be the presence of a stray sheep or cow," the register of the General Land Office in Los Angeles told one special agent in 1873.[2]

In Northern California meanwhile, gold had been discovered within weeks of the treaty's signing, dramatically changing the lives of the Indians in Northern California. Gold seekers rushed in from around the world, many of whom viewed local natives as simply an impediment to their search for wealth. "Extermination was embraced as one sure way of eliminating those obstacles," whether in a mineral or agricultural context, writes historian James Rawls. Indian lands were overrun, crops trampled, scarce water supplies diverted, and occupants driven from their homes. As the Indian population plummeted due to disease, armed attacks, and starvation, the white population soared.[3]

Southern California's Indians were spared much of this horror. Those who lived along the major overland trails served as guides to help miners cross the Colorado River, or sold foodstuffs, or even took in laundry. Some of the forty-niners, however, took what they wanted by force and allowed their livestock to break down Indian fences and overrun their cultivated fields. Their diaries are often full of negative comments about the "wild" Indians they met on the desert, although they tended to be kinder toward the villagers who had adopted a more European-style way of life, commenting on their adobe homes, farming activities, and civilized dress.

While these Mission Indians (as they came to be called) were stripped of the few legal rights they had enjoyed under Mexican rule, they were still sometimes expected to meet the responsibilities of the citizenship they were denied, including payment of property taxes. Indian stock was often forcibly taken in lieu of payment, an issue that led to open revolt in San Diego County in late 1851, when Cupeño leader Antonio Garra attempted to unite several tribes to drive out the interlopers. American soldiers and volunteer militiamen marched against the insurgents, and tribal leaders turned on one another to settle old scores or curry favor with their new American rulers. The Garra Uprising was brief and unsuccessful but left a lingering fear among the new settlers that lasted decades.[4]

By 1852 three federal commissioners were already negotiating eighteen treaties with 139 Indian tribes and villages up and down the state. Even before Antonio Garra was executed by a military firing squad, one of the commissioners had met with nearly fifty Southern California tribal leaders at Temecula and Santa Ysabel, where they signed treaties of "Peace and Friendship" recognizing federal authority. Among those who "made their mark" on these treaties were some of the most prominent tribal leaders of the day, including Cahuilla leaders Juan Antonio, who had captured Garra and turned him over to the Americans, "Old" Chief Cabezon from the Coachella Valley, and Juan Bautista from the Cahuilla Valley. Victoriano, the longtime leader at Soboba, signed, as did José Panto of San Pasqual. Other Luiseño leaders came from Pala, Pauma, La Jolla, and Aguanga, as did Kumeyaay headmen from Santa Ysabel, San Dieguito, Sycuan, Jacumba, San Felipe, and even as far away as Vallecito, on the desert.[5]

All eighteen treaties were similar. Indian groups agreed to live on reservations (some 7,488,000 acres' worth), to refrain from fighting with other tribes and local whites in return for food, tools, and livestock, and to accept instruction from teachers, farmers, and carpenters in the ways of the dominant white society. Like federal treaties with eastern tribes, these treaties divested the Indians of much of their land and attempted to convert them into productive, self-sufficient farmers under government control.

American settlers and the California congressional delegation opposed the creation of reservations, claiming they gave away half of the state's mineral and agricultural lands, although in fact, especially in Southern California, the lands were mostly barren and sterile, unfit for farming. Governor John McDougal, who viewed the Indians as a "source of much annoyance," even recommended their relocation out of state, reminiscent of the relocation of eastern tribes to lands west of the Mississippi. Following the lead of the state's congressional delegation, the U.S. Senate in June 1852 rejected the treaties. Because of their potential value as a labor force, however, the Indians were allowed to remain in California.[6]

To regulate Indian affairs, Congress in March 1852 created the California Superintendency, headquartered in San Francisco. Naval Lieutenant Edward E. Beale was appointed as superintendent. Unlike the federal commissioners, who had proposed setting aside several million acres by formal treaties, Beale, inspired by the Franciscan mission system, proposed instead a handful of modest, temporary "military or government" reservations of about seventy-five thousand acres each, protected by a series of military posts. The Indians were invited to settle on these reservations but would not receive title to the land. Indian agents would take over the former role of the *padres* and teach agricultural and mechanical arts, with the end goal of making the Indians self-sustaining.[7] Beale's "enthusiasm for the mission system may have been influenced by the views of Benjamin D. Wilson, his subagent for Indian affairs in southern California."[8]

Benjamin D. Wilson

A native of Tennessee, Benjamin D. Wilson (1811–1878) came to California in 1841 and married Ramona Yorba, the daughter of a prominent *Californio* family.[9] He soon joined the ranks of the California *rancheros,* serving as mayor of Los Angeles before his appointment in September 1852 as Indian subagent for Santa Barbara, Los Angeles, and San Diego counties under Superintendent Beale. Wilson was always proud of his efforts on behalf of the Indians, including distributing food, clothing, and farming tools, but he is best remembered for his 1852 government report on the status of Southern California's Native peoples—a report largely ghost-written by Judge Benjamin Hayes, a longtime advocate for the local Indians.[10]

At Wilson's recommendation, Beale appointed Cave J. Couts Sr. as subagent for San Diego County in 1853. Couts had come to California as a soldier in 1848 from his native Tennessee. Like Wilson, Couts married into a prominent Californio family, and he and his family lived at Rancho Guajome, only a few miles from what had been Mission San Luis Rey. Though charged with protecting the Indians, Couts was more often accused of mistreating and even killing both Indians and Mexicans. He resigned his position as subagent in 1856.[11]

Other subagents were appointed to keep an eye on Indian affairs in San Diego County in the 1850s, including W. W. Harvey, rancher John Rains, who had connections at both Temecula and Warner's Ranch, and even Jonathan Trumbull Warner, one of the first American settlers in Southern California, whose San Diego County ranch was a central point in much of the Indian history of the area. As George Phillips notes, these "civilian subagents also implemented their own Indian policy. Appointed with no salary and little oversight, they sometimes engaged in extralegal, if not unethical activities." He describes Couts as one of the most controversial.[12]

For the next several years government officials only occasionally visited the Mission Indians. In 1856 Capt. H. S. Burton, the U.S. Army commander at San

Diego, met at Temecula with Juan Antonio, who complained that settlers were already moving onto lands promised them by the 1852 treaties. "We wish the superintendent of Indians to visit us," Antonio informed Burton, "so he can see how we are living; we wish to tell him our wants. Why does he not come to see us as he does the Indians of the Tulare and the north? We want attention as much as they do."[13] Antonio's request went unheeded. As the demands of the Civil War and later Reconstruction dominated the attention of the government, California Indian affairs received even less attention, and in 1873, the California Superintendency system was abolished.[14]

John Quincy Adams Stanley

The condition of the Mission Indians continued to deteriorate as more settlers entered the state. Subagents and special agents were periodically appointed to visit their villages and advise the government on their condition. Because few California superintendents spent much time in Southern California, in the spring of 1865 several prominent citizens of Los Angeles County sent a petition to California Superintendent Austin Wiley, recommending that John Quincy Adams Stanley be appointed a special agent for the south. Stanley, a resident of the county since 1852, was politically active and generally well liked. Like Wilson and Judge Hayes, Stanley had an interest in Southern California's Native peoples, and like many Indians, he spoke Spanish.[15]

In his March 1865 report, Stanley urged that the Mission Indians receive "protection from a vagabond and desperate set of white men and Mexicans, who go among them to sell whisky, and induce them to steal and rob for their benefit." Of more immediate concern, however, was the Indians' inability to feed themselves because of the drought of 1863 and 1864. Stanley strongly recommended that seeds be purchased and he even offered to distribute them, requesting only his expenses. Fortunately, in addition to twenty pounds of melon seeds, thirty pounds of pumpkin seeds, and three thousand pounds of corn and bean seeds, Superintendent Wiley also authorized the purchase of ploughs, harnesses, and hoes.[16]

Aided by Special Agent W. E. Lovett,[17] Stanley handed out a portion of the supplies on April 28 to some fifty Indians at Temecula to enable them to begin planting. Lovett, who praised his companion for the diligence and patience he exhibited as distributing agent, sent out runners with written orders to all the neighboring *rancherias* (villages) to assemble on May 4 at Temecula for a meeting and a wider distribution of seeds and agricultural implements. Temecula, Stanley explained in his report, was a principal Indian village, which little more than a decade earlier, under the watchful eye of Luiseño leader Pablo Apis, had been in "flourishing condition," cultivating a large tract of land and producing a surplus of wheat, corn, and beans. Apis himself had a personal land grant of some half a league.[18] Since his death around 1853, unscrupulous whites had moved in, distributing whiskey, assaulting Indian women and luring them into prostitution, and forcing many Indian people into a virtual servitude. Without Pablo Apis's wise counsel, some of his heirs had already begun to mortgage their interest in his rancho. Now the Indians at Temecula were idle, neglecting their vineyards and peach and pear orchards, and letting their adobe homes fall into disrepair. The young had moved away to find work on neighboring ranches or in Los Angeles and San Bernardino, leaving behind only the elderly. What these people needed, concluded Stanley, was "a faithful and conscientious agent, who has the will and the power to protect them from the encroachments of the whites."[19]

Stanley and Lovett then traveled to Warner's Ranch to visit the Cupeño village of Agua Caliente, or Warner Hot Springs, the best known of the five Indian villages on the forty-four-thousand-acre ranch granted to Jonathan Trumbull Warner by the Mexican government in 1844. (A Connecticut Yankee, Warner Hispanicized his name as Juan José (J. J.) Warner upon receiving Mexican citizenship.) At Agua Caliente, Stanley found the remnants of an extensive village, with the ruins of several large adobe homes as well as "a vineyard of perhaps a thousand grapevines, quite a number of pear and peach trees and other evidences that a large number of Indians had formerly occupied the place." Returning to Temecula, on May 1 Stanley rode over the mountains some ten miles down to the old mission outpost of San Antonio de Pala to visit with Manuelito Cota, who had been appointed "chief" of the Luiseño by Cave Couts in 1853.[20]

Cota was a controversial figure, whose government-appointed leadership was not always accepted by local villagers. The illegitimate son of a Spanish soldier and an Indian girl from Mission San Luis Rey, he cooperated with the Americans but was never fully accepted by any side.[21] In 1846 he was accused of complicity in the Pauma Massacre—the murder of a group of Mexican soldiers who were staying at the Rancho Pauma after their battle with American forces at San Pasqual.[22] For much of the mid-nineteenth century he lived at Agua Tibia, above Pala. Stanley described him as "always truly faithful to the government," a temperate man who opposed liquor, and "an efficient and energetic administrator of the law," who had, however, become unpopular after one of the agents refused to sanction some of his decisions. Cota then resigned, moved to a thirty-acre parcel two miles from the Pala chapel, and was currently acting as a private individual.[23]

California Superintendent Charles Maltby, who accompanied Stanley on a later visit to Pala, believed much of the opposition to Cota was due to his anti-liquor stance and his efforts to stop the sale of Indian women into prostitution.[24]

Stanley then returned to Temecula for what was to be the first "major multi-tribal conference with federal officials in the region" for more than a decade.[25] Held on May 4 at Temecula, the gathering gave Stanley and Lovett not only the opportunity to distribute planting seeds and beef cattle, but time to listen to grievances and make an accurate count of the seventeen rancherias in attendance. Lovett's report on the gathering was critical of the treatment of the Mission Indians at the hands of whites, whom he described as vagabonds, often cohabiting with Indian women and fond of liquor. He praised the work of the Franciscan missionaries, noting that "under the mission system the Indians were far better cared for, and were much happier, more industrious, and less vicious than at present." He recalled that some fourteen hundred Indians attended, including "all of the San Luisena [*sic*], together with most of the Santa Ysabel and the San Diego Indians," and one hundred Cahuillas under Manuel Largo, who controlled most of the Mountain Cahuilla villages.[26]

In early 1867 Stanley made several visits to Southern California villages, continuing to distribute goods and tools. He visited a dozen Cahuilla captains (village leaders) at Palm Springs, where he also met with a representative of the Chemehuevi people from further out on the desert. In his reports to B. C. Whiting, then head of the California Superintendency, he continued to stress the need for a Mission Indian reservation and urged that a special travelling agent be appointed to visit all the principal villages to "direct and instruct the Indians in their labors, and prevent, as far as possible, intoxicating drinks being sold to them." Whiting in turn wrote Indian Commissioner Nathaniel Green Taylor in Washington, suggesting that Pala and the San Pasqual Valley to the south would make a viable home for all of the Mission Indians, as well as the Cahuillas in the San Jacinto Mountains.[27]

Augustus P. Greene

Although a reservation for the Mission Indians was not yet forthcoming, the Indians did benefit from a new federal Indian policy, inaugurated during the administration of Ulysses S. Grant. Called the Peace Policy, it included an ill-conceived attempt to improve the quality of Indian agents by assigning some agencies to various Protestant churches. For other agencies, the president appointed army officers because he believed "they furnished a corps of public servants whose integrity and faithfulness could be relied upon." A year later Congress would prohibit officers from accepting civil appointments, but for that short time period, First Lieutenant Augustus P. Greene, formerly of the Fourth Regiment U.S. Artillery, was appointed a special agent in Southern California, replacing Stanley in October 1869.[28]

Greene assumed his official duties on December 7. From available sources, he estimated that he was responsible for almost four thousand Indians, half of whom were Mission Indians. The remaining eighteen hundred were Cahuillas—six hundred, he said, living under the command of Manuel Largo; the rest, whom he described as "mostly pagan," lived in the Coachella Valley on the desert and answered to "Old" Chief Cabezon. Two days after relieving Stanley, Greene hired a driver and, accompanied by Stanley as interpreter, set out on the ninety-mile drive to Temecula to confer with the approximately 150 San Luis Rey Indians living there. He described them to Indian Commissioner Ely Samuel Parker as "Christians in their religious belief," following "the customs, dress, and habits of the whites," with fenced, cultivated fields and considerable livestock. He concluded they "would do well were it not for the whites and Mexicans, who degrade them and their women."[29]

Poor road conditions forced Greene and his party to travel by horseback the ten miles to Pala, where they found some one hundred residents and about one thousand acres that could easily be cultivated. Greene was most impressed with Manuelito Cota, whom he called the "head chief of all the Mission and Coahuila [Cahuilla] Indians." During the visit, Cota informed Greene that Pala could easily accommodate all of the San Luis Rey Indians; however, if the government preferred San Pasqual as a possible reservation site, "he would do all in his power to carry out the wishes of the government." Duly impressed, Greene hired him to accompany them on to the San Pasqual Valley, about twenty-five miles distant, where some 150 Indians lived in an old, established village now being crowded out by a growing number of white settlers. Here, Greene noted some two thousand acres of potentially valuable agricultural land.[30]

Describing the Indian's condition as "continually growing worse" and in desperate need of a government reservation where "they could live in peace and enjoy the benefits of their labor," Greene recommended that both San Pasqual and Pala be set aside and that white settlers there be required to vacate their homes without compensation for improvements. If the government intended to create a reservation for the Cahuillas, then he recommended the purchase of the Rancho Rincon del Diablo (near modern-day Escondido), which he and his party had visited on December 13.[31]

Finally, after nearly two decades of recommendations for a reservation, government officials acted. On January 27, 1870, Secretary of the Interior Jacob D. Cox submitted Greene's report to President Grant, along with supporting letters from Bvt. Maj. General John B. McIntosh, superintendent of Indian Affairs for California, and Joseph S. Wilson, commissioner of the General Land Office, requesting that all the public land in both the San Pasqual and Pala Valleys be set aside as reservations. On January 31, 1870, President Grant established the first two executive order reservations in Southern California, covering some 138,000 acres in San Diego County, one at Pala for the Luiseños and the other at San Pasqual for the Kumeyaays. Though physically separate, they were considered one single reservation by the government.[32]

In early January 1870, Greene moved his agency office from Los Angeles to Temecula, a more suitable location "for intercourse with and oversight of the Indians" under his charge. However, with the creation of the two executive order reservations at Pala and San Pasqual, he moved the office again on April 2, 1870, to San Pasqual, to better serve the 195 Kumeyaay Indians who lived in the San Pasqual rancheria, which occupied less than a quarter-section of the reservation.[33]

More than one hundred white squatters lived in the valley. Although they did not legally own their farms and homes, they immediately protested the establishment of the San Pasqual Reservation. They hired San Diego attorney Charles P. Taggart, until recently part owner of the influential *San Diego Union,* to begin the process of having Grant's executive order set aside. The squatters found supporters among a broad group of people, including the current editors of the *Union,* who Greene complained were "publishing some most wonderful curiosities in the way of newspaper incendiary literature," calculated "to throw oil on the trouble waters." According to Greene, none of these people had "the true interests of the Indian at heart." The situation for the 137 residents at Pala was less tense, for there were fewer white settlers in the vicinity.[34]

In a follow-up report, Greene explained why so many whites were living on the San Pasqual Reservation. These intruders, upon learning in 1867 and 1868 of the recommendation to establish the reservation at San Pasqual, had rushed to the valley, intending "to trade and sell liquor to Indians, others expecting to be bought off by the Government, and but very few, if any, to make permanent homes." The situation at Pala differed because of its isolation from the main routes of travel and because it was governed by Manuelito Cota, described by Greene as an "excellent" leader, giving "good counsel."[35]

Although he protected the Mission Indians, as was his duty, Greene at times agreed with the settlers that the Indians were "retarding the settlement of that portion of the state, inasmuch as they are in possession of public lands which they do not and will not cultivate to any reasonable extent." He recommended that the government either force them to locate on the designated reservation lands or make full citizens of them, letting them take "their chances in the race of life along with the white, and black races of the country."[36]

In January 1871, curious to see if other Indians had decided to move to the reservation, Greene made an extensive two-week inspection tour to various villages within his agency, reporting that their "feelings in reference" to relocating had "improved but very slightly." He was more concerned that they would go hungry because they had planted so little. At least at San Pasqual, he found the Indians had opened their irrigation ditches, anticipating the annual spring flowing of the San Bernardo River. If starvation became a reality, Greene feared the Indians would resort to killing stray cattle, bringing on a conflict with white ranchers—a situation that would end badly for the Indians.[37]

Greene's tour had revealed considerable population decline. At the Pauma village, located on the Rancho Pauma, a former Mexican land grant upstream from Pala, he counted only 67 residents, down from a total of 106 in 1865. At Temecula, on the Pauba ranch, he counted 237 residents, down from 525 in 1860. At Santa Ysabel, the last rancheria he visited, he found only 146 residents living on the rancho of the same name, owned by Capt. A. H. Wilcox of San Diego, who for years had squabbled with the Indians over ownership of the valley. Greene described the Kumeyaay residents as poor, "fearfully demoralized," and subsisting on acorns—which actually had been their staple food for centuries.[38]

In addition to undertaking investigative tours, Greene also dealt with rising tensions along the upper San Luis Rey River, where the agents' longtime practice of appointing specific Indians as tribal leaders had led to the emergence of rival factions. One of the more serious issues dividing the factions was the new reservation, which Manuelito Cota had supported. Tired of having Cota's will imposed on them, in July 1870 leaders of a dozen Luiseño villages had elected Manuel Olegario of Rincon as their new chief, even traveling to San Diego to seek certification of his election from local officials, including the county judge. Even though Olegario was duly elected by local captains, government Indian agents refused to recognize his authority.[39]

Olegario, who spoke both Spanish and some English and had been employed as an agricultural worker in Los Angeles, was a hereditary Luiseño tribal leader with broad support among the various villages. His rival, Cota, was not without his backers, both Indian and white. Olegario, in fact, complained that Cota was "the tool of certain large ranchers, who want to get possession of our lands."[40] As tensions between the two rival leaders increased, opposition to Cota at times turned violent. Greene reported that Cota was "virtually a prisoner" in his home at Agua Tibia, actually fearing that his life was "in danger from the party acknowledging Olegario as their chief."[41] One of Cota's relatives, Margarita Trujillo, owner of the nearby Rancho Cuca, was actually captured by some of Olegario's supporters, hanged by her wrists, and left to die, before being rescued by tribal elders.[42]

Both reservations were doomed from the beginning, not only because of white opposition but also because most of the Indians and all of the Indian leaders except Cota were dubious about giving up their homes for an uncertain reservation life. If the plan were to fail, they would have no place to return to. After barely a year, on February 17, 1871, just days before Greene submitted his final report, President Grant, at Indian Commissioner Parker's recommendation, revoked his own executive order, returning the land at San Pasqual and Pala to the public domain.[43] Just days later, the original Mission Indian Agency was abolished.

In the fall of 1871, as the rivalry between Olegario and Cota continued to fester,[44] frightening rumors began to appear in the press. The *Daily Alta California* had received numerous telegrams claiming that the Luiseño and Cahuilla Indians were combining to wage war on local whites. Older residents still vividly remembered the earlier Garra uprising, while newer residents had grown up on stories of Indian atrocities from across the nation. In a rare visit to Southern California, State Superintendent Whiting met with both sides of the rivalry at Pala in September 1871. At Olegario's request, J. J. Warner served as one of the interpreters. Christopher N. Wilson, a Los Angeles attorney, and Cave Couts, the former subagent, were also present. During the council Whiting suggested to Olegario that if he would "bury the past" and support Cota, he would be appointed Cota's second in command. Later Warner wrote that Whiting's proposal was "a most strange" one, since the superintendent "had so often repeated the declaration that they were in his opinion both bad men and not fit to be placed over the Indians." However, Warner concluded that he "had seen so many strange things at this meeting that [he] was not astonished at this."[45] Given only fifteen minutes to consider the proposal, Olegario and his followers refused. Whiting then asked Cota to resign and appointed one José Antonio Sal in his place as "Chief of all the Mission Indians in San Diego County." Whiting also recognized Manuel Largo's control over the Mountain Cahuillas.[46]

John G. Ames

The twin reservations had fallen apart, tensions between rival native leaders had the white public on edge, white usurpers continued gobbling up the Indians' land, and the government was still without a cohesive plan for its Indian "wards." The Indian Office's solution was to send yet another special agent, Rev. John G. Ames. Appointed on May 6, 1873, he was ordered to visit Southern California, investigate the condition of the Indians there, and make some specific recommendations to improve their condition.[47]

Detained from beginning his tour by a family illness, Ames set up his headquarters in Los Angeles on June 1, taking advantage of this delay to meet local citizens, confer with federal land office officials, and hold several Indian conferences. On June 12 he met with several Luiseños who were living in Los Angeles. Ten days later he conferred with Manuel Olegario, whom he described as the "actual chief of the majority of the San Luis Rey tribe, though not recognized as such by the late superintendent of Indian Affairs." Olegario, accompanied by ten of his captains, had traveled from Rincon to complain about being driven from lands "held in immemorial possession," requesting that the government "secure them in the possession of the lands now occupied by them." They also demanded the right to elect their own leaders—a reference to Cota's rule being forced upon them. Time had not lessened the rivalry between the two leaders.[48]

Ames began his investigative tour on July 7, 1873, accompanied by Luther E. Sleigh, recently appointed as government clerk by the Indian Office, and an interpreter. When Ames was taken ill, Sleigh went on ahead, the two agreeing to meet at Pala. Sleigh first conferred with José Panto, the longtime Kumeyaay captain at San Pasqual, who had summoned his people for a conference.[49] Those who gathered complained of continual land encroachment and of the failure of local ranchers to pay them for work done. In addition, they stated that when they made any land improvements, such as planting fruit trees or grape vines, whites simply came in and took over the land. However, when Sleigh inquired if they would like to move to a more protected area, they responded: "Our fathers lived and died here, and we would rather live here than at any other place." At the Santa Ysabel rancheria, Sleigh found the Indians busy reaping, thrashing, and grinding their grain. Conferring with Augustine, the village captain, Sleigh learned that their situation was different from that at San Pasqual. So far the Santa Ysabel ranch owners had not tried to eject them.[50] At the Cupeño village of Agua Caliente on Warner's Ranch, Sleigh met with the longtime village captain,

José Maria Moro, who reported that his village had 168 residents. A recent survey had revealed that the village, thought to be on public land, was actually within the ranch boundaries, and that the new owners were threatening to drive the Indians away.[51]

Once recovered, meanwhile, Ames headed for Pala, arriving on July 18. He immediately sent out runners to inform the residents of neighboring rancherias to meet on July 21 at Rincon if they were interested in learning the news from Washington. On July 19, he interviewed Manuelito Cota and José Antonio Sal. From there he visited the nearby Pauma rancheria, describing it as "flourishing," and then moved on to Olegario's village, Rincon, before a visit to the Potrero,[52] a mountain meadow on the slopes of Palomar Mountain some ten miles above the Pauma Valley. Here he met with Margarita Trujillo, who had inherited half a league of land, granted by the Mexican government to her Luiseño grandmother—land which, Ames noted, "she now holds by her mother's will in trust for the heirs of the same." Although her husband was absent that day, Ames described the woman as competent to manage affairs during his absence. On Sunday, June 20, now joined by Sleight, Ames conducted religious services at Rincon, reporting that most of the rancheria Indians attended and recited "a portion of the liturgy of the Catholic Church, one of their own number leading and the rest responding."[53]

Upon returning to Rincon, Ames had discovered so many tribal leaders gathered for the July 21 meeting that he had to hire two interpreters. He listened to the complaints of those gathered about continual "indignities from white neighbors," who wanted the local Indians' lands and stole their water. He addressed their concerns about government interference in their selection of a chief, agreeing to "refer the question to the Government for instructions," and he urged the attending leaders to keep the peace and "work together for the common good." According to his report, the assembled Indians agreed to live in peace and wait "for the Government to take such action as will secure them in the enjoyment of their rights." Ames, like other special agents, was impressed with Olegario, finding him above average in intelligence, peaceable toward whites, an enthusiastic defender of his people's rights, and capable of controlling them. "A more competent man altogether cannot be found in the tribe," he concluded. If an election for chief were held now, Ames believed "he would doubtless be chosen."[54]

Following a short respite in Los Angeles, Ames set out to visit the Cahuilla Indians, traveling first back to the Potrero (now known as the Morongo

Reservation) in the San Gorgonio Pass[55] to confer with "Old" Chief Cabezon, long a leader in the Coachella Valley.[56] The venerable old man, upwards of ninety, arrived about noon of the day designated, "with much pomp and noise," at the head of a single file line of horsemen, "heralded by a marshal in uniform." According to his captains, Cabezon was in control of a dozen rancherias with 1,080 residents, scattered across the desert and in the surrounding mountains, many of whom had been driven out of the settled areas around communities like San Bernardino. Ames described him as a "remarkable man," who exercised "a powerful influence" upon his people "in the interest of peace and good-will toward the whites" even in the face of great adversities. The old chief wanted two wishes granted before he died: the establishment of schools and to see his people "settled upon lands which they could call their own, and where they and their children could live unmolested."[57]

Following a roundabout journey via San Bernardino and Riverside to the San Jacinto Valley, then up to the Cahuilla Valley, Ames met with the remaining Cahuillas under Manuel Largo and several of his principal captains.[58] Then in his fifties, Largo, a traditional headman who had served as a lieutenant under Juan Antonio in the 1850s, succeeded him as "general" of the Mountain Cahuillas in 1863. His leadership was recognized by government officials, and he was not involved in the various controversies over leadership found among the Luiseños. Ames, however, reported that "this section of the Coahuila [*sic*] tribe is less peaceably disposed—more inclined to resort to force in the maintenance of what they believe to be their rights."[59]

In his October 28, 1873, report Ames stressed the issue of the Mission Indians' citizenship and their relation to the land. The citizenship question had already been discussed at length by State Superintendent Whiting in a May 19, 1873, report, which asserted that under the Mexican Republic, the Mission Indians had the rights of citizens, and that therefore by virtue of the Treaty of Guadalupe Hidalgo they were now citizens of the United States. However, three Indians who had recently applied in Los Angeles County to be registered as voters were denied.[60] Ames recommended that the government not only incorporate the Indians into "the body-politic at the earliest practicable moment" but also allow them to hold their own elections without interference from government officials.[61]

Even more problematic than citizenship was the question of land rights. The Indians, Ames explained, had been driven from their homes and cultivated fields like so many stray sheep or cattle. He hoped that "justice and humanity" would finally compel the government to provide for the few remnants of "these once

Chief Cabezon (with arms crossed) surrounded by other Indian leaders, circa 1895. Will Pablo stands directly behind him; Santos Manuel is on his right, in the top hat.
William H. Weinland Collection, The Huntington Library, San Marino, Calif.

populous tribes." Although Ames was aware that some officials preferred that all Mission Indians be located on one reservation, he cautioned that he knew of no single, large, well-watered tract of land available. He also believed that "progress toward civilization and citizenship" would best be promoted by separating the tribes rather than forcing them to share a reservation.[62]

Therefore Ames recommended a reservation for the Luiseños at Pala, the Kumeyaays at San Pasqual, and the Cahuillas somewhere near the base of the San Bernardino Mountains. Villages located on public lands should be set aside for Indian use, but those on privately held land would have to be moved unless the land could be purchased. Although grazing lands should continue to be held in common, he recommended that agricultural plots on these new reservations should be family-owned and family-farmed. Indians who owned "lands in their own rights should be strongly urged to retain them . . . and transmit them to posterity." With the goal of instilling the concept of private property, Ames recommended that on government lands, forty acres be given to heads of households and unmarried adult males.[63]

Ames further recommended that once these reservations were established (or re-established in the case of Pala and San Pasqual), schools be built to teach the Indians "the rudiments of education," particularly English, and a permanent agent, fully in sympathy with the Indians, be appointed. Once the Indians were given oversight, direction, and protection in the possession of their land, Ames cherished the hope that "they will at no distant day become prosperous and independent agricultural communities."[64]

The *San Diego Union* initially supported Ames's reservation plan, insisting the Indians needed to be "far removed from contact with farming and stock raising communities, and from lines of travel." They suggested the Cahuilla Valley.[65] But after Ames's report was released, they changed their tune. "The people of San Diego county will emphatically dissent from many of the views expressed by Mr. Ames, and will earnestly protest against the carrying out of some of his recommendations." They doubted he could "coax" even twenty Indians to his proposed reservation at Pala. "The Government ought to give the Indians the *Public lands* occupied by them and give them a *title,*" they continued. "To aggregate the Mission Indians is simply to destroy them."[66]

Charles A. Wetmore

Although Congress denied Ames's request for land and money, the Indian Office did not completely abandon the Indians. Instead it resorted to its standard approach—appoint yet another official. On August 1, 1874, Charles Augustus Wetmore[67] was selected as a special U.S. commissioner (rather than a special agent) to thoroughly investigate the Indians' circumstances and "devise some plan whereby favorable legislation can be had to relieve their present deplorable conditions." After consulting old mission records, he was to report "as fully as possible" on the "history and condition" of these Indians and to select reservation sites, which would be "vested in the Government."[68]

Eager for his proposal to be acceptable to local whites, Wetmore requested that government officials on all levels, as well as prominent citizens, consult with him at a public meeting in San Diego. He was particularly interested in hearing from land office officials, who were continually dealing with disputes between Indians and settlers. On October 20, 1874, residents and civic leaders assembled in the San Diego County courthouse to learn about his plans and, more importantly, to express their opinions. The *San Diego Union* reported a "unanimous endorsement of [his] general plan" and a willingness "to urge its adoption upon the Government by the people of this county."[69] A similar meeting was later held in Los Angeles, where Wetmore won additional support.

He recommended a partial revival of the old mission system: Once Indian-occupied lands were purchased and surveys were completed of villages and homes on public lands, lands were to be closed to white settlers and held in trust by the government. Indian villages would be organized and an invitation extended to the Catholic Church to establish a permanent presence. Wetmore reminded the public that many Mission Indians were already Roman Catholic. "The influence of such an institution might in a great measure restore the former prosperity of the Indians," noted a *San Diego Union* reporter. Finally, a resident agent would be appointed to supervise. The ultimate goal was to eventually transfer ownership of the land to the Indians, thus qualifying them for citizenship—"and the old mission idea would be fulfilled."[70]

In the wake of a late October meeting held in Los Angeles, the *Los Angeles Herald* described Wetmore's suggestion of giving small homes to the Indians to be "held in trust for them by some responsible party" as "decidedly sound and practical," as was the invitation to the Catholic Church to undertake missionary work. The *Herald* editor noted that "the most enthusiastic Protestant will admit that the Roman Catholic Church has dealt most generously with the red men and accomplished much good for them, and it is reasonable to expect that just as much good can be accomplished by them at this latter day." Calling this a "new deal," the editor predicted "that the Indian vagabondage which has proved such a shame and a curse will soon cease."[71]

During his investigation and prior to writing his report, Wetmore had visited Archbishop Joseph Sadoc Alemany to ensure the willing participation of the church. Alemany explained that even the church could not do anything for the Indians so long as the government's Indian policy was constantly in flux, with the creation of a reservation one day and its restoration to the public domain the next. The only way for the Catholic Church to succeed, he explained, was to "have a permanent control, and the Indians should have permanent homes."[72]

The implementation of Wetmore's proposal might actually have gone a long way toward solving the problems of the Mission Indians. However, the support of Archbishop Alemany and a positive reception by the *Union* and *Herald* and all of the other newspapers in Southern California combined would never be enough to bring about a federal Indian policy based on a role for the Roman Catholic Church. Evangelical Protestantism was too strong among the upper- and middle-class Americans who held governmental positions and who would soon emerge as leaders of a new Indian reform movement. Even President Grant's Peace Policy, which turned over the control of Indian reservations to church-appointed agents, was almost totally a Protestant effort.[73]

Either unaware of the strong Protestant bent of the newly emerging reform movement or believing it inconsequential, Wetmore submitted his report to the commissioner of Indian Affairs on January 9, 1875, trusting that he had devised plans that, if approved, would materially, morally, and physically advance both the Indian and the white communities in Southern California. Closely following orders, fully one-half of his report was historical in nature. To lend credence to his report, Wetmore submitted testimonials of prominent individuals, including the San Diego district attorney and a state assemblyman.[74]

By the middle of the 1870s both Indians and whites were growing increasingly frustrated with Washington's failure to act. "The Government has for a long time been pursuing a very bad policy concerning the Indians of Southern California," complained the *San Diego Union*. "It would have been better if it had done absolutely nothing at all." Special agents were sent, they conferred with the Indians, and in the end nothing got done. "What the Government means by its contemptible shilly-shallying policy of delay, no mortal man can tell."[75]

David A. Dryden

The *Union's* conclusion was on the mark. The shilly-shallying continued as yet another special agent, Rev. David A. Dryden, a Methodist minister, was appointed on March 31, 1875.[76] His appointment was not universally welcomed. The *Alta California* later complained that choosing an English-speaking Protestant with no Indian experience to deal with mostly Spanish-speaking Catholic Indians would accomplish little. The position, the paper claimed, had been "seized upon as legitimate [political] plunder" by one of California's senators, and those working to try and help the Indians were "disgusted."[77]

Nonetheless Dryden clearly took his job seriously. He submitted his report to Indian Commissioner Edward Parmelee Smith on June 30, 1875. Like previous special agents, Dryden held conferences with the leading men of various Indian villages, including Temecula, Pala, Rincon, San Pasqual, and Santa Ysabel. He was surprised to find the Indians "more numerous, civilized, and industrious" than he had supposed. Like his predecessors, he found their most pressing problem to be land tenure. "Either these helpless, non-resisting people will be driven from their lands as homeless wanderers," he wrote, "or [they] will be exasperated to violent deeds of self-defense."[78]

Meanwhile, the surveyor of San Diego County had received instructions to make a survey of Indian-occupied lands—a result of the wide local acceptance of Wetmore's plan. Pleased with this development, Dryden recommended that as soon as these surveys were completed, lands be set aside for the Indians' exclusive occupation, with the government holding the title. To implement the process, he recommended the appointment of a commission to estimate the value of settlers' improvements and then reimburse and remove them. With the government retaining title to the land, he hoped, the Indians would feel secure and be willing to make improvements.[79]

Dryden, however, failed to protect Indian land. Instead he was forced to stand by helplessly during the wrenching eviction of Indians from Temecula. In September 1875, barely two months after he submitted his report, the new owners of the Rancho Pauba at Temecula announced plans to evict any and all Indians living on the old Mexican grant—an action that had been a long time in coming. In 1869 the former owners of the ranch had filed a trespass suit against the Indians in the Fifteenth Judicial District Court in San Francisco. Records of the case do not seem to have survived, but the newspapers later reported that although the Indians were represented by counsel, when the case came to trial the judgment went against them. The verdict was not immediately carried out. Then in May 1873, three Spanish-born sheep ranchers who had settled in California bought Rancho Pauba and the adjoining Rancho Temecula. They initially informed the Indians that although they had no plans to evict them—in fact they expected to hire some of them as ranch workers—the Indians needed to understand that they had no legal right to their homes and fields. Then two years later the new owners changed their minds, turning the court-ordered eviction over to San Diego County Sheriff Nicholas Hunsaker.[80]

On September 9, 1875, Hunsaker served notice on all adult men in the village, announcing they had just ten days to move out or be thrown off the land. The next day—ignoring the government's denial of Manuel Olegario's status as leader of the majority of the Luiseños—Hunsaker visited Olegario at his home at Rincon to inform him of the impeding eviction. When the sheriff and his men returned on Monday, September 20, the Indians asked for more time to consult with Olegario. Hunsaker, however, insisted that they had all previously been notified and that the deadline was set. Juan Murrieta, who took care of day-to-day operations for the ranch owners, offered to let families stay up to forty days to harvest their crops and move their possessions, but they had to sign a lease acknowledging their lack of ownership. Seven families signed. The remaining two-thirds or so were evicted. The move was completed by Wednesday; the Indians and their livestock were "driven over the line" with only what they could carry. The *San Diego Union* described the Indians as "behaved very well," giving the sheriff "no trouble."[81]

When the sheriff carried out the eviction, Olegario was already in Los Angeles conferring with his attorney, Christopher Wilson. Dryden, out of town at the time, did not learn of the event until it was over. Returning from Los Angeles, Olegario immediately visited the agent, and together they set out for Temecula. There, on September 24, Dryden discovered what he estimated to be three hundred Indians, "thrust out of their homes, and in a destitute and deplorable condition; also much exasperated and threatening hostilities."[82] The *Los Angeles Star* reported that Olegario called the villagers together and advised them to return to the ranch and "fight till they died"; fortunately they listened to cooler heads, remaining beyond the boundaries of the ranch.[83] Soon rumors circulated that trouble was on the way. Francisco Estudillo, a county supervisor and later a Mission Indian agent, described Olegario as "threatening and defiant" and feared there would be violence. Sheriff Hunsaker and the county district attorney agreed and contacted the governor and the military commander at San Francisco for immediate assistance.[84]

Maj. Gen. John Schofield, commander of the U.S. Army's Pacific Military Division, scathingly replied on October 2 that he could not possibly send troops on such short notice. "This should have been thought of before the Indians were driven to desperation," he scolded. The *San Diego Union* expressed displeasure with his response, complaining there was too much sympathy for the Indians—ranch owners had rights, too—and blamed the government for not taking action sooner to solve the problem. The *Los Angeles Express* said the eviction proved that "our Indian system is a fraud—disgraceful to the Government and humiliating to every right-thinking citizen."[85]

Fears of an uprising quickly faded, and by mid-October Olegario was back to work in Matthew Keller's vineyard in Los Angeles, where a *Los Angeles Herald* reporter interviewed him and several other Indian leaders. The day after the eviction, Olegario told him, three thousand sheep had been run into the Indians' fenced fields, eating their entire winter crop of melons, beans, pumpkins, squash, and corn. With their people facing starvation, Olegario and several others had traveled to Los Angles, seeking help for the coming winter. The *Herald* reporter expressed hope that the rights of these civilized Indians would be protected "at all hazards and the carelessness or rascality of an Indian agent should not be allowed to work them injury." Why the reporter had singled out Dryden for criticism is unknown. It was a court-ordered eviction, and Dryden had no authority in the matter. His term as special agent had expired, although he was reappointed, perhaps in response to the removal.[86]

Commissioner E. P. Smith, like the *Herald* reporter, sided with the Indians, understanding the "exasperation and despair" they felt, deprived of their homes and crops and with "their little personal property [taken] in satisfaction of cost of judgment." Impressed with their "forbearance and peaceful disposition" in the face of adversity, Smith ordered Dryden to locate a suitable ranch to lease temporarily for them, with the possibility of purchase. Ashamedly, the commissioner concluded that "the embarrassments under which the Department has labored for the past two years in its efforts to rescue these Indians from their present condition still continue."[87]

Even the Indian Office was beginning to feel the pressure of a failed policy. Although it had sent agent after agent, who toured villages and wrote sympathetic reports, members of various congressional committees continually stalled the process of establishing reservations by failing to pass Indian appropriation bills. Now perhaps it was time for Indian leadership to become more involved. Indeed, the continual encroachment upon Indian lands and the eviction of his people from Temecula seemed to have worked a change on Manuel Olegario. Originally opposing the centralized reservations at San Pasqual and Pala, he now began agitating for reservations as a way to preserve and protect the remaining villages. He made numerous trips to Los Angeles and San Diego, pleading his case before judges, visiting newspaper offices, and conferring with officials to move reservation plans along for the ever-growing number of homeless Mission Indians.[88]

Not everyone was sympathetic, but Olegario had his proponents. With the support of Agent Dryden, attorney Wilson, and other government officials, as well as the apparent financial support of Los Angeles merchant Wolf Kalisher and others, Olegario traveled to Washington, D.C., and on November 15, 1875, accompanied by an interpreter, he met with Interior Secretary Zachariah Chandler. At the meeting, Olegario requested relief for the eight hundred members of his band who had been ejected from their villages and "some secure provision" for the rest of the Mission Indians. Chandler explained that Congress would have to take action in the matter. In the meantime the secretary agreed to try and arrange an interview with President U. S. Grant. The next day, Olegario indeed had his interview with Grant, "who promised them temporary relief and a recommendation to Congress for a permanent home."[89]

For almost three decades special agents, inspectors, and commissioners had recommended reservations, which had been established and then revoked, forcing an Indian leader to journey across the country to confer with the president. The *Sacramento Daily Union* may have been correct when it reported that "probably the best thing that could have been done was to send Olegario" to Washington. Now "some genuine sympathy will be expended in getting Congress to do justice to these unfortunates." The newspaper, wisely advising against collecting all of the Mission Indians on a single reservation or forcing them to move out of state, warned of the duel dangers of placing them on worthless land or placing them on land that would only provide a profit to the "Indian ring."[90]

On December 27, 1875, just six weeks after Olegario's visit, President Grant created nine small executive order reservations in present-day San Diego County, taking in some 52,400 acres. The reservations established at Pala, Potrero (including Rincon and La Jolla), and Agua Caliente (Warner's Ranch) would provide some small degree of security for Olegario's Luiseño and Cupeño followers—at least temporarily. Manuel Largo's home at Cahuilla was also set aside, as were the Kumeyaay villages of Capitán Grande, Santa Ysabel (including Mesa Grande), Sycuan, Inaja, and Cosmit.[91]

William Vandever

Wisely, Grant had created a number of small reservations instead of one centralized reservation. But officials in the Indian Office continued to seriously consider the idea. In November 1875 William Vandever, a U.S. Indian inspector, was ordered to find a single site to lease or purchase.[92] Working closely with Agent Dryden, Vandever personally visited most of the Indian-occupied localities in Southern California. In his report of January 31, 1876, he informed Indian Commissioner John Q. Smith that he had considered at least half a dozen of the old Mexican *ranchos* that had been offered to the government, finally concluding that the 17,712-acre Rancho Santa Ysabel was "the best adapted to the use of the Indian," with ranch buildings that could easily be put to use and the presence of an outpost of Mission San Diego, a favorite spot of the Indians. The property could be leased for five years for $5,000 a month, or purchased for $100,000 after three years—by far the cheapest sale price offered. Vandever informed Commissioner Smith that he had already negotiated an initial lease with the owners; only government approval was needed.[93]

There was "no body of Indians" anywhere who had "occasioned so little trouble" and "endured wrong and outrage with more patience than these Indians," wrote Vandever. And there were no Indians "more useful than these in developing the country, for their labor has been freely used by the settlers at a small cost," he continued. Therefore he warned that removing them "would be a detriment." Nowhere was there "to be found [a body of Indians] for whom a moderate expenditure would accomplish more good." However, he warned Smith that to secure harmony, the land acquired for a reservation "should be of such dimensions that bands known to be unfriendly toward each other can be separate." Unfortunately the 17,712 acres of the Rancho Santa Ysabel, spread along one long valley, did not offer much room to accommodate the estimated four thousand Mission Indians adequately.[94]

Commissioner Smith's recommendation to Congress for a $150,000 Indian appropriation to purchase reservation land and to establish a permanent agency for the Mission Indians was ignored, and Vandever's proposal to purchase Rancho San Ysabel never became a reality. Instead, on May 15, 1876, President Grant set aside eight additional small reservations in what is now Riverside County: Potrero, Agua Caliente (now Palm Springs), Torres, Martinez ("Old" Chief Cabezon's home village),[95] Mission (now Mission Creek, northeast of Morongo), and two small adjoining villages at Indian Wells. They totaled only about 6,000 acres; most were only a single section (640 acres) that, one could hope, took in a major village.[96] The reservations of Potrero and Martinez included state school land[97] and thus were not actually under the control of the federal government. As with the 1875 reservations, there would be many additions and deletions over the coming years.

The creation of these small reservations did little to stop white encroachment upon Indian lands. What was needed was a new Mission Indian Agency, with a permanent agent who would work full time on the Indians' behalf. This action would require congressional funding. But Congress refused to appropriate even enough money to continue Dryden's agency. "It is better it should thus be abolished than to be continued without power to accomplish satisfactorily the work which ought to be done," he told one newspaper. "And to me it is a relief to be released from responsibilities I was powerless to meet." Now, he told another reporter, "the Indians and settlers of San Diego county will have to adjust the difficulties between them as best they can. I confess my sympathies are largely with the Indians as the weaker party and the more liable to be wronged."[98]

J. E. Colburn

On July 12, 1877, the Indian Office appointed J. E. Colburn as agent to the Mission Indians. In the month between his appointment and his annual report, Colburn seems to have solidly grasped their desperate condition. Little had changed since Stanley's report more than a decade before. Colburn clarified the Indians' condition by identifying three classes of Mission Indians. The largest group worked on white-owned ranches or farms, earning about a dollar a day.[99] A second group, living in small native communities, farmed their plots of land and cultivated some fruit trees and vines but were often threatened by land-grabbers who viewed them as only so many "grasshoppers and coyotes." The smallest group, the "vagrants," hung about "the outskirts of towns, pass[ing] wistfully through the streets, seldom asking for anything, but silently begging with their longing, pathetic eyes." Colburn predicted that within a quarter of a century, the double curse of "bad whisky and the unscrupulous venders of it" would result in the complete "extermination" of the Indians save for a few "strolling bands of vagrants and beggars." He concluded, however, that there was still time to protect them from white settlers intent upon driving them from "the best places."[100]

During the summer of 1877 Colburn was forced to deal with just such a situation when Captain John Morongo[101] traveled nearly one hundred miles to Los Angeles to "lay the troubles of his people" before their new agent. Morongo was from the small village of Potrero at the mouth of a canyon in the San Gorgonio Pass,[102] where he and a few families of Cahuilla and Serrano people had lived for years. Diverting water from the nearby creek, they had successfully irrigated their crops. Recently, however, an American named Helmick had acquired land in the area under the Desert Land Act and was diverting their water onto his land, rendering the Indian village "uninhabitable." On August 3, Colburn wrote to Commissioner Smith that "the most speedy and certain method of protecting" this village would be to set aside the area by executive order. Describing the land as a mile and half from the Southern Pacific railroad tracks, he included the general township coordinates and recommended that the area be properly surveyed.[103]

The land situation in the San Gorgonio Pass would prove to be one of the most complicated in the history of the forthcoming Mission Indian Agency—not only because of land-hungry whites but also because of a checkerboard pattern of land ownership. The Southern Pacific railroad had been promised a government subsidy in land before it extended its line through the San Gorgonio Pass and out across the desert to Yuma in 1876–77. The subsidy promised land for ten miles on either side of the tracks. But to prevent a complete monopoly, the land was divided into alternating sections of 640 acres each, with the odd-numbered sections going to the railroad and the even-numbered remaining public land. Adding to the confusion, where the odd-numbered sections had already been claimed, the railroad's lands were simply pushed farther and farther from the tracks. Two of the thirty-six sections in each township had already been granted to the State of California, to be sold to raise money for school purposes. The result was a bewildering checkerboard of ownership, made even worse by a lack of accurate surveys in the field. The confusion would plague most of the reservations in what is now Riverside County for decades.[104]

The government had already tried to protect the Potrero village, establishing a reservation in May of 1876, but unbeknownst to federal officials, the village was physically located on Section 36, a state school section. Therefore on May 3, 1877, the land was restored to the public domain by an executive order from President Rutherford B. Hayes. Then on August 25, 1877, three weeks after Colburn requested an executive order for Morongo's village, President Hayes agreed to set aside another tract, hoping this time to include the village site. (It is unknown whether this executive order was already in the pipeline, or whether the president had actually acted that quickly to address Colburn's request.) The Potrero Reservation (as it was known in the nineteenth century) now totaled about 53,000 acres, mostly scattered in a checkerboard fashion. Some of the land had not even been officially surveyed, leading to future complications.[105]

After a quarter century of special agents and government reports, Southern California's Native peoples found their situation in many ways worse than when they had first come under American rule. In his only annual report, Colburn pointed out that the Indians had developed an understandable suspicion of government agents, who visited their villages and heard their troubles but seldom seemed to provide any relief. He cited the example of Martinez, an Indian leader in the Coachella Valley, whose lands were not yet "reserved" and like so many other Indian holdings were threatened by white intruders. Martinez believed that if Colburn were "a 'strong' and 'true' agent," he would give him a "'paper' to show those white men and warn them off." Colburn faced the same dilemma that many of his predecessors had. "If I decline to deceive him with a useless order, or if I give him an order which he finds the white men do not respect,"

Colburn wrote Smith, then "he thinks I am not 'strong' and 'true'" and "will always believe me a mere pretender." The only solution was for him "to secure the reservation of the Rincon before white settlers gain legal title to it."[106]

No doubt aware from past events that such a solution was not realistic, Colburn instead recommended that Congress appropriate no less than $150,000 to purchase permanent reservations. This task could be carried out by a commission authorized to visit the various Indian settlements, learn from the Indians what they wanted, visit prospective reservations, settle disputed rights, and finally address the issue of limited water.[107] Again, Congress not only refused to appropriate the money to implement Colburn's plan but refused to appropriate funding for his salary; his position was discontinued.

Colburn, like the special agents, inspectors, and special commissioners before him, had failed the Mission Indians not because the Indian Office was unsympathetic to their situation but because Congress failed to appropriate adequate funding. Not until 1878 did Congress agree to authorize the funding for a permanent Mission Indian Agency.[108] In mid-June 1878, Samuel S. Lawson became the first full-time agent at a newly created Mission Agency. For the next quarter century, seven different agents filled this post. Their successes and failures are presented in the following chapters.

CHAPTER 2

▼ ▼ ▼

SETTING THE STAGE

Samuel S. Lawson, 1878–1883

> The lands reserved for them are wholly inadequate to the support of older people, who must of necessity remain at home, and when others are forced by the absence of outside labor to return and subsist upon the same, want is inevitable. The necessity for providing suitable lands for them, in the form of one or more reservations, has been pressed upon the attention of the department in my two former reports, and I now for the third and perhaps, the last time, emphasize that necessity, by saying that whether government will immediately heed the pleas that have been made in behalf of these people or not, it *must* sooner or later deal with this question in a practical way, or else see a population of over 3,000 Indians become homeless wanderers in this desert region.
>
> —*S. S. Lawson, August 20, 1881*

Establishing Indian reservations in Southern California was not enough, as Samuel S. Lawson repeatedly pointed out in the early days of the Mission Indian Agency. Without sufficient land, especially sufficient quality of land, the Mission Indians would never be self-supporting. Genuinely concerned with their well-being, he found his efforts on the Indians' behalf repeatedly thwarted by government officials, causing the frustration that finally led to his resignation.

When word came that a regular Indian agent was to be appointed for Southern California, several local men began vying for the position. San Bernardino newspaper editor William D. Frazee even claimed to have the support of some Cahuilla leaders.[1] But this was a presidential appointment requiring Senate approval—a political process, where the opinions of the Indians mattered little. In the days of political patronage and the "spoils" system in Washington, appointees to any office were generally party loyalists rewarded for their support. Their qualifications were often secondary at best. Fortunately, the first regular

Mission Indian agent was a cut above a mere political appointee. On June 15, 1878, President Rutherford B. Hayes appointed the Rev. Samuel S. Lawson, a Midwestern minister, as agent for all the reservations in what was then San Diego and San Bernardino counties, to take office on July 1. He would report directly to the commissioner of Indian affairs in Washington, D.C., instead of to the California superintendent.[2] Although some would later question Lawson's qualifications, his devotion to the job was clear.

Lawson was born in York County, Pennsylvania, on November 24, 1838, to Rev. S. B. Lawson, a Lutheran minister, and his wife, Catherine. He attended Gettysburg's Pennsylvania College and began his ministry as a Lutheran pastor at Massilon, Ohio, in 1860. Two years later he was appointed pastor of the Evangelical English Lutheran Church in Chili, Choshocton County, Ohio, serving until January 5, 1864, when he enlisted in Company C, Fifty-First Ohio Infantry regiment—not as a chaplain, but as a private. He mustered out on October 3, 1865, at Victoria, Texas. Returning to Ohio, he resumed his ministry in Leesburg, Ohio, in 1866. In 1870 he moved to Illinois and served as a Lutheran pastor in both Ottawa and Freeport before moving to Morristown to assume the pastorate of the Evangelical Lutheran Church, a position he held at the time of his appointment.[3]

Tanis Thorne, author of the only study of Lawson's tenure as agent, claims that he was part of President U. S. Grant's Peace Policy program, which included apportioning the Indian agencies to various Protestant missionary societies in the hope that good Christian men would make better agents than political appointees.[4] Several Northern California agencies had been assigned to the Methodists, which may have influenced Rev. Dryden's appointment as a special agent in the south back in 1875. But of course the Mission Agency did not yet exist during Grant's time, and the Hayes administration had abandoned the policy. While Lawson mentioned in his 1882 annual report that his agency had been assigned to the Lutherans, he also questioned whether their missionary work among the largely Catholic Mission Indian population "would be justified by results, at least among the grown-up population, on account of the difficulty of communicating with them, and because of their fixed habits of thought and life."[5] In any case, as agent, Lawson removed his clerical collar, never presenting himself as a clergyman.

To become familiar with his far-flung agency, early in December 1878 Lawson set out on an eleven-day inspection tour of interior San Diego County, visiting all but a few of the smaller Mission Indian settlements. His first stop was the San Jacinto Ranch and the Soboba village, where he learned that land reserved for the

Indians adjacent to the ranch was "all inaccessible mountain land, except about two acres—this little spot being utilized by one Indian family." The following day he arrived at Temecula to find "unoccupied adobe homes," left behind when the Indians were evicted three years before. The few families who remained were living "among the rocks in the foothills, with no land to cultivate." At Pala, where the records showed some 240 acres reserved for Indian use, he found a small settlement of Luiseños. But government surveyors had not yet clearly defined the reservation boundaries and "disputes and trouble reign supreme."[6]

Twelve miles up the San Luis Rey River, at Rincon, Lawson discovered that the village was not within the boundaries of the 1875 reservation. Whites had already filed claims, putting the Indians' homes in jeopardy. Because the reservation land was almost worthless, it was useless to remove the villagers inside its boundaries. Lawson remained at Rincon for several days, awaiting the arrival of all the San Luis Rey Indians, who were still divided over the election of a headman following the death of Manuel Olegario the previous year. While waiting, Lawson was informed of numerous wrongs endured by these Indians at the hands of white men. Only four years earlier they had sheep, cattle, horses, and money—all lost through litigation, according to the correspondence of Chief Olegario. Only two years earlier, the Indians had paid out nearly $1,000 in legal fees to certain San Diego attorneys. In one case, the lawyer took thirty-one steers in payment when the Indians ran out of money. "The record of wrongs inflicted upon these unfortunate Indians, if written in full," Lawson reported to Indian Commissioner Ezra A. Hayt, "would mark the blackest page in our Indian history."[7]

Everywhere he turned, Lawson discovered rapidly deteriorating conditions, especially at San Pasqual since the death of José Panto in 1874. The hundred or so residents of neighboring Santa Ysabel and Mesa Grande had little useful land and no pasture for their horses. When their stock trespassed on public or private land, white settlers shot them, took them, or invoked the state's new "no fence" law and demanded cash payments for the damage they caused to crops.[8] "That these inoffensive Indians should be peaceable and patient under such treatment," Lawson retorted, "is more than would be expected, yet it is true." He confided to Hayt: "I could scarcely restrain my own combativeness, as these wrongs were recited to me in the presence of some of those *white men—so called*." On December 12, Lawson arrived at the village of Agua Caliente on Warner's Ranch to find the Indians as yet undisturbed, although a surveying party had recently staked their lands, raising their fears. He described the Cupeños living there as "steady, sober and industrious," although with insufficient land.[9]

On his way up to the Cahuillas, he visited a Luiseño family living at Aguanga on the eastern side of Palomar Mountain. They had come to see him at Rincon to complain about white intruders.[10] The father and mother, two sons, two widowed daughters, and their children were all living on a forty-acre parcel that had been their home for eleven years. With a comfortable home and fenced fields, they believed themselves secure in their little mountain retreat. Unfortunately they resided on public land, where, as Lawson cynically noted, "an Indian has no rights which a white man is bound to respect." A white man who lived on a large ranch a few miles away had filed on the land under the Homestead Act, signed into law in 1862. The Indian family did not immediately leave, and he had visited them a few days before Lawson's arrival, "with club in hand," threatening to kill them if they remained. The enraged agent wrote Commissioner Hayt: "[I]f I had the power I would annul the purchase and sale, for I found them most worthy and excellent Indians."[11]

Lawson found "the most serious trouble" in the Cahuilla Valley, where a reservation had been set aside for the Indians in 1875. Not only had the survey left out half of the main village, including Manuel Largo's comfortable adobe home, but the land actually contained within the reservation, except for 240 acres, was "inaccessible mountain, rock and brush land." A white man had recently purchased adjoining land, taken "forcible possession of the chief's house," and was threatening to dispossess those whose homes were on his land. The villagers responded aggressively by starting to tear down the man's corrals and fences. "[A]nd it is doubtful if they can be restrained," added Lawson. "I would not be at all surprised to hear they had killed the white man."[12]

Several months later, Lawson learned that this Indian village was actually on railroad land, and that another white man, who also threatened to drive the Indians from their homes, had already filed on that exact tract. Unable to tolerate the situation, Lawson contacted the land department of the Southern Pacific railroad, learning that the man had no "right or title to the land in question." The Indians, with their long residence, had a prior claim. Therefore the railroad official sent Lawson a blank land application and suggested that someone file a claim on the Indians' behalf so that if the Cahuillas decided to buy it when the land came on the market, "their claim would undoubtedly take precedence." Lawson located an individual willing to file on the Indians' behalf. However, the intruder, when notified to leave, refused. "He can not with safety be left to occupy their village," Lawson informed Hayt. "Has not the U.S. court jurisdiction in his ejectment."[13]

Lawson was often accompanied by Captain John Morongo, who not only served as his interpreter but was an "efficient fellow-helper at the agency." Lawson informed Hayt that Morongo's "service cannot be estimated by dollars and cents," and that a "nobler specimen of the possibilities of civilization upon those of his race" is "nowhere to be found."[14] Morongo's presence enabled Lawson to conduct enough investigative tours to get a good sense of the current population of the Mission Indians, estimating their numbers at three thousand, about fourteen hundred less than the previous count. This sharp decline concerned Lawson, who recommended that all the Indians he had visited in San Diego County be consolidated on land in the San Bernardino Valley, placed "under judicious management," and equipped with schools, enabling them to "become a thriving and industrious community." He suggested San Bernardino Valley because its land was less susceptible to frost and offered quick access to markets for Indian goods, accessibility to the railroad, and better employment possibilities. Lawson proposed a similar situation for the Desert Indians, who were also under his supervision and only twenty miles from San Bernardino.[15]

A New Home for the Potrero Indians

No doubt John Morongo kept Lawson apprised of the continual encroachment of white squatters on Indian lands in the San Gorgonio Pass, where he lived. The trouble in the pass was complicated by the fact that the Potrero village was located on state school Section 36 and thus not under federal control. The checkerboard railroad lands left Indian-occupied holdings scattered throughout the pass instead of confined to one area, and white settlers holding legal claims were not eager to be surrounded by Indian-held land.[16]

Because removing the Indians was seen as an easier solution than dealing with angry settlers, in November 1878, Hayt ordered Lawson to find a new home for the Potrero Indians. The commissioner seemed to believe that there was still sufficient land available in Southern California to successfully relocate them. Newly appointed and unfamiliar with the topography, Lawson consulted a deputy U.S. surveyor, who informed him that "there was absolutely nothing upon which [the Indians] could settle that would afford a living to one half" of them. For a first-hand view, Lawson made a thorough examination of the pass country, including a visit to the desert reservation of Agua Caliente (near today's Palm Springs) and the village at "Toros" (Torres).[17] Lawson informed Hayt on November 28 that all he found east of the city of San Bernardino was a sandy desert waste, "where neither vegetation or water is found for a distance of thirty miles." Water was available in only "a few places, and that in very limited quantities, and when the least water is found—you find some white settler owning it though he be 30 to 40 miles from any other habitation."[18]

Lawson informed Hayt that he trusted the Interior Department would not insist upon the removal of the two hundred Cahuilla and Serrano people until appropriate land was located. He believed that the white settlers who claimed Section 36, which contained the Potrero village, would not demand their immediate removal. This would buy some time to try another approach. During one of his inspection tours, Lawson had explored the area above the Potrero, at the foot of the San Bernardino Mountains, and had found six sections with a splendid stream and arable and pasture lands "sufficient to subsist, under proper management—all these Indians, as well as others"—a perfect location for a Mission Indian reservation. Furthermore, he was confident that $5,000 from the government would be sufficient to extinguish all the settlers' claims. Except for a certain Mr. Hickman, who was described as a fugitive from justice and known by locals as "a very bad man," the other claimants were currently giving the Indians no trouble.[19]

Rancho Cuca, the Other Potrero

The total disrespect for Indian land rights and the manipulative actions of lawyers employed by white interlopers proved a continual source of irritation for Lawson. One case in particular involved Rancho Cuca, also known as the Potrero, located at the southern edge of Palomar Mountain, east of Pala. Like Pablo Apis's grant at Temecula, the 2,174-acre Rancho Cuca was one of the small ranchos set aside for the Indians by the last of the friars at Mission San Luis Rey and later confirmed by Mexican Governor Pío Pico in 1845.[20] Margarita Trujillo was the daughter of the original grantee, Maria Juana de Los Angeles, a Luiseño woman. Trujillo was also often identified as a sister or possibly half-sister of Manuelito Cota. Reverend Ames had visited her during his 1873 tour, explaining that she held the land "by her mother's will in trust for the heirs of the same." An 1876 visitor had described Trujillo as "a fine looking and very intelligent woman," who "lives in a comfortable adobe house, as well furnished as those of half the white folks, and speaks Spanish correctly."[21]

In 1876 Trujillo had leased much of the rancho to a Los Angeles sheep rancher named Antonio Varela, who arrived early that summer with a flock of about four thousand sheep. Also living on the ranch were a dozen or so Indians who "recognize[d] the authority of the redoubtable [Manuel] Olegario," wrote a *San*

Diego Union reporter. Fearing that Varela's sheep would further deplete Luiseño food reserves, Olegario had gathered some sixty followers and forced Varela off the ranch. In retaliation, Varela had a number of the Indian men arrested and taken before the local justice of the peace, who claimed he had no jurisdiction and released them. According to the *Union*, Olegario, "[t]hinking that this ended the matter in their favor, and feeling quite jubilant," notified Trujillo that she also had to leave the premises, possibly as a way of settling an old score with her relative, Manuelito Cota.[22]

Olegario's "stand at Cuca was far too strident for many local leaders and ranchers," and they and the *San Diego Union* demanded his arrest. On July 14, 1877, Deputy Sheriff Ed Bushyhead arrived at Pala to serve papers on him. The *Union* reported that "Olegario was defiant, and had a hundred and fifty or more of his retainers at his back." In a threatening manner, they gathered about the deputy, "some of them proposing to tie him up." Bushyhead remained cool-headed, and Olegario and his followers concluded that the deputy "would not be a safe subject to experiment upon—an eminently sound conclusion." Instead Olegario traveled to San Diego to present his case before a judge. Then on July 31, 1877, Manuel Olegario suddenly died in his sleep.[23] Concern over the cause among Indians and whites alike prompted the county coroner, Dr. T. C. Stockton, to examine the body. He found an enlarged liver, "resulting in rupture of a blood-vessel and internal hemorrhage," but no traces of the poison some had suspected. Some followers, however, remained convinced that he had been killed by a *hechicero*—a witch.[24]

Much of this controversy at Cuca occurred before Lawson took office. Therefore it is unknown if he was aware of the circumstances prior to receiving a letter from one Chalmers Scott dated December 7, 1878. Scott introduced himself as the attorney for Margarita Trujillo, the present owner of Rancho Cuca, who had suffered "loses and abuses" because Indians had squatted on and thus monopolized her land. Scott's involvement raises some interesting questions. A well-known attorney, civil engineer, and former newspaperman, he was also the son-in-law of the late Cave Couts. How he became Trujillo's attorney is unclear, but with the Couts family busily trying to establish title to another of these small "Indian" ranchos—the nearby Rancho La Jolla, which all but surrounded the Cuca—his motives are questionable.[25]

Scott's letter explained that Trujillo held title by a patent issued by the federal government in July 1878 and that she was currently involved in two court cases against these Indians, pending in the district court, both of which stemmed from the Varela incident. *Trujillo v. Calac* sought the eviction of the Indians there (presumably not members of the family that she had previously allowed to live on the rancho) and *Varela v. Olegario* was for forcible trespass.[26] The lawyer assured Lawson that in both cases the intruding Indians "must necessarily be defeated, and a forcible ejection by the sheriff will follow." Already legal expenses had exceeded $400, which would be collected by the sheriff.[27]

Lawson immediately forwarded Scott's letter to Commissioner Hayt, commenting that the attorney had improperly counseled the Indians. "Between thieving white men who would defraud them of their rights, and *avaricious* lawyers who have robbed them of their money, they have been ground as between 'the upper and nether mill stone,'" he complained. Requesting advice, Lawson concluded that this was merely a repetition of "the state of things" he had found everywhere among the Indians.[28] Months later Scott was still threatening to evict the Indians from the ranch. By this time legal costs had increased to $1,000, and the lawyer had collected $200 and thirty-one head of cattle from his clients. The government "should come to their rescue," Lawson insisted, for this situation had been "caused by the neglect of the Govt. itself."[29]

As Scott had predicted, the eviction suit went against the Indians late in 1879. Soon after, one of the defendants, José Antonio Morano [*sic*—Moreno?], "a young Indian, speaking remarkably good English," along with eleven other Indians came to San Diego to consult with the judge in the case. When they found themselves without enough food, the judge wrote a letter explaining the situation, suggesting they approach the Board of Supervisors for help. Morano did, and the board agreed to supply them with "beef and bread."[30] But neither they nor the judge could do anything to stop their eviction. In his August 1880 annual report to newly appointed commissioner Roland E. Trowbridge, which began by describing the past year as "one of great expectations and great disappointments," Lawson noted that about fifteen families had been forcibly removed from the Cuca.[31]

One Big Reservation

Lawson, disgusted with attorneys who extorted money from the Indians, sought counsel outside of the Indian Office. On December 21, 1878, he wrote Peter D. Wigginton, a member of the House of Representatives from California, hoping to generate support for the establishment of a Mission Indian reservation during the current congressional session. Lawson explained he had just returned from an extended tour in early December, visiting the small Mission reservations and finding "their conditions pitiable in the extreme." Not one acre in a thousand was tillable, and now he was being ordered by the Indian commissioner to locate a new home for about two hundred Indians at the Potrero. "I am compelled to report to the Dept. that it is really impossible to find any land upon which that number can maintain themselves." The frustrated agent was "utterly unable to account for the indifference with which their situation has been regarded by the government, except upon the ground that they are peaceable through it all, and eke out an existence without the aid of supplies from [the] government."[32]

Lawson explained that the previous winter a resolution had been passed by the state assembly, requesting the purchase of one or more large reservations for the Mission Indians. A copy of the resolution, accompanied by a petition signed by hundreds of San Diego and San Bernardino county residents, including judges, attorneys, sheriffs, merchants, and other public officials, had been forwarded to Washington.[33] The resolution called for the creation of a commission to examine different locations for a permanent reservation. Concluding his letter, Lawson observed that it was now up to California's representatives to "press the matter to the speedy attention of Congress." On December 31, Wigginton forwarded Lawson's letter to Interior Secretary Carl Schurz.[34]

Struggling to comply with Hayt's request to locate land for the Indians on the Potrero in the San Gorgonio Pass, in early January Lawson again referred to the site he had found, only five miles from their village, describing it as offering "the best advantages at the least expense" and sufficiently large enough to "consolidate" all the Mission Indians. Although it was primarily desert land, water could be "purchased and flumed upon it which will irrigate all the land needed for cultivation by all these Indians." There was also sufficient land for sheep and cattle grazing. In addition, its location near the Southern Pacific railroad would enable the Indians to find employment milling railroad ties. Its purchase, he claimed, would enable the Indians to become self-sustaining—"an industrious and thriving community." One month later, still pleased with his selection, Lawson wrote Hayt that it remained the best he had seen. He also was pleased to learn that the House Committee had recommended its purchase as a reservation.[35]

The Indians did not share Lawson's enthusiasm for a single reservation. During a meeting he held at Old San Bernardino, "Old" Chief Cabezon made it clear that his people, the Cahuillas, were tired of being pushed out by the Americans and refused to move.[36] The Luiseños especially did not want to share a reservation with the Cahuillas. In fact, more than one thousand Indians signed a petition opposing removal from lands they had resided on for generations. Although recognizing their position as "critical," the petitioners described themselves as "honestly and peaceably living by [their] manual labor, and honest industry, without being in any way a burden to the government." They opposed removal to "the vicinity of San Gorgonio," which they described as "a sterile country well known to [them] to be unfit for [their occupation] and incapable of affording [them] the means of subsisting without aid from government as has been [their] custom heretofore." On March 26, 1879, a delegation of Luiseños delivered this petition to Lawson, requesting he forward it to the president and Congress. Lawson complied, expressing no displeasure with the petition other than to remind Hayt that all of the lands occupied by these various groups were "owned by private parties by whose grace they have been permitted to remain thus far."[37]

In early March 1879, still enthusiastic about his proposal and not yet in receipt of the Indians' petition, Lawson had informed Hayt that he was "in the possession of facts that *intensify* the necessity of making provisions for the Mission Indians." He hoped these additional issues would move the Interior Department to do something. Captain Wilcox, owner of the Santa Ysabel ranch, had notified Lawson that he "must demand" the removal of the Santa Ysabel and Mesa Grande Indians from his ranch within the year because he was unable to rent it due to their presence. Lawson also learned from the land office in Los Angeles that the Indians on Warner's Ranch and at Soboba on the San Jacinto Ranch faced imminent eviction. The Potrero village on the school section in the San Gorgonio Pass was also in danger. Lawson warned Hayt that there could be "serious trouble," for there was no place for the Indians to be removed to. "I fear Congress and the Department will not fully appreciate the condition of things in relation to these Indians until in their desperation they are driven to violence." To make matters worse, he had just learned from Horace F. Page, the congressman from California's second district and a member of the House Committee on Indian Affairs, that the proposed bill for "the relief of the Mission Indians" probably would not pass. Six days later Lawson wrote: "Congress has adjourned, and with it, seems to have passed away the last hope of a reservation for my Indians."[38]

Lawson's commitment to "his Indians" and the anger he felt at their worsening condition only intensified. In late April 1879, he wrote Hayt that with the petitions and appeals by influential men to congressmen, he found it "hard to understand" the "apathy that prevail[ed] on the part of Government toward these Indians." The previous week the last of the San Pasqual villagers had finally been evicted by the sheriff and were "forced into the desert mountains." The Santa Ysabel ranch owner had informed Lawson that he had "sustained twenty thousand dollars damages by their residence there," complaining that he was unable to rent the ranch "because Indians kill the stock." Furthermore the Rancho San Jacinto would be partitioned in a few weeks, and the Indians at Soboba forced out. "So a general rout is pending all along the line," he concluded. Prostitution and the attendant diseases, as well as drunkenness, were also on the rise. Still holding out for his concept of one big reservation for both Mountain and Desert Indians, he argued that all of these problems could be solved if only the Indians were consolidated on a suitable reservation, under the direction of an agent.[39]

By year's end Lawson was still convinced that his proposed reservation at San Gorgonio was the best solution. During a visit to the area in mid-December, he met with almost every settler in the immediate area and estimated that $25,000 would be sufficient "to extinguish all the claims of private parties" within the six townships he had selected. William Hickman, the owner of the San Gorgonio Flume Water Company, was demanding $10,000, but because Hickman had a large mortgage against his property, Lawson believed he could be bought out for $1,500 or $2,000. Getting this water supply would "make a reservation in that desert locality feasible," Lawson declared.[40]

During this visit, Lawson learned more about the potential of his proposed reservation, informing Hayt that he was "more fully settled in [his] conviction that it is the only suitable place in Southern California." His preference was so firm that he even objected to a proposal to buy the Santa Ysabel ranch as a central reservation for the Indians of San Diego County. He wrote letters to Washington, engaged the *San Diego Union* in debate, and "registered his disapproval" with California Congressman Page when the purchase of the Santa Ysabel ranch was proposed in Congress.[41]

To promote his one big reservation idea, Lawson visited the Indian Office in Washington in October 1879 to call upon Secretary Schurz and Commissioner Hayt. He was assured "that steps would at once be taken to bring the matter before Congress," leading him to believe that "his visit was an assured success," as he would inform Trowbridge, Hayt's replacement. But beyond "the offering of a bill by a California member," Lawson later reported that nothing was actually accomplished, even though he believed the Indian Department was doing what it could.[42]

Others were not so sure. The *San Diego Union* argued that Lawson himself was the problem. "He is an importation from Ohio," the paper complained, "who never saw a live Indian till he reached his 'Agency,' utterly ignorant of the Spanish language, and altogether the most thoroughly incompetent of the many incompetent men sent to California from the East to mismanage Indian affairs." The *Union* added a day later that however "*well meaning* he may be . . . in *action* he is most lamentably incapable."[43] A petition for Lawson's removal was circulated in San Bernardino in early 1880. He ascribed the movement to "the whiskey element" and "the rabble," writing to one of the local papers, "I hereby give notice that, barring a change in Administration. . . . I am here to stay." He even went so far as to threaten to stop making agency purchases in San Bernardino. "I want no further business relations with a community who repays patronage with insult and abuse."[44]

The Plight of the Warner's Ranch Indians

In addition to the eviction at Cuca, Lawson's agency suffered through another potential eviction, a result of an action taken by President Rutherford B. Hayes. On January 17, 1880, Hayes rescinded Grant's 1875 executive order creating both the Santa Ysabel and Agua Caliente reservations. The latter consisted of some 1,120 acres on Warner's Ranch, which by the spring of 1880 was owned by former California governor John G. Downey.[45] Thoroughly displeased with this cancellation, Lawson informed Acting Commissioner E. J. Brooks in early March that the situation now "should *magnify* the necessity of making strenuous efforts to secure beyond a doubt, the proposed reservation during the present session of Congress." Lawson saw little that gave him "much encouragement."[46]

As he was completing his second annual report, Lawson learned from Downey that since the Agua Caliente Reservation had been cancelled, he intended to sell Warner's Ranch—the Indians would have to move. It was the start of more than two decades of threats, court cases, and uncertainty. On the positive side, Lawson noted that an agency physician had been appointed. Unfortunately the doctor's isolation from most of the Indians made it "difficult to afford all benefits of his service."[47]

Insufficient Gains

Although Lawson never achieved his goal of one big reservation, he did achieve a few small victories. On January 10, 1881, he requested that Commissioner Trowbridge set aside certain lands for the "permanent use and occupancy" of about eighteen Luiseño families, who had been doing well at Rincon for a dozen years. Three years earlier "certain parties" had filed on the land under the Desert

“House of Indian Agency Doctor,” San Bernardino. Henry Sandham, who traveled with Helen Hunt Jackson, made this sketch for the 1900 edition of *Ramona*.

Land Act, but Lawson, after inquiring at the land office in Los Angeles, learned that the entries were fraudulent. Therefore he “earnestly” asked that these lands be set apart for the Indians, explaining that it would support not only these Luiseño families but other “landless and homeless Indians” as well. The Indians, willing to build a school and a grain mill at their own expense, wanted to be assured that their labor would not be lost. Two months later Lawson received a copy of an executive order dated March 2 “withdrawing from sale and setting apart a reservation for the permanent use and occupancy” of these Indians.[48]

A second small triumph occurred that summer at the village of Capitán Grande along the upper San Diego River, where in 1853 a small band of Diegueños had been moved from San Diego by Lt. John B. Magruder of the U.S. Army.[49] Some nineteen sections had been set aside as a reservation in 1875 by President Grant. Apparently Lawson had not yet visited Capitán Grande, but in early July 1881 he received a letter sent from the village, written on behalf of Ignacio Curo, the village captain. Despite describing the reserve as “uninhabitable” (“a mountain of granite boulders where a goat could not live let alone a man trying to live and gain a living from it") and lacking water, Curo wanted Lawson to try and set aside this land "if possible for him at once."[50]

Lawson informed Hiram Price, recently appointed Indian commissioner, that Curo had been troubled the past winter by a white squatter, who after establishing an apiary on his land, had refused to move. Lawson suggested to Price that Curo and others pay to have surveys made of their property. Enclosing Curo's map, Lawson "respectfully recommended" that Price set aside some eight sections as an executive order reservation instead of invoking the government policy of encouraging Indians to take up land individually (in severalty) under the Indian Homestead Act.[51] Describing this legislation as "objectionable to these Indians" and believing the homestead policy was premature, Lawson explained that while the Mission Indians had "adopted civilized habits in a great measure, they are not yet willing, in individual cases, to sever their tribal relations and assume the role of citizenship." Instead, an executive order reservation would "stop further encroachments into this canyon by white men and [would] rid the settlement of the man who has lately gone in."[52]

Lawson waited almost two years for Price's response, no doubt becoming increasingly frustrated. Apparently several of his letters had been overlooked because of the transfer of a clerk to another division of the Indian Office. Therefore not until early March 1883 did he receive an answer to his July 1881 letter. Price responded that an inquiry at the General Land Office had turned up homestead entries by a Charles Hensley and a James Meade on the same land claimed by Curo. "If the circumstances justify it," wrote Price, "these entries can be contested."[53] Unfortunately Lawson would not have the honor of officially removing Hensley; that task would be carried out by Horatio Nelson Rust, a future Mission Indian agent.[54]

Lawson's respect and appreciation for the hard-working Mission Indians was evident in his annual reports and letters, as was his growing frustration with the inactivity of the Indian Office and what he perceived as its mistreatment of him. Although this frustration was not as apparent in his official reports, it manifested itself in his personal letters to Indian Office officials. In late December 1881, he complained to Commissioner Price that since taking charge of the Mission Agency over three years earlier, all his letters on the subject of one large reservation for all the Mission Indians had resulted in nothing except "to make more clear the actual condition and needs of these Indians." Furthermore, his efforts "to adjust the varied and complicated difficulties arising from conflicting interests between Indians and whites" had failed to command "the attention of the Department"; as a result, his questions for both advice and instructions had gone unanswered.[55]

Part of the reason for the inattention, Lawson believed, was the sheer distance between California and the nation's capital. It was difficult through mere letters to make government officials understand the true condition of these Indians. Although he did not want to leave his post, he was willing to travel east and serve in the Indian Office or appear before the House Committee on Indian Affairs. He could more easily describe their situation in person. Already headmen from several tribes were determined to travel to Washington on their own. "They are growing impatient at what they considered the inability of the agent to do anything for them," confided Lawson. "It is useless to try to explain to them why I fail in my efforts [on] their behalf." He found the situation quite vexing, and "growing more complicated every day."[56]

A New Reservation

Lawson continued to deal with the issues as they presented themselves. In early February 1882, he informed Price that the captain of a band of Luiseños, numbering about thirty families, visited his San Bernardino agency "to consult on the subject of securing for them the land on which they live." These were some of the families who had formerly lived at Temecula and were driven from their homes in 1875. For the past decade they had "repeatedly been driven from other localities." However, within the past two years they had finally settled at Pechanga, "on a mountain, adjacent to the above ranch where they found spots of table-land which they cultivate, and in which, at great labor, they developed water by sinking wells." Although it afforded only "a scanty subsistence," it was nevertheless "their last refuge," and they feared, "with good reason, that when white men find they have improved and made it habitable, this also, will be taken from them." Although aware that the current government policy was to avoid creating more "small and isolated reservations," he queried: "[Y]et, what is to be done if government withholds from them this boon, small though it be, and fails to provide larger." He stood between the Indians who occupied the land and whites who had filed a claim, swearing it was "uncultivated, unoccupied, and not in the adverse possession of another." In frustration, Lawson explained that he could no longer simply watch "the Indian driven away, simply because he [is] an Indian and has no rights under the law." If he had his way, he would reserve from sale "every acre of government land now occupied by them."[57]

To learn first-hand more about their situation, in June 1882 Lawson visited the Pechanga village, witnessing their successful harvest of wheat and barley. Fortunately, on the 27th of that month, President Chester A. Arthur had set aside the area as an executive order reservation. In his August annual report, a delighted Lawson boasted that he had kept his promise to the Indians. "To me, as well as to these Indians," he wrote, "it was the most gratifying incident of the year."[58]

Soboba

There were setbacks as well. The Rancho San Jacinto Viejo in the San Jacinto Valley was finally partitioned in 1882, and Matthew R. Byrne, a San Bernardino businessman and investor, had acquired seven hundred acres in the northeast corner of the rancho, which included the two-hundred-acre village of Soboba. Originally, in 1842, the rancho had been granted to José Antonio Estudillo, and he and his heirs had always respected the Indians' right to live there. Granted an eviction order by the Superior Court of San Diego County, Byrne now demanded their removal.[59]

On March 21, 1883, Lawson wrote E. L. Stevens, acting Indian commissioner, informing him that Roques (or Rogas) Jauro, the Soboba captain, had visited him at the agency headquarters to report that a surveyor was now running lines north of the village on land occupied by two Indian families. To protect this land, Lawson recommended to Stevens that this tract be immediately set aside by executive order. In May Lawson received support from an unexpected source. Helen Hunt Jackson, a special commissioner appointed to investigate the "conditions and needs" of the Mission Indians, was in California at the time, touring Mission Indian villages. She had written Commissioner Price requesting that certain lands, including tracts adjacent to Soboba, be set apart for Indian use. Two days later Price recommended to Secretary Henry M. Teller that these lands be included in an executive order. On June 19, 1883, President Arthur concurred, setting aside the lands above Soboba.[60]

Thus in four short months Lawson, with unexpected help from Jackson, had secured the first lands for the Soboba villagers—even if those lands did not include the village itself. He believed the remainder of the Indians' land could and should be purchased by the government, but in the meantime Byrne filed his eviction suit. A long legal battle had begun.[61]

Reservation Day Schools

Lawson was given authority to open the first two Indian schools in Southern California in 1880, though neither were to be located on a reservation. The first, at Soboba, was taught by Mary Sheriff, who years later related its beginnings. In the summer of 1880 Roques Jauro had "asked the government to give them a school for their children." Lawson in turn had "urged the organization of one at

A peon game at the Soboba fiesta, circa 1910. In this popular gambling game, the men holding the blanket on the right are shifting the markers around before the other team tries to guess who is holding them.
Courtesy of the San Jacinto Museum.

Soboba as a test, not quite sure it would be a success." In November an old adobe house was set up as a school building.[62] A San Diego newspaper correspondent praised Sheriff's "industry, tact, earnestness and sympathy in the management of the Indian school," which had "four classes in reading," as well as "classes in geography, grammar and construction of sentences."[63] The second school, established at Agua Caliente, in the Cupeño village at Warner Hot Springs, was taught by Flora Golsh.[64]

These government day schools (as distinct from boarding schools) and their teachers became important day-to-day contacts between the agency and the Indians. Agents seldom visited reservations, but the teachers, mostly women, were present daily, living either in attached housing at the school or in the village. They did much more than simply educate the children—they taught housekeeping skills to their mothers and English to their fathers; they held Sunday School classes and formed temperance societies. They treated the sick, distributed food and clothing, and served as interpreters. These teachers helped the Indians successfully deal with the white world around them.

By the end of his tenure, Lawson had founded five day schools. In his third annual report (1881) he informed Price that he was "firmly convinced" that the expenditures spent building schools would "be more than justified by the results obtained." The latest census revealed more than seven hundred children of school age. "It is not a question any longer whether Indian children can be educated or not," he reported, "but a demonstrated fact that they have capacities equal to those of white children." Further, schools had at least some supporters among the Indians. In some villages, such as La Jolla, the Indians began making adobe bricks, believing that if they constructed a school house, a teacher would be sent. But that required specific approval from Washington. Lawson, like other agents who followed, believed that day schools could not adequately educate the Indians because of their scattered settlements. Therefore in his fourth annual report, dated 1882, he recommended the building of two boarding schools located "away from the influences of village or camp life."[65]

Lawson's successor, John G. McCallum, noted in his first annual report the presence of six active day schools, the last of which had been established at Rincon in April 1884. Attendance at all had been good until the heavy rains started. McCallum also mentioned the first attempt at a Catholic boarding school in Old Town San Diego, which closed after two months because most parents objected to sending their children that far from home. By the time of McCallum's second annual report, the number of reservation day schools had grown to eight, with an average attendance of twenty-three and a half.[66]

McCallum's successor, John S. Ward, was also active in advocating for schools. He disapproved of the Indian Office's 1887 decree that those with an average daily attendance of less than twenty be closed, a policy he viewed as unfair to villages with small populations. He recommended the minimum be lowered to fifteen.[67] The government insisted on its new rule, and by 1887–88 the agency had only four schools open all year. Three others ran only part of the year. The death of longtime teacher Nancy Ticknor at Cahuilla on May 7, 1888, so affected the entire tribe that Agent Joseph W. Preston deemed it advisable not to reopen it for the remainder of the term.[68]

When Horatio Rust took over the agency in 1889, there were eight government day schools, operating at Agua Caliente (present-day Warner Hot Springs), Cahuilla, Soboba, Potrero (present-day Morongo), Pechanga, Rincon, Mesa

Grande, and La Jolla. He recommended five more and an industrial school at Agua Caliente on Warner's Ranch.[69] None were approved. Rust believed the best way to elevate the Indian people was to first educate Indian children in a reservation day school, especially with kindergarten teaching, to "overcome the natural timidity" of the Indian child. Then the student should be sent on to a manual training school "entirely away from the reservation and all the old camp life and associations."[70]

A Female Special Commissioner

One person especially appreciative of the government school teachers was Helen Hunt Jackson, the New England–born poet, essayist, and recently turned Indian reform advocate.[71] Jackson had initially come to Southern California in the winter of 1881 to research articles for *Century Magazine.* After visiting Mission Indian villages and seeing their struggle first-hand, and aware of the threatened eviction of the Soboba village, she had written Secretary Teller to offer her assistance. In the summer of 1882 he appointed her an official agent (commissioner) of the Interior Department, authorized to visit the Mission Indian villages, secure lands for reservations, and write an official report, including recommendations to improve their conditions. She returned in February 1883, accompanied by Abbot Kinney of Los Angeles, whom she had met during her previous visit.[72] She also called upon former special agent John Q. A. Stanley to visit the Coachella Valley villages for her, incorporating his observations into her final report.[73]

Isolated at the Mission Indian Agency, Lawson was perhaps unaware of Jackson's reform writings or of her book *A Century of Dishonor,* published in 1881. Their paths had not crossed during her initial 1881 tour of the Mission Indians, but her official government appointment made a meeting necessary. They immediately got off on the wrong foot, misreading each other's intentions. Ironically Lawson, in his published annual reports, and Jackson, in her government report, agreed about the condition of the Mission Indians. Each in their own way used the limited powers they had to protect Indian lands.

Part of the misunderstanding was no doubt due to the failure of both Secretary Teller and Commissioner Price to alert Lawson of Jackson's appointment. Instead she had written directly to Lawson on February 26, 1883. "To my surprise," he responded to her on March 2, "the Indian Office has not up to date apprised me of, or given me any instructions relation to the mission upon which you have been sent."[74] He was already displeased with his treatment by Indian Office officials, and this oversight regarding Jackson could well account for their contentious relationship, an unfortunate situation considering they were both working for the Mission Indians' common good. They met only three times in March 1883; during one meeting he temporarily assigned his interpreter, Jesús Lopez, to serve as her driver and guide.[75]

As Jackson and Kinney toured his agency, Lawson began to hear disturbing rumors. He complained to Price that her meddling was stirring up "discontent and bad feeling." She had come "ostensibly to inquire into the Condition of the Indians," but instead she had "assumed the prerogative of the agent," causing him grief. During his last visit to Pechanga the Indians had even asked him whose orders they should follow. Furthermore, she had "restored the office of general" in the village—appointing a tribal member and giving him a commission—a position that Lawson had previously abolished. Describing Jackson as armed "with a mere sentiment, and no knowledge, practically, of the Indian character," he believed she was "seriously" compromising the "interests of the service," doing more harm than good. "All I have to say, and I say it reverently,—from future female commissioners, Good Lord deliver us!"[76]

Three weeks later Lawson wrote Price that he wanted to take back his earlier criticism of Jackson. It was not Jackson but Lawson's interpreter, Lopez, who was "the real author of the mischief," making statements and taking action on her behalf without her knowledge or approval. He believed the interpreter had a grudge against him for prosecuting "many of his [Mexican] countrymen for selling liquor to Indians." In the meantime, Lawson had written to Jackson, explaining the situation and admitting that Lopez was the real instigator of much of the unrest he had blamed on her. Upon returning to the agency, the interpreter had "openly boasted that he [had] gotten even on me, that Mrs. Jackson was going to raise h——l with me." However, to prove that he was still in charge, Lawson reminded Jackson that no matter what her instructions had been as a commissioner to investigate the condition of the Mission Indians, "it was clearly not" her duty "to assume authority in the Government or conduct of the Agency." In no uncertain terms, he declared: "That is what I am here for."[77]

During her investigation Jackson brought some issues directly to Lawson. She had learned that Arthur Golsh, the teacher at the Temecula Day School at Pechanga, had fathered a child at Pala, driven four families off their land, patenting it for himself, and had had relations with a young woman at Pauma. Because Golsh's sister, Flora, was a well-respected teacher at Agua Caliente, Jackson chose to contact Lawson instead of reporting Golsh directly to the Interior Department.[78] "If he will immediately resign, we will make no farther allusion to him," she wrote

Lawson, who responded bitterly that if her instructions from the government embraced "jurisdiction in such cases," and if she had thoroughly investigated the matter, he would of course comply. He, however, was skeptical of the rumors and wanted to investigate the charges further, requesting her sources of information.[79]

On May 13 Lawson agreed that the information Jackson had provided was reliable, and he would request that Golsh resign. Then, after meeting with Golsh one week later, Lawson informed Jackson that the teacher had denied all the accusations, claiming that Jackson had merely listened to his enemies. Peeved at Jackson's interference, Lawson informed her that "a better knowledge of the Indian character before starting on [your] mission would have been of incalculable value in [your] service." Golsh had engaged legal counsel, he claimed, and was determined to bring a suit against both Jackson and Kinney for "defamation of character." (Apparently no suit was filed, for Jackson made no further mention of the incident.) In his monthly report to Washington for May 1883, Lawson complained bitterly that Jackson had ordered him to ask for the teacher's resignation "under a threat of reporting certain matters respecting him to the Department." He felt the whole business had been forced on him in a very arbitrary manner, and asked to be pardoned if "any expressions in this report indicated insubordination."[80] In the end, Arthur Golsh lost his job.

Early on in their relationship, before misunderstandings and pride got in their way, Lawson actually turned to Jackson for assistance. Concerned about the fate of the Soboba village in the San Jacinto Valley, he had written her in March 1883, declaring emphatically that "in the name of justice and humanity they ought not to be removed from their present homes." It seemed to him that the seven hundred acres in question at Soboba could easily be bought at a fair price, and its purchase was "exactly in the line of duty" of her commission. Because there was "land trouble connected with almost any settlement," he suggested they meet, either in Los Angeles or at his agency, to consult directly rather than confer through letters. He expressed the belief that it would "become a question" for her to "settle upon the best plan of providing for homeless Indians like the San Jacinto, Agua Caliente and San Ysabel Indians."[81]

Although Lawson and Jackson continually butted heads, her investigative work made it possible for Price to cancel Mead's and Hensley's homestead entries at Capitán Grande—something that Lawson had wanted done. According to the commissioner, the General Land Office cancelled both entries "on the ground that the lands covered thereby had been occupied and cultivated by the Indians for a period of thirty one years and therefore were not open to settlement."[82]

The End of the Road

In Lawson's fifth and final annual report, dated August 13, 1883, he described his three thousand Serrano, Cahuilla, Diegueño, and Luiseño charges as "peaceable and law abiding." He pointed to various achievements, especially in the area of education; there were now five schools in operation, there were none when he was appointed. He also had made some headway in finding jobs for the Indian men, ensuring fair wages. He stressed that their biggest problem was the liquor traffic, which, through rigid enforcement, he had tried to contain even though the district judge in San Francisco regarded the sale of liquor to the Indians as "trivial." He concluded that the Mission Indians would only prosper and be self-sustaining "in proportion as the liquor traffic among them can be suppressed."[83]

Opposition from the whiskey sellers and continued misunderstandings with Jackson may well have finally pushed Lawson over the edge. Sometime in the first half of July 1883, he resigned as Mission Indian Agent.[84] On August 4, the *San Luis Rey Star*, quoting the *San Bernardino Times*, reported that he had resigned "preparatory to his being removed." According to the news item, Lawson was feeling "a sense of relief" for the first time in five years. He no longer had "Indian troubles or whisky traffic to fight" and was thinking about a trip East since he was entitled to a free trip back to where he had been appointed from. "He had better stay East," added the editor, "as the people have no used [*sic*] for him here." The editor also recommended the removal of that "busy body" Mrs. Jackson, whom he described as a "meddlesome feminine pet of the Hon. Secretary. In our opinion, no woman should occupy the position of Indian Commissioner; it is no place for any member of the femine [*sic*] gender."[85]

The rantings of the *San Luis Rey Star* appeared in print about the same time that Lawson resigned and Jackson completed her official report. Jackson and Kinney had recommended the resurveying and patenting of reservations to Indian residents, with a twenty-five-year trust period; removal of white trespassers; the purchase of the Santa Ysabel ranch, which Lawson opposed, as well as the Pauma Ranch; and at least two inspections annually of all reservations and villages. In addition, a law firm should be hired to represent the Indians; a more judicious distribution of farm equipment was needed; and a fund should be established for food and clothing for the aged and sick. And finally, the co-commissioners had recommended the establishment of more schools, especially at Rincon and Santa Ysabel.[86] It is likely that Lawson would have approved of most of their recommendations.

Jackson's dislike of Lawson was reflected in a comment she made in November 1883 to a friend: "Of course you have observed that Agent Lawson has been removed. I think he was a bad man." Although accused of having orchestrated his removal, in a November 1884 letter published in the *Council Fire*, a publication of the National Indian Defense Association, she denied it. "Grave charges had been preferred against Mr. Lawson by one of the California judges," she wrote, "and his removal already determined upon, before we [she and Kinney] went out; though of this I did not know till after my return." Although she did not think of Lawson as a "clear-headed or a discreet man," they "did not learn anything which proved him to be dishonest."[87]

Lawson, convinced that Jackson had cost him his appointment, may have been the author of an 1884 letter, sent from Colton and signed "Justice for the Indian," which appeared in the *Council Fire*. The writer described Jackson's role in the removal of an agent "against whom the Indian Office had had no previous complaint," and who had a "record of five years' faithful service." The writer complained that after Jackson, "without authority," had "interfered with the conduct of the agency," the agent, firmly and courteously, had pushed back, raising her "ire." In response she had written Secretary Teller, who removed the agent.[88]

T. A. Bland, editor of the *Council Fire*, informed his readers that the conflict apparently sprang from Lawson's opposition to Jackson's recommendation of the purchase of the Santa Ysabel ranch. According to Bland, the *Colton Semi-Tropic* had suggested "that as Agent Lawson opposed the scheme to Mrs. Jackson's face, and he was dismissed from the service soon after her return to Washington, she probably had something to do with his dismissal." Jackson, however, pointedly denied both accusations, noting that she had suggested the purchase only if the government needed a new reservation. She expressed sorrow that Lawson was so bitter. She also denied having any influence over Teller.[89]

It is difficult to define Lawson's legacy as the first Mission Indian agent. On a personal level he seemed to genuinely respect and appreciate these hard-working Mission Indians. As early as 1881 he had bragged that they were "as much civilized as the population by which they are surrounded; and if they are not up to the full standard, it is because of their surroundings."[90] Like the *San Diego Union*, which conceded that Lawson had "an honest desire to do his duty," historian Tanis Thorne describes the agent as "clearly and sincerely" focusing "his energies as an advocate for Indian people." She views his tenure as influencing the role of the Mission Indian Agency to expand and defend the Indian land base, although she faults his interference with the government purchase of the Santa Ysabel ranch and criticizes his "one reservation" policy as an attempt to consolidate Indian peoples against their wishes. She finds value in his correspondence with the Indian Office, describing it as revealing a "glimpse into the passing of the independent *rancheria* era for Southern California Indians" during a time when they had "enjoyed a modicum of prosperity and security." However, she accuses him of not learning their language or their culture—although it must be said that none of the other agents were familiar with their culture, and only Francisco Estudillo spoke Spanish. In his defense, Lawson had defended executive order reservations, thus preserving "communally-held reserves" in lieu of implementing the Indian Homestead policy, which would have forced the Indians to end tribal ties. His legacy was therefore "well-meaning" but "mixed."[91]

Lawson remained in Southern California the rest of his life, living in San Bernardino and Los Angeles. He still attempted to insert himself into agency affairs from time to time. In the mid-1890s he passed the bar and became an attorney, practicing law in Los Angeles off and on until shortly before his death at the Sawtelle Veterans' Home in December 1908 at the age of seventy-one.[92]

CHAPTER 3

▼ ▼ ▼

THE NEED FOR WATER

John G. McCallum, 1883–1885

> Nine-tenths of this [reservation land] is practically worthless, rough mountains and desert land; half of the remainder is good land, having sufficient water and timber, and the remainder would be valuable if water should be brought upon it; otherwise it is worthless. The Indians have not the capital or the enterprise to bring water on such lands. They are therefore useless to them now, and would likely continue so, at least until the next generation. At present they do not cultivate an average of one acre in one hundred of the lands reserved for them.
>
> —*J. G. McCallum, Annual Report (1884)*

It is hard to underestimate the value of water in Southern California, especially in the desert, and water remains an issue on local reservations to this day. But Agent John McCallum's words have a certain irony about them. While he did develop the first irrigation system at Palm Springs, the lion's share of the water went not to the Agua Caliente Indian Reservation but to his own nearby development. While affecting to be the Indians' friend, he could not protect them from his own ambitions, tainting his two-year tenure and leaving behind a questionable legacy.

At the time of his appointment McCallum had been a loyal Republican for years, and no doubt it was because of his long political service that U.S. Senator John F. Miller of California proposed him for the position of Mission Indian agent. He "is as honest a man as any now living," the senator wrote to Interior Secretary Henry Teller on July 17, 1883, "and a man of fine ability." Miller explained that McCallum was "not doing much" at the time and would be willing to accept the position, even though the original salary of $1,500 had been reduced to $1,300. "You can rely on him with perfect faith," continued Miller. "[H]e is a good lawyer, a good natured kind-hearted man, truthful, sensible and of high character."[1]

Teller agreed, forwarding his recommendation to President Arthur. After a little confusion in filing his performance bond, McCallum was confirmed, took the oath of office, and began his duties on October 1, 1883. The *Overland Monthly* "hoped that his thorough knowledge of the public land laws and of Mexican ranch titles" would be beneficial to his "Indian 'wards' in their conflicts with intruders."[2]

John Guthrie McCallum was born in Indiana on August 10, 1826. He practiced law there before coming to Northern California in 1854, settling initially in Placerville. Like other politically minded men of his day, he turned to the press to promote both his party, the American, or "Know-Nothing," Party, and his own political ambitions. He purchased an interest in the *Georgetown Weekly News* in El Dorado County, which he edited until his election to the state senate in 1855. In 1860 he supported Democrat Stephen A. Douglas for the presidency while he was publishing another newspaper in Placerville. During the Civil War he joined the new Republican Party and in 1868 was appointed register of the Government Land Office in Sacramento. He eventually moved to Oakland, where he practiced law. From 1878 to 1879 he served as a delegate to the convention that wrote California's current constitution. He had hoped to be elected to the new Railroad Commission, created to rein in the political power of the Southern Pacific railroad, but failed to win. Known in later years by the courtesy title of "Judge" McCallum, he never served on the bench.[3]

McCallum was attracted to the position of Indian agent in part because Southern California's warm dry climate would be especially healthy for his oldest son, who suffered from tuberculosis. He moved his family to San Bernardino in the summer of 1883, even before his appointment was complete. In October he began his first tour of the reservations, visiting the schools at Potrero (present-day Morongo) and at Soboba, both established by his predecessor, Samuel S. Lawson. In November McCallum took a week-long tour of nearly three hundred miles, visiting the other three agency schools and finding all the students "making remarkable progress in learning the elementary studies." The tour began in mid-November, when he reached the Pechanga school, where in the past water had to be carried nearly half a mile to the school. He was pleased to report to Commissioner Hiram Price that work on the new well there was progressing, and he had been able to purchase the supplies needed to complete it. The Indians "assembled to learn the policy of the government towards them, and to tell their wants." They requested a government wagon, and as the other schools had been given one, the agent respectfully asked the government to supply one.[4]

John G. McCallum.
Courtesy of Palm Springs Historical Society.

During this visit, McCallum also attended what he described as an annual feast of the San Luis Rey tribe, which was more than likely a Luiseño funeral ceremony. He described a gathering of "a few hundred Indians" a mile from the Temecula schoolhouse, with dancing and singing. Although he found the ceremonies "harmless in every aspect," he objected to the burning of Indian baskets and other goods, trying unsuccessfully to convince the leader of the feast that "it was very wrong to destroy their property when there were so many poor Indians who needed it." These ceremonies, he informed Price, "furnish arguments that it is very difficult to civilize the older members of the tribes." But McCallum believed that through education these various cultural practices would soon end. "The contrast between the Indian school children and their parents is so great," he explained, "that it is hard to realize that they are of the same family or even of the same race."[5]

McCallum and his party arrived at the Cahuilla Valley Indian school after dark on a very cold night and were forced to bunk down in the school room, wrapped in blankets because there were no beds. He commended the school teacher, who had done the best she could for her visitors. The agent described her as "evidently in earnest," and her reports as reflecting a "large monthly average attendance," with the children "fast learning to speak English." After a brief inspection, the group left early in the morning for the government school at Agua Caliente on Warner's Ranch. The Cupeño children there were "progressing rapidly" under their teacher, who was "earnestly and intelligently engaged in her work." He reported that they had written several letters to McCallum, showing "remarkable progress in penmanship and composition."[6]

The Cupeños had suffered a serious setback in January 1880; Warner's old Mexican land grant had finally been confirmed by the U.S. government, and the official survey included the village at the hot springs. Accordingly, President Rutherford B. Hayes had seen no choice but to rescind the 1875 executive order reservation. Because both the village and the school were within the limits of the confirmed grant, McCallum now met with the John Downey, the current owner. Downey informed him that "with great reluctance," he planned to evict the Indians within the year "to avoid the operation of the California Statue of limitations." Unsure if Downey was correct, McCallum later examined "the original grant of Agua Caliente at the U.S. Surveyor General's at San Francisco, and found that it contained the usual exception in favor of the [I]ndians who were on the grant."[7]

From Warner's Ranch, McCallum continued on to Santa Ysabel to look into the possibility of constructing another school, as instructed by Commissioner Price in his November 6 letter. The agent met with the nineteen-year-old captain, José Pablo, who informed him that the population of his village was 159, about 80 of whom were children. Although it was too late in the season to build an adobe structure, McCallum explained to Price that it was possible to construct a one-story frame school house, twenty-four by thirty feet, at a cost of $250. The Indians had agreed to help haul the lumber to the site. Heading back, down the San Luis Rey River, McCallum conferred with the captain at Rincon about the possibility of a school there but was unable to learn anything about the proposed school house at nearby La Jolla.[8]

One month later, McCallum's report to Price painted a very bleak picture. The case to eject the Indians from Soboba, long threatened by Matthew Byrne, had begun in the superior court of San Diego County; white settlers at the Potrero in San Gorgonio Pass were threatening to cut off the Indians' water supply; and drunkenness continued to plague the Indians in San Diego County. He concluded his report with a mention of the convictions of whites who supplied liquor to

The government school on the La Jolla Reservation, 1901.
Courtesy of the San Jacinto Museum.

the Indians, an issue that also had troubled his predecessor's administration, forcing Lawson to spent a great deal of time trying, mostly unsuccessfully, to get convictions. On a positive note, McCallum reported that school attendance was "good under the circumstances," despite Indian festivals and public holidays. He had received authorization to rent a suitable building for a school at Rincon and had conferred with a builder on the cost of constructing a school at Santa Ysabel. He concluded that a farm and a training school should be established at the agency, the latter especially because the boarding and day school started in San Diego in March had lasted only two months. Education was becoming more important since "public sentiment" was currently in accord with the government's educational policy, especially for any practice that would make the Indians "self supporting and qualified for citizenship."[9]

Eight months later, in his first published annual report, McCallum informed Price that the Mission Indians lived in about twenty villages, mostly in San Diego and San Bernardino counties. They were Spanish-speaking Catholics, with only about one in five speaking English. Wearing "the costumes of civilized people," they engaged in civilized pursuits, with few depending upon fishing and hunting. They were "peaceable and honest with but few exceptions," "show[ing] no disposition to resist the policy of the Government." Although not always following their agent's advice, they always respected "the orders of the Government." They were "subdued in manner," presenting "little self-reliance," much "like people who had been accustomed to bondage or other great wrongs." He concluded that given their recent progress, all indications revealed that the Mission Indians would "before long become a part of the people of this State having and exercising the rights of citizenship."[10]

In actuality the Mission Indians were not always subdued. Inadvertently or not, McCallum would soon choose sides in the running power struggle at Morongo, firing John Morongo as agency interpreter and replacing him with his political rival, Will Pablo, "who became not only his aid[e] but his fast friend." The agency physician, Dr. Albert Thompson, was retained at his post, and McCallum hired one of his own sons (probably Harry) as agency clerk to handle paperwork.[11]

Soboba Goes to Court

Legal troubles soon enveloped the Soboba village, requiring McCallum's attention. On December 10, 1883, the agent informed Commissioner Price that Byrne "had engaged counsel to commence proceeding to eject the Indians living in the San Jacinto Indian village" and that in turn the government had engaged a special counsel to defend them. This latter fact he had learned unofficially, and now requested more details.[12] The long-threatened case by Byrne to evict the Indians began in the Superior Court of San Diego County that same month. Earlier that year, Helen Hunt Jackson, at her own expense, had hired the Los Angeles law firm of Brunson & Wells to prepare a legal opinion on the Indians' rights. The lawyers concluded that the villagers held a legal right to remain on the land because Mexican law stated that land occupied by Indians could not be granted as a rancho without respecting their possessory rights, and it had been a consistent policy of the United States to respect property legally recognized by prior sovereigns.[13]

The government appointed Brunson & Wells as special counsel for the Mission Indians in this and all other eviction cases. On April 7, 1884, McCallum delivered to the law firm a copy of Byrne's complaint, along with a copy of the summons served on the Indians. The lawyers immediately requested a sixty-day extension to "appear and plead or file" any necessary motion. At the same time, the law firm suggested to the U.S. district attorney in San Francisco that this case (*M. Byrne v. Antonio Alas, et al.*) was appropriate for transfer to the federal court. After a consultation with the U.S. attorney general, the district attorney was instructed to assist Brunson & Wells "in protecting the interest of the Government." It was agreed that because local county influence might be unfavorable to the case, the law firm was to take appropriate steps to have the case removed to the federal court.[14]

Squatters at Morongo

Instructed to report specifically on the conditions at the San Gorgonio Reservation (Potrero) and the incidents of illegal white entry there, in early June 1884 McCallum arrived at the reservation, some thirty miles from his San Bernardino agency office. During the recent unprecedented rainy season, a dozen new cabins had been built on reservation lands by white trespassers, most of them in March and April. Although the cabins were not yet occupied, McCallum assumed they had been built so these intruders would "be first on the ground" when and if land became available to homestead. He had learned from his inquiries in the nearby town of Banning that residents believed this land would soon be restored to the public domain. After assuring them this would not happen, McCallum ordered the squatters to remove their cabins; most refused. Therefore he asked Price for "special instructions" that he could show the trespassers, as well as inquiring if he had the authority to "remove or cause the removal of such persons and their cabins."[15]

Commissioner Price responded with an announcement that all persons "occupying or having improvements on the Potrero Indian Reservation without authority of law" were to remove them. McCallum had these orders copied and posted at several locations, including the post office in Banning. Although the squatters took no notice, McCallum reported a few months later that no new trespass had occurred. He told Price that Agent Lawson had previously advised the white residents that they could occupy what they assumed would be railroad lands, but the area had still not been officially surveyed, so it was impossible to know exactly where these sections were located. Most of the settlers were on such lands, but a few had expanded their occupancy onto the reservation. McCallum could only report these facts since he had no means of enforcing the removal of these intruders. He asked Price to provide him with more detail so that, "[i]f force must be used, the instructions in that regard may be full and specific."[16]

McCallum—unlike Lawson—was also moving toward the idea that the reservation system in Southern California should be replaced by individual Indian homesteads. The sooner this happened, "the better it will be for the Indians as well as for the whites," he claimed.[17] In this view he was simply expressing what was becoming the mantra for the late-nineteenth-century Indian reformers—to break up reservations, allot the land, and turn the Indians into self-sufficient, pseudo-Jeffersonian farmers. In their official report, Jackson and Kinney had recommended the resurveying and patenting of reservation lands to a few Indians, with a twenty-five-year trust period. However, they cautioned: "Some of them are fit for it now, and earnestly desire it, but the majority are not ready."[18]

Incorporating the Jackson/Kinney recommendations, Commissioner Price had drafted a bill for the relief of the Mission Indians, and on January 10, 1884, he sent the draft and a printed copy of the report to Interior Secretary Teller, who forwarded them to President Arthur. The bill was presented to Congress on July 3, 1884, and it passed the Senate but failed in the House.[19] In November 1885, Commissioner John D. C. Atkins resubmitted a draft of the bill along with a copy of the Jackson-Kinney report to Interior Secretary Lucius Q. C. Lamar, who sent it on to President Grover Cleveland. In his annual report, the commissioner described this proposed bill as "the most feasible and satisfactory solution" to the inevitable starvation and extermination awaiting these people, "who, by the treaty with Mexico, were received on an equal footing with other citizens of that republic." Again the House of Representatives rejected the bill.[20]

Congressional failure to pass this legislation meant business as usual in Southern California, with little or nothing done to stop intrusion upon Indian lands. In the spring of 1885 McCallum was ordered to move the agency headquarters from San Bernardino to or near Banning. With its three saloons, one boarding house, one store, and a depot for the Southern Pacific railroad, Banning was not much of a town.[21] Unable to find anything suitable during his April visit there, he recommended to Price that a building be constructed at a cost not to exceed $3,500. Leaving Banning, he visited the nearby Potrero Reservation, which he described as "the largest and the best of all these reserves." The Indians there, he noted, had cultivated "four or five times as much land" as they had the previous season, in part because seeds had been furnished them by the government and there had been "recent copious rains." The fact remained, however, that "those Indians prosper best who work among the whites." McCallum believed that one of the chief duties of an agent was to induce his charges "to labor in civilized pursuits."[22]

Pressed from All Sides

The Mission Indians required more than just farmland; many also raised cattle and horses, grazing them on the open range. Just as with their farmland, white settlers had pushed onto the open range, forcing the Indians to move farther and farther into the hills. McCallum continually dealt with the Indians' complaints on this score. In May 1885, he received two letters from José Maria Moro, Cupeño captain at Agua Caliente (Warner Hot Springs) for more than thirty years, alerting him that a notorious white man, Bill Fain, had recently laid claim to the Indians' mountain pastures in Lost Valley, on the north side of Hot Springs Mountain. Writing on behalf of all the men of his village, Moro informed McCallum that Fain had demolished their corral and was now occupying land that they had used for more than forty years as pasture for their livestock. "We are most anxiously waiting for your reply," he wrote McCallum, "as said land is the only place where we can have our animals now that all the fields are under cultivation & planted with wheat, barley, potatoes, corn, beans peas etc." Fain, he added, was a bad man who "killed his own uncle and an Indian in San Diego and he is only a boy as yet."[23]

McCallum forwarded the letters along with two of his own to Wells, Van Dyke & Lee, Brunson & Wells's successors. He explained to Wells that as agent he had no authority to remove trespassers outside of the reserves. "I think it is clear, that all such matters are for the Courts," he noted, "and of course must be brought before the Courts by Attorneys for the Indians." Wells in turn submitted the letters to Secretary Lamar on August 18, but no further action seems to have been taken.[24] Fain filed his homestead and took control of the valley.[25]

Months earlier McCallum had received a letter from Capt. José Pablo at Santa Ysabel, advising him that "the new owners will be here to take possession in a few days." After explaining that the reservation was unfit for his people to live on and that there was currently no government land available for their settlement, Pablo nevertheless "kindly" asked McCallum to take steps to protect their interest. Enclosing this letter along with those written by Moro, McCallum explained to Wells, Van Dyke & Lee that he knew nothing of the situation at Santa Ysabel, noting that all lands referred to in these Indian letters were outside of the reserves on land over which he had no control.[26]

Charles C. Painter and the Indian Rights Association

About the time McCallum learned of the Cupeños' problem with Bill Fain, Charles C. Painter, the full-time agent for the Indian Rights Association (IRA), and Joshua W. Davis, a member of the Boston Indian Citizenship Committee, began an investigative tour to assess the condition of the Mission Indians.[27] Founded in 1882 by prominent evangelical Christian reformers interested in promoting their ideas of "civilizing" the Indians, the IRA employed Painter to work the halls of Congress. He had left his Massachusetts home in late May 1885 and headed west for a three-month tour of Indian reservations, beginning in Indian Territory (modern-day Oklahoma) and then on to California. Having read Helen Hunt Jackson's novel *Ramona* and her government report, he was eager to visit the Mission Indians, making a quick tour of some villages before visiting the ailing author in San Francisco in late June. He believed she was comforted, in "her closing day," to know that the IRA had sent him to investigate the Mission Indians, "whose sad story she had told in Ramona with such moving pathos, and whose wretched and hopeless condition weighed so heavily upon her heart."[28] She was indeed pleased with his visit, asking that he make a more detailed tour through the Indian villages. To Antonio F. Coronel and his wife, Jackson wrote: "I have been much cheered by an interview with Prof. Painter," and "if he really undertakes to get something done for those Indians, he will be worth more than all the Senators and Congressmen put together."[29]

Enlisting the help of Coronel, Abbot Kinney, and Horatio Rust, a member of the Los Angeles branch of the IRA and later a Mission Indian agent, Painter and Davis had arranged a meeting with various village captains at Pala.[30] Painter had specifically requested that the captain at Santa Ysabel assemble as many Indians as possible. Almost four hundred, including twenty-eight village captains, gathered on July 15, 1885, some traveling great distances. Painter and his party failed to appear, however, disappointing the Indians. Three days later the captain received a letter explaining that the hot weather had made it difficult for the women in his party to travel; Davis's wife and Rust's daughter had accompanied them. Painter did, however, send ten dollars to Father Antonio Ubach, a long-time friend to the Mission Indians, to help defray the expenses of the village captains.[31]

Father Ubach was also displeased with Painter and Davis's conduct, commenting to General William S. Rosecrans, "[W]hat *report* can these two gentlemen make to the Government after acting in such a manner." It is not known if Ubach was aware that Painter and Davis were not official agents of the government; his comment leads one to believe that he assumed they were. He concluded that "this kind of behavior has been the same by every special delegation sent out from Washington for the past 20 years," except for that of Jackson and Kinney. They had "done their duty nobly and faithfully," visiting one Indian Pueblo after another and seeing the real condition of the Indians for themselves. Their official report "will be an eternal monument of the truth, justice and fair play which has received the applause and admiration of everyone that has read it."[32]

Ubach may have viewed Painter's actions negatively, but the IRA agent proved to be a consistently strong advocate for the Mission Indians. He visited their villages in 1886 and 1887, and in 1891 carried out one of the most extensive and successful investigative tours in the history of government Indian affairs in Southern California, leading to the establishment of a number of new reservations. More important, after each of his investigations, Painter wrote extensive reports, published and widely circulated by the IRA. In this manner the public, government officials, and Indian reformers were kept current on illegal encroachments, the liquor traffic, removals, and any other problems faced by the Mission Indians. These issues were then discussed at the annual fall Lake Mohonk Conference of Friends of the Indian (LMC).

Painter soon assumed a much larger role in the Soboba case. By mid-1885, following his appointment to a judgeship, Anson Brunson had retired from Brunson & Wells. Then Painter learned that G. Wiley Wells had withdrawn from the case, "because the Government refuse[d] to allow even his necessary expense account," he explained to Coronel in a letter written in late June. Because the eastern "friends of the Indian" were "much disappointed" with Wells's "professional conduct in the case," Painter asked Coronel to organize a conference at his home, to include Congressman Henry Harrison Markham, as well as Kinney and Rust, so they could all "settle on a practical line of conduct to be pursued." Out of their talks Painter hoped that some action could be taken to establish "that under the Treaty with Mexico these people [Mission Indians] were citizens of the United States." Personally interested in the fate of the villagers at Soboba, Painter now brought the powerful IRA into collaborative effort with prominent local "friends of the Indian" to defend this village as well as support the struggle for Mission Indian rights.[33]

The literary world and the Indian reform arena lost a most able advocate when Helen Hunt Jackson died on August 12, 1885, of cancer. Already her articles, her novel *Ramona,* and her report to the government, authored with Kinney, had drawn Painter and the IRA to the Mission Indian cause. The Women's National Indian Association (WNIA) and the LMC would soon follow. The LMC was an annual three-day forum bringing together a diverse group of individuals, including government officials, representatives from various religious societies, clergy from all denominations, members of congressional Indian committees, army officers, heads of Indian schools, presidents of universities and colleges, members of the national Indian reform associations and the Board of Indian Commissioners (BIC), and editors of secular and religious newspapers. In this forum, conference attendees determined the government's Indian policy.[34] Individually and collectively these reformers carried on Jackson's work among the Mission Indians of California. While the IRA provided financial and legal support, the LMC served as a strategic nerve center and the WNIA established missionary work in remote Mission villages.[35]

Health Care in the Mission Indian Agency

The Mission Indian Agency was not provided with a government physician until about 1881. The results were far from satisfactory. Every agent from Samuel S. Lawson to Lucius Wright called for the establishment of a hospital and home for the elderly, where long-term care could be provided—to no avail. But that was not the worst of it. The physician, once appointed, was always stationed at the agency headquarters—first in Colton/San Bernardino and later in San Jacinto—and he generally expected his Indian patients, no matter how ill, to come to him. To make matters worse, in the early years the agency physician also served as the agency clerk, tying him to a desk and dominating much of his time.

Jackson addressed this situation as early as 1883 in one of the recommendations in her *Report on the Conditions and Needs of the Mission Indians*. The physician, she wrote, should be "young, strong, [and] energetic" and "willing to make at least four circuits a year through the villages." Furthermore, he should be "bound to go when called in all cases of epidemics, serious illness, or accidents occurring among the Indians within one day's journey of the agency headquarters." He should be paid an adequate salary, "or else the office of agency physician to the Mission Indians should be abolished." She concluded, "[A]nything less than this is a farce and a fraud."[36]

Even after a physician was actually in place, problems emerged. Former Agent Lawson accused Agent McCallum's physician, Dr. Thompson, of taking government-issued medical supplies for his own use, "with the tacit approval" of the agent. In 1885 Special Inspector Robert S. Gardner was sent out to investigate the accusation and reported that Thompson was "a good physician . . . both honest and capable" of giving "satisfaction to the Agent and to the Indians." The inspector had made a "particular inquiry touching the character of both Dr. Albert Thompson and S. S. Lawson for Truth and Veracity," describing Thompson's character as "above suspicion and beyond reproach" and pointing out that he had "not been the subject of criticism." Lawson, however, he noted, had "to some extent been the subject of criticism by some of the leading citizens of this place."[37]

Lawson made another complaint in 1891—this time to the newspapers. The agency physician, he wrote, was "utterly needless and useless." He claimed that "not one in a hundred ever applies for or receives [medical care] once in three months." Instead, he accused the physician of spending much of his time investing in real estate. The Indian, he notes, fails to see "why he should be told to work and earn his living, when he sees a useless official, receiving a salary for no other reason that he knows of, except that he may have the opportunity for personal gain in outside business ventures."[38]

These outside complaints joined the stream of protests found in the Mission Indian agents' annual reports to Washington officials. Nearly seven hundred Indians came asking for medical help in 1885–86, Agent John S. Ward would report. But there were hundreds more too feeble to make the trip. "To make the medical arm of the service useful to the Indian," Ward informed Indian Commissioner Atkins, "the physician should be furnished with horse and buggy and medicine and sent" once a quarter among the Indians. He should be paid $1,000 a year.[39] A year later Ward explained that although Dr. W. E. Ferrebee had done much to convince the Indians of the effectiveness of the "white man's medicine," there had been epidemics of whooping cough and measles, and worse, reports of smallpox in Los Angeles. Understandably the Indians greatly feared this disease, and some had "broken out" of the reservations to escape infection. Ward asked for vaccine, and many accepted the procedure, he said—except for Cabezon, who refused to allow the children of his village to be vaccinated.[40]

In 1889 Agent Rust recommended the establishment of a government hospital at Warner Hot Springs, with the agency physician stationed there. "It is a pitiable sight to see these confiding people bring their invalids 30 to 125 miles in a wagon to be treated," he noted in 1890 in his report to Commissioner Thomas Jefferson Morgan.[41] He was less than impressed with Dr. Ferrebee, writing confidentially to Morgan in 1891 that the medical services he provided were "not what white people would desire," although the doctor "discharged his duties faithfully." At times Rust had been forced to ask local doctors living closer to the reservations to care for some Indians—but he had no money to pay them.[42] In his annual report in 1891 he was at least able to report that the duties of clerk and physician had finally been separated.

When the agency physician ventured into the field, that meant he was not at his post when Indians came to the agency. Pointing this out in 1893, Agent Francisco Estudillo recommended contracting with a local doctor to fill in when needed. "The sick of the many reservations in my care are certainly in a very sad condition," he reported a year later. There had been no provision made for their comfort or for their support. "The insane are in no better condition," he continued, "without a place to confine them they become a serious charge and care to this agency." The aged and infirmed were yet another problem, many of whom he described as "homeless and without shelter." Estudillo again recommended a hospital and also a safe place for "the few insane Indians."[43]

When Estudillo moved the agency to San Jacinto, Dr. Charles C. Wainwright, the agency physician, moved with him.[44] The doctor provided his own annual report for 1894–95 to accompany Estudillo's report. Wainwright had visited nearly every village four times that past year, teaching the Indians "the use of domestic and simple remedies." He listened to their maladies, promising them only what he could perform in the hope of gaining "a better foothold on their confidence and trust." For assistance, he asked the day school teachers and government field matrons to hand out the medical supplies he provided to cure simple ailments like colds, and fevers, "thereby strengthening their influence over the Indians." He reported that more and more people were turning away from the "medicine men," and even some of the *hechiceros* (witches) he knew agreed with him. "[I]ndeed, some of them are my most ardent supporters," he claimed, "and never want to be without some of my medicines in their houses at all times." In his lengthy 1897 report, Wainwright listed numerous diseases, such as "[l]a grippe, consumption, scrofula, idiopathic anemia, disease of the heart and its appendixes, venera, and pneumonia," that preyed on the Indians, partially because many slept in dirty, unventilated houses and had insufficient food. "To reach the most people," he reported, he spoke to all residents whenever he visited a reservation. In this way he also gathered vital statistics, "the only correct way." He defined this as "a very important part of the service."[45]

The Office of Agency Physician for Southern California was finally abolished on June 30, 1901. "I believe this was a step in the right direction," Agent Wright reported. The various reservations were "so scattered and separated as to make it impracticable for one physician to give prompt and efficient treatment to the Indians." Instead local physicians were employed, and as agent, he issued medicines from his office and while visiting reservations. In addition simple medicines continued to be furnished by all day school teachers and were distributed when needed. "This plan is more economical and satisfactory," Wright concluded.[46]

"The present system, if it can be called a system, is very unsatisfactory," Agent Charles E. Shell reported in 1904 after he had taken charge of the southern portion of the old agency. Because of the scattered reservations, he found it impossible "to decide intelligently in all cases whether it is wise to call a physician or not." He was forced to defer to the judgment of either the teacher, if there was one, or the Indian captain. "The teachers generally use good judgment, while some of the captains do not." Then, of course, there was always the "inclination on the part of some physicians to make as large a bill as possible," he noted, "under the popular impression that the Government is rich and legitimate prey."[47]

McCallum's Departure

The slowly emerging interest among Indian reformers on behalf of the Mission Indians unfortunately did little to benefit them during McCallum's tenure. He tendered his resignation on August 22, 1885. By then, a number of complaints about his activities (or inactivity) had already reached Washington. In July, James Faris, a deputy marshal at San Bernardino, complained that he and other law enforcement officers had been working hard to arrest men selling liquor to the Indians, "without encouragement or assistance of Agent McCallum," and asked that they be reimbursed out of government funds. In August one S. K. Lankston informed the commissioner that McCallum had allowed his friend "Dr." Welwood Murray to hire the Indians to cut wood on the Potrero Reservation, which Murray then sold, and that McCallum had inflated school attendance figures so that Mrs. Murray could keep her job as teacher on the reservation.[48]

Early in September, a few days before McCallum's resignation became official, Father Ubach wrote General Rosecrans, sending him San Diego newspaper articles with references to McCallum. Ubach asked Rosecrans whether he thought it prudent that he show this information to Secretary Lamar "so that he may see for himself and appoint to such an office some other person who will in a more conscientious manner discharge his trust." General Rosecrans forwarded this information to Washington officials.[49]

By then, McCallum was on his way out, but he insisted on submitting one last annual report at the end of the month. He presented a seemingly detailed census report, showing a total of 3,070 Indians under his agency (770 of them children, ages six to sixteen). He broke the number down further: 1,142 Luiseños, 793 Cahuillas, 745 Kumeyaays, and 390 Serranos, living in thirty-two villages totaling from just 18 to 236 residents, and twenty-one scattered reservations with a total of two hundred thousand acres. McCallum reported that they had received "an unusually liberal allowance of agricultural implements" during the past year, as well as seven more wagons and a large supply of grain seed.[50]

For some unexplained reason he added to the census figures over 100 Chemehuevis in San Bernardino County, plus other Indians living in and around Los Angeles and San Diego (many of the latter, he noted, were born in Baja

California but had been living in the United States for more than thirty-five years). The numbers get even shakier when he admitted that an actual census was conducted only in the eight villages that had schools, with the remainder of the figures being estimates. Thus his totals—and presumably all those before and after this report—must be treated with care.[51] Obtaining an accurate census always presented a challenge, and fifteen years later Agent Wright provided an interesting reason for the dilemma. "The Indians[,] not understanding the design nor appreciating the efforts of the Government to count and classify them," suspected "some sinister motive," and "many positively refused to answer the questions of the census agent." As a result totals are "perfectly unreliable and worthless, some reservations not being visited at all."[52]

McCallum, like Lawson before him, had achieved considerable gains in education. There were now eight schools within the agency, five of which were in newly constructed frame buildings, two as replacements for adobe structures ruined in 1884's heavy rains. Two others were in rented buildings. A ninth schoolhouse for Santa Ysabel had been authorized. McCallum reported that as a group, the schools had an average attendance of some twenty-three students.[53]

McCallum's Later Activities

Although Indian school children seemed to have benefited during McCallum's two-year administration, in the end the agent himself benefited more, mostly to the detriment of the Cahuilla people at Palm Springs. Seeking a better climate for his tubercular son, McCallum took the advice of Capt. Will Pablo and began acquiring land in the Palm Springs area. The family moved to the valley in 1887, making them among the first permanent non-Indian residents in the area. Around 1880, two San Bernardino investors, W. E. Van Slyke and Matthew Byrne, the owner of the Soboba tract, had begun buying adjoining land from the Southern Pacific railroad and together established the Palm City Land and Water Company. On March 24, 1885, well before leaving office, McCallum had purchased some 320 acres, or one-fifth interest in this land, as well as an equal share of the development company.[54] He continued his purchases until he reputedly owned more than 6,000 acres. In 1887, when Southern California real estate was booming, he incorporated the Palm Valley Land and Water Company, which laid out the first subdivision of modern-day Palm Springs, setting McCallum on a collision course with the Indians who had lived there for centuries.[55]

In early November 1885 more of McCallum's questionable activities were exposed to the Indian Office by his successor, John S. Ward, who—McCallum's biographer complains—had been "swept into the opposition camp."[56] Ward accused McCallum of using his knowledge of the availability of land, which he had garnered as Mission Indian agent, to illegally acquire thousands of acres in the vicinity of modern-day Palm Springs. Before McCallum had left office, a number of applications under the Desert Land Act were cancelled, and the land returned to the public domain. Within a few days of his retiring, McCallum was employed as attorney for most of these applicants. He argued that "inasmuch as these filings were allowed by the Government officials"—meaning himself—"they ought not to be canceled now."[57] He then led "an effort to re-enter these lands." In many cases McCallum even filed the applications personally in the Government Land Office in Los Angeles. During his investigation into the matter Ward had learned that "not a person now living in and around these lands ever heard of the names of the persons in whose names the Desert Land entries were made." McCallum "may have had the *legal right* to act as attorney against the Indians, within a few days after he retired from the Agency," Ward concluded, "but I think he had no *moral* right to assist in defeating the Indians in their efforts to get lands."[58]

Ward pointed out that McCallum had also purposefully failed to inform the Cahuillas of their "equal rights with the white man to enter homesteads or other entries on these lands." Ward concluded that this "large land grabbing scheme" could easily be upset by "prompt action on the part of the President" to withdraw the forfeited desert lands from settlement and "set them aside as part of said Reservation."[59] Following up on these accusations, a special agent named Heath was sent out to look into the matter. After he met with Ward he went out into the field, investigated the wood-cutting incident, accusations that "Dr." Murray had stolen water from the Indians, and McCallum's assistance to other investors evicting Indians from lands they had purchased. Given the chance to respond, McCallum denied all these charges. Strangely, it was the least of the charges—the wood cutting—that finally landed McCallum (and Murray) in court. But in 1889 they were acquitted when the district judge in Los Angeles ruled that the wood had come from railroad land.[60]

All this would be a little less offensive were it not for the way McCallum's family later praised his work as Indian agent.[61]

CHAPTER 4

▼ ▼ ▼

A BRIEF, BITTER TENURE

John Shirley Ward, 1885–1887

> Clothe the Indian with the insignia of citizenship, and invest him with title to land in fee simple, and it still does not make him a man without he has been taught the arts of industry and has solved the problem of self-support. The transition from the lounging, loitering, lazy, lousy son of the forest, to the full stature of self-supporting citizenship, is one which demands the highest order of practical statesmanship for its solution. . . . He must be taught to work by persuasion if possible, by force if necessary. I hear a righteous howl from some well-meaning but impractical enthusiasts, saying this would be "an abridgment of man's personal liberty." The pilgrimage through the desert was a necessary preparation to those who were to enter the land of promise.
>
> —*John S. Ward, Annual Report (1887)*

By the 1880s, attitudes toward the American Indian were changing, but many people still believed they were nothing but "lounging, loitering, lazy, lousy" savages. It is a pity that one of these believers became the third Mission Indian agent. The Biblical allusion in John Shirley Ward's final annual report cannot hide his contempt for the people he was charged with helping. His report also betrays his firm belief that he alone knew what was best for the Indians and could offer the only way to bring them to that "promised land." Denied that opportunity, after less than two years in office, he resigned in a remarkable (and very public) display of frustration.

Ward assumed the duties of running the Mission Agency on October 1, 1885. Born in Madison, Alabama, on August 25, 1834, he was living in Nashville when the Civil War broke out. A staff officer in the Confederate Army, he was captured, spending two years as a Union prisoner. At war's end he returned home and worked for a time as editor of the *Nashville Union and American* before becoming

John S. Ward.
Confederate Veteran magazine, February 1905.

editor of the *Ladies' Pearl,* a literary and religious journal associated with the Cumberland Presbyterian Church. In 1873, he moved his family to Southern California, seeking a milder climate for his son, Shirley C. Ward, who in early 1886 would replace G. Wiley Wells as attorney for the Mission Indians and in this capacity would work closely with his father on the Indians' behalf.[1]

One of Ward's first actions as agent was to return Captain John Morongo to the role of agency interpreter. Not everyone was pleased. Months later, Chief Gervasio Cabezon, son of "Old" Cabezon and a respected Cahuilla leader in his own right, met with U.S. Inspector Robert S. Gardner to complain about "all the wrongs done" his people by Morongo, "who claimed to be Chief." The inspector and Agent Ward decided that in the government's eyes, Morongo would no longer hold that position, "that he had no commission to be Chief." He was now simply an interpreter and a teamster—"nothing more."[2] His duties as interpreter, however, were by no means light; his work took him everywhere.

Because each branch tribe in the district spoke its own dialect, Morongo had to learn all of these as well as Spanish and some French. He was also "a familiar figure in many courts . . . intimately known by government and state officials."[3]

More Trouble in the Pass

Like his predecessors, Ward dealt with the continual encroachment of white settlers upon the Potrero Reservation (the present-day Morongo Reservation) in the San Gorgonio Pass. In early November 1885 he made a thorough investigation of the Indians' numerous complaints, reporting that a Mr. Jost had settled on a stream above the Indian village near the mouth of Potrero Canyon and that his fences were blocking the passageway from the reservation to the Indians' mountain pastures. Actually, C. F. Jost and his wife Margret had moved in before the land was set aside as a reservation. They were living on Section 25, an unsurveyed tract, and therefore held the land only "by occupancy." Ward reminded Assistant Commissioner Alexander B. Upshaw that according to the presidential executive order of August 25, 1877, all unsurveyed parcels in the area were reserved for Indian use. Therefore the agent suggested that the government pay Jost $2,000, the estimated value of his home and improvements, and order him to leave. This would remove "a source of present and future trouble and give great happiness to the Indians." He trusted the commissioner would give this prompt attention.[4] The Josts were eventually bought out, but not for several years.

Barely three months later, Ward informed Commissioner Atkins that any hope of the Indians getting a crop planted at Potrero for the spring had been dashed by trespassers who had sown "nearly all the land fit for cultivation," forcing the Indians to plant only where they could "find a vacant spot." Ward concluded that the "Indians and their friends hope the Government will soon decide to act in the matter." On the positive side Ward reported to Atkins that the agency schools were doing well and the health of the Indians was "generally good."[5]

In June 1886 Ward made a hasty return to the Potrero at the behest of Assistant Commissioner Upshaw. Alerted by a letter, Upshaw had telegraphed Ward that someone was diverting Indian water there. Ward, accompanied by Captain Morongo, examined every stream, enduring heat that rose to 120 degrees. Finally, out on the desert, six miles from where any Indian lived, they found two men engaged in such activity; Ward ordered them to cease. The agent assured Upshaw that this incident amounted to nothing—this water had never been used by the Indians, and furthermore "they express no concern about it." Hoping to interview the individual who had alerted Upshaw of the water theft, Ward requested a copy of the original letter. Apparently the letter writer had made some negative comment on Ward's lack of knowledge about the reservation. It is unknown whether Ward ever saw this letter. In his defense, Ward wrote Upshaw: "My facilities for a knowledge of what is being done at the Potrero could not be better if I lived on the Reservation." Morongo, whom he described as "the most intelligent Indian in the Mission Agency," did live there, and he was "wide-awake to every interest of the Indian." Ward assured the commissioner that "the Potrero Indians are happy & contented & keep the Agent thoroughly posted as to all their wants."[6]

The Potrero was again on Ward's mind as he wrote his first annual report on August 14, 1886. He described the reservation as "covered over with squatters who have settled there long since the lands were set aside for Indian purposes." They were openly defying the law, and some had even brought cases for adjudication before the Interior Department. Ward concluded that the "squatters should never have a standing in court till after they [are] dispossessed." In their cases before the secretary of the interior at least some of the squatters were represented by former Agent McCallum; but he failed to sway the secretary, who ruled against them.[7] Ward reported yet another trespasser at Potrero in mid-November. For several weeks, "in open defiance of [Ward's] orders," this particular intruder continued to plow and sow, "preventing the Indians from putting in their grain." Ward also complained of still one more trespasser who was building a house on the land—the same land whose filing had been rejected by the General Land Office. The agent viewed all intruders as simply laughing at the government's efforts to aid the Indians. "What shall I do?" he asked.[8]

Meanwhile, Agent Ward's son, Shirley Ward, was busy juggling the various cases arising from the complicated land situation at Potrero. In an October 1886 letter to Henry S. Pancoast, a Philadelphia attorney, the younger Ward explained that in August 1877 President Hayes had withdrawn the even-numbered sections and some unsurveyed parts of Township 2 South for a reservation. Unfortunately when the executive order expanding the reservation was issued, there were already several desert land filings in the area, parts of which had not yet been officially surveyed. These claims had later been abandoned and, Ward argued, had thus automatically become part of the reservation under the executive order. But since then, other individuals had filed on the same lands, claiming instead that when the old entries were cancelled, that land had reverted back to the public domain. Using the argument that the land was now part of the reservation, Ward had filed objections before the commissioner of the General Land Office, winning several cases.[9]

Although squatters at Potrero remained an issue, in his first annual report Agent Ward took pride in announcing that he had added three new schools, making a total of eleven, with some 222 students. He later told a reporter that his "motto" was "Education and Agriculture; the only hope of the Indian."[10] He described his charges as occupying "a rather anomalous position," under a "most dangerous condition." "They are a little too much civilized to be an Indian and not civilized enough to be a white man." However, like his predecessors, he still faced the pernicious problems of relentless white intrusion everywhere and illegal liquor traffic.[11]

Ward devoted a lengthy paragraph to his personal attempts to remove liquor from the agency, which almost always were to no avail. Although all but one case that he brought before the U.S. commissioner in Los Angeles had been bound over to appear before a U.S. grand jury in San Francisco, "not one has ever been punished." The only case that ever reached the San Francisco court was thrown out without an investigation. He did acknowledge that he had some success in state courts, but the penalties were so light "as not to deter a vender from continuing the nefarious practice."[12]

The Liquor Traffic

Prohibited by federal and later by state law, the sale of alcohol to the Indians remained a perennial problem throughout the second half of the nineteenth century—not just the crime and the social problems alcohol caused, but the way it was perceived by outsiders. It took only a few drunken Indian men for some whites to conclude that all were drunkards. Yet a number of contemporary observers concur that the Mission Indians were no more addicted to alcohol than their white neighbors. For the Mission Indian agents, prosecuting these cases was a constant struggle. First, federal charges were presented to the U.S. commissioner in Los Angeles. If the case was sent to trial, a hearing was held in the U.S. District Court in San Francisco—requiring defendants, attorneys, witnesses, and often the Mission Indian agent to travel halfway up the state. Conviction was never guaranteed, and fines were often small. In 1883 Agent Lawson had declared that the liquor traffic had been "[the Indians'] greatest curse in the past." He complained that because the U.S. district judge in San Francisco regarded "the selling of liquor to Indians as a 'trivial offense,'" he meted out "trivial" penalties, thus encouraging rather than suppressing the traffic.[13]

During his tenure, John Ward presided over one of the most convoluted liquor cases of the time, which began at Capitán Grande in July 1887 when seven "hard looking" men were arrested. Among them was a certain Patrick Cody. Ward brought them for a preliminary hearing before U.S. Commissioner William M. Van Dyke in Los Angeles; the men all pled not guilty. Their bail was set at $500 each—which none of them were willing (or able) to pay. All seven were packed off to the county jail.[14]

The sale of alcohol by these men had been discovered by Charles C. Painter. On yet another investigative tour on behalf of the IRA, he had been visiting Capitán Grande when he discovered "five liquor saloons in full blast on the reservation." He informed the authorities, including John T. Wallace, a special inspector with the Justice Department. Eventually Wallace, a U.S. marshal named Dunlap, and troops under General Nelson A. Miles were involved in the roundup of the seven men. According to Painter, their supplies of beer and ale were destroyed and a wagon load of whiskey and wines was confiscated. In a July 17 letter to Joshua W. Davis, Painter explained that the raid was scheduled for early the following morning, concluding, "I hope it will be a success." Taking credit for the situation, Painter wrote, "[I]t is a commentary on the way officials discharge their duties that this raid had to be instigated by the agent of the I.R.A." He complained that Ward had ridden by at least two of the saloons last spring, taking "all his information of things there from the keepers of two others; and left them undisturbed."[15]

Several of the men eventually pled guilty and were fined. But Cody held out for a jury trial. His case finally came up for a hearing in August 1888, and trial was set for September but was then continued.[16] In the meantime, U.S. District Attorney J. Marion Brooks fought to block the return of liquor and saloon fixtures that had been taken from several of men, including Cody. Brooks petitioned the district court to sell the confiscated goods to help pay for their prosecution, which he estimated at about forty-five dollars per man.[17] When Cody's case finally went to trial in February 1889, he claimed he was unaware that he was even on an Indian reservation, producing several witnesses to testify on his behalf. He was acquitted.[18]

Despite such disappointments, most of the Mission Indian agents, especially Lawson, Estudillo, and Wright, continued their efforts to fight against the liquor traffic. When California lawmakers finally banned sales to Indians around 1884, higher fines were set and it became possible for them to prosecute cases in the local courts.

The Soboba Case

Other issues besides liquor cases were also moving through the courts. On October 28, 1885, Assistant Commissioner Upshaw ordered Agent Ward to visit the Soboba Reservation and investigate the requests of two Indians, Rosario

Osia and José Jesus Castillo.[19] They were asking to have their lands set aside in severalty as personal property. The Byrne eviction suit (see chapter 3) no doubt had prompted Osia and Castillo to make this unusual request. It was the village that was in dispute in the Byrne case; the two Indians lived farther up in the hills on the reservation that had been set aside two years earlier. The Indian Homestead Act of 1875 had made it possible for Indians to obtain land on their own, but this legislation applied only to land in the public domain. "Until there is some law by which Indians can secure Homesteads within Reservations," wrote Ward to Upshaw, he would have to deny both requests.[20]

Around this time Ward's son Shirley had stepped in as legal representative for the Soboba villagers, as well as all of the Mission Indians. The young lawyer was born near Nashville, Tennessee, on June 30, 1861, and had moved with his family to Southern California. After graduating from Hastings Law School, he was admitted to the California bar in 1885 and formed the partnership of Wicks & Ward in Los Angeles, specializing in water rights, corporate law, and Mexican land grants.[21] In the fall of 1885, the younger Ward requested a letter of recommendation from L. D. McKisick, attorney for the Southern Pacific railroad, for the purpose of applying for the position of attorney for the Mission Indians, the job originally held by Brunson & Wells and later by G. Wiley Wells. McKisick complied, informing Commissioner Atkins that he knew the young lawyer well; he had examined Ward when he applied to practice in the California Supreme Court, and therefore his letter was "not a mere perfunctory recommendation." Ward, he explained, was "a very bright lawyer, an ardent student, and clear thinker. He is a gentleman of unexceptional character, conscientious and honorable."[22]

Even before receiving his appointment, Shirley Ward had been preparing an argument to be filed on behalf of the Indians on the Potrero Reservation in several land disputes currently before the General Land Office. He informed Upshaw that at least twenty lawsuits had already been filed by white interlopers.[23] At this point the younger Ward was apparently acting of his own volition. That would change in mid-January 1886, when he was formally appointed special assistant U.S. attorney for the Mission Indians of California by Attorney General A. H. Garland.[24] His efforts would become a major part of the story of his father's tenure and beyond.

The case of *M. Byrne v. Antonio Alas, et al.* had already been decided in favor of Byrne by default, in part because Byrne's attorneys had moved ahead with the prosecution after promising the government attorneys to hold off on the case until certain other matters could be settled. Somehow the government attorneys were not notified and therefore were not present in court to provide any defense for the Sobobans. The circumstances were long and complicated, and total blame for this defeat should not be assigned entirely to Brunson & Wells or their successor, Wells, Van Dyke & Lee. Wells, in a lengthy June 20, 1885, letter to California Congressman Henry H. Markham, explained in detail the circumstances.[25]

When the original firm of Brunson & Wells had been hired to represent the Mission Indians on June 26, 1883, the lawyers had left the amount of their fee up to the discretion of the Department of Justice. Six months later Attorney General Benjamin Harris Brewster determined their expenses could not exceed $200 a year. The lawyers were therefore serving without compensation. Because Brunson & Wells believed that the Indians "had been robbed, abused and mistreated," they had taken the case both because of a "professional interest in the matter" and because they "individually felt a responsibility" to maintain the Indians on their homelands. "We felt it a burning shame upon the Government, and a duty neglected, that these Indians had been allowed to be driven from their homes, time and time again, without awakening any feeling of interest in the Indian Agents who had been sent here to look after their interest," Wells had declared. Despite the disappointing compensation package, Wells and his partners nevertheless made visits to San Francisco to consult with the U.S. attorney, to San Diego to examine court records, and to San Bernardino to confer with Agent McCallum, who provided them with a list of witnesses to interview. They also wrote numerous letters, prepared briefs, and attended to the other duties necessary to bring the case to trial. By this time, they had run up expenses totaling five times their proposed compensation; when they submitted an invoice for only $200—it was denied.[26]

In addition to preparing for trial, Brunson & Wells had also begun to make arrangements to have the case transferred to the U.S. Supreme Court—an action that required the payment of a bond. At their request the Interior Department had authorized Agent McCallum to prepare the bond, but instead of the paperwork being returned to the law firm, it was forwarded to the Indians. Although it took time, the bond was finally executed with the help of the Soboba schoolteacher Mary Sheriff. Unfortunately too much time had passed, and as Wells later wrote, "a default had been taken against the Indians" in "violation of a stipulation entered into with us by the attorney representing the plaintiff."[27]

Therefore on July 3, 1886, the San Diego County superior court in *M. Byrne v. Antonio Alas, et al.* ruled against the Indians. This setback did not discourage

Shirley Ward. He wrote Attorney General Garland that he intended to appeal the ruling to the California supreme court and that, if necessary, he would take it all the way to the U.S. Supreme Court.[28] His father noted the appeal to the California supreme court in his August 1886 annual report, but he stated that he feared, based on the "general trend of the Supreme Court decisions," that the Indians at Soboba, along with those at Santa Ysabel and Warner's Ranch, would all "eventually be ejected."[29]

With the loss of the case and the threat of eviction for the Soboba Indians, Herbert Welsh, long-time executive secretary of the IRA, personally paid the $3,300 bond—giving Ward, who had been in charge of the case since January, time to prepare the necessary legal papers to vacate the judgment, retry the case, and carry it to the California supreme court—this time with legal representation for the Indians.[30] Meanwhile, J. M. Dodge, the superior court clerk, wrote that Byrne, whom he described as "sincerely humane," did not wish to evict the Indians if there was a speedy way to get them to move on their own, or if the lands could be purchased for them by the government—neither of which was a likely prospect.[31]

Receiving payment from the government for legal services proved to be as problematic for Ward as it had been for his predecessor. However, unlike Wells, who by continuing the case could well have endangered his firm's financial future, the younger Ward had the support of the IRA, which stepped in and covered his expenses. Painter, as the group's agent and congressional lobbyist, also worked on his behalf. In addition, the larger Indian reform community, including the members of the LMC, added their support in 1886 after listening to Welsh's address, explaining his role in paying the bond. "You must depend upon your own arm and public sentiment," Welsh had informed his fellow reformers. "If this is not a sham sentiment," he declared, "we must act ourselves." The power of public sentiment was needed to push Congress forward—indeed, "public sentiment . . . is the only power," he concluded.[32]

Welsh was not the only reformer at that October 1886 LMC meeting to actively take up the Mission Indian cause. He was joined by Mrs. Osia Jane Joslyn Hiles, a well-to-do Milwaukee widow with a long history of humanitarian work, and Amelia Stone Quinton, general secretary of the WNIA. Hiles, inspired by the writings of Helen Hunt Jackson, had personally visited a number of Mission Indian villages. In the ten minutes allotted to her during the conference, she described the Indians' banishment to desert and mountain wastelands, where she found them starving in "both soul and body." Their "exceedingly pitiful" condition so moved her that along with thirteen other Lake Mohonk members, she agreed to contribute $5,000, and the LMC Committee for the Legal Defense of the Mission Indians was established.[33]

On the third and closing day of the conference, Quinton took the floor to report on her association's work that year.[34] Founded in 1879 in Philadelphia, the WNIA already had more than seventy branches scattered across twenty-three states and was just beginning missionary work in California, having received permission from Assistant Commissioner Upshaw to send missionaries to Round Valley in Northern California.[35] Within a few short years, the WNIA would open up their Ramona Mission field among the Missions Indians, supporting government day school teachers, providing medical doctors, and planning a hospital.

Mere addresses and resolutions at Lake Mohonk were not sufficient to save Soboba, though. Therefore on January 9, 1886, Painter, joined by Welsh and Dr. James E. Rhoads, president of the IRA, met with Commissioner Atkins, who expressed pleasure with Shirley Ward's conduct of the case so far. The commissioner's major regret was that Ward was not being adequately compensated by the government. Painter would later explain to Ward that the main reason the IRA had agreed to meet his expenses was that the association did not want the case "to suffer because of red tape."[36] The IRA delegation then visited President Cleveland, arguing that the only way to settle the land rights of the Indians at Soboba was through the courts. The president concurred and recommended that Painter confer with Attorney General Garland. Finally, after much delay and a great deal of consultation, government officials agreed that since *M. Byrne v. Antonio Alas, et al.* was already in the courts, "they would let it be decided, and by it settle the cases of all the other Indians in southern California."[37]

Painter was favorably impressed with the young attorney, describing him as "earnest and vigilant in the discharge of his duties." He was confident that Ward would "honestly make the best fight he can for his clients." To ensure that the legal theories used by Ward were the most appropriate and well thought out, the IRA's Law Committee reviewed his legal brief, a copy of which Ward had forwarded to Painter in mid-May. Pleased with the brief, the chair of the committee conferred with Ward not only to familiarize himself with the case but also to gather valuable first-hand details about Soboba and other Mission villages to include in the association's widely distributed pamphlets.[38]

Hampered by the lack of funds to carry on his work, Ward was forced to continually write prominent public officials, including the attorney general and Henry Laurens Dawes, the senior senator from Massachusetts, about adequate compensation. Commissioner Atkins also wrote the IRA, requesting the association's support in bringing the issue of compensation for Ward before Congress. Welsh responded that the most effective approach was to gather as much support as possible for the passage of Senate Bill 53, authored by Dawes. This legislation, which had already passed the Senate, included a section providing for the defense of Indian rights—"secured to them in the original grants from the Mexican Government." If in the commissioner's judgment this clause would secure the necessary compensation, then Welsh urged him to encourage Interior Secretary Lamar to write a letter to Olin Welborn, chair of the House Indian Affairs Committee, pressing the need for its passage.[39] Unfortunately, none of this would solve Ward's immediate needs for compensation.

Now Santa Ysabel

With his son busy working on behalf of the Soboba Indians, the senior Ward continued to look after agency business. In early February 1886 the owners of the Rancho Santa Ysabel, through their lawyer, F. Orleans Brackett, informed Ward that they would soon begin removing Indians from the ranch if they did not leave of their own accord. Brackett complained that lately the captain of the Indian village had been "very saucy to the owners of the ranch." When the Indians were offered work, according to Brackett, the captain forbade them from. Ward forwarded the letter on to Commissioner Atkins, requesting instructions.[40]

Days later Agent Ward informed Atkins that a delegation from Santa Ysabel had just visited him, begging for "subsistence & blankets." Although there were 183 Indians still living in comfortable homes in the ranch's old village, the adjoining reservation, consisting mostly of hills and mountains, could barely support one-third of that number. Some 50 of the Indian residents were able-bodied men capable of earning a living on neighboring farms, while the rest were women, children, and the elderly, who would have no means of subsistence for the coming year because the grant owners had forbidden any Indian from farming on the ranch. Starvation now "stares them in the face," Ward concluded. He had advised the Indians not to leave until legally evicted by an officer of the law. Turning to the courts, he believed, was the only possible solution, and he hoped that his son would be instructed to take action on their behalf. Less than one month later, E. L. Lippitt, another attorney representing the Santa Ysabel ranch owners, informed Agent Ward that the Indians must be removed, asking that he use his "personal influence in getting them to go off quietly." In the meantime, Ward was still awaiting any advice or instructions from the commissioner.[41]

Ward's problems with the inactivity of the Indian Office were similar to those of his predecessors. Because the Mission Indians were only a few small tribes compared with the scores of larger tribes the Indian Office had to deal with, no doubt the staff's attention was focused elsewhere. Ironically, the fact that Southern California's Indians were generally peaceful and self-supporting also gave Washington little cause for concern. Although the Plains tribes had all been driven onto reservations by this time, the military was still active in the Southwest, where Geronimo and his Chiricahua Apaches would not surrender until August 1886. Without the efforts of Eastern Indian reform associations and the activities of their members, even less might have been done for the Mission Indians.

In the meantime, the ranch owners turned to the secretary of the interior, with Lippitt adopting a more conciliatory tone than he had used with Agent Ward. He reminded the secretary that a Santa Ysabel reservation had already been set aside on Volcan Mountain and suggested that the few Indians then living on the rancho should be "kept wholly upon this reservation." Lippitt even offered the ranch owners' assistance, "believing that to be the easiest solution of the problem of their removal."[42]

Perhaps his change of tone was based on Shirley Ward having taken up the matter. Lippitt had already received a no-nonsense letter from the attorney, informing the ranch owners that "no compromise is practicable and the matter can only be settled in the courts." Now Lippitt wanted to know from the commissioner if the younger Ward actually had any official authority. Had he been appointed "to contest with the owners of lands patented to them by the United States?" he inquired. Lippitt was distressed that the government seemed to be "fighting against its own patents to protect the Indians in possession of lands not included in their reservation." Noting that the state supreme court did not recognize Indian land titles, Lippitt wondered if Ward's desire was only "to black mail us or involve us in a tedious litigation resulting only in bad feeling between the Indians and the Ranch owners." Since the land reserved for the Indians was more than sufficient, Lippitt asked why the government could not simply "remove them a short distance," off of ranch lands, "peacefully placing each party in sole possession of their respective lands."[43]

Other Lands

During the fall of 1886, Agent Ward informed Commissioner Atkins that a number of Indians were applying for homesteads, both on and off the reservations, no doubt because they believed that was the best way to protect their land rights. The agent described the Indians as being "as ignorant as children as to what they want and . . . so timid that they had rather abandon the Homestead, than to undertake a trip to Los Angeles to find the Land office." If he accompanied them, the process went more smoothly; however, each trip cost the government four dollars and fifty cents. Trying to be economical, he queried: "What shall I do in such cases?"[44]

Meanwhile his son was also working on a case before the state courts which he hoped would settle the question of Indian citizenship and by extension their opportunities to obtain their own lands. It involved a Luiseño from La Jolla named Felix Calac, who had tried to buy some adjoining state school land that he had lived on for years. His application was denied because he was an Indian. The denial was appealed to the state attorney general, arguing that because he was a Mission Indian he was "as such a citizen of the United States." In the meantime, W. B. Ferguson, a white settler, tried to buy the land for himself, claiming that not only was an Indian not entitled to purchase the land but that as a white man, he had a better right. The case of *Calac v. Ferguson* was heard in the San Diego County superior court, and thanks to Shirley Ward's skillful defense, Calac won.[45]

Ward's Resignation

During the summer of 1887, Ward welcomed Painter on his third visit to Southern California. On this visit, not only was Painter looking after IRA interests, since the association had taken on the responsibility of paying Shirley Ward's expenses, but he was also tasked to explain to the Indians the provisions of the Dawes Severalty Act, which had passed that February.[46] Ward, who had originally agreed to accompany Painter, then suddenly informed him that he had just telegraphed the Interior Department of his intention to resign, asking to be relieved at the end of June. He explained to Painter that he had made this decision because of a telegram from Washington that "he regarded as insulting." He had received other telegrams and letters "of which no official ought, or could, under a decent administration, be made the subject." In addition, the government had informed Ward that it was closing four of the agency's schools for low attendance. Painter described this school order as "simply infernal and worthy of the contemptible scrubs who are running the Bureau."[47]

Painter later explained that he had, upon Ward's authority, reported "the utter incompetence of a teacher" who was in charge of the new Indian school at San Bernardino. "A war was begun at that time and never ceased until he [Ward] had been forced, as he says, in self-respect, to resign his position." The teacher, it turned out, had connections in Washington and was considered something of a protégé of Assistant Commissioner Upshaw. On the basis of this relationship, Painter claimed, she had "attempted to run the Agency," leading to the clash with Ward.[48] Despite what certain officials might have thought of Ward as an agent, the *Los Angeles Times* praised him for uniformly performing "his official duties in an able and impartial manner," taking "with him the highest esteem of those officially connected with him."[49]

A marked bitterness permeates Ward's second and final annual report, written in mid-August. For years, he complained, the very name "Indian agent" had "savored of fraud and robbery." When he took the office, it "took a strong personal character to hold its own against the malodorousness of the name." Now at the end of two years he was "perfectly willing" for someone else to "try his hand at civilizing the Indian." Even with all the education provided for them, Ward wrote, the children still did not have "one practical idea how to make a living." The adult Indians were in a worse predicament. He described them as neither knowing how to work nor even desiring to learn. The Indian "must be taught to work by persuasion if possible, by force if necessary." The government's policy of handing out food and supplies had "smothered out nearly every particle of native self-reliance among them," he claimed. "They are content to lie in the shade and wait for the annual appropriation." The only success he could claim was due to the "earnest and intelligent co-operation" of the agency physician, Dr. W. E. Ferrebee, and the agency's eleven "heroic" teachers.[50]

But Ward saved his strongest criticism for the recently passed Dawes Act, describing government officials and "outside enthusiasts" as bespangling "the Indian's sky with cabalistic signs of the coming jubilee" by passing this legislation, which had "been promised as the keynote in the grand chorus of emancipation from the thralldom of the white man." This legislation was viewed by most Indian reformers as a panacea for the Indian problem. Designed to individualize and civilize the Indians by breaking up tribal lands, it called for the allotment of lands to families and individuals in parcels of 160, 80, and 40 acres, along with the granting of citizenship. A twenty-five-year grace period would follow, during which time the land could not be sold or taxed. Although this time of "tutelage" and "almost military discipline" might turn the Indian into a self-sufficient farmer, Ward stated, without coercive power the Indians would "make but little advance in the march of civilization." They would not be qualified for "the battle of life." Ward clearly did not put much faith in this new legislation to transform what he described as the "lounging, loitering, lazy, lousy son of the forest" into a self-supporting citizen. That, he wrote, demanded "the highest order of practical statesmanship for its solution."[51]

Painter was not impressed with Ward, describing him as intending "to go out in a blaze of glory, in the estimation of the people of California among whom he lives." Ward had taken the unusual step of giving his last annual report to the public press of Los Angeles. It was a report in which he belittled the Indians, Painter said, made "contemptuous flings at every one else," and showed "how easily the whole problem would be solved if his practical common sense could only be utilized."[52]

Ward remained in Los Angeles for the rest of his life, even running unsuccessfully for mayor in 1890. But unlike some of his fellow agents, he does not seem to have tried to insert himself into later agency affairs. When he died in November 1904 the *Confederate Veteran* eulogized the former agent as "a man of rare mental attainments," describing him as a "fascinating writer, a magnetic public speaker," and "a genial companion." His greatest charm, however, was "the spirit of his strong, pure heart, his gentle dignity, his exquisite courtesy, his rare chivalry, and his warm human interest in every life he touched returned to him a hundredfold in the deep affection felt by all who knew him."[53]

It is difficult to square these genial traits attributed to Ward by the *Confederate Veteran* with the bitter agent who in his reports and letters shows so little respect for the Mission Indians. Even allowing for the hyperbole of a eulogy, it seems Ward was not always the angry man portrayed in his official correspondence. Instead, his low opinion of the Indian, combined with his high opinion of himself, seem to have collided with the limitations of his office, and rather than seek out what could be done, he chose instead to rage against his circumstances, with the Mission Indians left out in the cold once again.

CHAPTER 5

▼ ▼ ▼

A SHOW OF FORCE

Joseph W. Preston, 1887–1889

> The condition of these Indians may be stated as fair. If they could be entirely free from the influence of the liquor traffic, the gamblers, and the trespassers they would be greatly relieved. They are located in a healthful climate, with splendid water. Their land yields food crops of cereals, grasses and fruits, and by proper guidance and a little aid from time to time there seems to be no reason why they might not become on a level with the average laboring agriculturalist. But this feeling of insecurity, clearly the result of the knowledge of so many wrongs in the past, seems to follow them and keep their spirits subdued and their hopes and energies weak, and on [this] account their feeling of dependence is profound. To the agent they look for everything. All their hopes are center[ed] in him. An agent should be a good man and kind. They deserve and need kind treatment.
>
> —*Joseph W. Preston, Annual Report (1888)*

A decade after the creation of the Mission Indian Agency, the various agents had established themselves as a force in local affairs, both on and off the reservations. Joseph W. Preston may have overstated the Indians' dependence on the agents in his 1888 annual report, but there is no doubt these men had a role to play. Some played it better than others, as we have already seen. As for Preston, he seems to have tried to be "a good man and kind," but he was also willing (albeit reluctantly) to use force when needed. Not, in this case, against the Indians, but against white Americans engaged in thefts of Indian land.

Preston, another Southern Democrat, succeeded John Ward in 1887. Born in Georgia in 1839, Preston (like Ward) had served in the Confederate Army. In 1868 he began a law practice and later served one term as a state senator before his appointment by President Grover Cleveland as the agent for the newly conceived Mission-Tule River Consolidated Agency. He assumed his duties on August 16, 1887.[1]

The enlarged agency now had responsibility for over four thousand Indians, spread out over half the state of California, from the Tule River Reservation near Porterville in Tulare County, nearly five hundred miles away from agency headquarters, to Fort Yuma on the Colorado River.[2]

A Different Kind of Removal

One of Preston's first duties as agent was the implementation of an order from Washington that had authorized his predecessor to remove any and all white intruders at Capitán Grande, along with the thirty-eight trespassers on the Potrero Reservation (the present-day Morongo Reservation), by September 1, 1887. Preston now had less than two weeks to comply. The previous March 9, Commissioner Atkins had somewhat reluctantly issued this notice for the removal of all intruders on Mission Indian reservations following Congress's latest failure to pass the Mission Indian relief bill, earlier that month. Having learned that the trespassers were applying for legal injunctions to prevent their removal, the commissioner had requested that the War Department provide troops to aid in the process.[3]

Agent Ward, Preston's predecessor, had viewed the situation in his all-too-often jaundiced way: "There are on the Banning reservation (Potrero) thirty or forty trespassers who have established good homes, with vineyards and orchards. These homes will have to be given up by the white man. The Indian now sits in the shade of the trees meditating on which particular well-improved home he is to get." Some Southern California newspapers agreed. The *Redlands Citrograph* later quoted with approval the *Chino Champion:* "Any officer who is truly a good man would flatly refuse to be a party to the eviction."[4]

Ward's resignation at the end of June had freed him from having to carry out the order. Removal was left to Colonel Preston, who reported that most of the fifteen or twenty families on the Potrero had purchased land from the Southern Pacific and made improvements. Others were on government land, and "still others had squatted without pretense or color of right." Three settlers could honestly claim they had been there since before the reservation was established, and the removal order recognized their equity in the land. Finding the trespassers to be "clever, intelligent, law-abiding people," he informed Atkins: "I therefore . . . obtained an audience and submitted to them my instructions and stated, as diplomatically as I could, the case." Those who were notified to vacate agreed "that they would not take legal steps nor offer physical resistance." Two, however, "fearing that they might waive their rights to test the titles in the courts, and acting under advice of counsel and in no captious spirit, declined to vacate without a show of force." Preston had these two, along with their cattle and movable effects, removed. Not so much settlers as investors, they were John G. North, son of Riverside's founder, and Richard Gird, owner of the Chino Ranch in San Bernardino County.[5] Just before the September 1 deadline, North and Gird had filed for water rights on Potrero Creek; eventually they would hold eleven claims to the canyon waters above the Potrero village. Without access to this water, the Cahuillas would be unable to farm their newly recovered lands.[6]

In late September 1887, Preston and John Morongo, accompanied by an army corporal and three or four soldiers, removed the trespassers. The settlers had "refused to vacate, hence the necessity of calling in the aid of troops," reported the *Los Angeles Times*. "There is no likelihood of bloodshed."[7] Those with crops still in the field were allowed to remain until they had been harvested—a privilege almost never given to Indians who were ejected. This removal freed up some six to eight thousand more acres for Indian use, half of it good land,[8] and it also opened the government up to a legal challenge when Gird and North filed suit on November 5, 1887. The case of *John G. North et al. v. Joseph Preston et al.* was initially heard in the Superior Court of San Bernardino County, but Mission Indian Attorney Shirley Ward, at the request of the Indian Office, managed to get it transferred to the U.S. Circuit Court for the Southern District of California in Los Angeles on November 27, 1887. Over a year later, in late April 1889, with the agent present, various Cahuilla and Serrano people, including John Morongo, would give their testimony in the case relative to the length of their occupation at Potrero. Former agent S. S. Lawson testified that he was acquainted with the Potrero as early as August 1878, and that the Indians had been using the lands for cultivation and pasturage then.[9]

On October 17, 1888, Shirley Ward filed a countersuit on behalf of the Indians against North and Gird, *John Morongo et al. vs. John North et al.*, "to quiet the title of 45,000 acres." This case would take precedence, as the suit against Preston had been stayed until the precise rights of the Indians could be ascertained. Since the Potrero was not part of a Mexican rancho, Ward presented a variation of his argument in the recent Soboba case, contending that these Indians, too, enjoyed the rights of U.S. citizens descending from Mexican rule by way of the Treaty of Guadalupe Hidalgo. North and Gird's attorneys, on the other hand, tried to show that the Indians were in fact late arrivals at the Potrero, only moving there in the 1850s.[10]

North and Gird's own land claims were convoluted. They had bought "possessory rights" from both the state and the railroad in 1884, but the railroad land was then unsurveyed. When lines were finally run, this land was supposedly incorporated into the reservation. But more importantly, they had received a patent for the state school section they had purchased (#36), and it included the main Potrero village site. Between that and their water claims, North and Gird were a serious threat to the entire reservation. "The case involves some very fine legal propositions," Shirley Ward told a reporter, but with help from Agent Preston he hoped to see it through.[11]

As the legal wrangling dragged on, there were rumors that some of the evicted squatters planned to force the issue by defying the government order and returning to their claims.[12] Agent Preston accused the *Banning Herald* of inciting the squatters into an "unpatriotic disregard of law and order" through its "scathing invective against the government" and "ruthless ridicule" of the Indians in "issue after issue" of the paper. If the editor would go out and actually see what was happening to the Indians, the agent suggested, he might have a different opinion.[13]

When Preston was replaced as agent by Horatio Nelson Rust in 1889, he also became a defendant in the original North and Gird suit. In his 1891 annual report, Rust informed Commissioner Morgan that several squatters had been living for years on the reservation. Although his predecessor, Preston, had removed them, some "returned, determined to hold the land at all hazards, but have again been removed." The final decision, he noted, "will now await the decision of the commission."[14]

He was referring to the California Mission Indian Commission, created by legislation based on the Jackson/Kinney report that had finally passed Congress in 1891. Settling matters at Potrero would be one of the commission's most complicated tasks. Eventually, on November 11, 1892, both cases were closed by the court, with each party paying their own court costs. Morongo and his followers, with Ward's support, had successfully defended the rights to their lands.[15]

Capitán Grande's Woes

Some ninety-two Indians lived on the 17,580-acre Capitán Grande Reservation. In October 1886 the Interior Department had ordered any intruders removed from there. However, not until March 1887 did Commissioner Atkins authorize the use of military force. That June Charles C. Painter returned to the Mission villages on another investigative tour, at which time Agent Ward informed him that all intruders had left but the Indians had not as yet returned to occupy the land. Painter, diligent in his efforts to protect Indian rights, made his own personal inspection of Capitán Grande and discovered that only one white man had actually moved off. That individual had merely moved his saloon a short distance away into a shanty located on public land, leaving his cattle behind on the land he had been occupying. The task of removing trespassers at Capitán Grande, as at Potrero, again fell to Agent Preston.[16]

Finally, on November 24, 1887, Preston arrived at the reservation with an army corporal and five privates. The very next day they evicted the intruders (including saloonkeeper Patrick Cody). Although Tanis Thorne's study lists about a dozen men, plus their wives and children, the situation was more complicated because four of the men had Indian wives, who "more or less lived with them." Preston was sympathetic, even allowing some of the families to return to their homes pending the outcome of their litigation against the government, provided they did not cause any trouble. Most of these men, he suspected, had married Indian women only to get a hold of their property. As for the rest of the Indian residents at Capitán Grande, he recommended that the entire reservation be cancelled and the Indians be removed to a less isolated area, where their children would have a better opportunity to receive an education. The Indians, he claimed, "seem to be perfectly indifferent about the white occupancy." Thorne suggests that the agent may have mistaken indifference for hopelessness.[17]

Illegal intrusion was not the only problem that the Indian residents of Capitán Grande faced. During his June 1887 visit, Painter had also discovered a massive wooden flume being constructed right through the reservation by a San Diego water company employing hundreds of men on the job—none of which Agent Ward had ever reported to the government![18] The San Diego Flume Company, which had been organized the previous May, had built the Cuyamaca Dam that same year. But this dam was worthless without a way to get the water to the city. A second dam was built just north of the reservation, and the flume began from there. One month after Painter's visit, the company finally filed its application with the government, requesting the right to cross the reservation. Although the request was denied, construction continued.

Presumably Preston was unaware of the flume project as late as the fall of 1887. In his formal published report to Commissioner Atkins for 1888, he wrote he had "no previous knowledge of this work," apparently unaware of Painter's earlier report. Describing the flume project as a "gigantic enterprise," of "incalculable public benefit to the city and county," the agent pointed out that it would, however, deprive the Indians below the flume of all water. Assuming such a major project would have required permission from the government, he inquired of George D. Copeland, president of the company, if he had made arrangements with the government to build across the reservation. When Copeland answered in the negative, Preston immediately informed Commissioner Atkins, who promptly instructed the agent, on December 23, 1887, to order work on the flume stopped unless the company "should make satisfactory arrangements by which the Indians would not be deprived of their water." Preston requested a formal meeting of company officials. "[P]erceiving their embarrassment" but also well aware of the potential loss of their investment, the officials agreed to submit to any arrangement Preston "might dictate." The commissioner had authorized the use of military force and legal proceedings if needed.[19]

Working together, Preston and company attorney Olin Wellborn drew up an agreement in mid-January 1888 that was favorable to the Indians. The flume company agreed to pay one hundred dollars per mile per year for a thirteen-mile right-of-way, plus a promise (not quantified) to provide the Indians with water for irrigation and domestic use. William H. Waldby, a member of the BIC who was on a two-month investigative tour in Southern California, praised Preston for his "amicable settlement and adjustment with the San Diego Flume Company."[20] That August, however, Frank D. Lewis, recently appointed attorney for the LMC's Committee for the Legal Defense of the Mission Indians, informed the newly appointed Agent Rust that Preston's contract had not yet been approved by Congress, and that the company felt that "it should not be compelled to pay so heavily for the right of way for so great a public benefit as the San Diego Flume." During the financial recession of early 1890s, the company continued to object to the annual right-of-way payments. With the support of the 1891 California Mission Indian Commission, the government finally agreed to drop these payments in 1892. During her research on the reservation, Thorne came to the conclusion that one reason for the long delay in creating the California Mission Indian Commission was that "Washington representatives may have been instructed by their constituencies [in the San Diego environs] to obstruct" its passage until the flume being built across the Capitán Grande Reservation was completed.[21]

Former Agent McCallum

Just a few days after arriving at his post, on August 22, 1887, Preston received an order from Commission Atkins to once again investigate the possible fraudulent activities of former agent J. G. McCallum on the Agua Caliente Reservation at Palm Springs. The Indians had complained about McCallum's water claims to former agent Samuel S. Lawson that summer; he had passed the complaint on to then-agent John Ward, who decided the Indians were already getting their fair share of the limited water available.[22] Now it was Preston's turn; he would spend almost six months piecing together the facts of McCallum's devious activities. Preston learned that while still in government service, McCallum had purchased 480 acres of railroad land within the reservation. His partner, W. E. Van Slyke, had purchased part of the same sections and built a flume to divert water there from Andreas Canyon, depriving the Rincon village near its mouth of a water source. Van Slyke had attempted to justify his acts by paying "Old Andreas," the Cahuilla man who gave the canyon its name, $150 "to remove from that place, (the point of diversion) and to aid him in procuring the consent of the other Indians there, to the diversion of said water." Preston informed Atkins that Old Andreas did in fact "leave the place, and is now dead; and, I am not prepared to say, that Van Slack [*sic*] did not, in some way, procure the temporary acquiescence of the few Indians at that place."[23]

Since McCallum's parcel also benefited from this water source, Preston assumed that he had approved of his partner's action and then had "the audacity to publically assert title to this water, to which, it is believed, he has no sort of right." As his investigation continued, Preston learned that both McCallum and Van Slyke had then sold their rights to the Garden of Eden Land Development Company. With cash in hand, McCallum continued to accumulate other lands and formed the Palm Valley Land & Water Company. Unable to discover just how the former agent had acquired all this property, building up a fortune estimated at $80,000, Preston concluded "that it originated in *fraud*; and, involved the grossest dereliction of official duty." Preston enclosed a contract treating McCallum's property "as that of the government," ignoring the former agent's title and placing "the onus upon him of establishing a clean title, if he has it." McCallum and Van Slyke, he concluded, were both "snakes" in this particular "Garden of Eden."[24]

McCallum's deviousness seemed to have no bounds. In 1887 his company built a nineteen-mile water system running all the way from the Whitewater River by way of a wooden flume and an eight-mile-long stone-lined canal to bring water to the lands he now offered for sale. However, the water had to cross over a portion of the Agua Caliente Reservation. "Fortunately," McCallum's biographer writes, Preston "proved to be a man of perspicacity," and after investigating the situation he proposed that McCallum be given a right-of-way for his already-built ditch, provided the "Indians shall have the first right" to a set amount of water.[25] In February 1888, Preston signed an agreement with McCallum's Palm Valley Land & Water Company, giving it the right to develop water from Tahquitz and Chino canyons, provided they paid one hundred dollars per mile for the right-of-way for any ditches across reservation land and agreed to deliver water free of charge to the Indians. Burleigh B. Barney, the promoter of the Garden of Eden tract, Preston judged innocent in the matter, and he worked out a separate agreement for Barney to develop water from Andreas Canyon, provided he not "hinder, obstruct, or prevent in any manner, the said Indians from the full and free use, occupancy, and enjoyment of their rights to their said reservation."[26] The Indian Office agreed and probably thought the matter settled. But not for long.

Water on the Desert

In addition to dealing with McCallum's frauds, Preston soon found that lack of water was a serious ongoing problem on all desert reservations. As developers and settlers purchased alternating sections of railroad land in the Coachella Valley, demand for water only increased. Some pushed for rights-of-way for ditches and flumes across reservation lands; others simply trespassed, building their water systems without any thought to Indian land or water rights. Whenever possible, Preston tried to negotiate deals that protected the Indians' water rights and guaranteed them a share of the waters flowing across the reservations.[27]

Palm Springs itself, in Section 14, was already a popular destination for the sick, who hoped to find relief in the waters of the hot springs—although, as Preston explained to Atkins, the springs was clearly Indian property. A hotel built nearby, run by "Dr." Welwood Murray and his wife, only increased the demand for access. The hotel owners offered to build a new bathhouse for the Indians as well as a second one for their guests, paying the Indians an annuity, beginning at one hundred dollars for the first year. Some of the Indians were in favor of the proposal, but Preston was fearful that Washington would view it as too favorable to the whites. Still, he supported the plan, claiming "there is no reason on this earth why this valuable water should be so, exclusively, held, when the Indians rights can not *but* be increased—and better enjoyed by them, under this improved condition of things."[28] The Murrays went on to run their little hotel for years.

In March 1888, Preston supported three white settlers, who had petitioned him to allow them to build a pipeline across the Potrero Reservation to bring water down from the canyons above the reservation to their lands near Beaumont. The sources they wanted to tap were not on the reservation. However, while exploring the area, they had discovered some undeveloped water resources on the reservation that could also be tapped and delivered to Indian lands by the same

Indians building an irrigation ditch on the Morongo Reservation in the 1890s.
William H. Weinland Collection, The Huntington Library, San Marino, Calif.

pipeline. Preston approved the arrangement on March 31, 1888, with stipulations, subject to the approval of the Indian commissioner. He may have been inclined to do so because of the new potential water sources for the Indians.[29]

Soboba Survives

As Preston was investigating McCallum and dealing with water questions, news arrived that the California state supreme court had—in an almost unprecedented move—ruled in favor of the village of Soboba in the case of *M. Byrne v. Antonio Alas, et al.* Shirley Ward had appeared before the court on October 13, 1887, arguing that the original Mexican grant to the Estudillos had protected the Indians' right of occupancy—a right the U.S. government was bound to recognize and protect by virtue of the Treaty of Guadalupe Hidalgo. While the January 31, 1888, decision did not confer title on the Indians, their village would be allowed to stay on this possessory right.[30] Ward sent a copy of the decision to IRA secretary Welsh, adding that he had thrown up his hands and shouted for joy when he heard of it. But Ward also cautioned Commissioner Atkins that the ruling would not help the Indians still living on public lands.[31]

Settling the Byrne suit only secured the Indians' possessory rights, preventing their eviction. The government would confirm and enlarge the existing reservation at Soboba in 1891, but the Byrne tract remained in private hands until it was seized by the state in 1903 for failure to pay delinquent taxes. The federal government then bought the seven-hundred-plus acres from the state in 1911. Byrne had sold his water rights in 1889, and through a long series of sales, the Citizen's Water Company, which served part of the San Jacinto Valley, eventually acquired those rights. In 1916 the company sued to remove the Indians, arguing that subsequent court rulings had invalidated the 1888 state supreme court decision.[32] The federal government stepped in, and in January 1920, after long negotiations, an agreement was reached between the Citizen's Water Company and the secretary of the interior whereby the water company would drop its eviction lawsuit and quitclaim any rights to the land, in return for the right to maintain its own water system across the reservation—provided it did not disrupt the Indians' water supply. Water would remain at key issue at Soboba for generations, but the land question was finally settled once and for all.[33]

Special Attorneys

For all his good work, Shirley Ward was still having trouble getting paid. In May 1888 he complained to Preston that he had already worked on three other cases on behalf of the Mission Indians but had still not received any compensation. He sent the agent a bill for $4,000, asking that he take steps as "he may see best to have same allowed and paid." Preston forwarded Ward's letter to Washington, explaining that the amount requested was "not only reasonable, but below—far below the usual fees for services in the line of his profession." He assured Commissioner Atkins that there could have been "no better selection" than Ward, and he endorsed and recommended the payment "without unnecessary delay," suggesting that Ward be given an annual salary of $2,500.[34]

Ward received some assistance when the LMC Committee for the Legal Defense of the Mission Indians agreed on February 23, 1888, to hire attorney Frank Lewis to assist the Mission Indians with any legal problems at a salary of $1,000 a year. Lewis moved to California shortly before his appointment. His duties included serving as committee attorney as well as field agent and legal adviser, preparing the groundwork for cases and assisting IRA agent Painter whenever needed. According to committee treasurer Joshua Davis, the young attorney was expected to "respond promptly in case of need, restoring long-lost courage in the Indians and checking their timid surrender of rights."[35] In mid-1889 Lewis received a government appointment after funding was finally approved by Congress.

The work that Lewis did for the LMC brought praise from Treasurer Davis during the proceedings of the seventh annual LMC gathering in early October 1889. He explained that in two cases, the attorney had corrected errors in government surveys and records of long standing. Lewis had carried out his work "with deep, conscientious interest on his part, securing the confidence alike of the Indians and of disinterested white residents." To emphasize that outsiders were also aware of the good work that Lewis was doing, Davis presented conference attendees with a letter from Jacob Bergman, a longtime local rancher, who declared that Lewis had accomplished more in his two years of service "than the Indian agency has in twelve years." Bergman explained that the Indians "placed explicit confidence in him." There were other testimonials outlining how Lewis had given the Indians "new courage," prompting them to plant more crops and build new homes. "This moral as well as material result is easily underestimated," concluded Davis.[36]

While Ward and Lewis received high praise from prominent reformers, officials, and residents, others also spoke highly of Preston's attributes. During the September 1888 LMC meeting, Davis described the colonel as possessing a "vigorous grasp of his manifold new duties, reaching out as speedily as possible, inspiring the respect of all, and giving assurance of even-handed justice to white and red man alike." BIC member William Waldby, investigating Indian schools during his two-month tour, had conferred with Preston in San Diego. Waldby spoke very highly of the agent during his address before the Lake Mohonk proceedings.[37]

The following year Albert K. Smiley, another BIC member and founder of the LMC, also praised Preston's competence.[38] Twice Colonel Preston received Smiley at his agency office in Colton, where they conferred at length. When Smiley and his wife, Eliza, expressed a desire to visit the Potrero Reservation near Banning, Preston sent his interpreter, Captain Morongo, to drive them all around, giving Smiley an opportunity to study reservation conditions in detail, thus gaining a better understanding of the true situation at Potrero for a presentation before the next LMC. Based on his tour and Preston's knowledge, both men came to agree that the president should send a commissioner to examine the situation more fully and arrange with the Southern Pacific for some land exchanges "so that the Indians can have their land in a body and their water under their full control." Preston's professionalism impressed Smiley, who described him to BIC secretary Eliphalet Whittlesey as "a most excellent man and good agent, firm and judicious." "All of the conflicting parties speak well of him," concluded Smiley, who was fearful that if Preston's salary was not increased, "as was promised when agencies were consolidated," he would resign.[39]

Preston's resignation, predicted by Smiley, was confirmed by Frank Lewis in a letter to Joshua W. Davis in late 1888. Believing that agents "should be politically in sympathy with the incoming administration," Preston, whom Lewis described as an "uncompromising Democrat of the Jeffersonian school," resigned on March 4, 1889—inauguration day for the newly elected Republican president, Benjamin Harrison. Preston later claimed he was invited to continue in his appointment but was dissatisfied with the wages he was receiving. The increase in salary promised with the consolidation of the agencies had not been forthcoming. Instead, the government had enlarged the jurisdiction of the Mission Agency to include the Hoopa Valley Agency and the Klamath River reserve. With the incoming administration, Preston saw little hope for an increase in salary.[40]

The WNIA in the Field

Although Preston formally resigned in March, his replacement was not yet in place when Rev. William Henry Weinland, a Moravian cleric employed by the WNIA to begin missionary work in the Cahuilla Valley, arrived in San Jacinto on June 19, 1889. The minister was accompanied by his wife, Caroline, and his sister Sadie. Months earlier Amelia Stone Quinton, now president of the WNIA, had written Indian Commissioner John H. Oberly requesting the use of an abandoned reservation school building, suitable as living quarters for missionaries to begin Christianization and industrial educational work among the Indians in Cahuilla Valley. Although Oberly informed her it was not the policy of the government to give missionary associations the use of government property, Quinton, undeterred, wrote again requesting the loan of a five-acre plot for a missionary cottage—land that Preston and the agency physician Dr. Ferrebee would select. To this Oberly agreed.[41]

With all official permissions in order, on June 21, 1889, Preston accompanied Reverend Weinland to the Cahuilla Reservation to select a five-acre parcel that had been granted to the WNIA for a missionary cottage. The following day the two attended a three-hour meeting in the school house at Cahuilla. Although the village captain had originally given his consent to turn over the land, the Indians had changed their minds. At Preston's recommendation, Soboba was chosen instead as headquarters for the new WNIA missionary work. The agent also suggested that instead of moving onto the reservation immediately, the Weinlands wait until they had won the hearts of the people. Eventually this missionary endeavor expanded to include the Potrero Reservation near Banning and other Indian villages and was designated the Ramona Mission, in honor of Helen Hunt Jackson's heroine. In the future Preston's successors, Horatio Nelson Rust and Francisco Estudillo, would not only have to deal with problems facing the Mission Indians but with complicated issues involving WNIA missionary work.[42]

Attorney Frank D. Lewis did not see Preston's resignation as a negative. Although sorry that the Indian service was losing "so good a man," Lewis informed Davis that Preston had already been offered a partnership in a San Diego law firm, where his "ability [would] undoubtedly place him in a prominent position at the California Bar and give him an income very far beyond his present salary." Because he had been "thoroughly interested" in his work, Lewis concluded the Indians would find in Preston "a sincere friend while he remains in California."[43] His stay was short; by the spring of 1890 Preston was back practicing law in Georgia. He retired in 1915 and passed away several years later.

CHAPTER 6

▼ ▼ ▼

A CONTROVERSIAL COLLECTOR

Horatio Nelson Rust, 1889–1893

> In September, one year ago, I attended [the Yumas'] annual mourning feast, when it is their custom to gather together and . . . mourn aloud for their dead of the past year. . . . [A] great variety of pagan ceremonies are enacted, with dancing, racing, chanting, recounting the virtues and deeds of the dead, etc. . . . [T]o close the festival, they burn the booths which have been used during the week, also all the gifts which they would send to their departed friends. Heretofore they have killed horses and burned many valuable goods, thus impoverishing themselves, but as at this time no animals were sacrificed and few valuables, we have reason to hope that our efforts to prevent this had some influence. It is customary to allow no white man on the grounds at night, but as I was there to learn all their customs and a friend, I was permitted to remain. . . . At night they sit and lie around the open fires, presenting a strange, weird scene, never to be forgotten.
>
> —*Horatio Nelson Rust, Annual Report (1891)*

No doubt Horatio Nelson Rust had a fascination with American Indians and valued the opportunity his role as Mission Indian agent gave him to observe some of their ceremonies. Unfortunately, his interest too often centered more on their artifacts and handicrafts than on their conditions and needs. Indeed, his penchant for collecting and selling Indian artifacts while in office would result in more public criticism than anything done by the other Mission Indian agents—even those who accomplished far less on behalf of the Mission Indians.

Rust was appointed by President Benjamin Harrison as agent for the Mission-Tule River Consolidated Agency on June 17, 1889, at an annual salary of $1,600.[1] Six years earlier, in the fall of 1883, both Helen Hunt Jackson and Abbot Kinney had recommended his appointment, to replace Agent Samuel Lawson. Jackson had written Commissioner Hiram Price that Rust and Kinney were the "only two men [she] knew in all Southern California that [she] would trust absolutely in all matters affecting Indian interests."[2] Her trust was misplaced.

Rust was not the effective agent Jackson assumed he would be. Born in Amherst, Massachusetts, he was a supporter of abolitionist John Brown, and he dressed wounds and drove an ambulance during the Civil War. Later he operated the largest warehouse in Chicago before moving to California and settling in Pasadena in 1881, where he established a nursery. He helped found the Pasadena Public Library and served on its board of directors with Kinney. He also became an avid collector of Indian artifacts.[3]

Less than one month after his appointment, on July 4, 1889, Rust wrote his superior, Thomas Jefferson Morgan, congratulating him on his recent appointment as Indian commissioner. In response, Morgan asked if Rust could find a teaching job within the agency for his sister "without displacing a worthy and efficient teacher." If so, he would nominate her. Morgan also informed Rust that LMC attorney Frank D. Lewis had been recently appointed as a special Indian agent, "a position for which he seems peculiarly adapted."[4] Later that month Interior Secretary John W. Noble advised Rust to consider his appointment as "one of far more than ordinary importance, both for the interests of the government and of the Indians." He expected Rust to not only practice sobriety and integrity but to improve conditions at the agency "within a reasonable time." He was directed to pay special attention to the "education and proper training of the Indian children," as well as agricultural and industrial pursuits for the adults. Noble admonished him to endeavor to further the department's twin goals of advancing the Indians "in the ways of civilization" and promoting their self-support.[5]

The Mission-Tule River Agency had grown considerably since Preston's administration, supposedly as a cost-saving measure. The two reservations within the Hoopa Valley Agency, nine hundred miles away in Northern California, which had been managed by army officers since 1877, had recently been "consolidated" with the already far-flung Mission-Tule River Agency. Commissioner Morgan admitted to Rust that serving this large agency would be a challenge, especially since the Hoopa Valley Reservation people were making good progress toward "civilization," while the Klamath River reserve's two hundred or so Indians needed "to be constantly within reach of an agent who has experience, energy, good sense, and some legal acquirements." The newly configured Mission-Tule River Consolidated Agency presented Rust with a "sufficiently onerous" job, he concluded.[6]

Rust agreed. Writing former Congressman Henry Markham, who was investigating conditions at the Mission Indian Agency, the agent complained that simply to visit the eight government day schools in Southern California required a trip of 290 miles.[7] If extensive traveling was not enough, Rust also complained about his salary. Although Congress had increased the agent's work load in merging the agencies, it had failed to increase his pay. Rust claimed that other agents with less work received $2,300. Furthermore, the previous agent had been allowed an interpreter, which he had been denied, and in the past there had been two government farmers to help the Mission Indians. Now there were none.[8]

Unlike his predecessor, Agent Preston, who had been living in Georgia at the time of his appointment and was totally unfamiliar with the Mission Indians, Rust had lived in Southern California for more than seven years. A childhood interest in archaeology had brought him West in 1880 to Arizona and New Mexico, where he saw "evidences of the greatest antiquity of man's occupancy in the Cave dwellings, the Cliff dwellings, and ruins of the plains." He and his family made a permanent move from Chicago to Pasadena in January 1882. Through his efforts to build a public library, he became acquainted with Abbot Kinney, who had served ably with Helen Hunt Jackson as a special commissioner to the Mission Indians. No doubt the two men often conferred on Indian issues. Rust, a member of the Los Angeles branch of the IRA and later its secretary,[9] had been consulted by Charles C. Painter during both his 1885 and his 1887 investigative tours. Thus Rust was already acquainted with the condition of the Mission Indians in a general way. Despite his contacts and experience, his would be a tumultuous administration, with much bitterness on the part of the Indians. For one thing, he was anti-Catholic, while many of the Mission Indians still adhered to their Catholic faith. He also took sides in tribal and intertribal politics, and his buying and selling of native artifacts during his tenure raised questions about his integrity.[10]

Into the Field

A few weeks after Rust took charge of the agency, he began an extensive tour of all its twenty-one reservations, including the distant Hoopa Valley Reservation, which he found ably run by Capt. William E. Dougherty of the U.S. Army. On September 4, he toured the 4,400-acre Tule River Reservation. Late in the month, accompanied by Dr. Ferrebee, the agency physician, he left the agency headquarters in Colton with two buckboards "loaded with school supplies" to visit the nineteen reservations in Southern California—a total journey of more than six hundred

Horatio N. Rust.
William H. Weinland Collection,
The Huntington Library, San Marino, Calif.

miles. Because Secretary Noble had admonished him to specifically address Indian education, Rust's 1889 diary of his reservation visits focused on the eight reservation day schools. At the Potrero Reservation he counted 150 residents, forty of whom were of school age. He described the Potrero schoolhouse, built on proceeds of a barley crop and owned by the Indians, as the best on any of the Southern California reservations, and the teacher, Sarah E. Morris, as "doing well."[11]

At Soboba, Rust recorded 200 residents, fifty of school age. The schoolhouse, entirely unfit, was "an old worthless adobe" that was much too small. The government was renting it for five dollars a month from Roques Jauro, who for the past eleven years had served as village captain. Learning that some residents were displeased with Jauro, reputedly a drinker, Rust ordered and supervised a new election. Pedro Chino won with eighteen votes to Jauro's seven. Although some Indians may have been displeased with Jauro, they had high praise for the village school teacher, Mary L. Noble, who drove in daily from San Jacinto to teach.[12] On Sunday, September 22, Rust and his party attended Rev. Weinland's regular service at the Soboba schoolhouse. "[S]aw a large part of the Indians [in attendance], much pleased with Rev. Weinland's manners," Rust noted.[13]

Rust's party then set out for the Cahuilla Reservation, where they counted 275 residents, forty of them school age. The schoolhouse was poorly built, and the teacher, a Mrs. Thayer, who was sick most of the time, did not like the Indians. The feeling was mutual. Describing Thayer as "out of joint," Rust closed the school with the comment: "[N]o use for such teachers here." Continuing down the valley, Rust and his party spent the night at Oak Grove, arriving at Warner's Ranch and the village of Agua Caliente (known by its Indian residents as Cupa). Here Rust found 149 residents, forty-eight of them of school age. He was impressed with the villagers, describing them as more industrious than others and "doing very well." Although the school teacher, Mrs. Florence M. Curry, a middle-aged widow, was content with her students and lived "quite comfortably" in her attached quarters at the schoolhouse with her little niece, Rust recommended her removal because she did not seem to have her students' confidence. He also recommended repairs and improvements on the school.[14]

In the rolling hills above the valley at the Mesa Grande village, Rust recorded 140 residents and thirty-five to forty students. Although the schoolhouse was old, unfit to repair, and in a bad location, he allowed the newly hired teacher, Mrs. Hylena A. Nickerson, to begin teaching, a position she would hold for many years. By 1890 the school had been repaired with two new rooms added for Nickerson's living quarters. Turning down the San Luis Rey River, Rust continued to Rincon, where he found a village numbering 160 residents. The thirty-nine school-aged children and the teacher, Miss Hattie E. Alexander, were doing well. Her schoolhouse, made of rough boards with no living quarters, was sorely in need of repair. Rust diagramed in his notes a new sixteen-by-thirty-foot schoolhouse. While in the village, he took time to confer with José Albanez, the newly elected captain and son of the old captain, giving both Albanez and José Calac, the *alcalde* (or judge, as Rust called him), commissions showing his approval of their elections.[15]

At La Jolla, Rust found the existing school, an old adobe structure, in need of repairs. New seats for the students were also necessary. The teacher, Miss Ora M. Salmons, was "doing well [and] generally liked by the Indians." Salmons, Miss Alexander's niece, had been appointed to her position in 1886. From La Jolla, she would later transfer to Rincon, where she remained for many years before moving on to Pala to teach.[16] Climbing up toward Temecula to the Pechanga

Reservation, Rust counted a population of 130, of whom thirty-eight were school age. The rough board schoolhouse was in extremely bad condition; Rust noted in his diary that it should be the first one to be repaired. He found that the teacher, Mrs. Mary J. Platt, was "newly appointed but appears remarkably well." In his next published annual report, Rust noted that the school house was now in good order and Platt's "Sunday-school and temperance society [were] doing much good, and the Indians respond generously."[17]

Later, Rust visited the Coachella Valley, beginning with the Agua Caliente Reservation at Palm Springs. On this trip he was accompanied by LMC founder Albert K. Smiley and "Dr." Murray. To avoid confusion with the Agua Caliente village on Warner's Ranch, Rust designated this reservation as Agua Caliente No. 2, a designation that appeared often in later government reports. During his visit he handed out rations to several sick, elderly women, and he called for a new election when he learned from some residents of their dissatisfaction with Capt. José Rafael. Francisco Patencio won the election, although Rust personally believed that Rafael, whom he described as stubborn, was the better candidate. Several months later Chief Gervasio Cabezon asked Rust to reinstate Rafael; Rust complied, ordering that henceforth all village elections be held annually on the final Tuesday of November.[18]

Indian Education

Rust's investigative tour had revealed that about half of the Mission Indians lived on worthless land in remote villages and that all of the government schoolhouses were in poor repair. During his first year in office he had three of them rebuilt, with hopes of improving the others. In addition to the eight government schools, there were also two Catholic-run contract boarding schools for the Mission Indians, each educating about one hundred students. The government paid these schools ten dollars per quarter per student up to a set maximum; beyond that, the schools had to find their funding elsewhere.[19]

The first Catholic boarding school in the region was St. Anthony's Indian Industrial School, founded in Old Town San Diego in 1886 by Father Antonio Ubach. The Sisters of St. Joseph of Carondelet served as teachers. Even the beloved Father Ubach had difficulty convincing parents to send their children so far from home, but by 1890 enrollment had reached ninety-five. In 1891 two large wooden buildings were built next to the ruins of Mission San Diego. Government funding ended in 1900, but the Bureau of Catholic Indian Missions stepped in to fill the gap, and the school continued until shortly after Father Ubach's death in 1907.[20]

Founded in 1890, the St. Boniface Indian School in Banning was administered by the Bureau of Catholic Indian Missions. It would play an important role in the education of Southern California's Indian children for more than eighty-five years. Most of the original funding came from Katherine Drexell, a wealthy Philadelphia heiress who supported a number of Indian schools. The original three-story brick building opened the year of its founding, with the government promising to help pay for up to one hundred students. There was always opposition in Washington to public funding going to religious schools; federal support ended in 1901. Much of the school's early success was a tribute to Father B. Florian Hahn, who supervised St. Boniface until 1913, ministering whenever he could at villages and reservations.[21] Rust's concern about the impact of St. Boniface on attendance at the government schools resulted in an arrangement in the fall of 1890 with Father Hahn, who agreed not to solicit students from within three miles of a government school.[22]

Less successful was the Anaheim Indian School, which operated briefly in 1884–85. Unlike the other contract schools, it was run by a local Presbyterian minister, Rev. J. M. Roberts, and his wife, under the auspices of the Presbyterian Home Mission Board. The Robertses had previously run a boarding school for Mexican-American children in New Mexico. By January 1885 construction had begun on a combination dormitory/classroom building. The students were all girls, apparently, including one of John Morongo's daughters. The curriculum included not only the "three Rs" but Bible study and training in housekeeping and other domestic skills. The effort was short-lived, and Roberts and his wife soon turned their attention to the children of Mexican immigrants.[23]

The Perris Indian Boarding School

The federal government also operated its own boarding schools. Under the leadership of Commissioner Morgan, Indian education assumed a new priority, and Rust eagerly pitched in. Morgan, a professional educator, viewed education as a key to Indian advancement. He had a distinguished career serving as principal of several state normal schools, as well as teaching at the Baptist Union Theological Seminary in Chicago. Promoting the government's key civilizing tools—education and Christianization—Morgan envisioned a "comprehensive system of training and instruction which [would] convert" the Indians into productive American citizens, bringing them "into fraternal and harmonious relationship with their white fellow-citizens."[24] One of his visions was the establishment of a Mission Indian boarding school.

As early as 1885, Agent McCallum had recommended such a school at Morongo. His successor, John Ward, agreed that "a boarding and industrial school, where the youths [could] be educated in the parts of practical life" was needed.[25] Although Rust believed that Indian children made "as ready progress in education as any other class who have had so little opportunity," he stressed the importance of education for all ages. As a case in point, he related the situation of five Indian men he had recently appointed as agency police. Unable to sign their names for their pay, Rust had encouraged them to learn to write. The Indian men went to the government teacher and requested that she open an evening school; they learned to write and signed their next pay checks.[26]

In addition to promoting education in his annual reports, Rust also publically addressed the values of education before audiences in Los Angeles and Pasadena. During a speech to the second meeting of the Pasadena Teachers' Institute, after giving a brief history of the government's Indian policy, he told his audience that statistically, the Indian race was not dying out but "uniting with the white race and being absorbed," and that therefore "[I]t is our duty to educate them."[27]

Later, in Los Angeles, Rust explained that the best way to elevate the Indian people was to initially educate their children in a reservation day school, especially one with kindergarten teaching, to best "overcome the natural timidity" of the Indian child. He strongly advised that "a missionary with good practical ideas of life and duty should be established and sustained near each of these day schools." Their presence would give the Indian student "the advantage of education among our own people and industries."[28] He was referring to one missionary in particular, Miss C. M. Fleming of Riverside, who had recently begun work on the Cahuilla Reservation, where she spent time in Indian homes, instructing both the women and other students in "the arts of housekeeping." Rust believed this kind of missionary work was a very important part of the educational service. In late August 1891 both Rust and Fleming spoke at the newly organized Pasadena branch of the WNIA. While Fleming spoke about her work at Cahuilla, Rust addressed the needs of all the Mission Indians and praised the missionary work of the association's California members.[29]

Rust strongly believed in the importance of an off-reservation manual training school, where students could learn the arts and trades, thus becoming self-supporting. In 1890, he was instructed by the Indian commissioner to select a site for just such a government boarding school, based on the Carlisle Indian Industrial School model.[30] Determined that the location should be near some "thrifty settlement" to bring the students into contact with "civilization rather than their home influences," he conferred with G. B. Knight, a resident of Perris, a small community south of Riverside. Through Knight, who was familiar with the Carlisle School, Rust met a number of local businessmen and civic leaders, including J. W. Nance, who subscribed to the project and arranged for eighty acres near the town to be donated to the government.[31] Commissioner Morgan personally visited the site, imagining the potential of planting a "splendid fruit farm" where the students would learn a trade that would provide profitable employment.[32]

After giving his approval, Morgan ordered Rust to have plans drawn for a campus to accommodate one hundred students. Multiple rooms of various uses were designed for both male and female students, as well as for teachers and the support staff. Modern conveniences such as indoor bathing and shower facilities were included, along with a sewing room for the female students. In the tower on the third floor was a ward "for isolated cases," presumably a reference to students who had contracted a contagious disease. Following approval of the plans, a contract for construction was issued on May 5, 1892, at a cost of $25,000. Under the direction of M. S. Savage, the school opened that October with only eight students.[33] Within three years the student population had grown to 130, and eleven instructors.

The location proved unfortunate. "This school was built on the kind of land usually finally selected for an Indian reservation—the poorest in the locality," School superintendent Edgar Allen noted a few years later. The acreage was level ground with no drainage and adobe soil that baked hard after becoming wet—not conducive to planting. As on many reservations, water became a serious problem. The Perris Irrigation District, formed in June 1890 to provide water for nearby citrus groves and vineyards, simply could not supply enough water to the valley. Allen complained that the irrigation district "at a very high price, [was] able to furnish only enough water to keep a few plants and a very small patch of grass alive." Since the teaching of agriculture was a key element in the school's curriculum, this scarcity was doubly fatal. The school was replaced by the Sherman Institute (today's Sherman Indian High School), established in 1902 in nearby Riverside.[34]

Land Battles

Rust all too quickly came to learn of the continuing battles over Indian lands, both large and small. In late August, shortly after taking charge of the agency, he received a lengthy letter from attorney Frank D. Lewis, informing him of the current status of several pending claims by whites on the reservations. For the past eighteen months Lewis had been acting as the LMC attorney for the Indians. At the end of his letter, Lewis appended a list of illegal entries and claims filed upon the executive order reservations by whites. Because a "strong sentiment" against the reservation system existed in Southern California, Lewis cautioned Rust that he would find a "persistent, energetic and systemic effort brought to bear to have as much of the land now held as reservation for the Indian thrown open" for white entry. Although there was insufficient land reserved to give out the 80–640 acres each of the Indians was entitled to under the 1887 Dawes Severalty Act, Lewis cautioned that allotment still needed to move forward lest the "popular clamor for the reduction of the reservations" led to an even worse outcome. Already, he explained, the San Diego press was "teeming with articles the sole effect of which is to create an erroneous impression in the public mind regarding the size and extent of Indian reserves in San Diego County." Their intent, he believed, was "part of the scheme for the general abolition of the reserve system and the extermination of the Indian in California."[35]

Lewis's letter explained, reservation by reservation, the situation that Rust would encounter and what Lewis and fellow attorney Shirley Ward had been doing to defend Mission Indian land. Some reservations were better off than others. For example, the Cahuilla Reservation was in good shape, but Lewis recommended that Rust use his influence to enlarge it "by having the unsurveyed township lying south of the reservation added." Although that spring he had been able to have the Los Coyotes Reservation created to protect the villages of San Ysidro and Los Coyotes, above Warner's Ranch, Lewis reported there were still white men claiming some of the land. Reminding Rust that he and Ward had been working on other cases that would demand "much care, patience and attention" from him as agent, Lewis reported that the case of *The Mission Indians v. John J. Walsh* at Warner's Ranch had been decided by the local land office in the Indians' favor.[36] Because the question involved in *U.S. v. Richard Gird and John North* had brought the legality of the executive order creating the Morongo Reservation into question, Lewis suggested that Rust try to "bring about a compromise" between the government, the Southern Pacific railroad, and settler claimants "whereby the Indian lands can be consolidated and the dispute concerning the odd sections ended."[37]

At the end of his letter, Lewis informed Rust that he would soon be leaving his position as legal counsel for Lake Mohonk; however, he added, since the LMC's "committee on mission Indians has taken a decided hold upon this work," it would no doubt "probably wish to open a correspondence" with him as agent, asking him to lend assistance. The conference was determined to see that "justice is at last accorded to a people who have been heavily oppressed and systematically robbed of everything that was dear or of value to them by representatives of all classes of the white people from the poorest and most desperate outlaw to the most prominent dignitaries of the Christian churches."[38]

Heeding Lewis's earlier concerns about the Potrero Reservation, in February 1890 Rust escorted several men on a tour: Albert K. Smiley; Philip C. Garrett, a member of the Executive Committee of the IRA; and Joshua Davis of the Boston Indian Citizenship Committee, who with Garrett was a member of the LMC committee to protect the legal rights of the Mission Indians. Charles O. Barker, secretary of the Banning Land & Water Company, had recently presented a proposition through Shirley Ward that Garrett thought "plausible" and "worth considering"—hence the tour and the inclusion of these high-powered Indian advocates.[39]

Rust and his party held several interviews with Barker, met with Will Pablo and John Morongo (the latter they described as "the most influential man in the village"), and then drove over much of the reservation to get a feel for the land. They observed that it was "practically valueless," except for a beautiful fertile valley in which most of the arable land was now occupied by white settlers. The Indians had been left with "a limited strip at the mouth of one of the canyons," some mountainside grazing lands, and the "rocky mountain tops, sides and cañons." Although Rust and the reformers agreed that the Indians at Potrero possessed the right of occupancy on the land upon which their village stood, they also agreed that their possession of the entire reservation was in "a state of uncertainty and complication."[40]

On February 21, 1890, Rust, Garrett, Smiley, and attorney Ward presented Barker's proposal to Commissioner Morgan in the hopes of unraveling the "hopeless tangle" of conflicting land claims on the Potrero Reservation between the Indians, the Southern Pacific holdings, state school lands, the Banning Land & Water Company, and those white settlers who had purchased land from them. Some of these claims had actually been granted before the executive order reservation had been established. The proposal was to reduce the current reservation from 144 sections to 26 sections with water rights, including upland grazing lands and some 1,500 acres in and near the canyon. The sacrificed land would go to quiet the settler, state, and railroad land claims. While at first glance the proposal would "seem to be a great sacrifice to the Indians," it still would give the Indians an "undisputed possession of a definite portion of good land," an adequate supply of water, and enough "tillable land" for six to ten acres per resident. However, at the time of this letter to Morgan, the Southern Pacific had not yet signed off on the proposal, and the deal fell through.[41]

In November 1890 Rust informed Morgan that Barker had decided to travel to Washington to appear before Congress in the hopes of getting the Mission Indian Relief Bill passed as a solution to the land title settlement on the Potrero Reservation. This was an old bill, based on the Jackson/Kinney report of 1883 and persistently but unsuccessfully presented to Congress by the Indian Office. Believing its passage seemed to "underlie all our work here," Rust suggested that in addition to Barker's visit, it might be advantageous to bring a delegation of representative Mission Indians to Washington to "secure the attention and influence of any congressman." Therefore he requested that Morgan give him the authority to take to the capital no less than six well-dressed, English-speaking Mission Indian men who through their "intelligent manner" would prove that they were "entitled to the rights of citizenship." He also wanted to add three Indian women who had families "and who at home command[ed] the respect of their white neighbors." No further mention of this planned visit was made, however, and Rust and his delegation did not appear before Congress.[42]

A Missionary Movement

Shortly after assuming his position as agent, Rust's predecessor, Joseph W. Preston, had informed Commissioner Atkins that there were "*no* churches, missionary, education or religious societies located within the limits of Mission Agency."[43] A Protestant, Preston seemingly ignored the agency's several small Catholic chapels and the missionaries who served them. It was Preston who in 1889 escorted Moravian minister William Henry Weinland, recently arrived to begin missionary work for the WNIA, to the Cahuilla Reservation to negotiate for a five-acre parcel for the building of an association cottage. The Indian Office, recognizing that the WNIA's "civilizing" and Christianizing goals matched its own, opened up reservations to these resourceful women reformers, granting them small plots of land and free use of unused federal buildings for housing and educational work. When the Cahuillas refused to give their consent, Preston had suggested that Weinland begin work instead at Soboba.

Shortly thereafter, Rust took over from Preston, and in December 1889 Rust informed Reverend Weinland that he had received instructions from Commissioner Morgan to "select and set apart," with the consent of the Potrero

Indians, a tract of land on the Potrero Reservation not to exceed five acres for educational and missionary purposes. Rust asked Weinland to meet with him before December 22. Rust would soon come to appreciate the Reverend's abilities, describing in his first annual report how the Indians had "cordially welcomed him." Attending Weinland's "simple, instructive services," Rust saw their interest manifested: "I wish that Christianity could put such a man in every Indian village on this coast," he commented to Morgan. In 1890 Rust reported that Weinland had constructed a comfortable residence and a neat chapel on the five acres that had been set aside for his use at Potrero, where he was "daily giving valuable object lessons to the Indians in building, and especially in cultivating the land, setting trees, and making permanent improvements."[44]

Indian Police

Law enforcement was an issue both on and off the reservations. The Indians themselves had long since developed their own justice system, and most larger villages had their own *alcalde,* or judge (by the later nineteenth century usually an elected position), who handled internal matters. Disputes were settled, and crimes were punished—with flogging, seemingly one of the most common punishments, and with hanging for capital crimes, at least in earlier years. For other offenses, banishment was sometimes imposed, and goods and lands were also at times confiscated.

Reporter John Hamilton Gilmour described these native courts in action among the Cahuillas at Palm Springs in the early 1890s. "[W]hen there is an offender to be judged the entire village takes part in the trial and, from what I can learn, there has to be a consensus of opinion as to the punishment before sentence is given," he wrote. Besides the judge, a jury of village leaders also helped to pass sentence. At least among the Cahuillas, flogging was no longer used by that time. When a fine was ordered, the men first considered the "financial status" of the individual, and "the condemned is made to pay about as much as his estate will allow or his patience suffer." Gilmour also noted that this tribal justice system was declining, as more and more of those who had been convicted appealed to the whites to escape their sentences and "now often condemn the actions of their courts and refuse to abide by their judgments."[45]

By the 1880s, Mission Indian agents began asking for their own Indian police force; Agent Preston had also recommended an agency court system with Indian judges.[46] Officials turned him down, citing lack of funds. A few years later Rust argued that both policemen and jails were needed. The Indians, he pointed out, could punish their own offenders if they could hold them by some way other than tying them to a tree, and just "the sight of a jail will do much to deter wrong-doers."[47] But it was not until 1890, under Rust's tenure, that the government finally approved the creation of an Indian police force. It started small, with just half a dozen officers selected by Rust, who appointed John Morongo chief of police. The men were charged in a general way to keep the peace and to keep an eye out for liquor sales, trespassers, and other criminal activity on their reservations by both Indians and whites. They could also be called in to help the agent deal with problems on other reservations.[48]

By the mid-1890s, Rust's successor, Agent Francisco Estudillo, employed fifteen policemen, whom he scattered over the reservations where most needed. He recommended issuing uniforms and badges. The uniforms never seem to have been approved, but a number of early photographs show the officers proudly wearing their badges. Estudillo's successor, Agent Lucius A. Wright, kept his men stationed on those reservations with day schools, where they also served as truant officers. "They are attentive, and obey instructions very well," he noted.[49] Village alcaldes and police officers (again, apparently sometimes elected) continued to exercise some control even after the establishment of an agency police force, but these local institutions eventually faded away.

A Man Was Lynched Today

While physical violence against the Indians was on the decline, it still occurred from time to time. Rust noted in his annual report for 1890 one of the more egregious cases: "An Indian, supposed to belong to a gang of horse-thieves, was arrested near Banning by a Banning officer, lodged in jail at San Bernardino, taken by the same officer back to Banning ostensibly for a trial, allowed to escape at evening and next morning was found half a mile away hanging to a telegraph pole."[50] Two months earlier, Rust had written a letter to Morgan concerning the circumstances behind this incident. Justifying the outcome, he had written that he had no doubt that the individual was "a Horse thief and probably a murderer" and if he "had had a chance [he] might have induce[d] him to confess and so secured the gang." Rust also blamed the Banning officials. "Their own version," he informed Morgan, "looked very much as if they took him back to have him get away and be hung." Believing that "untrue statements were being published," Rust informed Morgan that he had written a letter to the editor of the *New York Tribune*.[51] Enraged by Rust's insensitivity, WNIA member Osia Hiles sent a copy of the news item along with her own letter to Interior Secretary Noble.

She was most upset about the fact that Rust, the official in charge of "the lives and interests of helpless people," had closed his *Tribune* letter with a mere regret that the death prevented him from being able to "draw from him [the murdered man] the names of the gang."[52] This was the only lynching mentioned in the annual reports of the Mission Indian agents. Of it, the *Redlands Citrograph* noted: "It is surmised the injured stockmen know something about the affair. In the meantime there is 'another good Indian.'"[53]

The California Mission Indian Commission

The year 1891 would prove to be a pivotal one for the Mission Indians and a trying and busy one for Agent Rust. He would host a commission empowered to create new reservations and tour Amelia Stone Quinton, the feisty WNIA president, around the reservations and to Reverend Weinland's missionary outpost. This was the first of many trips that Quinton would make to California. Previously, WNIA missionary work in California had been supported entirely by eastern branches and auxiliaries. That changed with Quinton's visit; now future association work in Southern California would be funded and run by local women, giving the organization the resources to undertake more missionary work among local tribes. Thus the powerful collective voice of the WNIA had joined those of the IRA, the LMC, and the Indian Office. Congress was soon battered by even more demands to aid the Mission Indians.

Although both the California Mission Indian Commission of 1891 and the WNIA had an impact upon the Mission Indians, it was the commission that more directly affected them. The commission was a direct result of the Jackson/Kinney report, which eight years earlier had recommended the resurveying and patenting of reservations to the Indian residents, with a twenty-five-year trust period, and removal of white trespassers.[54]

In January 1891, more than five years after Jackson's death, "An Act for the Relief of the Mission Indians in the State of California" passed both houses of Congress and was signed into law by President Harrison.[55] As part of the legislation, Congress authorized the appointment of a three-man commission "to arrange a just and satisfactory settlement of the Mission Indians residing in the State of California, upon reservations which shall be secured to them as hereinafter provided." The three members of the California Mission Indian Commission were Albert K. Smiley, Charles C. Painter, and Joseph B. Moore, a Michigan attorney.[56] They were to gather in San Francisco in late February 1891.[57]

The three men were about to undertake an unparalleled and arduous task for the paltry government compensation of eight dollars per day. In a twelve-page letter, containing pertinent summaries of past agents' reports, Commissioner Morgan charged them with the selection of a reservation for each band or village—to include, as much as possible, lands and villages currently occupied. Quoting Agent Rust's report of May 9, 1890, Morgan explained that besides the existing reservations there were also thirty-seven separate Indian villages in Southern California, six of which were located on private lands, eight on patented grants, and three on government lands. One village of forty-eight Indians was partly on private and partly on government land.[58]

It was a daunting task. Not only were they to create new reservations for over one thousand Indians, they were also to check existing reservations to make sure that all the lands described in the original executive orders had been included and if not, submit a description to correct the situation; appraise the value of improvements made by settlers with valid claims; and locate vacant public lands upon which to settle all Indians currently living on private grants. Since some reservations and other Indian-occupied lands were located on railroad land, the commissioners were also forced to arrange a complicated exchange of railroad and Indian lands to achieve their goal.[59]

The commission was also required to make full descriptions of the "character of the land in each reservation," specifying the amount of arable, grazing, and other lands. If Indian communities held excess lands that were not needed, a reduced reservation should be recommended. To carry out their assignment, commission members were authorized to hire a surveyor and assistants to define boundaries of selected tracts and to confer with Frank Lewis, special attorney for the Mission Indians, and attorney Shirley Ward.[60] To ensure that Lewis would be included, on March 27 Rust requested that Morgan instruct him to accompany the California Mission Indian Commission, all expenses paid. On May 20, 1891, Lewis was officially appointed to serve as the commission's clerk.[61]

Often called the Smiley Commission (for its chairman and most prominent member), the California Mission Indian Commission might better be called the Painter Commission, as most of the work fell to the energetic IRA agent, who labored almost continually for the entire year.[62] How much help, if any, Painter received from Agent Rust is difficult to ascertain. No letters between the two have been located. Rust was aware of the commission, writing Morgan in February that he was "pleased to learn" of it. In his September annual report, he noted that until its work was completed and the reservations divided in severalty, he could not "hope to report marked progress."[63]

By year's end, the commission had completed its report. At least thirteen new reservations were established, home to some six hundred fifty people in total: San Manuel, Ramona (north of Cahuilla), La Posta, Manzanita, Cuyapaipe or Long Canyon, Campo, and Laguna, all in the mountains of southern San Diego County;[64] Pauma and Rincon along the San Luis Rey River; Augustine Reservation and a new Cabazon Reservation;[65] Santa Ysabel; and Twenty-Nine Palms. Thirteen previously existing reservations had their boundaries clarified, adjusted, and in some cases reduced. The Morongo Reservation (formerly Potrero) was reduced from 88,475 acres to 14,560; Agua Caliente, from 60,870 to 4,480; and Capitán Grande, from 17,340 to 12,480; while the Torres Reservation was enlarged from one section (640 acres) to forty-five sections, taking in the villages of Torres, Martinez, Alamo Bonita, and Agua Dulce.[66]

In his 1894 annual report Agent Estudillo summarized the new reservations created by the California Mission Indian Commission as varying in altitudes "from 260 feet below to 3,500 feet above sea level," with temperatures "from 120° to 80° in the shade." He concluded that "with water many otherwise dependent families of Indians can be made self-sustaining." He also included a brief description of each reservation, with varying amounts of detail. Cuyapaipe, for example, he described as "located in a long narrow canyon, inaccessible by wagon, containing not 10 acres of arable land." The population of thirty-nine industrious Kumeyaays lived on acorns and hunting and "would make good farmers if they had any land to farm." Considering how poor they were, Estudillo described them as possessing good homes. He recommended that "steps be taken to secure them some farming land at the mount of this canyon," and that a school be built and a field matron sent to live among them. He concluded that "they have been totally neglected heretofore." The small population at Twenty-Nine Palms Reservation lived in reasonably good houses and were "quiet, law-abiding people; their lands are all that they require." As for the few Indians residing on the Augustine Reservation, they mostly worked for Southern Pacific Railroad Company. The same was true at Cabazon: "This reservation is not susceptible of cultivation to any extent." The Indians were either employed at the railroad company or worked cutting wood to be shipped to Los Angeles, and their chief food source, the mesquite bean, was disappearing rapidly. Although the Ramona Reservation was "little more than pasture land for the few families living thereon," they were well off and lived in "reasonably good houses." Two years later Estudillo added that some of these lands "would not support a horned toad, let alone supporting an Indian—a human being endowed with thoughts, feeling, and a soul as immortal as our own."[67]

Reading Estudillo's descriptions of the reservations might lead us to conclude that the commission members had failed. Their choices were not always easy, even though they tried to respect the Indians' natural desire to stay in their homes. Painter was well aware of the inequities. He reported, for example, that the "reservations of Laguna, La Posta, Manzanita and Cuyapipe [*sic*] are on the mountains overlooking the desert, and were unwillingly set apart by the commissioners as homes for Indians who were moved, years ago, from near the missions, to serve as a protection to the settlers against the wild Indians of the mountain and desert." While three families at Laguna had sufficient land and water, "the other three villages are exceedingly poor, and can never be otherwise."[68]

In some places the commission's work settled years of conflict and confusion. The original Mexican land grant at Pauma made provision for three villages to remain on the rancho. The property later passed into the hands of Bishop Francis Mora of Monterey and Los Angeles. He had tried to sell the land, but as the title was clouded by the Indian occupation, the deal fell through. In 1890 he leased the land, but the lessee found his use restricted by Indians and opted to cancel. In 1891 the bishop went to court to define and limit the Indians' rights. The commission finally made a deal with him to quitclaim 250 acres, with water, to the government, which gave a life lease to an Indian family.[69]

Smiley remarked that the commission's most difficult task was trying once and for all to settle the complicated claims and counter-claims on the Morongo Reservation.[70] The squatters' claims were not the real issue; it was the individual claims to land, sometimes patented, that whites had acquired before the executive orders that created and then later enlarged the reservation. These included the claims of C. F. Jost and his wife, Margaret; Walter S. Hathaway;[71] and Welwood Murray and his wife, Eliza, who had also figured in a number of Agent McCallum's schemes. Then there was John North and Richard Gird, who claimed most of the available water and much of the Potrero village, including "nearly all of the houses, ditches and considerable orchards and vineyards of the Indians." Finally the Southern Pacific railroad still controlled a number of alternating sections.[72]

Attorney Barker, who managed the Banning Colony tract adjoining the reservation to the west, represented the claimants and negotiated an agreement with the commission that the claimants would give up their claims and water rights in return for patented land elsewhere. The Murrays took their in-lieu land at Palm Springs, where they had long been living. The Southern Pacific also agreed to release its remaining rights in return for other lands. Another settler on the eastern edge of the reservation, a Mrs. Toutain, received ten acres near the Whitewater River. These land swaps eliminated much of the checkerboard pattern of ownership, especially in the central part of the reservation where the most productive lands were located. The drier, more mountainous lands on the northern end of the reservation were then returned to public domain. The *Banning Herald* thought all this would be very good for the community and believed the Indians would also now be happy—and prosperous.[73]

On November 11, 1892, the North and Gird case against the government and the Indians' countersuit against them were dismissed, with each party paying their own court costs.[74] The only lingering problem was Mrs. Toutain. In 1894 Agent Estudillo reported that she was still "a thorn in the side" of the Indians, and he recommended she be removed and her land taken for reservation purposes. But at late as 1909 she was still there, demanding much more money to sell out than the government was willing to pay.[75]

Predictably, there was criticism of the commission's work. "[S]ome errors of omission were made, greatly to the damage of the Indians," the *Sacramento Record-Union* noted. For example, the commission should have included an adjoining section at Torres. Agent Estudillo later had the area resurveyed and discovered the schoolhouse and the homes of a number of families were left out. He recommended that the land be closed to entry until the problem could be solved. The errant section was state school land, so it would take an act of legislature to deed it to the Indians.[76]

In their annual reports from the mid-1890s, Agents Estudillo and Wright listed several reservations that were mislocated. Estudillo explained that "the reservations call for certain lands upon which the Indians do not, never did, and will never be able to live for want of water, etc." This included Cosmit, Laguna, Campo, La Posta, Manzanita, Twenty-Nine Palms, and the Martinez village, which was supposed to part of the Torres Reservation.[77] The lack of water was not the only problem that the six industrious families on the Manzanita Reservation endured. According to Estudillo's 1894 report, a certain Mr. McCain, following in his father's footsteps, had enclosed and improved a portion of the reservation. "The Indians have never claimed this land or in any way shown that they owned it or thought they owned it," wrote Estudillo to Commissioner Daniel M. Browning. Unfortunately a survey revealed that McCain's property was actually "within the lines of the reservation as described and defined by the commission." Therefore

Estudillo recommended that "some immediate action should be taken looking to a speedy settlement of the boundaries of this reservation."[78]

Estudillo was also concerned with the situation at Cosmit, which he described as worthless. "Had the Indians received the lands they formerly owned or were in possession of years past they would have a comfortable place to live and would have good homes, as they are somewhat industrious," he informed Commissioner Browning. Painter agreed with Estudillo's assessment. "The little Reservation of Cosmit as set apart embraced nothing but dry pine bluffs," he admitted, "while the good land, with water, on which stood the Indian Rancheria, was left outside for a white man who had squatted down by the side of the Indians." Painter remarked that the man's wife had said: "It was very kind of the Commissioner and surveyor to run the line as they did and give us this land."[79]

Finally at Laguna, cattleman Eli A. Harper held a patent for some of the supposed reservation land that included lands used by the village captain, Valentine. Even a part of the village cemetery was involved. According to Estudillo, Harper claimed to have a deed from the state. "This would have been avoided had the commission described properly the lands occupied by the Indians," announced Estudillo to Commissioner Browning. By 1897 Agent Wright could report that surveys had recently been completed at Laguna and Campo, while the survey at Twenty-Nine Palms was under way. He also thought those at La Posta, Inaja, and Manzanita were completed. Unfortunately the Martinez village was not even on the Torres Reservation. Despite these missteps, almost everyone agreed that the commission deserved much credit—especially in dealing with squatters, private inholdings, and railroad lands.[80]

Government Day Schools

Rust's 1891 annual report listed other improvements on the reservations. At Soboba a new schoolhouse accommodating forty students and including living quarters for Mary Noble had finally been constructed. Mrs. Nanie J. Salsberry was doing an excellent job as the teacher at Cahuilla, and she had been joined by Miss C. M. Fleming, who had been appointed to assist her as an industrial teacher and to work directly with Indian girls and their mothers in their homes. Her efforts were appreciated, Rust informed the commissioner. He also reported that the teacher at Agua Caliente, Mrs. Josephine Harlan Babbitt, was proving to be very valuable, exerting a "strong influence among the people for good."[81] The Mesa Grande teacher, Hylena Nickerson, was making "commendable progress," as were Ora Salmons, now at Rincon, and Flora Golsh at La Jolla. But Rust saved most of his praise for the work of Mary Platt, who had taken over the school at Pechanga, previously abandoned because of the presence of whiskey and "low white" influence. Many of the Indian adults were now reclaimed by Platt's temperance society. For those isolated families living where schools were not available, Rust believed that a good educational solution would be the establishment of a boarding school, teaching manual training. He ended his report on a positive note. He could see a "marked improvement in public sentiment" toward the Indian. "Prejudice is giving way to reason."[82]

Rust's educational plans would get a boost in the summer of 1891, when he escorted Quinton through various Mission villages and reservations. Although the WNIA did not establish schools among the Mission Indians, it did build and support various missionary sites and worked closely with Reverend Weinland, Fleming and others, financially supporting government school teachers and field matrons, thereby improving the quality of education for Mission Indian students.[83]

Medical Missionaries

Health care, like education, was another perennial issue for Indians and government officials alike. Here again Quinton's arrival in June 1891 was fortuitous. At the Cahuilla Reservation, she visited with C. M. Fleming, whose ongoing medical missionary work would soon be partially funded by the WNIA, including the construction of a cottage for her. When Fleming was appointed as a government field matron in July 1891 by Commissioner Morgan, the association became involved in that important government program. Whenever the WNIA sponsored government field matrons, members from across the country would send supplies to these chronically underpaid women to support their work, which among other duties included basic health care.[84]

While visiting the village of Agua Caliente on Warner's Ranch, Quinton determined that the hot springs there would be ideal for an association-funded hospital, with the healthful mineral waters piped directly into the building. At year's end Quinton wrote Morgan, offering to build such a hospital and support a doctor if he would grant her association a tract of land and supply the salary of a field matron to live with the doctor and "teach Indian women and girls practically, domestically and morally."[85]

Rust, too, had seen the need for a hospital and believed, like Quinton, that the best location would be in the village of Agua Caliente with its abundant hot springs. He had made that recommendation as early as his first annual report in 1889. One month after escorting Quinton on her tour, Rust again brought up the idea of building a hospital, informing Morgan that although Dr. Ferrebee "discharged his duties faithfully," there were still times when he had to turn to local doctors to care for the Indians. More medical help was needed. "I still believe the Hospital feasible, reasonably and the best possible way to spend the money we now have," he stressed. Because a new school was needed at Agua Caliente, the agent suggested that the old structure temporarily be used as a hospital.[86]

With Quinton now involved, it appeared that the Indians might actually get a hospital. However, Rust for some reason was reluctant to support the WNIA efforts. Perhaps he wanted to take credit for the project himself. His reluctance took the form of advising the villagers not to make a formal agreement with the WNIA until Commissioner Morgan had given his approval. Quinton, of course, could not have known how eager the agent was to have a hospital at the hot springs. Based on her anti-Catholic feelings, she had initially assumed that the Indians' reluctance to grant the land was due to interference by a priest, but she had soon shifted the blame to Rust.[87] Kept apprised of the situation by the government school teacher, Josephine Babbitt, Quinton went over Rust's head to the commissioner, who agreed to send a letter to both the Indians and Rust. In mid-March 1892, Rust informed Quinton that he had now prepared an agreement, requesting the village captain to give his consent for a plot of land upon which the WNIA could build its hospital. "I shall be pleased to do all I can to forward your plan," he wrote, "and hope for success."[88]

Commissioner Morgan took almost a month to respond to Rust's May 6 letter. After a thorough investigation by his office, the commissioner wrote that they could not "see that the Indians will be otherwise than benefitted by the proposed hospital." The Indians would have a facility "established and maintained solely for their welfare" and in the end would probably end up owning it. "I do not see why there should be any trouble whatever in their consenting to the arrangement," he concluded, "unless interested parties are trying to prejudice them against this hospital with some ulterior purpose in view, which cannot be the best good of the Indian." Morgan ordered Rust to use all of his influence to make the Indians understand that this hospital "can be only a benefit to them" and therefore not to "cheat themselves through misrepresentation or other influence of a good which is waiting for them."[89] But in the end—even after Mrs. Babbitt's best efforts to convince them—the Indians still refused to give up any land. They claimed they were pleased with their present physician and did not need a hospital, although they would "consent" if their agent ordered them to do so. Rust, however, told Morgan that he did not "feel justified to order them to sign."[90]

Bitterly disappointed that the hospital project had been stalled, Quinton wrote Rust, requesting that he use his persuasive powers with the Indians. Her association had already collected money and had two "admirable ladies" ready to begin their medical missionary work. Months passed, the agent dragged his feet, and then the August 1892 issue of the WNIA's monthly newsletter, *The Indian's Friend,* published a small article announcing that plans for a hospital would be suspended because "ex-governor Downey will at once begin suit for the ejectment of these Indians."[91] In September, Morgan received a letter from Frank Lewis, now special assistant U.S. attorney, reporting that Downey and the Merchants' Exchange Bank of San Francisco had begun an action of ejectment against the Indian villages of Agua Caliente, Puerta la Cruz, La Puerta, San José, and Mataguay. The Indians, Lewis explained, had immediately notified him, giving him time to "secure from the attorneys of the ranch owners a stipulation" and to appear on their behalf.[92]

Neither Rust's reluctance nor Downey's suit deterred Quinton. The WNIA rented quarters from the Indians and in January 1893 authorized Dr. Rebecca C. Hallowell, an 1878 graduate of the Woman's Medical College of Pennsylvania, to proceed to Agua Caliente as the association's medical missionary. In addition, the WNIA also supported Hallowell's friend, Julia M. French, as government field matron. Although Quinton had been unable to build an actual hospital, she and her association had at a minimum provided a resident physician to meet the Indians' medical needs, as well as providing housing and some support for a government field matron who would educate Indian women in the "civilized ways" of the dominant white culture.[93]

Years later Rust's bitterness over the whole incident was palpable. When Morgan had originally decided to build a hospital, the agent claimed to have chosen the location and sent building plans to Washington, and then Quinton had agreed to use WNIA funding. Rust expressed his profound displeasure with Quinton to a reporter of the *Los Angeles Times* in May 1902. "My plans were all frustrated, my promise to the Indians broken," he complained, especially when he learned that the primary function of Hallowell and French was to engage in missionary work—and even for that task, Rust described them as "poorly equipped." He also claimed they had no idea how to conduct a hospital; instead they remained in their rented adobe for five years, accomplishing "nothing more than to draw their salaries and make missionary reports."[94]

The record, however, shows that Rust's evaluation was inaccurate. The two women accomplished a great deal more than he probably knew or would admit.

In December 1893, for example, Dr. Hallowell reported forty sick calls to her home and twenty-one home visits, giving out forty-two prescriptions as well as bandages and other supplies. The following month she had thirty-five official visits to her home, made thirteen house calls, and filled sixty-eight prescriptions. French busied herself teaching Sunday school and running sewing and quilt-making classes, as well as showing the Indian women how to make basketry for chairs and stools.[95]

Although Rust, possibly out of pure spite, deliberately hesitated to help the WNIA at Agua Caliente, his actions at Cahuilla are even less understandable. When Fleming resigned her post as a government field matron in the fall of 1892, Quinton recommended Dr. Anna Hayward Johnson to Commissioner Morgan and requested the grant of a five-acre parcel for "educational & missionary purposes" upon which to build a missionary cottage.[96] Johnson, a graduate of Vassar and the Woman's Medical College of Pennsylvania and a former teacher at Hampton Institute, arrived at Cahuilla on January 20, 1893, two days after Hallowell and French arrived at Agua Caliente. Dr. Johnson immediately began her duties as both field matron and physician, making 322 medical calls during her first five weeks.[97] Although the details are shadowy, it appears, at least according to Quinton, that Rust prohibited Dr. Johnson from occupying the recently built WNIA missionary cottage. Always ready to defend her association's missionary efforts, Quinton immediately pointed her finger at Rust, who in turn called her accusation a "*base falsehood.*"[98]

Writing Morgan on February 20, 1893, Rust reported that he "never thought of 'forbidding Dr. Johnson from going to Coahuilla [*sic*] and occupy that cottage,'" which, he explained, had been constructed without his knowledge. Quinton scoffed, noting that Reverend Weinland, Captain Leonicio Lugo of the Cahuilla village, Mrs. Salsberry, the government school teacher, and Fleming, the field matron, had all conferred and agreed upon the location. Meanwhile, Rust maintained that he had done nothing but try to please Dr. Johnson and help her in her work. "I wish to be fully understood," Rust emphatically wrote, "when I say there *is no truth in Mrs. Quinton's statement* to the contrary and if I were to remain as agent I should heartily wish she would keep out of the state for I know she has only made trouble from the day she began what she calls her work in So. Calif."[99]

A Newspaper Critic

While Rust was dealing with the negotiations for a WNIA-sponsored hospital at Agua Caliente, the *San Francisco Chronicle* published a series of letters, later reprinted in other newspapers, including the *Los Angeles Herald* and *Los Angeles Times*. Written from the Coachella Valley by correspondent John Gilmour, several of these articles were critical of Rust's dealings with the Cahuilla Indians in the valley, with Gilmour accusing Rust of "causing discord" among these Indians. "Since the advent of Mr. Rust, the present agent for the Mission Indians," he declared, "there has been bad blood among the Cahuillas."[100] Using an exaggerated, uneducated dialect to mimic Rust, Gilmour described the agent's appearance before a mixed company of Indians and whites: "I am going to break up this here tribal relation and that feller Cabazon [*sic*] ought to be locked up, for he is a bad, wicked Indian." According to Gilmour, when Rust was asked by a woman in the audience if he ever felt his life was in danger, his answer was, "Frequently." Then Gilmour's Rust declared, "[Cabezon] is always a tryin' to incite them to violence. He is a bad Indian and won't let them work. He won't do what I tell him, and I am going to make him, and if he don't do what I want him to do I'll lock him up. Jail ain't good enough for him."[101]

Incensed with the "most imaginary western dialect" that Gilmour had put in Rust's mouth, Jessie Benton Frémont, widow of John C. Frémont, wrote to Anna Dawes in Rust's defense. Explaining that she rarely allowed herself to "feel indignant," Frémont said that Rust was "highly educated" and a "valued member of all the ethnological societies of Europe." A "remarkable archaeologist," he combined the "true care of the Indians with researches that make America honored among scientific bodies here and in Europe."[102]

The recipient of Frémont's letter was an active member of the WNIA and the daughter of Henry L. Dawes, the powerful Massachusetts senator who served as chair of the Senate Committee on Indian Affairs and authored the 1887 Dawes Act. Frémont had hoped that Anna's father would somehow be able to protect Rust. Gilmour's article was a "concerted attack" that would no doubt reach Washington, remarked Frémont. "Stronger than laws are the slanders of the Press," she continued, and this "modest and proud man" was being unfairly criticized and undervalued as an Indian agent. At her father's request, Anna Dawes forwarded Frémont's letter to Morgan.[103]

Obviously Rust did not speak in the vernacular portrayed by Gilmour, but the journalist was correct in asserting that Rust was attempting to break up tribal relations. Indeed, he was under orders from the Indian Office to do so. His job was to implement the provisions of the Dawes Act, which called for the dismemberment of tribal land holdings and the subsequent allotment of these lands. Rust's methods, though, are open to criticism. Not only did he attempt to implement the legislation, but he had replaced Cabezon with William (Billy) Williams, an action Gilmour described as raising "much bad blood." Gilmour, who was impressed with Cabezon's "manliness and his spirit of fair dealing," criticized Rust as ignorant about the Cahuillas and their work ethic. He suggested that it was the agent, not Cabezon, who was keeping the Indians agitated. These "desert Indians unhesitatingly declare that their troubles have commenced since the introduction of this Indian agent."[104]

In his defense, Rust responded that Gilmour's attacks were instigated "by a certain widow in Palm Springs, with whom the newspaperman roomed." This widow was angry that water had been diverted from her property on Rust's orders. Gilmour, of course, denied the charge, accused Rust "with falsehoods galore," and replied that he lived alone, adding, "the woman whose ditch Rust closed and subsequently had to reopen is the wife of a prominent San Francisco businessman, well known in Los Angeles." The ditch in question had been closed by Rust in mid-April. This water source had long been used by Indians, and it had been used by local whites for the past six years; all parties involved were angry and had signed a petition. According to the *San Francisco Chronicle,* when Rust received the petition, he "insolently told the Indians to go about their business."[105]

Besides defending himself in the press, Rust also wrote Commissioner Morgan, assuring him that because he had been warned ahead of time about Gilmour's character, he had treated the correspondent "with politeness" and was "guarded in speech as he would be likely to misrepresent me." Rust explained that some Cahuilla Indians had come to him more than a year before, requesting that Cabezon be deposed and "obligated to return to them some $372," which they had raised to pay for his trip to Washington—money he then supposedly squandered. Rust had encouraged them to "drop the matter," but when they returned, he informed them they could hold an election and remove Cabezon. Because the election results were 102 votes for Williams and only 36 for Cabezon, Rust felt obligated to give the commission to Williams.[106] This had only resulted in Will Pablo and Cabezon conspiring "to make all the trouble they can," Rust concluded. The final straw was Gilmour's article in the *Chronicle.*[107]

Rust assured Morgan that most of the tribe had "shown a disposition to accede" to his wishes because for years Cabezon had "refused to receive anything from Agents." The agent's solution was to arrest both Cabezon and Pablo and confine them "until they would promise to stop their opposition to reasonable regulations." Rust explained that Pablo had recently come to see him, agreeing to end his opposition. Although they shook hands, parting as friends, Rust had "no confidence that [Pablo] was honest." Rust disliked having to trouble the commissioner with this situation, but he concluded that "the morbid desire of an unprincipled newspaper correspondent to create a sensation regardless of facts" to be a valid reason for his letter.[108]

Gilmour ended his lengthy critique of Rust with Will Pablo's petition calling for Williams's removal and the return of Cabezon to his rightful position. The journalist seemed impressed with Pablo, the Potrero village captain, describing him as "a remarkably able Indian" who was both literate and politically savvy. A strong leader, "his soul is in the task of returning to power the hereditary chieftain of his tribe," exclaimed Gilmour. "He feels bitterly the injustice done the Cahuilla Indians."[109] However, a few months later, Gilmour, like Rust, would become markedly critical of Pablo, describing his "mania for writing letters and issuing manifestoes." The captain was deluging "the various settlements with his orders and instructions that the majority of the Indians believe he has some mysterious connection with the President, and his words have weight in the councils of the State." Not only did he write "at least four letters a week" to Congressman W. W. Bowers, but he ordered friendly captains around, telling them what to do and say "and how to treat the Indian agent or offensive whites."[110]

Gilmour's complaints about Rust did not stop at his treatment of the Cahuillas but were also aimed at his "predatory relic-hunting tours." In mid-March the journalist accused Rust not only of taking valuable official time "in traveling from house to house trying to sell a car load of date palms to enterprise rancheros" but also of "fill[ing] in the interstices of his time by trying to find metates (milling stones) and other relics."[111] In August Gilmour repeated the same accusations, but more strongly. Instead of devoting his time "to looking after his wards," the agent had been busy collecting their handicrafts and then selling them for "many thousands of dollars." In the three or four sales he had held since his appointment as agent, Rust had realized "something like $18,000 from the enterprise," noted Gilmour. The Indians even accused their agent of taking "whatever he wants without making any recompense." He visited the more remote villages only when he thought he could obtain valuable curios there. Gilmour concluded that it was not "archaeological enthusiasm which actuates him, but simply a spirit of commercial enterprise."[112]

Rust did collect and sell Indian art and artifacts at the same time as some Southern California Indians were trying to make money selling their handicrafts. He admitted his strong interest in archeology and archeological relics in a brief biographical sketch, explaining that he had started out collecting minerals but

A previously unpublished portrait of
Captain John Morongo, circa 1895.
Courtesy of the San Jacinto Museum.

soon found the field of archeology "rich and attractive." His interest increased after visiting a Mound Builders site in Ohio in 1855, but it was not until 1879 that he was he able to engage in digging in a mound in Missouri, returning the next summer. He soon acquired some eight hundred vessels, which he sold to Yale University. After he settled in Pasadena, he enjoyed traveling the West, from Oregon to Mexico, in search of relics. By the summer of 1894, he explained that his collection "had grown upon [his] hands far beyond [his] expectation."[113]

Continuing Controversy

Rust's confrontational approach as agent predated Gilmour's critical articles. As early as 1890 former Mission Indian Agent Lawson (who remained in Colton following his resignation) had written his former interpreter, Captain Morongo, inquiring how he was getting on with Rust, noting that a government inspector was now in the area. "If you mean to get rid of Rust," Lawson wrote, "and want my help—we can do it." He cautioned Morongo to keep this quiet, however. Lawson added that he would like to "make a fight for [re-]appointment," but only if Morongo would be willing to "come into the service" with him again. Lawson claimed Indians "from over the mountains" were also coming in daily, asking him to return to the agency. How much further this collaboration went is unclear.[114]

Morongo's role in all this is unclear. It appeared that the captain, who served as agency interpreter, and Rust, who was willing to appoint him as Potrero captain, had a good working relationship. In a December 1891 letter to Morgan, Rust described Morongo as "the most intelligent, careful, and reasonable Indian" in Potrero. He supported his family, did not drink, and was a Christian, having been baptized by Reverend Weinland. Early in 1893 a reporter asked Morongo: "Is it true that Mr. Rust is not popular and should be removed as agent?" Morongo, without hesitation, said no, explaining that "some of the people do not like him" because "he will not let them have their own way." Then he talked about Will Pablo, claiming Pablo had abandoned his wife and two babies and killed another Indian when he was drunk. Although some of the tribe wanted Pablo as their chief, Morongo added, Rust refused to appoint him, claiming that "if he could not take care of his family he could not take care of the reservation." Morongo also told the reporter that Chief Cabezon did "nothing for his people and they got tired of him." Morongo explained that these were the only complaints against Rust, and they were made "by the bad fellows of the reservation. The good ones are satisfied with Mr. Rust."[115]

Like Morongo, Will Pablo also turned to the newspapers. A reporter for the *San Bernardino Daily Courier,* especially impressed with him, wrote that although Pablo enjoyed greater support on the Potrero Reservation, "Morongo exercises the authority in agency affairs, whether he is formally called Captain on not." Morongo, Pablo told the reporter, "boasts of his power and of his influence with the Agent"—controlling, for example, the use of the farm wagons provided by the agency. The journalist inquired if their use was "to subserve the malicious vanity of a Morongo or to gratify the bigoted spleen of a Rust?" In conclusion, the article described the agent as "too narrow, too egotistical, too discriminative, [and] too much prone to prejudice and bigotry," and that both he and "his *protégé* Morongo ought to go."[116]

Rust's conflict with Will Pablo dated back several years. At the end of 1890 the young Indian had succeeded his father, Pablo Gabriel, as captain at Potrero, but Rust refused to recognize him in that office. "I knew he was a hard case," wrote

Rust to Morgan at the time, characterizing Pablo as a "drunken, idle captain." Morgan "sanctioned" Rust's action toward the young captain, replying that only "industrious and sober" men should occupy the office.[117] In early February 1891, Rust again complained to Morgan, accusing Pablo of doing "very little work," failing to "support his wife and child," and fomenting "trouble among the Indians constantly." Pablo had not only threatened to bring enough Indians to Potrero "to drive out all the whites and take all the lands" but had already sent to Washington a petition with two hundred signatures requesting the agent's removal. In July, Rust described him as representing "the worst element among the nonprogressive Indians of Potrero." Like his father before him, Pablo was a respected Cahuilla shaman, perhaps one of the reasons Rust characterized him as a bad influence. Furthermore, Rust was angry because Pablo had become involved in a brief "Messiah" movement on the reservation.[118] This "Messiah" was expected to arrive around July 4, 1891, and already, Rust complained, some fifty families were camped on San Jacinto Mountain awaiting his arrival, expecting him to "run down the whites."[119]

Rust was concerned enough about the potential disastrous consequences of the Messiah craze at Potrero that he included a lengthy paragraph on the situation in his third annual report in September 1891. He informed Morgan that only a few people were influenced "by the statements of the medicine men, who said that the white man would be destroyed and that they [the Indians] would possess the land." When the Colorado River "began to fill up the Salton Sea" and after runners told "wild stories of the waters to come," many "good faithful Indians . . . fled to the mountains in wild haste; but a few days of fasting reassured them and they returned disappointed." But even so, the agent concluded, there may have been a political aspect to the movement. The medicine man had also "told them that the most progressive Indian of the tribe, John Morongo, must be driven out or die. Constant threats are made, and his haystack of 10 tons of hay was burned."[120]

Months earlier Rust had complained that Pablo had joined hands with Chief Gervasio Cabezon, San Bernardino "shyster lawyer" John Brown Jr.,[121] and "disgraced" Indian Agent Lawson in keeping the Indians stirred up. Rust believed he could not control the Indians "and benefit them" so long as Pablo was permitted to go about at will. Numerous times he requested permission to construct a jail in which to lock up the troublesome Indians. Rust bitterly complained to Morgan that Pablo was constantly "influencing" other Indians against him and against the government-run day school, with its mostly Protestant teachers, encouraging parents to enroll their children at St. Boniface instead. At one point the Potrero school was forced to close because of lack of students. No doubt Rust's strong anti-Catholic bias was part of the reason he so disliked Pablo.[122]

Matters came to a head in April 1891, when Will Pablo prepared seven specific charges against Rust. Initially printed in the *San Bernardino Courier,* most of them were reprinted by the *Los Angeles Herald* under a catchy title: "Too Much Bric-A-Brac," a reference to the agent's buying and collecting of Indian relics, which Pablo severely criticized. According to the charges, the Indians were displeased with the time and attention Rust gave to gathering their basketry, relics, and other "curiosities" without even offering them any money. These items were then sold but "not for the Indian's benefit." Pablo accused Rust of being incompetent, due to a "crankiness that amounts to imbecility," as well as arbitrary and tyrannical. As a result of the ill-will toward the agent, the Indians of Morongo refused to send their children to the government day school. The agent was perceived not only as "their worst enemy" but as unwilling to even "hear the Indians when they come to transact business." Tired of him, they had sent a letter, signed by all the chiefs and captains, to Noble, asking for his removal.[123]

The following month, former Agent Lawson went public with his attack on Rust. In a letter to the *Los Angeles Times,* Lawson described a meeting between Rust, a special inspector, and the Indians at Potrero, who were interested in airing their grievances. "Charges and countercharges were made by Indians and agent," wrote Lawson. He described "the wily 'Captain John'" (John Morongo), coming in for a "good share of abuse by his dusky colleagues, because he has now taken sides" with Rust "against the Indians, in all matters of controversy between them." Morongo's defection, Lawson claimed, was prompted by the gift of the agency's two-seat carriage, which was "not 'tony' enough" for Rust. Lawson also addressed the "useless position of agency physician," located at Colton, miles from where the majority of the Indians lived, as well as the issue of leasing Indian lands to white men. The Indians, noted Lawson, were intelligent enough to know that under the rules and regulations of government agencies, an agent "must have their consent and the approval of the Secretary of the Interior" to engage in such practices.[124]

A week after the publication of Lawson's letter, John Morongo explained to a *Times* reporter "that there were one or two matters in it he wished to deny." It was true that Lawson had previously offered to aid the Indians in Rust's removal so he could be reappointed. After an interview with Morgan, Morongo realized there was "no hope of success" in this plan because the "Commissioner refused to listen to such petty troubles." The captain, therefore, abandoned the matter. However, during another meeting with Lawson, the former agent tried again to encourage Morongo to forward to the interior secretary the petition to remove Rust "for malfeasance of office." Ultimately it was Morongo's refusal that was the "reason for Lawson's animosity" toward him. As for the carriage, Morongo claimed it was an old one that had not been used for three or four years, and it cost him thirty-nine dollars to have it fixed up. This gift, he claimed, "had not influenced him one way or the other." Furthermore, Morongo wanted it understood that "he did not stand up for the agent as against the interests of his people." If the Indians were in the wrong, he would have defended Rust, or any other agent.[125]

Dr. Ferrebee also defended the beleaguered Rust from some attacks by the press. However, the *San Bernardino Daily Courier* was having none of it. Rust, they insisted, was disliked by "the overwhelming majority of the Indians." The *Courier* continued to attack Rust in no uncertain terms, declaring that "men who do not consider themselves as divinely commissioned to reform the world" should be selected as Indian agents, instead of "narrow, bigoted, harsh, obtuse fanatics" like Rust.[126]

It is true that almost from the beginning Rust had meddled in village politics. It was, however, his attempt to control the political structure of the Desert Cahuillas that finally brought his actions into question. During the summer of 1892 the volatile situation between Agent Rust, Will Pablo, and the Cahuillas at Potrero began to reach an audience outside of Southern California. In mid-May, Interior Secretary Noble forwarded a May 12, 1892, letter written by Saint Louis attorney Alexander J. P. Garesché, along with a newspaper clipping from the *St. Louis Republic* relative to the condition of the Cahuilla Indians, to Acting Commissioner R. V. Belt. As reported in the news item, Pablo had accused Rust of taking away his land, renting it to a white man, and then, after collecting the rent, refusing to pay him—even threatening to jail him. Belt acknowledged receipt of Noble's letter, concluding that "the charge of wrongful conduct on the part of the Indian agent" in regard to Pablo's land would "receive proper attention." Two days later Belt informed Noble that based on "repeated complaints" from Rust, he recommended an investigation by an Interior Department inspector of the charges against Pablo and his followers, Rust's actions, including his rental of lands at the Potrero, and "the general management of the affairs of the agency."[127]

In early June 1892 the U.S. Senate passed a resolution directing the interior secretary to inform the Senate on three points: whether or not the department had instructed Rust to remove Cabezon,[128] what caused the "discontent" within the tribe, and what steps or legislation was needed to "allay" the Indians' fears.[129] A week later the *Los Angeles Herald* reprinted a lengthy article, initially published in the *New York Sun*, reporting that Will Pablo's petition and complaints about Agent Rust had finally reached the halls of Congress. Missouri Senator George G. Vest personally decided to investigate the Cahuilla crisis, insisting that the Senate contact Secretary Noble to find out what had "caused the discontent now existing in said tribe" and "what steps have been taken to remove this discontent." Vest had learned that the Cahuillas had been governed by the Cabezon family for decades, and that Rust, who considered the current Chief Cabezon "as a bad Indian," had removed him. The accusations against Cabezon were "unjust," claimed Vest. Now familiar with Will Pablo's petition protesting the appointment of William Williams as chief, the senator began his own inquiries.[130]

In early July, Arthur M. Tinker, a U.S. Indian inspector from the Interior Department, arrived in Palm Springs. Although his primary function was to explain to the Indians the workings of the allotment process under the Dawes legislation, he was also to investigate the Indians' complaints. Although Gilmour, in his article on the visit for the *San Francisco Chronicle*, did not address Tinker's role in the investigative process on behalf of the Cahuillas, he definitely criticized the inspector's explanation of the Dawes Act. Gilmour complained that Tinker knew little about the law's provisions, promising the Cahuillas "an abundance of water." "This rather astonished the white residents who were present," noted Gilmour, "and who are stockholders in the water system which irrigates the valley." Despite all of the positive comments made by Tinker about the allotment process, Gilmour remarked that "to a man" the Indians were opposed.[131]

In his fourth and final annual report, written in September 1892, Rust acknowledged that Will Pablo's influence had reached as far as the capital and that a special inspector had been appointed to "investigate" his complaints. The remainder of the agent's report was generally positive. He described the Indians as raising more crops than ever before, improving their homes, dressing better, and working harder to keep their children in school. They also were paying less attention to the "medicine men" and their feasts. Rust again praised the government day schools, seven of which had been rebuilt or repaired, and noted the construction of the two substantial school buildings at Perris.[132]

At year's end, Rust's troubles with the Cahuillas were again publically aired, and to an even wider audience. Displeased with the response to his May 12 letter, Saint Louis attorney Garesché again wrote Interior Secretary Noble. This time his lengthy letter, dated November 14, 1892, along with an appendix that included some remarks made by Senator Dawes, was privately published and circulated. Garesché requested that Noble give him the opportunity to collect evidence to prove that Rust was "dishonest in the conduct of his Agency" and "that his hatred of [Will] Pablo and of Cabezon has no other reason than their courage in defense of their people against his dishonesty and his wrongs." The attorney believed that only Rust's removal would result in the restoration of reservation peace. Of the few remarks from Dawes, Garesché noted that the senator had written that "matters of complaint" against Rust had been sent to the Senate Committee on Indian Affairs, which he chaired, and that there was opposition to him. However, Dawes also acknowledged that the last time he had inquired, the Interior Department believed that Rust was doing his duty "in a proper spirit."[133]

In his letter to Noble, Garesché had also included excerpts from Inspector Tinker's report on Rust, which he described as "unconditional absolution." Although the attorney was displeased that Tinker had exonerated Rust—describing it as "an infamy for its gross outrageous bias"—he nevertheless believed that the inspector had made a good enough case for removing Rust. Tinker had described Rust as honest, possessing a moral character, and energetic, although spending only one-third to one-half of his time on agency business. The special inspector's final assessment was that the agent possessed a manner that was "most unfortunate, calculated unintentionally to make enemies." Based on Tinker's report and what he had learned during his two visits to Potrero, Garesché concluded his letter to Noble with "one qualification"—that the interior secretary "force Rust's removal or resignation."[134]

The controversy continued with articles in other newspapers. On January 1, 1893, the *St. Louis Western Watchman* ran a story, including an attack by Senator Vest calling for Rust's removal.[135] Yet after all this unfavorable publicity, what finally brought about Rust's departure was the return of a Democratic administration with the election of Grover Cleveland in 1893. The Republican Rust knew it was time to go. Even in resigning he created a controversy—leaving his post without officially being relieved of his duties. He later claimed that he left in "disgust" over his lack of influence with the Indian Office, but the specific instance he cited was Washington's refusal to give him a leave of absence so he could participate in the World's Columbian Exposition in Chicago. This final action earned him a rebuke from Tinker.[136]

The reports of Rust's contentious dealings with Chief Cabezon were still following Rust two years later when a *Los Angeles Herald* reporter wrote that until Rust became the agent, the tribe had been peaceful, with Cabezon ruling supreme. The *Herald* quoted claims from the Indians that during his time as agent, Rust had traveled from village to village, robbing them "of the baskets they make and other curios which they manufactured to sell to tourists."[137] Despite these ongoing complaints, Rust continued collecting and selling Indian art and artifacts for the rest of his life. He sold large collections to Yale University and the University of Pennsylvania, and even had a retail shop near his home in Pasadena. He died in 1906. As historian Donald Chaput concludes, "the collecting and selling of materials was so important to Rust, that it added unnecessary tarnish to his reputation as agent to the Mission Indians."[138]

CHAPTER 7

▼ ▼ ▼

A TROUBLED TENURE

Francisco Estudillo, 1893–1897

> As reported previously, I have every variety of land on the 32 reservations in my care—covering, as they do here and there, a space of country in extent larger than several of our small States. For example, from Campo Reservation, next to the Mexican line, to Tule River Reservation, on the extreme north, is a distance of 450 miles in nearly an air line, while by the way of travel it is nearly 600 miles. From east to west it is quite 250 miles. Therefore I say that upon these reservations, scattered as they are over such a space of territory, I have such land as would support an orange grove, while I have other lands that would not support a horned toad, let alone supporting an Indian—a human being endowed with thoughts, feelings, and a soul as immortal as our own.
>
> —*Francisco Estudillo, Annual Report (1896)*

Francisco Estudillo brought a special empathy to the role of Mission Indian agent that none of his predecessors could match. A native Californian, he knew both the Indians and their homeland well. In fact, he counted California Indians among his relatives, and his father had tried to protect the village at Soboba during his ownership of the Rancho San Jacinto Viejo. Yet Estudillo's ties to the land and its people could not save him from the trials and tribulations of his office, which took him from one end of Southern California to the other.

Because of Agent Rust's confrontational personality, both Indian leaders and many whites employed on the reservations, especially teachers and WNIA workers, were eager to have a replacement they knew and trusted. In early March 1893, Mrs. Isabella M. Cadwallader, a representative of the Southern California branches of the WNIA and an association-sponsored missionary worker in Fall River Mills, California, wrote President Grover Cleveland recommending Reverend Weinland for the position. Weinland wrote directly to Interior

Secretary Hoke Smith, "respectfully" requesting to be appointed. He explained that he had lived among the Indians for the past four years, was a graduate of the Moravian College in Bethlehem, Pennsylvania, and had successfully managed two expeditions to northwestern Alaska. He agreed to follow the directives of his superior officers and would "aid and stimulate *all*, regardless of creed, who are doing true, honest work for the good of the Indians."[1]

On March 16 three more WNIA-sponsored workers added their support. Mary Sheriff Fowler, who had taught at Soboba for many years and whose missionary work was now sponsored by the WNIA, wrote the most complimentary recommendation. She described Weinland as honest, efficient, moral, and practical, capable of helping the Indians "upward to self-respecting and self-supporting manhood and womanhood." Two days later, more letters were sent by Weinland supporters. Among these were school teachers Ora Salmons and Nanie J. Salsberry and field matron Dr. Anna Johnson. (Interestingly, although they had worked with Agent Rust, they gave no hint of their opinion of the outgoing agent.)[2]

Weinland would have been a good choice. He not only had good rapport with the Indians, especially John Morongo,[3] but he was more diplomatic than Rust. Although his Protestant preaching might have divided him from the many Catholic worshippers on the reservations, Weinland would not have engendered such extreme distrust on the part of the Indian leaders. The cleric also had been respected by Rust and Preston, so he worked well with government officials. Most importantly, his appointment would have benefited the WNIA, enabling Quinton to expand the association's missionary work into other villages.

However, on April 12, 1893, President Cleveland appointed Francisco Estudillo.[4] John Morongo, on a pleasure trip to Riverside in June, informed a *Los Angeles Herald* reporter that he was personally acquainted with Estudillo and believed the Indians would "no doubt find him the best agent that ever presided over their wants." When asked his opinion of Rust, Morongo, ever the diplomat, explained that although the former agent had mistreated some of the Indians, others on the Banning reservation "liked him very well, and thought him a model government official."[5]

Morongo appeared pleased, but Amelia Stone Quinton was not. In support of Weinland, she wrote James K. Jones, Arkansas senator and chair of the Senate Indian Committee, who advised that if she could give the committee proof that Estudillo, as she suggested, was "an intemperate man, or otherwise unfitted," they would not confirm him. Requesting that Senator Jones delay the confirmation, Quinton wrote Weinland: "Do all you can, please, & so will I to prevent his confirmation." Quinton's reaction was typical; she never hesitated to engage in battle when she believed that the missionary efforts of the WNIA were endangered. Upon learning that Estudillo had been confirmed, she advised Weinland that they had to be "all the more diligent & watchful & alert for our poor Indians."[6] Failing to prevent Estudillo's appointment, Quinton was prepared to make sure he did no harm to WNIA missionary work. Based on his past reservation dealings, Estudillo no doubt expected outraged Indian leaders, but not a self-righteous Indian reformer, who from her headquarters in Philadelphia appeared to exert great influence on the Indian Office. Their clashes were inevitable.

Francisco Estudillo was from a prominent Californio family. His grandfather had come to California as a Spanish soldier around 1800, and his father, José Antonio Estudillo, served as a public official under both Mexican and American rule. The family home in Old Town San Diego has been preserved by the state as a historical landmark. Many other family members held public office over the years. An older brother, José Guadalupe Estudillo, served as state treasurer from 1875 to 1879—the last Mexican-American to hold statewide office until the late twentieth century. Francisco, the youngest son, was born in San Diego in 1844, in the waning days of Mexican rule. His family owned a number of Southern California ranchos, including the Rancho San Jacinto Viejo, where the cities of Hemet and San Jacinto now stand. Francisco moved there around 1865 and built an adobe home (now gone) and then in 1885 a fine, two-story brick residence (which still stands). He served as a San Diego County supervisor from 1876 to 1879 and was San Jacinto's first postmaster and second mayor. He was an active Democrat, and it was probably his many political connections that led to his appointment.[7]

Estudillo was welcomed by a great number of the Mission Indians in a way none of his predecessors or successors could match. They seemed to feel a closer connection to this Hispanic, Spanish-speaking Catholic. In June 1893, some four hundred Indians gathered to welcome him during a fiesta at Morongo. Chief Gervasio Cabezon and Will Pablo greeted him warmly, and Father Hahn and San Bernardino lawyer John Brown Jr. also spoke. "Representatives were there from San Diego, Mesa Grande, Warner's ranch, Coahuilla [*sic*] Valley, San Jacinto, San Bernardino and vicinity, and the desert, including Agua Caliente, Martinez, Torres and other places," the *Los Angeles Herald* reported.[8]

Controversy at Cahuilla

It took only three months for Estudillo to become embroiled in a controversy with Quinton. The actual cause remains a mystery. It appeared to begin with Quinton's repeated request for a five-acre parcel on the Cahuilla Reservation for

Francisco Estudillo.
Courtesy of the San Jacinto Museum.

missionary purposes and to end with the Indians' refusal to grant the land and the threatened expulsion of Dr. Johnson, who served as physician and government field matron. Of the four-way exchange of letters, only those written by Estudillo, Quinton, and the new Indian commissioner, Daniel Browning, are extant.[9] It is impossible to get a clear picture of Johnson's role because her side was filtered through Quinton. The situation placed the WNIA president squarely in the center of a controversy not of her own making, as she mediated from afar, determined to protect the WNIA missionary work from a newly appointed agent who was perhaps trying to assert his power.

The picture becomes cloudier still because Johnson, in the few extracts from her letters quoted in WNIA's monthly newsletter, painted an idyllic scene. Two months after she arrived at Cahuilla early in 1893, she informed her sponsors: "The Indians are very good to me thus far. The young captain, Gabriel Costo, is indefatigable in his assistance" while also helping, she added, to advance his people in every way possible. Even the former captain, Leonicio Lugo, had "been most kind" to her, but unfortunately he lived a distance away. She described her days as extremely busy. "To-day I have ridden thirteen miles," she wrote, "calling on eight patients, have given medicine to twelve here and food to three very old, and to five very sick ones." On her first Sunday, she had sixteen at her little service; the previous Sunday she had twenty-seven. One month later she enthusiastically wrote that "young and old are kind and cordial to me." She described her new home in the most loving terms: "The rocks, the hills and mountains are dear to me already, and the meadow lark fills me with joy and thanksgiving."[10]

It is hard to understand how this seemingly blissful situation turned nightmarish. It is also impossible to clearly judge Estudillo's role—was he culpable in some way, or was he simply defensive because he was new on the job and unaccustomed to dealing with an irate female reformer, whether Quinton or Johnson? In the past Johnson had difficulties with former Agent Rust; therefore, was she partially or totally responsible? Or in the end, was the issue simply the site she had chosen to rent? In any case, in mid-July 1893, Estudillo informed Commissioner Browning that the Cahuilla captain and several tribal members had visited him at the agency, declaring they had no desire to give away five acres of land to Johnson, or anyone. According to Quinton, Johnson was eager to get her missionary work started and, without informing her WNIA sponsors, had rented a plot of land, one that she and Agent Rust had selected because it provided access to water. Then for sixty dollars she had bought the "*tribal* rights to it" from the owner.[11]

Ordered by Browning to investigate, Estudillo visited the reservation and was met at the government schoolhouse by a large group of Indians, who vigorously protested giving land to anyone. The land in question included springs that were used in common by the villagers, and it was considered by the Cahuillas to be "the only valuable part of the reservation." In Johnson's presence, the Indians claimed they had been deceived about the "true nature of the paper" that she had them sign—a paper requesting the land on behalf of the WNIA. The Indians presented Estudillo with their own petition, signed by thirty-six men, sixteen of whom had been among the twenty-five signatories of Johnson's original agreement. Now, before both Johnson and the agent, these sixteen denied that "they ever knew of the nature of the paper they signed." Estudillo reported to Browning that after he translated everything for Johnson, "her feelings were sorely tried." Because the Indians wanted her removed "on the grounds that she had deceived them," the agent recommended to Browning that the land grant be suspended until things settled down. Heeding Estudillo's observations and recommendation, on August 14 Browning formally turned down the WNIA request for that particular parcel.[12]

Prior to this cancellation, Estudillo and Quinton had engaged in a series of terse and carefully polite letters. On July 25, for example, Estudillo wrote Quinton that he had just returned from the Cahuilla Reservation, where he found "everything that is unpleasant." (Interestingly, the agent had informed the commissioner that he did not go to the reservation until July 26. Quinton questioned this discrepancy in her August 17 letter to Browning.) Reinforcing what he had said to the commissioner, Estudillo's letter went on to explain to Quinton that he had met with a large delegation of Indians, who charged Dr. Johnson with "openly" deceiving them. "Her prestige is lost with that tribe," he explained, "no matter what she did now, her accomplishments would be nothing." Estudillo blamed much of the "mischief" upon a surveyor who apparently had included the spring in the parcel. "I am sure you do not wish to take all the valuable water that the Indians have," he politely challenged Quinton, "besides their best land."[13]

Quinton responded on August 9 explaining, presumably on Johnson's word, that unfortunately—because of the timing of Estudillo's visit—the Indian delegation he met was composed of the more conservative tribal members, with few of the "*progressive* elements" present. The latter were more accepting of change and of the services that Johnson was providing. If his visit had taken place when "*all* the Indians could have been present," Quinton believed his impressions would have been different.[14] To reinforce her argument, in mid-August Quinton wrote Commissioner Browning, hoping to persuade him to side with Johnson. "These awakening, industrious, and more progressive young men and women should, *in this free country,*" she wrote, "have the opportunity for this help which they *appreciate,* leaving the others perfectly free to stand aloof if they choose to do so."[15]

In Quinton's August 9 letter to Estudillo, she described the good doctor as earnestly devoted to her work, "awakening the ambition & right aspiration of the people." But to mollify Estudillo, she agreed that Johnson had erred in renting the five acres as pasture for her horse and then buying out the Indian owner's interest—all without informing the WNIA. Yes, Quinton confirmed, the land had been surveyed without Estudillo's "knowledge & approval," and that was a mistake. Had she known the land in question contained "all the springs & the hot springs," she would never have approved of the arrangement. Describing Estudillo as kind, fair, and courteous and, possibly to stroke his ego, referring to his "*power* as agent," Quinton asked for his help not only to get enough land so her association could build a "little home," which the "Indians may be stimulated to imitate," but also to reconsider Johnson's removal. After all, the doctor was "greatly liked by the *best elements* among these people & by those who have had a fair opportunity of knowing her work."[16]

In response, Estudillo disagreed that the timing of his visit had been "an unfortunate affair" and complained that Johnson had misrepresented his acts toward her. Eight out of every ten of the villagers, he claimed, "did not want her there any longer." He excused Quinton for not knowing about the water situation, but surely the doctor had known. Estudillo stood firm on his refusal to grant this piece of land but agreed to search for another suitable location. Explaining that he had "forty years experience among the Indians," the agent assured Quinton that what he had said about Johnson losing her prestige among the Indians was "worth some consideration."[17]

Quinton's August 24 response was a bit testy, claiming that the agent had misunderstood several of her points. When she said his timing was "unfortunate," she was referring only to the fact that fewer progressive Indians were present. After fourteen years working in every state and territory among the Indians, Quinton felt that she had learned that the progressive tribal members "make the element of hope for the future." She also asked Estudillo to look over her letter again. "I have not said that she [Johnson] blamed *you*"; the person at fault was the village captain, who would not allow the progressives to speak on the doctor's behalf. Calling the opposition to Johnson as "new, & temporary," Quinton again appealed to Estudillo's ego, stating that she believed that with his "protection & *moral support*" the entire situation could be righted.[18]

Possibly to appease Quinton, and to assure himself that his original decision to deny the land request was valid, Estudillo returned to Cahuilla in early September 1893 and again met with Johnson and thirty-one Indians, ten of whom had been among the original signatories of the land donation. Because twenty of those present opposed the land deal, he informed Commissioner Browning, he saw no reason to change his opinion. He again asked the Indians if Johnson should remain without the land, and "the vote stood the same." He described the villagers as civilized, "law abiding people harmless, and industrious," governed by a captain who was well respected by both Indians and whites. His only fear was that "under the existing circumstances," there would be more "trouble and annoyance." His intention was to keep the Indians "as contended and happy as possible and to cause them to follow the path of industry and frugality," which he believed would be difficult with the "uncertain condition of affairs." In the end Quinton prevailed; Johnson remained at her post until early 1895, when she resigned to care for her ailing mother.[19]

Although Estudillo disapproved of Dr. Johnson, others valued her work. For example, a five-year resident of the area—signing himself only as "F. M. C.," probably Floyd M. Casner, storekeeper and postmaster at the nearby white community, also known as Cahuilla—wrote the editor of the *San Jacinto Register* describing the field matron as having "gained the confidence of this tribe" and saving the lives of at least two young Indian women. Working night and day, she set a "noble example" worth "much more than what it costs to keep her here." The writer claimed that the united efforts of Johnson and Mrs. Salsberry, the government teacher at the Cahuilla school, were "enough to insure prosperity and true citizens to this tribe of Indians."[20]

Salsberry's work was also praised by several of the local cattle ranchers, who along with many other white residents of the area attended the 1893 graduation exercises at the Cahuilla school. "The entertainment opened with the song 'America' and how well they did sing," attendees wrote. An ode of welcome followed, with a greeting by eleven-year-old Martin Costo, who was well spoken. Then more singing, student recitations, and an exhibition of arithmetic assignments, ending with a farewell by student Ventura Saubel. Equally as important as the graduation ceremonies was the attendance at the school. Locals recorded that "some of the children walk 8 miles to attend school, have no mid-day meal and they are glad to come and come regularly. We wonder how many of our white children would care enough for school to do this." Adult men were also in attendance, "willing to go into a class with younger children"—including a thirty-year old man who had nothing to do for two weeks and asked if he could attend classes during that time.[21]

Land Allotment

Allotment was the key provision of the 1887 Dawes Act, which proved to be one of the most destructive pieces of Indian legislation ever passed. The idea was to break up communally held Indian reservation land, allotting it in severalty (individually) to families, single adults, and orphans, with the land protected from seizure for twenty-five years. Millions of acres of Indian-held land across the United States was lost until the legislation was abrogated in 1934. Although Horatio Rust had insisted that the local Indians "anxiously await the allotment of land,"[22] the process did not begin until Estudillo's tenure. Opponents ranged from Will Pablo to William Collier, who preferred patents being issued to each village to avoid any entanglements if the patentee died during the twenty-five-year trust period.[23] Estudillo reported in 1893 that "at first the Indians at Rincon and

Pala refused to allow their lands to be allotted." He wrote the commissioner: "I however succeeded in showing them that it would be a benefit to them in many ways. I have no fear that any trouble will arise or difficult[y] occur on any of the reservations in the matter of allotting lands."[24] Two years later he reported a similar situation at Santa Ysabel and Mesa Grande. He was bitterly disappointed with the situation at Mesa Grande, where "an element of rebellion" blocked allotment.[25]

Allotments were generally made by special agents sent in for just that purpose. Some were Californians familiar with the region; others were outsiders, including Indian reform advocates. For example, Kate Foote, president of the Washington, D.C., auxiliary of the WNIA, was the allotting agent for the Rincon Reservation in 1893.[26] As of 1895, in addition to the 51 parcels at Rincon, there were 156 at Potrero (La Jolla), 17 at Sycuan, 92 at Pechanga, 37 at Capitán Grande, and 12 at Pala, allotted to those already farming their fields. Because there was so little land available, the rest of the Indians had to be given land at Rincon or Potrero.[27]

The Indian Office asked for special reports on the status of allotments in each agency. In 1898 Agent Wright would report that in Southern California only 361 allotments had been made, and none for the past two or three years. Of these, only 117 Indians at Pala, Pechanga, and Sycuan had actually received their patent in severalty. "Practically all" of the allottees occupied their parcels and were farming and improving their homes. He was not aware of any who had leased their land to others. Still, friction between Indians and whites continued, in part because reservation boundaries were poorly marked.[28] A year later Wright added that of the reservations allotted, only La Jolla had enough decent farmland to make the tiny (ten- to twenty-acre) parcels worthwhile. "I can not understand why the other five reservations were allotted, as they contain but few 'patches' of good land." In some cases he had not even been able to deliver the patents because the Indian allottees, unable to survive on the small amount of land, had already moved elsewhere "seeking a livelihood."[29]

No additional allotments (or patents, apparently) were issued until well after 1900. In his regular annual report for that year, Wright noted that the Indians generally appreciated having their own lands. In fact for years the Indians "under the leadership of chiefs, captains, and headmen, [had] made informal allotments of their lands, and these individual rights have been very well respected." However, "this crude method of partitioning the land [had] resulted in considerable dissatisfaction." According to Wright, notable examples were at Tule River and Agua Caliente (Palm Springs), where just four or five families now claimed all the proceeds from tourists using the hot springs there.[30]

The failure of allotment in Southern California was graphically described in 1906 by Charles E. Kelsey, a special agent for the California Indians and general secretary of the Northern California Indian Association, a WNIA affiliate. Allotment, Kelsey explained, had come too late for California's Indians because most of the best land had already been preempted by white settlers. Furthermore, the mission reservations were so small that it was impossible to grant even the minimum amounts specified by the law. Kelsey reported that some 1,400 allotments were located in the southern part of the state, and of that number, over 300 allotments were "absolute desert, being sage brush plains without water or the hope of water." On a more serious note, he discovered that the process in California did not include protection for the allottees, either in the ability to use their land as they saw fit or the availability of water. "Anyone can jump an Indian's allotment," he reported, "and there seems no practical remedy." The intruder could move a fence or divert water, and "it is not even a misdemeanor."[31]

The struggle between Will Pablo and John Morongo at Potrero that had plagued Rust continued, though Estudillo felt confident that he would soon "have all the trouble settled and matters running smoothly between them" because they realized "that only justice will be given them; both factions, therefore, are anxious to outdo the other."[32] A few months later the *Los Angeles Herald* reported that under Estudillo's direction "peace has been brought among the several factions of the tribe, and the energies of the Indians for some time past have been expended in cultivating the soil and in improving the irrigation ditches." One reporter interviewed Will Pablo, who was in town buying food and supplies for the annual tribal elections and reportedly said that things had never been "more satisfactory nor more promising." Pablo was described as the head of the "Catholic element" on the reservation, with John Morongo as head of the "Protestant faction." Morongo "is now a very good Indian, trying for peace," Pablo informed the reporter. "[H]e makes no more trouble, and we are good friends."[33] However, their struggle really only ended with the 1898 death of John Morongo from complications of a serious fall. Agent Wright praised him as "an efficient officer, a true and trustworthy friend," and the *Los Angeles Times* gave him a glowing obituary.[34]

More Troubles with the WNIA

In August 1893, Estudillo again faced a controversy over the presence of a WNIA-sponsored missionary, this time at the village of Agua Caliente on Warner's Ranch. In his annual report he noted that a doctor and field matron in the village "are not liked or wanted by the Indians, and . . . have been of recent date the subject of correspondence between this agency and the Department."[35] He was referring to Dr. Rebecca Hallowell and government field matron Julia French. Letters and accusations were traded between Estudillo, Quinton, and Commissioner Browning. No extant letters written by either Hallowell or French exist, therefore it is impossible to get a full picture of the events at Cahuilla and to know with certainty the role that Estudillo played.

The catalyst for the disturbance was the theft of a watch belonging to French, an incident that Quinton shared with Commissioner Browning in an August 22, 1893, letter. Quinton was informed, possibly by Hallowell, that during a visit to the village Agent Estudillo had learned that a boy had stolen the watch and had threatened to have the boy punished. The agent's threat had so upset the Indians that they demanded the two women leave the reservation. In the meantime, Estudillo had promised to protect them. The watch would never have been stolen, the Indians explained, had Hallowell and French not invited the children into their home. When Quinton received a telegram in which the Indians denied that Estudillo actually had the power to protect the women, she immediately asked Browning to telegraph the agent and his interpreter to "protect the ladies at once." Concluding that the commissioner's authority would, no doubt, be obeyed, Quinton described the incident as "part of a plan to drive out Protestants, for threats of this sort have from time to time come to us."[36]

A week later, on August 29, Estudillo informed Quinton that he had received a telegram from Washington, stating that a "disturbance [was] reported among Indians at Agua Caliente and that Matron and Missionary need protection, what are [the] facts?" He had heard from French that same day, and she had mentioned nothing about any disturbance. Estudillo wrote Quinton that although he had concluded that the report was "without foundation in fact or truth," he had nevertheless "commanded" that the women "be fully protected." Upon receipt of Estudillo's letter, Quinton made a copy and enclosed it with a letter to Commissioner Browning, notifying him of an August 14 letter from Hallowell, claiming that the Indians were giving her and French thirty days to vacate the village. Hallowell's letter went on to say that the agent had assured the women of his protection. Although she described Estudillo as "friendly in *manner,*" she stated that he had nevertheless advised the women to leave because the Indians despised them. Then, on September 4, Quinton wrote Browning that she had received a telegram from Hallowell that read: "Ordered out. Send protection. Indians deny Agent's Power. Reply by Letter." This was the wire that had initially prompted the Indian Office to write Estudillo about a "disturbance" at Agua

Caliente. Quinton then assured Browning, "It is all, we think, simply an incited caprice that will pass over."[37]

Two days after writing Browning, Quinton wrote Estudillo. Superficially courteous, she thanked him for protecting the two women. She had learned that during an Indian council he had informed Hallowell and French that the Indians wanted them to leave. Then during the second council the Indians had denied the agent's power to protect the women. This evidence, Quinton concluded, was "considerable 'foundation'" for the report of a disturbance. Although polite throughout the letter, Quinton felt she had learned enough to disagree with Estudillo's assessment of the situation. She assured him that she and the two women fully understood that he did have the power to protect them. Because no mention of the incident appeared in WNIA literature, and because Hallowell's and French's letters do not survive, it is impossible to know the truth. Hallowell and French, however, like Dr. Johnson before them, remained at their posts.[38] On the surface, it seems apparent that Indian Office officials saw sufficient value in the work being done by WNIA missionaries and chose not to order their removal, no doubt much to the chagrin of the agents who had to deal with these often pesky activists.

As 1893 drew to a close, Estudillo was still dealing with an irate Quinton and defending his actions to Commissioner Browning. This time it was again at Cahuilla, with Quinton in exasperation writing the commissioner that she had learned of a new scheme to remove Dr. Anna Johnson and asking that he "arrest" the matter until December, when she would have an opportunity to meet with him personally. Quinton wanted to prove to Browning that there had been "gross misrepresentation & injustice of the whole affair." She traveled to Washington to confer with him and Interior Secretary Smith, later writing Weinland that she had succeeded in saving Johnson's position.[39] Without documentation, it is impossible to know what went on in the commissioner's office and what evidence Quinton presented. However, by the following May, Quinton wrote Browning that Estudillo "was becoming very suave to us all, as he finds that he cannot upset us in Washington." Quinton believed that the agent was "being converted to *her* [Johnson] also, at least-*outside,* and I think will find it to his interest to co-operate, or take the risk of losing his own head."[40]

Legal Battles at Warner's Ranch

In his 1893 annual report, Estudillo informed Commissioner Browning that several villages were now facing legal challenges. Five villages on Warner's Ranch (most notably Agua Caliente) were threatened with eviction by ranch owner John

Downey, as was the Kumeyaay village of San Felipe, located on the Rancho Vallé de San Felipe on the edge of the desert to the southeast. Estudillo described the sixty-nine people living at San Felipe as "inoffensive"—self-sustaining and happy except for the lawsuit "now pending to eject them from the ranch." Because they had no title to these lands, Estudillo could see "no help for them at this time." It was a shame, he informed the commissioner, but it seemed "inevitable."[41]

Residents in another Kumeyaay village, at the lower end of the Rancho Vallé de San Felipe near Sentenac Cienega, had been run off by force some years before, with no consequences for the white perpetrators. According to Indian scholar and photographer Edward H. Davis, a resident of nearby Mesa Grande, the surviving Kumeyaay village farther up the valley, called We-nelschi by the Kumeyaays, was "picturesquely situat[ed] on a small bench or mesa at the foot of Volcan Mountain," commanding a view "of the half-desert ranch of San Felipe." The village itself consisted of "ten or a dozen adobe and grass huts with a little white-washed chapel." The residents, Davis explained, were poor; and because their small cultivated fields did not afford enough food, most the men had found employment outside the village. Another observer noted that even this "poor refuge, the destitute village with its few pitiful acres, has been coveted by the white man, with whom to covet is to acquire, where Indian land is concerned."[42] In October 1891, a few months before the Warner's Ranch lawsuits began, the ranch owners filed an eviction suit in San Diego County superior court, in an attempt to remove the "Indian squatters" who "in fact claim it as their own."[43]

These suits were no different from the Soboba case, and Shirley Ward set out to defend these villages on the same basis—this time with assistance from Frank Lewis. The cases generated intense public attention and drew powerful supporters to the Indians' cause, especially the IRA and the LMC. Quinton and the WNIA were eager to protect their missionary work at Agua Caliente, sending a resolution to Congress in 1892 urging "an immediate appropriation" for compensation for legal fees and "for the necessary expenses of such suits."[44]

The initial suit to dispossess the Warner's Ranch Indians (*John G. Downey v. Alejandro Barker, et al.*) had been filed in the Superior Court of San Diego on July 27, 1892, by Downey and the Merchants' Exchange Bank of San Francisco, which held a large interest in the ranch, basing their claim on the confirmation patent issued by the federal government in January 1880. Several months later Lewis informed Browning that the Indians had notified him of this action, and that he had "secured from the attorneys of the ranch owners a stipulation giving [him] time in which to appear for the Indians."[45] For some unknown reason this suit covered only the Cupeño village of Agua Caliente, known to the Indians as Cupa, and the nearby Luiseño village of Puerta la Cruz. Alejandro Barker, captain at Agua Caliente, headed the list of eighty-six defendants. A second suit, *John G. Downey v. Jesus Quevas, et al.* (181 U.S. 481), was quickly filed, seeking the eviction of the Luiseño village of La Puerta, near today's Lake Henshaw, and two small Kumeyaay villages, San José and Mataguay.[46]

The two cases were combined for trial, which began in June 1893 with the taking of depositions and the usual exchange of documents; Judge George Puterbaugh presided. During the trial Ward and Lewis not only argued in favor of the Cupeños' possessory rights, descending from Mexican law by way of the Treaty of Guadalupe Hidalgo, but emphasized their long occupation at the hot springs. Some of the oldest members of the tribe testified, including Machola Moro, the widow of longtime captain José Maria Moro.[47] Depositions on the Indians' behalf were also provided by Pío Pico, the last Mexican governor of California, and eighty-five-year-old Juan José Warner, who dealt firmly with Downey's lawyers.[48]

Thirty-nine-year-old Barker, the only registered voter at Cupa, served as translator for the village elders. He was portrayed by the *San Francisco Chronicle* as "a man of unusual intellectual attainments," who "took charge of the litigation" and hired the best legal counsel. A *San Diego Union* reporter remarked that Barker was "deeply interested in the ultimate outcome of the suit." The Cupeño leader, continued the *Union,* "may consider himself highly honored by the council for the plaintiff," who by "allowing him to interpret the remarks of his fellow citizens in a tongue that nobody but himself understood, evinced a faith in his honesty that should be gratifying in the extreme."[49]

In contrast to the 1892 trial over the same land, Governor Downey was clearly no longer in control of himself, or the case. "[E]x-Gov. Downey was present and made himself conspicuous by interposing questions to the witnesses, much to the annoyance of attorneys on both sides," wrote a reporter for the *Union.* His attorney, Senator Stephen M. White, became impatient during cross-questioning and had to "remind the childish old man that he was trying the case, and that matters would be much facilitated if the ex-governor would keep still." When he did not like an answer to one of the questions presented during the trial, Downey would mutter under his breath "That's a dum [damn?] lie."[50]

Downey's case did not depend on undermining any Indian testimony. In fact it was deceptively simple. The government patent had confirmed the legality and boundaries of Warner's Mexican grant, which he now owned and paid the taxes on—and the patent said nothing about any Indians or their rights. Anticipating

Ward's possessory right arguments, Downey's lawyer also made the remarkable claim that there had been no Indians living in the valley at the time of Warner's grant in 1844! To do this, they deliberately misinterpreted a letter from the time concerning the lack of any improvements on the land belonging to the former Mission San Diego—despite Warner's best efforts to set them straight.[51] The court, however, never considered Warner's testimony. Downey's attorneys argued that the patent to the rancho was binding between the plaintiffs and the government, and thus any testimony that tried to question it was inadmissible. And Judge Puterbaugh agreed, tossing out all of the testimony and evidence presented on behalf of the Indians. Ward and Lewis presented a parallel defense for the people from San José, Mataguay, and La Puerta when that case came before Judge Puterbaugh shortly thereafter and again placed some of the oldest village residents on the stand. They also asked to introduce all the evidence submitted in their first case, but once again Downey's lawyers objected. After the hearing, the two suits moved together through the lower courts, eventually reaching the U.S. Supreme Court.

Other events combined to delay a ruling for three years. On March 1, 1894, Governor Downey died, and his will went missing. Eventually his nephew, J. Downey Harvey, was substituted as plaintiff.[52] The lead case now became known as *J. Downey Harvey, et al. v. Alejandro Barker, et al.* Then in November 1895, Judge Puterbaugh disqualified himself because of a conflict of interest. He was involved in a plan to build a dam and reservoir on the lower end of the ranch to provide irrigation water for the white communities below—a project that could move forward only when the villages of La Puerta and San José were removed.[53] Yet before disqualifying himself, he had made the key ruling that all of the testimony on behalf of the Indians was inadmissible. The case was then transferred to another department of the superior court, with Judge W. L. Pierce presiding.

Pierce did not submit his ruling until December 29, 1896, just before he retired. The government patent, he held, was conclusive as to property rights—in other words, the Cupeños were left with absolutely no defense in the eyes of the court. "Thus," Shirley Ward and Frank Lewis later wrote, "*the entire issue between the parties was and is one of law and not of fact. It is as to the materiality and admissibility of defendant's evidence, and not as to the sufficiency or weight thereof.*"[54]

Ward was disappointed but perhaps not surprised. "I cannot account for the decision of the Superior Court of San Diego County," he confided to Herbert Welsh of the IRA. As he pointed out, however, "It is a matter of fact . . . that may or may not be entitled to serious consideration in this action, that the Judge who decided the case was a very intimate friend of the plaintiff." While the case was under submission Pierce "was quite frequently 'dined and wined'" by J. Harvey Downey. Then after Pierce retired, Ward added, he moved to San Francisco to become the plaintiff's private attorney. "I think we are justified in believing that our chances for success before the Supreme Court of the State are really just as favorable now as they were prior to the decision by the lower Court."[55] Downey's lawyers may have thought their job was done after getting a judge to set the highest appeal bond possible to discourage any further litigation. However, they did not take into consideration Ward's determination and the support of the growing number of "friends of the Indian."

Troubles at Yuma

Drinking and gambling were perennial vices and a challenge for every Mission Indian agent. The addition of the Yuma Reservation to the Mission Agency brought unexpected consequences in this regard. Although this reservation was primarily in California, much of its external relations naturally flowed across the Colorado River to Yuma, Arizona, the only town of any size nearby. In his 1893 annual report, Estudillo wrote that ex-chief Patrick Miguel of the Yuma Reservation had actually been selling young Indian women "to the whites for immoral purposes"—often the daughters of his enemies. They were sold for between five and twelve dollars each; one went for as high as twenty-one dollars, Estudillo explained to a reporter.[56] The *Yuma Times* reported that "these facts have been well known around here for some time, and hence a change of chief and agent was very much desired." The *Los Angeles Herald* previously had reported that "the harm done by old Miguel, however, can never be undone, and no steps have been taken or even devised to punish him for his crime." Even more unsettling was the fact that several of Miguel's own daughters were among those sold.[57]

Miguel continued to make trouble throughout the summer. Then in September he reportedly sent some of his followers to kidnap a reservation policeman. These same men also "forcibly entered" the local Catholic Indian boarding school and "violently laid hands on one of the sisters." Eventually they were arrested. Miguel's inappropriate actions may have been partially due to his removal as chief by Estudillo.[58] However, he was also angry with the teachers, who, "inspired by a desire to improve the moral status of the tribe," had opposed his re-election.[59] The new chief was Jose Pama, son of the former chief, Pasqual, who had supported the nun's efforts. Pama had Miguel arrested; he was given twenty-five lashes by his own police before being turned over to Estudillo, who took him to Los Angeles to face American justice. The whole incident had the area on edge for several weeks.[60]

Troubles across the Border

Estudillo's responsibility for the residents of the Yuma Reservation took him into Baja California in 1897, where several dozen Yuma Indians had settled on the Rancho de los Algodones, living along the west side of the Colorado River. The owner, Guillermo Andrade, who had recently become the Mexican consul in Los Angeles, was busy colonizing the ranch. His agreement with the Mexican government stipulated that a portion of the rancho was to be set aside for the native Cucapá Indians, but the presence of the Yumas was problematic. Andrade took the matter before the Mexican government, and the Mexican ambassador brought it to the attention of the U.S. State Department, which in turn involved the Interior Department and the Indian Office. Ordered to investigate the matter, Estudillo interviewed the Yumas, who refused to leave their homes, claiming they had lived there for ages. Shown commissions given the Indians by a former governor of Baja California, Estudillo recommended they be allowed to remain.[61]

Acting Indian Commissioner Thomas P. Smith would have preferred that the Indians be moved to the U.S. reservation in the United States, but if they wanted to remain in their Baja California home, there was little the Indian Office could do. The secretary of state concurred. On April 24 Sister Mary O'Neil, the superintendent of the Catholic boarding school at Yuma, was contacted for both investigative and reporting purposes. She acknowledged that the Yumas living on the Rancho de los Algodones had always recognized the authority of the tribal chief at Yuma and had sent some of their children to her school, but that prior to 1894, they preferred to live off the reservation. She clearly favored their return, or at least that their children attend school, but she preferred that the Mexican government take the initiative and evict them.[62] In the end Smith concluded that this particular case did "not appear to be one covered by the provisions of the extradition clause" with Mexico, "unless the Indians shall be charged with some crime, as provided in said treaty,"[63] and the wayward Yumas remained south of the border.

Santa Ynez

Agent Estudillo's travels also took him to Santa Barbara County, where he visited a small village of Chumash people living on an old Mexican rancho located a few miles from the former Mission Santa Inés. According to Charles Painter of the IRA, these twelve or fifteen Indian families dated their occupation back to 1835. The rancho, La Cañada de los Pinos, commonly known as the "College Rancho," had been granted in 1844 to a group of Franciscan missionaries who planned to build a college and seminary on the site, with title later vested in the name of the bishop of Monterey. Their College of Guadalupe survived until 1882.[64]

About that same time, the archbishop of San Francisco sold twenty thousand of the rancho's original thirty-six thousand acres to a development company and turned the remainder over to Bishop Francis Mora of Monterey-Los Angeles. This sale put the Chumash Santa Ynez village in an untenable position. As he had done at Pauma, Bishop Mora allowed the Indians to remain. However, their village straddled the Zanja Cota Creek, which served as the dividing line between the Catholic property and the Santa Ynez Land & Improvement Company's holdings. The issue finally came to a head when the members of the 1891 California Mission Indian Commission made a deal with the Santa Ynez Land & Improvement Company and the bishop whereby the company would provide eighty-five acres for the dozen or so remaining Chumash families. This land was to be divided into five-acre fenced plots, each including a two-room frame house built by the co-owners of the grant, with piped water for both irrigation and domestic use.[65] The Indians, in return, had to leave the land and homes they occupied on the diocesan side of the creek (something less than thirty acres) and renounce all claims to the land. "I have labored strenuously and unremittingly to induce the Indians to accept this proposition, without success," wrote a frustrated Frank Lewis in 1896, when he was serving as Mission Indian attorney.[66]

Estudillo, who had visited the Chumash several times by 1896, had also attempted to convince them to accept the offer. They preferred to remain in their existing homes, provided they were protected in their possession; Estudillo agreed to have the area surveyed and forwarded their request to Washington.[67] Meanwhile, Lewis had arranged for the bishop to bring suit to quiet title to the diocese's share, by which he hoped that about half the Indians could secure the rights to their homes. "This proceeding would cut out, in my opinion, one-half of the Indians on the grant, but I can see no other course to pursue," Lewis explained.[68]

This controversy dragged on into Agent Lucius Wright's tenure. As early as 1899 he believed the issue could be settled, but in September 1901 he was still reporting delays. The agent was eager to have matters settled in order to build a school for the children. William Collier, the special attorney for the Mission Indians, who was collaborating with Wright, reported in October 1902 that he had arrived at "terms of adjustment," embodied in a contract signed by the agent and the corporation, and forwarded it to the Indian Office. The "friendly suit" between the bishop and the Indians to determine their rights, however, ran into a snag. One member of the band "set up a defense," claiming rights against the bishop which differed from those of other members. The case was then pending in the Santa Barbara Superior Court. Not until 1903 was a "satisfactory solution" arrived at. The land company agreed to sign over the lands occupied by the Chumash to the government, and a similar agreement was made with the diocese, giving it "a splendid piece of well-watered land for the use of the Indians as long as they or their descendants shall live."[69] As late as 1906 the matter was back in court, as another lawsuit sought to establish the precise boundaries of the deeded tracts.[70]

The Village at San Luis Rey

Francisco Estudillo's annual reports not only discussed conditions on the reservations, but also included those rare surviving villages in the backcountry. One of these had long been located near Mission San Luis Rey, where during the 1890s about fifty Indians lived in brush huts. The village site, the agent noted, had been patented to white settlers, and the Indian residents would ultimately be evicted, "as they utterly refuse to move from the home of their fathers and their childhood days."[71] His successor, Agent Wright, mentioned them as late as 1899; after that they disappear from his annual reports.

Government Schools

When Estudillo took office in 1893 there were eight government day schools, the boarding school at Perris, and three Catholic schools, partially subsidized by the government. The day school teachers, paid $720 annually, mostly lived in tiny apartments attached to their schoolhouse. Funds were also available for the hiring of a housekeeper at thirty dollars a month; sometimes Indian women were employed, sometimes it was one of the teacher's relatives.[72] During 1893–94 Estudillo added another day school at Martinez, constructed two replacement schoolhouses, and made necessary repairs to the remaining schools, except the one at Soboba, which was in excellent repair. He informed the commissioner that in his opinion, the school at Pechanga was not worth repairing.[73]

To further strengthen the agency schools, in April 1894 Estudillo brought all his teachers together for a three-day teacher's institute in Colton, with featured guest speakers and training sessions. Institutes such as this were common among public school teachers in the late nineteenth century, but this was the first such event for agency schools in the Mission Indian Agency. Estudillo opened the institute with an address, followed by presentations by Professor M. S. Savage from the Perris School and various reservation day school teachers, including Mary Platt, whose topic was "How to Interest Children and Parents in Schools," and Ora Salmons, who

Schoolboys working in the garden at Soboba, circa 1896.
This is probably the "industrial garden" launched by Agent Estudillo to teach "practical gardening," including fruits, vegetables, and flowers.
Courtesy of the San Jacinto Museum.

addressed the issue of the "Government School-Teacher's Duty on a Reservation." Attorney John Brown discussed the general issue of the "Welfare of the Indians," while Dr. Wainwright, agency physician, spoke on the issue of "Sanitary Condition of Indian Schools." Among the dignitaries that participated was Redlands resident Albert K. Smiley, founder of the LMC and member of the 1891 California Mission Indian Commission. He presided on the third day. The four-day event, covered by the *Los Angeles Times,* brought the agency good publicity.[74]

Estudillo's fourth annual report, in August 1896, continued to reflect his strong interest in education. He was now responsible for eleven agency schools, including those at Capitán Grande and Tule River, which had just reopened. Although he reported that school attendance had fallen off considerably since his last report due to increased student illness, he nevertheless made a point to mention each of the schools individually, listing the teachers and average attendance. He seemed especially pleased with the success of the industrial garden he had instituted adjacent to the school in Soboba. The teacher, Charles Burton, was instructing both children and adults in practical gardening, and the men of the village had taken a great interest in growing flowers, vegetables, and fruit.[75]

Estudillo's hard work to improve the government Indians schools was indirectly recognized in the fall of 1897 in Newton H. Chittenden's lengthy illustrated article in the *San Francisco Chronicle.* Although Estudillo was no longer agent, most of the credit for the condition and successes of the schools belonged to him. Chittenden made his tour in late 1897, visiting with "hundreds of intelligent, sturdy, healthful, orderly and good-manned native boys and girls . . . full of promise for the future of the race." Shown through Perris Indian School by Superintendent Allen, Chittenden described the facility as the Carlisle of the Pacific Coast, successfully carrying out its goal of "training the Indian in the self-supporting pursuits of civilization."[76]

At Cahuilla, Chittenden wrote, Mrs. Salsberry had been teaching for seven years and had sent thirty of her students on to Carlisle or St. Boniface in Banning. He found the Cupeño village of Agua Caliente on Warner's Ranch to be the most interesting of all, with its 150 residents living in "an exceptionally promising condition," although they were much alarmed "over an adverse decision recently rendered [by the courts], which threatened to dispossess them." The teacher, Mrs. Babbitt, had been there six years and had sent twenty-seven of her students on to Carlisle, Perris, or St. Boniface. Anyone reading this article would come to the same conclusion that Chittenden had—the government's investment in education for the Indian people was paying off.[77]

Tragedy at Temecula

There was still real conflict as well. On the night of September 20, 1894, the burned body of Mary Platt, the teacher at the Pechanga School, was discovered in the charred ruins of her schoolhouse and attached living quarters. Fortunately her ten-year-old niece, Hattie Leslie, who was visiting her, escaped the fire. Platt had written Estudillo a day or two earlier "that she believed herself to be in danger" and asking him, if he did not hear from her in a few days, to come to her "at once, for there will be trouble." Her letter arrived almost at the same time as the telegram informing him of her death. He immediately set off to investigate.[78]

Platt, who had been at Pechanga for about three years, was "a middle-aged and matronly widow, who having been bereaved of her husband and children early in married life, had given over her life to teaching." She also distributed government rations and helped care for the sick, held Sunday school classes, and advocated temperance among the villagers. She told several visitors over the years that her predecessor had been scared off by the harassment of a few of the Indians, but because she had ignored them, she had won the respect of

Mary Platt (*center*) poses with a group of Indian children and adults outside the Pechanga School, circa 1893.
C.C. Pierce Collection, The Huntington Library, San Marino, Calif.

the village captain, Mateo Pa. He had since taken it on himself to look after her and encouraged the village children to attend her school. Even so, the school had burned down mysteriously in 1891.[79] According to newspaper accounts, a rumor had been circulating at Pechanga that the Indian students at the Perris School were starving, and Captain Mateo Pa had visited Platt on the evening of the twentieth, demanding money so he could go to the school to see for himself. When she refused, instead offering to drive him to the school in a day or two, he angrily left, threatening to have the school closed.[80]

Estudillo was cautious in assigning blame, preferring, at least publicly, to let the courts settle the matter. But Quinton and Weinland blamed a white perpetrator. A lengthy article in the November issue of *The Indian's Friend* described Platt's "intrepid work in way of protecting her Indians from the temptations of strong drink and the impurity of outside whites," which "had awakened the malice of those who saw their profit in these terrible traffics." In an article for the *Christian Herald,* Reverend Weinland claimed that while trying to break up the "debauchery and prostitution" brought upon the Indians by "unprincipled white men," Platt had placed herself in danger. He concluded that the details of the crime pointed to "the brain of a fiendish white man [rather] than to that of the sluggish Indian."[81]

Los Angeles photographer C. C. Pierce reported that Platt had previously tangled with white men who came to the fiestas at Pechanga to run gambling games. On learning of this, Agent Rust had given her a revolver and said, "Keep that always loaded and handy, and if any of those scoundrels come around to bother you or the girls, shoot them." Pioneer Aguanga rancher Jake Bergman told Pierce, "I knew that woman to take a six-shooter from the school and go into the woods and drive white men away and bring her girls back from the brush."[82]

Captain Pa and two other men were eventually charged with her murder. In late March 1895 Pa was tried in the U.S. district court in Los Angeles. Estudillo, Dr. Wainwright, and Platt's niece all testified for the prosecution. The government's chief witness against Pa was Francisco Guavish, another one of the accused. Longtime Temecula Justice of the Peace John Magee was called by the defense and testified that he had known Pa since 1860, and that he was always quiet, honest, and peaceable, friendly toward whites and supportive of the school. Guavish, on the other hand, had a "doubtful reputation, and was considered a tramp and a vagabond." Former Indian agents John Ward and Samuel Lawson, agency physician Dr. Wainwright, and Frank Lewis also testified to Pa's good character.[83]

Captain Pa testified that he was fifty-two, born at San Luis Rey, and had become captain fourteen or fifteen years previously. He spoke only "broken Spanish" and no English, so he had asked Guavish to accompany him when he confronted Platt. He was interested in visiting Perris because he wanted to meet with the new superintendent and get his assurance that he would regularly report on the Pechanga children in attendance. When Platt refused to give him money, Pa admitted threatening to close the school by not bringing children there any more as he had been doing. Other witnesses confirmed that he had been home the night of the murder. In the end, it took only twenty minutes for the jury to acquit him.[84]

Attention soon turned to Guavish and three other men, Venturo Molido, Francisco Rodriguez, and Decco (Anthony) Trujillo. Guavish, it seems, was the one who had started the rumors about mistreatment at Perris after he himself had been expelled for "maltreating a lame boy" at the school. After Pa's trial he had gone to Los Angeles, where he was implicated in a number of petty crimes. Meanwhile, Captain Pa's attorney and the prosecuting attorney from his trial had joined forces to gather evidence against Guavish, and Agent Estudillo asked his nephew, former Los Angeles County Sheriff Martin Aguirre, to keep an eye on Guavish and learn what he could. Aguirre was assisted by Deputy A. C. Marsh, who had known Platt.[85]

In January 1896 Guavish was arrested for stealing a cow. Once he was in custody, the lawmen quickly rounded up his suspected accomplices and some witnesses. Molido confessed, swearing that Guavish was the ringleader who had led the others to Mrs. Platt's apartment, abducted her, raped her, strangled her, then piled wood over her body, poured kerosene over it, and set her on fire. Molido was tried first, in the Riverside County Superior Court. He repeated his testimony and was sentenced to life in prison. Guavish, Rodriguez, and Trujillo were tried in April–May 1896. Guavish's testimony from the Pa trial was used to impeach his testimony in his own trial, and it also came out that he had intimidated at least one other witness at the previous trial into backing his claims. Mateo Pa now had his chance to testify against Guavish, while other witnesses corroborated Molido's testimony. In the end the jury was dead-locked. Rodriguez and Trujillo were set free, but Guavish was held and later convicted of his other crimes in Los Angeles County and sentenced to twenty years in prison. "All the Indians say that Guaves [*sic*] should have been hung and not sentenced to imprisonment," Agent Estudillo reported.[86]

Water on the Desert

Since much of the land occupied by the Mission Indians was desert, the availability of water had been a major concern for all agents. During his tenure Estudillo secured funding for several water projects, including a new well at Martinez and a $5,375 stone-lined irrigation canal at Morongo, built over a two-year period and paid for by the government, which employed the residents to construct it. An outside well-driller had been hired to bore the well next to the schoolhouse at Martinez. The summer heat took a gruesome toll; Estudillo reported that two of the workmen died on the job.[87]

Estudillo alone cannot be credited for bringing a reliable water supply to the villagers at Martinez. Part of the credit must go to Amelia Stone Quinton and the WNIA. Reverend Weinland had been preaching at the village on a monthly basis, but the Indians wanted their own permanent resident missionary. Quinton agreed that if the Moravian Church would pay for a missionary, the WNIA would build a chapel and a missionary cottage. In the fall of 1896 the WNIA established its desert mission in the village. The water supply, however, was inadequate.[88] Long experienced with petition drives, Quinton encouraged the Indians to petition the government for new wells. She promised that the WNIA would endorse their efforts. After considerable correspondence with Estudillo, the Indian Office agreed to pay $2,100 to have a well drilled.[89] Additional wells were put in at Martinez in the early 1900s, including three in Section 16, where the government school was located. A few small reservoirs were also constructed, with pipes to carry water to the fields. But funds ran out before all of them could be completed.[90] Some of the construction work was apparently done by the Indians, using their own teams and equipment. "They will not be paid in cash," Dr. Wright told a reporter in 1899, "but will receive rations and whatever they need. Thus they will be given a chance to earn their living, which is the government's plan in dealing with them."[91]

At Agua Caliente (Palm Springs) there were problems of a different sort. The Palm Valley Land & Water Company, headed by former agent John McCallum, refused to provide a dependable supply of water to the Indians in return for the irrigation ditch crossing their reservation. The lengthy drought that plagued Southern California in the 1890s made agriculture difficult for whites and Indians alike. McCallum, favoring white settlers over the Indians, easily overlooked the 1888 right-of-way agreement, and by 1894 almost no water was reaching the Indians.[92]

"Some government officers who have acquired a grandiose style of talking, not unaccompanied with vague threats, plainly say that if the Palm Valley Company does not give the required twenty-seven inches [of water], then the government will step in and seize the flow of water coming from Chino, Taquitch [*sic*] and Andreas Canyons," the *Banning Herald* complained. But the company judged this threat "trivial" because so little water came down these canyons, and only two settlers were tapping it. Then, perhaps predictably, company officials insisted that the Indians should be removed by the government, or at least that it should reduce the size of the reservation, which had only thirty residents, most of whom worked for white ranchers rather than farming their own land.[93]

Finally in 1895 Estudillo had a showdown with McCallum, demanding that the former agent immediately surrender all sections of the water company's canal that "touched any portion" of the reservation. If McCallum did not comply within ten days, Estudillo threatened to return with his Indian police and forcibly remove the company's employees from the reservation.[94] Estudillo's threat finally forced McCallum to the bargaining table, and in 1896 the two negotiated a new right-of-way agreement that guaranteed the Indians their share of the water. Submitted to Washington for confirmation, the agreement was rejected by the government, which insisted on the Indians' right to water not just from the irrigation ditch, but from Andreas and Tahquitz canyons as well. McCallum refused. "The blow was too much for his weakened heart," his biographer writes.

The Henry Block in San Jacinto became the agency offices in 1897.
Courtesy of the San Jacinto Museum.

"John McCallum succumbed without medical attention on Feb. 5, 1897, in Palm Springs." The water wars at Palm Springs were far from over, but for better or worse, McCallum would no longer be part of the fight.[95]

Estudillo's Exit

Although Estudillo was not as combative as Rust, after four years of his administration some Indian leaders demanded a change. In the spring of 1897, Will Pablo prepared a petition for the incoming U.S. president, Republican William McKinley. Identifying himself as captain at Potrero and a "special attorney" for various Mission Indian groups, Pablo presented the hopes, wishes, and true condition of his people, who could not remain "good and loyal subjects," trying to "improve their morals and manners," as long as government Indian agents like Estudillo kept them as "peons and slaves," watching over them as if they were "ignorant children." They were citizens, Pablo declared, made so by the Treaty of Guadalupe Hidalgo and entitled to 160 acres of land, instead of the paltry 20 acres of allotted land that Estudillo was forcing them to accept.[96]

Pablo presented a number of reasons why he wanted Estudillo removed, including the agent's failure to prevent the liquor traffic that was ruining the lives of the young people; his "selfish motives" behind the small land allotments, attributed to ensuring that his son Frank, who was doing the land surveys, was paid for each survey; and his slandering and persecution of friends and supporters of the Indians, especially the removal from office of one of the most respected captains at Mesa Grande because he opposed allotment. Pablo stated that Estudillo had replaced the captain with a drunk who was easily manipulated. The personal reason for Pablo's opposition was that the agent had threatened to arrest and imprison him at Alcatraz for opposing allotment. Pablo hoped that the incoming president would appoint "only good and true men to look after [the Indians'] welfare."[97]

Complaints against Estudillo also came from the non-Indian communities. For example, like his predecessor, Estudillo was sometimes subject to scrutiny from the press. The *San Francisco Call* claimed alleged irregularities. In 1895 Estudillo had finally succeeded in getting the agency headquarters moved from Colton to San Jacinto, closer to more of the reservations. However, for his new offices, Estudillo had selected a building that he owned, charging the government rent. His previous agency building had been rented from Noel Davenport, the agency clerk, whose son, although attending school in Los Angeles, was being paid forty dollars a month as the agency's issuing clerk and was required to be present when rations were distributed. All of these irregularities were investigated; little seems to have come of it.[98] And ultimately such criticisms probably had little to do with Estudillo's departure, which was ultimately caused by the November 1896 election, bringing in William McKinley as the new occupant of the White House.

Estudillo's tenure may have cost him, personally and financially. He still owned a large tract in the San Jacinto Valley, and as the new century began he found himself deep in debt. Whether he had neglected his own interests during his term as agent is unclear, but at the end of 1901 he lost his land and home to foreclosure.[99] He moved to Los Angeles, where he lived the remainder of his life quietly. He died in 1921 at age seventy-six, following a long illness.

CHAPTER 8

▼ ▼ ▼

THE CONTINUING STRUGGLE

Dr. Lucius A. Wright, 1897–1903

> [The Indians] are not (save in a few instances) provided with suitable land, with water for irrigation; hence they can not make an independent and comfortable living by tilling the soil. . . .
>
> Southern California has had five successive years of severe drought, and . . . many industrious white men have been compelled to . . . seek a more favored locality. We can not expect Indians to be successful in farming where white men, with their superior knowledge and judge[ment,] have failed. . . .
>
> Under these adverse conditions, . . . the Mission Indians have done remarkably well; they have shown conclusively that they are not beggars, not lazy, but faithful laborers. Upon their own land they would have starved, consequently they have sought labor in irrigated districts already spoken of. . . . This gypsy-like method of Indian employment does not tend to the best standard of citizenship, for the home is neglected, but it shows that when the improvements now under way for the betterment of their condition are completed the Indians will make good use of the facilities given them.
>
> —*L. A. Wright, Annual Report (1902)*

It would be unfair to suggest that in 1897 there had been no progress in the Mission Indian Agency since its establishment in 1878. Reservations had been created and protected, schools had been established, water systems developed, farming equipment distributed,[1] and medical services provided. The new agent, Lucias A. Wright, may have had cause to face the future with hope. But many challenges still remained. Old prejudices remained strong in some quarters, reservation boundaries remained in dispute, poverty and disease were still all too common, and Indian lives and lands were still threatened. The coming years

Dr. Lucius A. Wright.
Los Angeles Times, August 21, 1897.

would see the last of the village "removals" in Southern California, a growing resistance to government restrictions on the reservations, and the end of the Mission Indian Agency.

Even before Republican William McKinley was inaugurated president in March 1897, the scramble for government appointments had begun. J. Hamilton Gilmour—Agent Rust's old nemesis—watched the process with a jaundiced eye, commenting that "the lucrative office of Indian agent—$1600 per annum and perquisites—is one that is being sought after with an avidity which alone would make a person believe that in these times $1600 is an immense sum." Many were lining up support, he noted in a letter to the editor of the *Los Angeles Times*; even Francisco Estudillo was circulating a petition among the Indians to endorse his reappointment. One hundred applicants had come in from Riverside County alone, along with an equal number from Los Angeles and about a third as many from San Bernardino. "There is really no shame-facedness about these gentlemen in showing-up their claims." Instead, Gilmour argued, the government should "do what it has long threatened to do" and appoint army officers as Indian agents. "Let them, at least, earn their living. Mere civilian appointments are simply outrageous."[2]

Dr. Lucius A. Wright, a loyal small-town Republican politician, was appointed as the new Mission-Tule River Consolidated agent in June 1897.[3] Learning of his appointment, Amelia Stone Quinton, who continued to support Rev. William Weinland, wrote President McKinley questioning the new agent's qualifications, even accusing Wright of "all sorts of iniquities, including drunkenness." McKinley referred her letter to his newly appointed interior secretary, Cornelius N. Bliss, who informed Quinton that following "a very thorough investigation," he was satisfied that she had been "misinformed" about Wright's habits and that his commission would be issued at once.[4]

Dr. Wright was born on March 21, 1852, in Mexico, Ohio, and his father, Bushnell A. Wright, also a physician, was superintendent of the insane asylum in Toledo. After reading medicine with his father and obtaining a degree from a Cincinnati medical institution, the younger Wright became an assistant physician in the asylum as well as an assistant physician for the county and city hospital. Four years later he resigned and purchased a drug store in Sylvania, Ohio. Failing health forced him in 1881 to move, first to Fresno, California, then four years later to Pasadena, and eventually, in May 1890, to San Jacinto, where he opened another drug store. He was soon elected a school trustee; and eventually, the city treasurer.[5]

Two months after taking over the agency, Wright sent his first annual report to Indian Commissioner William A. Jones,[6] noting that nothing more had been done toward allotment but that the eleven day schools under his jurisdiction were all "in a thrifty condition." Jones, an educator by profession who supported a practical educational system to aid the Indians to assimilate and take advantage of land allotment in severalty, was no doubt pleased to learn of the condition of the schools. Thanks to the work of the California Mission Indian Commission, Wright was able to report, there were now thirty-two reservations with a population of some 3,848, scattered over "an immense section of the country." Water, or rather the lack thereof, was the most serious problem, especially at Pechanga, Morongo (the old Potrero Reservation), Torres, and the new reservation at Twenty-Nine Palms, where he described the Indians as "destitute and without a chance to advance in the line of civilization."[7]

Desert Irrigation

Like Estudillo, Wright repeatedly emphasized the need for irrigation projects—especially in the lower Coachella Valley because of water diversion by white settlers.[8] There were only four reservations in all of Southern California "where anything like a system of irrigation [was] put in practice"—at Morongo, Agua Caliente (Warner Hot Springs), Palm Springs, and Rincon. He suggested allotment on the reservations with good land and water (and secure title) to encourage the Indians to farm more. As for the Desert Indians, they should be gathered together on the "best portions" of the Torres Reservation, near Indio, where the government should sink artesian wells and help them become self-supporting farmers.[9]

Wright got ahead of himself in December 1902, ordering several desert villages to relocate to a central location before wells had been drilled. The Indians, understandably, objected, well aware of the pending evictions at Warner's Ranch and fearful that the order was a ploy to enable white men to claim their village lands. Three days later—as Wright was on his way to Washington, D.C., to discuss this and other matters—the Indians met at the Martinez schoolhouse. Julian Lopez, previously confirmed by Wright as chief of the Indians on the Torres Reservation, led the meeting. A petition, signed by Chief Lopez and the captains of the Torres, Martinez, La Mesa, and Alamo Bonito villages, along with two dozen heads of families, was addressed to now President Theodore Roosevelt and Commissioner Jones.

"We have never made any trouble for anybody," they wrote. But now they were being pushed to the "extreme northwest corner" of the reservation so that white settlers could "apply for the larger portion" of their land. They concluded: "[T]his is the first time we have made known our wants and necessities." They were asking only for "one artesian well at the following Indian villages: Walters, Cabezon, La Mesa, Alamo Bonito, Agua Dulce, Agua Dulce Tuba, and four artesian wells each at Martinez and Torros [*sic*] Indian villages. With this distribution all of the Indians will be supplied with sufficient water for the present, and will thus be made happy and self-supporting."[10]

The petition seems to have had its desired effect. Several more artesian wells were drilled across the reservation during Wright's tenure. In 1903 he proudly reported to Jones that "the Indians on the desert are very well pleased: many are building new houses near the wells and what they desire now is to have apportionment or allotment of lands to them so that they may know what they may call their own."[11] Four years later, Wright was still seeking some sort of distribution of land, "either formal or informal," where the artesian wells were located on the Torres and Cabazon reservations. He informed Commissioner Francis Ellington Leupp[12] that the "desert Indians, who formerly raised practically nothing in the way of subsistence and led idle lives, depending on mesquite beans and the forage of the country for themselves, families and animals, have done remarkably well since water has been furnished them." Imitating white farmers, they soon began to raise cantaloupes "and such things as pay best in that peculiar locality." However, because their lands were not subdivided at the time they began moving there, the situation was in a "chaotic state." Wright continued: "When I first spoke of allotting the land none of the Indians were in favor of it"; however, now they "say they would like to have it divided up so that each family may know where his permanent home is to be and make such improvements as they see fit."[13]

Indian Education

Judging the "material welfare" of the Indians as not at all satisfactory, Wright in his 1899 report nevertheless gave an upbeat report on the eleven reservation schools. Although attendance was declining and the buildings all needed painting, the facilities were otherwise generally adequate. He singled out the school at Cahuilla, which he described as not worth repairing. Despite their sometimes dilapidated conditions, he described the government day schools as a "great civilizer . . . benefiting the Indians very materially." Several years later he reiterated his appreciation for them, informing Jones that Indians who lived on reservations with day schools "are more enlightened and conform more to the habits and customs of civilization than those who live at remote distances from schools."[14] He had high praise for government school teachers and their role on the reservation. "A zealous and kind-hearted school-teacher is a very material aid in the improvement and advancement of the older Indians," he reported to Jones in his 1902 annual report. But teachers should not limit their activities to only educating Indian children, he opined; their "good offices should extend to all the Indians of the reservation."[15]

In his annual report for 1900, Wright included an interesting summary of school attendance for the eleven reservation day schools:

Students attending school as of Nov. 15, 1899

	Day	Perris	St. Boniface	Carlisle	Phoenix*	Not in School
Agua Caliente	22	5	9	7	1	3
Cahuilla	17	14	12	0	7	10
Capitan Grande	18	0	0	0	0	12
La Jolla	25	31	0	0	0	1
Martinez	39	0	0	0	0	0
Mesa Grande†	23	10	7	0	0	15
Morongo	36	18	7	0	0	11
Pechanga	24	15	2	4	0	0
Soboba	23	4	5	0	5	0
Rincon	30	12	1	0	6	0
Tule River	23	9	0	0	0	21

Source: "Wright to Jones, September 20, 1901," *Annual Reports of the DOI, 1901*, part 1 (GPO, 1902), 211.
*The Phoenix Indian School was a government boarding school, established in 1891. Like the Sherman Institute, it later became a high school. It closed in 1990.
†Plus 3 at St. Anthony's and 4 in public school.

Unfortunately Agent Wright's list does not include statistics for the reservations without day schools; at least some of their children would have been enrolled at either the Catholic or government boarding schools.

The tension between the boarding schools and the day schools continued to be an issue. In his annual report for 1903 Wright complained that day school attendance on the reservations suffered because "the boarding schools select pupils from the reservations in a most indiscriminate manner, without regard to age, educational qualifications, or other requisites for transfer." He blamed the Catholics for making "strenuous efforts to obtain every child possible for enrollment in their mission schools"—two of which were located within agency limits.[16]

At Mesa Grande, some of the children attended the local public school. Although this was apparently rare, it happened at one or two of the smallest San Diego County reservations. Indian children from Palm Springs, Santa Ysabel, and Sycuan were also attending public schools.[17] Wright noted that encouraging Indian children to attend public schools was often difficult because older Indian children were sometimes placed with much younger white students. "The Indian children are sensitive, as are our own, and do not like to be classed among the younger and more advanced white children," he reported.[18]

Drought and Disease

In the late 1890s Southern California endured a serious drought, resulting in crop failures on many reservations. Conditions became even worse in the winter of 1898–99, when harsh weather led to an outbreak of the flu, which in many cases turned into pneumonia. Then in the spring and summer of 1899 an epidemic of "a malignant form of measles" swept through many villages. As always, children and the elderly were especially hard hit.[19] "Something must be done," Wright told a reporter. "[T]he Indians have never had such a year before." Not only did they need food and clothing but many were sick with consumption (tuberculosis). At his headquarters in San Jacinto, he noted: "I have been dealing out sick rations to them. They are a stoical, patient people, but they are coming to me and begging for help."[20]

The government had long provided some food, but mostly for the sick and elderly. Now—even with private donations—the widespread poverty of the late 1890s taxed the system to its limit. As a special contributor to the *Los Angeles Times*, Reverend Weinland had written a lengthy illustrated article on the condition of the Mission Indians, describing them as a race "rapidly growing extinct" due to the "ravages of disease and the evils of civilization." His article was reprinted in three successive issues of the WNIA's monthly newsletter.[21]

In the past, when the Indians' crops failed they found work with local ranchers, but now the ranchers too were suffering from the drought and had little need for extra hands. "For three successive years both whites and Indians have been compelled to endure this water famine," Wright reported in 1899. According to the *Hemet News*, at Cahuilla the Indians' crops, "like those of their white brothers yielded no returns," and many had fallen ill.[22] On the desert, the drought was exacerbated by the continuing water struggles at Palm Springs. "Five years ago," a reporter noted in 1900, "a number of fruit ranches in the valley gave regular employment to most of these Indians, but mismanagement of the water supply has led to the abandonment of nearly all the ranches." As a result, the Indians had their water supply for irrigation cut off and were "dependent upon a few days' chance work in a month and upon desert products like the mesquite bean." Several died. "The government should do something for these Indians, as they are good workers and have never made any claim on the nation so long as the means of support were within their reach," concluded the reporter.[23]

Wright's 1900 annual report was equally depressing. After visiting each reservation during the year, he found the Indians with insufficient food and clothing.

"The balance of the reservations" he described as a "worthless lot." "[N]o white man, with his superior education and training, could take any one of them as a gift and raise and educate a family of six children from the products there from."[24] Part of the problem, Wright felt, was California's reputation as an agricultural paradise. Officials in Washington did not have a proper understanding of the Indians' extreme plight. "The fertility of California soil, and the splendid products are so renowned that it hardly seems creditable to an Eastern person that a great number of our Indian reservations are a worthless lot," he contended. Unfit for agriculture, they are "made up in many cases of land that an intelligent white man, with his superior knowledge of farming, would not accept as a gift."[25]

The situation worsened when an epidemic of measles killed several children, and on Christmas morning, 1899, a strong earthquake centered in the San Jacinto Valley caused six deaths at Soboba and several other injuries when adobe homes were "crushed like eggshells." The adobe school house at Agua Caliente was also destroyed.[26] The building that housed Wright's agency office had moved an inch or more off its foundation, scattering his papers and supplies and leaving his office in shambles. Although rumors were circulating about extensive destruction at the nearby Cahuilla Reservation, Dr. Wainwright had informed the papers that he had heard from the village that no houses had been destroyed and that, as reported earlier, the "topography of the country had not been changed."[27]

By 1902 the drought was in its fifth year, and even many of the "more industrious white men" have been forced to give up their ranches. Some Indians were now forced to travel more than one hundred miles seeking work, taking their families with them and disrupting home life and schooling for their children. For Wright this showed they were "not lazy."[28] Indeed, Wright varied his portrayal of the condition of the Mission Indians depending on circumstances. When bragging about their success, meaning more funding for agency projects, he praised them. When that funding was threatened by others who claimed the Indians were self-supporting, he could be quite negative. On the whole, he did not hold a high opinion of the Indians' abilities to take care of themselves "under existing conditions"—that is, poor land, lack of water, unsettled boundaries, and "meddlesome" Mexicans and whites.[29]

The Last Removals

Wright also inherited the eviction lawsuits at Warner's Ranch and San Felipe. Government attorneys Shirley Ward and Frank Lewis had moved to set aside the judge's decision in the twin Warner's Ranch cases based on numerous errors in law. In his first annual report to Jones, Wright had expressed "great hopes of the Indians' final success." He vowed to give them all the help he could, but because he had been in office only a short time, he had been unable to "be of much service so far." Several months earlier, on April 24, 1897, the motion for a new trial had been denied.[30] The Indians would have been evicted on July 15, 1897, had their case not been appealed with the help of the IRA. Supported by the LMC Mission Indian Committee, the IRA— believing the Indians were "morally and legally the owners of these lands" and unwilling to see four hundred innocent Indians "homeless and without a roof to cover them"—provided the $6,100 for an appeal bond so Ward and Lewis could carry the cases to the California state supreme court. According to *The Indian's Friend,* the bond had deliberately been set high in the belief that "no one would be found willing to furnish it."[31]

A backlog of cases prevented the California supreme court from hearing arguments until April 19, 1899. On October 4, in a split decision, 4 to 3, the court found against the Indians, upholding the earlier decision of the superior court. Since the days of the Soboba case, several new justices had been appointed, and this new court was not as sympathetic to the rights of Indians as the previous one. The decision, quoting extensively from the Soboba case, maintained that the Warner's Ranch case "differs materially" because the land "was vacant and unoccupied at the date of the grant"—a fact easily disproved by the evidence ruled inadmissible by Judge Puterbaugh (see chapter 7).[32]

D. L. Withington, one of the Downey family attorneys, while welcoming the verdict, was mild in his comments to the press: "There is and never has been any indications of any unfairness to the Indians on the part of the owners of the ranch, whose standing in the community is such as to insure the utmost fairness towards the Indians."[33] An application for a rehearing was turned down, but the growing notoriety of the case prompted the U.S. Attorney General's Office to file an appeal to the U.S. Supreme Court. Shirley Ward and Agent Wright, trying to keep the Cupeños informed on the status of the case, wrote both the village captain, Salvador Nolasquez, and the government schoolteacher, Mrs. Babbitt, a vocal advocate of the Indians' right to remain. These letters, assuring the Indians that everything possible was being done on their behalf, were read to the Cupeños during a meeting on November 6, 1899.[34]

Ward traveled to Washington to plead the Indians' case before the Supreme Court on March 20 and 21, 1901. He was assisted by Henry M. Hoyt, assistant attorney general of the United States. They had written two exhaustive briefs and participated in oral arguments. "I must confess that I felt very confident after the oral argument that we had impressed the Court," Hoyt later wrote. He described Ward as having devoted himself to the hearing "with the same energy, zeal and ability he has shown in the previous stages of the case." The court, Hoyt explained, had "refused to consider the equities," instead resting its decision upon legal principles it "considered to be well established"—that "under the Act of 1851 the Indian claim should have been presented to the Commissioners of the Act." Because the Cupeños failed to follow the letter of the law and present their claim for confirmation, the land was viewed as abandoned. Further, since the case of the Kumeyaay villagers on Rancho Vallé de San Felipe had been conjoined with that of the Warner's Ranch Indians, they would share the same fate.[35] On May 13, 1901, the U.S. Supreme Court upheld the prior decision of the California state supreme court. Ward and Lewis had presented the Indians' claims with clarity and diligence, but they managed only to delay the inevitable. After nearly thirty years of threats, lawsuits, and intimidation, the Warner's Ranch Indians lost their homes. "It is hard to exaggerate the severity of their fate," wrote Philander C. Knox, U.S. attorney general.[36]

The Cupeños and the other villagers on the ranch had been defeated at every step of the way through the court system. Even if they had held rights under Mexican law, they had lost them because some government clerk had failed to mention them in Warner's grant. And even if his grant had included the required language, it would not matter because Downey's attorneys had "proven" that the Indians were not living in the valley in 1844. And even if they had lived on the ranch then, they lost their rights when they failed to file a claim with the Land Commission in the 1850s—even though the Land Commission was supposed to deal with the rights of Indians separately. While the courts could not find any record that the commission had studied the question of Indian property rights, they took it for granted that a report had been made, and having not seen it, they naturally assumed that it had gone against the Indians. The disappointment of Eastern Indian advocates was immediate. Amelia Stone Quinton, whose association had sponsored a physician and helped support a field matron among the Cupeños since 1893, was especially "heart sick." She wrote Weinland, the WNIA's former missionary superintendent, that "we are all helpless together in this case."[37]

For Agent Wright the loss was equally as devastating; he described it as "the most noteworthy and unfortunate event" of the year. Now that the court had decided against the Indians, over two hundred people had been "deprived of their homes." The Indian Office had informed him, however, that the land owners had agreed to wait until the next session of Congress to enforce the eviction decree, giving the government time to take steps for their relief. "Thus the matter stands at present," Wright informed Commissioner Jones in his September 1901 report.[38] A year later Wright was still upset about the decision, describing it as "the event of paramount interest this year as well as last," exciting "unusual interest and sympathy all over the country."[39]

In October 1901 U.S. Senator Thomas Bard of Ventura County, a member of the Senate Committee on Indian Affairs, visited Agua Caliente (Cupa) along with Agent Wright and William Collier, special attorney for the Mission Indians.[40] They also visited Puerta la Cruz, Mataguay, San José, and La Puerta, the other villages on Warner's Ranch. After their meetings, Bard reported that the Cupeños "won't entertain for a moment the possibility of being removed from the reservation." Informing them of the "great possibility of them not being allowed to remain," Bard asked where they would prefer to live. "The chief replied that if they were compelled to leave their present home they would all die; they want to remain where they have buried their fathers."[41] The federal government attempted to purchase the village lands at Agua Caliente from J. Downey Harvey, but he refused to sell any smaller parcels, offering only the full thirty thousand acres for $245,000—a cost far beyond the government's willingness to pay. A new location had to be found.[42]

The *San Francisco Call* reported that the government had already "given up the idea that there is any Government land in this section of the County which is suitable for a reservation." All tillable land, the reporter noted, had already been taken by white settlers. The only land left was on "the sides of mountains where the Indians have a hard time to exist."[43] Therefore in late November 1901, the Indian Office sent Inspector James McLaughlin, a special agent of the Interior Department,[44] to California to confer with Wright. According to Wright's report to Commissioner Jones, they spent over a week in December examining numerous pieces of property to purchase as a new home for the Warner's Ranch Indians. Their choice—the Monserrate Ranch in the hills between Bonsall and Fallbrook in northern San Diego County—did not meet universal approval.[45] Nevertheless, in January 1902 the Indian commissioner asked Congress for $100,000 to buy the property.

Wright had initially suggested purchasing land in the San Pasqual Valley but eventually came to support McLaughlin's recommendation. The agent explained to Commissioner Jones that he initially disapproved of Rancho Monserrate because it only had a small supply of surface water. Irrigation was essential in Southern California, and this property would not provide sufficient water.

Ultimately there was "so much protest against its purchase," wrote Wright, that the government was forced to appoint a special committee to find a more suitable location.[46] One of the most prominent—and most vocal—critics had been Los Angeles author and editor Charles Fletcher Lummis.[47]

In June of 1901 Lummis had formed the Sequoya League, a West Coast–based reform organization hoping to work with the government on what he considered common-sense policies with Indian consent.[48] He used his position as editor of *Land of Sunshine* magazine (later renamed *Out West*) to promote the league's policies and projects, and the Warner's Ranch situation was their first big cause. Through the pages of *Out West* and personal letters, Lummis insisted that Washington disregard the inspector's recommendation and authorize a group of knowledgeable Southern Californians to make a more proper selection.[49]

In his vigorous defense of the Warner's Ranch Indians, Lummis turned for support to President Roosevelt, whom he had met while attending Harvard University years before. The president in turn recommended the establishment of a special Warner's Ranch Indian Commission, with Lummis as chairman. He was joined by Indian advocate Charles L. Partridge of Redlands, and another former Harvard classmate, Russell C. Allen of San Diego, who managed a large ranch at Bonsall, not far from the Rancho Monserrate.[50] They were joined by Special Attorney William Collier; Judge Richard Egan of San Juan Capistrano, a surveyor and longtime Southern California resident; and a stenographer to take down their comments.[51] Former Mission Indian Agent Horatio Rust was pleased with the appointment of the commission, confident that the work would be "intelligently and honestly carried out and that the Indians could have no better representatives for this work."[52]

In March 1902 they held a "junta" (as Lummis like to call it) with the Indians at Agua Caliente, where the commission members learned what they should have already known—the Cupeños had no interest in giving up their ancestral home. Lummis was impressed with "the unvexed truth, the simplicity, the directness, the earnestness, and yet the perfect self-control of these aboriginal speeches." Through an interpreter, Captain Cecilio Blacktooth informed Lummis that there was "no other place" for them. "We do not want you to buy any other place. If you will not buy this place we will go into the mountains like quail, and die," he declared. They did "not want any other home." Although they were a proud people, they would not fight.[53]

Lummis then set out to do exactly what Blacktooth had begged him not to do—buy the Cupeños another home. He asked the tribe to select two representatives to accompany the commission members on their search. Former captain Salvador Nolasquez and future captain Ambrosio Ortega, who served as lay reader at the little chapel near the hot springs, agreed to go.[54] The commission made two tours of inspection through Southern California during the summer of 1902. Agent Wright had hoped to accompany them as an advisor, but the Indian Office refused him permission. The commission considered forty-five possible reservation sites and visited twenty-eight of them. The locations considered included parcels at Santa Ysabel, Pauma, Moosa, DeLuz, Guajome, Los Flores (in San Bernardino County—not the old Las Flores ranch on the coast), Ethanac (now Romoland), Jurupa, San Pasqual, Agua Tibia, and Descanso. Nolasquez and Ortega rejected them all.[55]

In late July Nolasquez and Ortega, accompanied by three other Cupeños, traveled the 150 miles to visit Lummis and other commission members in Los Angeles. They had also expected to confer with Commissioner Jones. When Jones did not show up, the Indian delegation headed for San Bernardino to visit and confer with Attorney John Brown Jr., a longtime supporter. While there, Nolasquez and Ortega drafted a petition to be delivered to Jones.[56] They also wrote President Roosevelt, asking him "to delay the removal of the tribe to Pala valley until he [had] personally inspected their present reservation and the lands chosen by the commission." They explained: "[W]e reported for our Indians to such Commission that none of the places were satisfactory." They were displeased, "owing to want of sufficient water for domestic and irrigating purposes and also for the want of sufficient agricultural land on which we could support ourselves . . . but the Commission did not regard our wishes which were to retain our old homes." Not until December did the delegation receive a reply from the president, who found it impossible to comply with their request. He assured them, however, that "every assistance will be given them in removing from Agua Caliente, and becoming established wherever the Indian commission decides is a suitable location."[57]

Nolasquez and Ortega finally arranged to meet with Commissioner Jones in Redlands in late July 1902. The Cupeño delegates again renewed their request to remain in their homes. Charles Partridge reported to the *San Francisco Chronicle* that Jones informed the Indians that the government "had done everything in its power to keep them in their old reservation." "The Indians had heard Jones quietly" and "agreed to go when the Government should require it," noted Partridge. Presumably during this meeting the Cupeños gave Jones a letter. The commissioner's eventual reply echoed what had been reported in the *Chronicle*.

He was sorry they could not remain at Warner's Ranch. The only thing left was to return home "and be ready to move peacefully to the new place when the legal authorities notify you to move." Jones sounded sincere when he concluded: "I am very sorry for you from my heart, and so are we all. But we have done all that could be done."[58]

In the end, the commission selected the Pala valley, site of the old Franciscan *asistencia* of Mission San Luis Rey and a small Luiseño reservation nearby.[59] Located on the west side of Mount Palomar on the San Luis Rey River some forty miles from Warner's Ranch, the site included over 3,300 acres, of which 2,000 were arable and 700 irrigable. Frank A. Salmons, a local trading post operator, had arranged the purchase. In addition, there were about 5,000 adjoining acres of public land that could be added by executive order, although most of it ran up the steep brushy sides of Palomar Mountain.[60]

The circumstances surrounding the fate of the Warner's Ranch Indians led to several unfortunate situations and misunderstandings, one involving WNIA president Amelia Stone Quinton and Charles Fletcher Lummis, and indirectly bringing Agent Wright into the fray. Quinton had originally visited the village in 1891, returning in 1895. In May 1902 she visited again, in the company of Reverend Weinland, and observed the sadness that "pervaded the assembly" that had gathered. She encouraged the Indians in their desire to send a delegation to Washington and explain to the president what was in their hearts and "see if he might help [them] or move Congress to find some way to buy [their] own home."[61]

When Lummis learned of Quinton's visit, he misunderstood or misinterpreted her intentions and wrote Agent Wright, requesting information about the WNIA. Like some bureaucrats, Wright held a low opinion of Eastern reformers, describing Quinton as having "considerable power in the East" but as appearing to him to be "a hindrance rather than a help to the work." Wright's reaction to Quinton suggests that, like Agent Rust, he did not appreciate an active, assertive woman infringing on what he considered "his" struggle for the betterment of the Indians. At the same time Lummis had come to regard the Warner's Ranch situation as his own private crusade and objected to anyone else muscling in. Months later, when Lummis and Quinton finally met face to face, he was forced to admit that "her motives at Warner's ranch, which appeared so insurrectionary at the time, were misunderstood."[62] In the meantime, however, Lummis seems to have arranged for the *Los Angeles Times* to publish a front-page article attacking Quinton.[63] Wright was glad to see the "roast" she received in the paper. "These same people have made life a burden for me since I have been Agent," he noted.[64]

In a similar way, Lummis attacked the Indians' attorney, John Brown Jr. of San Bernardino, in the pages of *Out West*, complaining that the lawyer had the nerve to write President Roosevelt, telling him that only he had the true interests of the Indians at heart—not their agent, not the Indian commissioner, and not the Warner's Ranch Indian Commission. In a meeting in Los Angeles, Lummis forced Brown to admit that there was nothing to be done about the Supreme Court decision and publicly shamed him for taking the Indians' money. Nevertheless, Brown remained a trusted advisor to many of the Cupeños for years.[65]

In May 1903, on the brink of the removal, Attorney Brown arranged for a group of Cupeño leaders, including Nolasquez and then captain Juan Maria Cibimoat, to meet with President Roosevelt during his goodwill tour of San Bernardino. Unfortunately, it was a futile gesture. The Cupeños had brought a petition to present to Roosevelt but were "jostled away from the president's carriage" after shaking hands with him. By then, even Brown realized there was nothing the president could do.[66]

On the sixteenth of the previous month, Lummis, Agent Wright, Special Agent Frank Conser, and Special Attorney William Collier had visited Agua Caliente to discuss removal plans. The Indians received them "sullenly and almost defiantly."[67] Lummis's arrival especially disturbed them. The Cupeños dubbed him the "Thin Liar."[68] Despite his sincere desire to help them find a new home, his tendency to thrust himself into the center of everything he was involved with made him an easy target for the Indians' wrath. Lummis never quite grasped that by continually bragging that he had arranged for a better home than their native village, he was taking credit for the single biggest disaster in the tribe's history.[69] As for their agent, Dr. Wright, one newspaperman reported, "The Indians do not entirely like him, or trust him, but they feel that he is doing his best. They say that they prefer him a thousand times to Mr. Lummis [to] whom they have taken a strange, unreasoning dislike."[70]

Lummis, Wright, and Collier called a meeting at the schoolhouse. The Cupeños, holding their own gathering beforehand, arrived an hour late, but they listened as Wright and Collier explained the government's position. Although officials wanted this move to be as painless as possible, it was also made clear that nothing would stand in its way. Father Hahn, the Catholic priest from St. Boniface who ministered to the villagers when he could, called upon the Cupeños to go peacefully. Lummis then rose and expressed the same sentiment, adding in no uncertain terms that if they refused, force would be applied—their homes would be torn down and soldiers would come to make them move—or shoot them, if necessary.[71] Lummis wrongly believed it would take the army to dislodge the Cupeños—"[I]t will be the height of folly to attempt anything without troops," he wrote to Wright soon after—though publically he always denied making such threats.[72]

Fortunately, the Indian Office understood that Lummis was not up to the delicate task at hand and at the last minute sent James E. Jenkins, one of eight special inspectors in the Indian service, to take charge of the removal, supplanting both Lummis and Agent Wright.[73] Through the thankless task that followed, Jenkins displayed patience, diplomacy, and ultimately firmness in seeing things through. He proved Lummis wrong; armed troops were not necessary to remove the Indians. Instead of soldiers, Jenkins hired some forty local ranchers and teamsters to transport them and their belongings. The teamsters arrived on the ranch on May 8 or 9, while Jenkins was busy negotiating with the Indians. Agent Wright had arrived a day or two earlier. His agency clerk, M. Matthews, wrote to Special Agent Conser on May 7: "Dr. Wright left [San Jacinto] this morning for the battlefield, Warners Ranch, with forty teams. A few more days will tell the story. He received all sorts of warnings not to go, but Mr. Jenkins assured him over the phone that they [the Cupeños] were ready to move peacefully as we trust and that all will be well."[74]

Jenkins showed remarkable tact, and he never doubted his duties. He could be patient, but ultimately, he expected to be obeyed. His diplomacy was helped along by the absence of the new Cupeño captain, Juan Maria Cibimoat, and the other more vocal opponents of the removal. They had traveled to San Bernardino as part of John Brown's futile scheme to try to secure a reprieve directly from President Roosevelt. Jenkins agreed to wait to take any action until the delegation returned. That gave him more time to try and win over the rest of the Indians. Meanwhile, Wright, who had been keeping a low profile for several days, left the ranch for Pala to supervise arrangements.

When Cibimoat and the others returned, the captain insisted that nothing could be done until he could consult once again with attorney Brown. Therefore, accompanied by Ambrosio Ortega, Cibimoat rode more than five miles to Mesa Grande, waiting three hours for a telephone connection to San Bernardino. Finally, around nine o'clock in the evening, they were able to get through to Brown, who promised to come immediately. The following morning, May 11, Jenkins was ready to begin the removal. He roused the teamsters and had them move their wagons into the village. News reports of the Cupeño response to this "aggressive move," as the *Los Angeles Times* termed it, varied considerably. Citing an eyewitness, the *Times* reported that "when the Indians saw the white men and wagons coming they locked and barred the doors of their cabins and threatened to shoot anyone who should dare to disturb them." But Joseph Schirmer, a *Riverside Daily Press* correspondent who was on the scene, wrote that there was little resistance; some of the adobes already had piles of furniture, boxes, and bedding in front of them, ready to go.[75]

Cibimoat continued to insist that removal not begin before Brown arrived, and Jenkins relented, agreeing to give them until noon. Meanwhile, Brown was driving virtually nonstop from San Bernardino, passing Wright, who was on his way to Pala. "I wondered what he [Brown] was up to," Wright later told a reporter.[76] Brown arrived around two o'clock in the afternoon and immediately sat down with Cibimoat and the other village leaders, informing them they must leave peacefully. Schirmer reported that this brief meeting "left a gloomy look on the dusky faces" of village leaders.[77]

Jenkins called one last meeting. John Brown spoke first, advising the Cupeños to go peacefully. He was followed by Cibimoat, who in an impassioned speech maintained "to the last that he would rather die than be moved." However, Schirmer reported, "one could see the bottom had gone out of the opposition and his following had forsaken him." Jenkins questioned whether Cibimoat was still acting as captain; he seemed to be speaking only for himself. Perhaps, Jenkins suggested, each man present should be allowed to speak. Yes, Cibimoat shrewdly replied, ask them if they would rather stay here or go to Pala. But Jenkins ignored that suggestion, knowing full well the answer. While many of the Cupeños were ready to move, none wanted to leave their homes. Jenkins continued to focus on Captain Cibimoat, reminding him that he had promised to do what was right if they waited for Brown's arrival. The captain replied that Jenkins was breaking his promise. At that point Jenkins rose; he had reached the end of his patience, and he expected the Cupeños to obey the government's orders and move.[78]

Tuesday, May 12, 1903, dawned bright and pleasant. The temperature began to rise; by mid-morning it was clear it would be a hot day. All through the village the Cupeños were rushing to finish packing for the move to Pala—furniture, clothing, kitchen items, pets, potted plants, chickens, even doors and window frames. Eleven-year-old Roscinda Nolasquez remembered the confusion of that last morning, with Jenkins giving orders in English, which most of the Cupeños could not understand. "We were so scared," she said. "We didn't know what he was saying. We didn't know what was going on. We saw old people running back

The Cupeños begin their "trail of tears" from
Warner Hot Springs to the reservation at Pala, May 1903.
Out West magazine, July 1903.

and forth. We cried, too, because we were afraid."[79] For most of the Cupeños there was only weeping or stunned silence.

Grant Wallace of the *San Francisco Bulletin* could not stand by and simply cover the day's events for his paper. "While I helped lay-reader Ambrosio [Ortega]'s mother to round up and encoop a wary brood of chickens," he later wrote, "I observed the wife [Jacinta] of her other son, Jesus, throwing an armful of books—spellers, arithmetics, poems—into the bonfire, along with bows and arrows, and superannuated aboriginal bric-a-brac." Jacinta's response when asked why she was destroying everything was that "now they hated the white people and their religion and their books." While helping the "dogged and dejected" Captain Cibimoat hitch his bony horse to a buggy, Wallace saw "a tear or two course down his knife-scarred face; and as the teamsters tore down his little board cabin wherein he kept a restaurant, he muttered, 'May they eat sand!'"[80]

Wagons were loaded and ready to go by mid-morning. A number of Cupeños had gone on ahead in "their own light wagons," driving rapidly ahead of the wagon train, "too proud and heartsick to witness the desecration of their ancient homes."[81] Jenkins also set off for Pala, leaving the teamsters in charge. A little after ten o'clock, John Brown climbed up onto the seat of the lead wagon next to Ambrosio Ortega and shouted "Vamoose Pala!" and the journey began. Captain Cibimoat was the last to leave. "We will go to Pala," he said, "but I cannot say that we will stay."[82]

"Indians Bundled away Like Cattle to Pala," read the banner headline in the *Los Angeles Times* the next day (much to Jenkins's disgust). When the wagons reached Puerta la Cruz, a few miles down the road, several other wagons were waiting to join the sad procession. It was a different story at Mataguay and San José, however. When the teamsters arrived early that morning, they found the villages deserted. The inhabitants—two families at Mataguay and three at San José—had fled. Some of the Mataguay villagers were later gathered up. "Only one village," the *Los Angeles Times* reported, "San Jose, with its dozen unbleached American citizens, escaped. Its captain, on seeing the heavy farm wagons approaching to carry away his people's lares and penates, fled up the mountain side and hid among the greasewood, and his people said they would go, but not to Pala; they would rather die in the cañons. They will be fetched later."[83] La Puerta was removed even later still.

Stopping for lunch near the edge of the ranch, Grant Wallace noted that the Cupeños "lingered long on the last acre of Warner's Ranch, as though loath to go through the gates."[84] Roscinda Nolasquez rode in a buggy with some of her family. "It was a hard trip," she later recalled. "[T]hey wouldn't let up stop to drink water."[85] Thirst was always one of Roscinda's strongest memories of the trip. "We were all crying," she said on another occasion, but "the drivers were all laughing and singing."[86] The Indians camped at Oak Grove that first night. They were offered rations, but many refused; they were not beggars who needed charity. Others refused because of rumors that circulated through the camp. "Don't eat anything," Roscinda remembered hearing that night, "because they might poison you."[87]

The next evening the caravan reached the lower end of the Pauba Valley, a few miles south of Temecula. There they were joined by Luiseños from the nearby Pechanga Reservation (who had themselves been "removed" almost thirty years before), bringing oranges and other small gifts. On May 14 the Indians began the descent down the canyon to Pala, with wagons strung out along the steep, dusty grade—the final leg of the journey. By nine o'clock that morning they slowly rolled into Pala. "Why do we stop here?" some asked. Cibimoat finally came—the last to arrive. "Is this home?" he asked. "*No muy bueno,*" he exclaimed, and broke down again and cried.[88] Seventy-five years later, Roscinda Nolasquez still recalled her first impression: "It was dirty," she said, "nothing but trees. We had no homes . . . we had nothing, we had nothing to eat."[89] The people huddled together; grown men were in tears. Hoping to defuse the situation, Jenkins asked the Cupeños to help set up the forty-odd tents—their homes for the next six months. They had not expected to go from living in solid adobes to canvas tents. "They promised us good homes," Roscinda recalled, yet there they were, camping down by the river, "like gypsies." Over the coming weeks many of the people became sick. At Cupa, Roscinda remembered, "we were never sick, because we were bathing [in the hot springs] every day."[90]

Lummis, whom the *San Diego Union* claimed was still "bitterly disappointed over his lack of success in bringing about the removal himself," maintained that Jenkins's success was based as much on good luck as any talent he might possess. He continued to insist that soldiers should have been brought in. "[Y]our method of moving the Indians has bred a running sore with which the [Indian] Department will have to deal with for years to come," he wrote in an angry eighteen-page letter to Jenkins in September. He complained to President Roosevelt that Jenkins had accomplished the task "in a wrong and hazardous way"—a view no one else seemed to share.[91]

There were numerous newspapermen and photographers at Pala when the Cupeños arrived. Most of them, except for Grant Wallace, would leave within a day or two. "At the end of my two weeks stay," he later reported, "I found that many of the older people were still 'muy triste' [very sad]. They had not yet ceased wasting fresh tears over old griefs, and still their 'sorrows crown of sorrow is remembering happier things,' for their love of home is stronger than ours."[92]

Home—or rather, homes—became one of the most pressing issues. The trouble began when the government rejected the idea that the Cupeños build their own adobe houses, as they had done at Cupa. The suggestion that the government provide lumber for wooden homes was also rejected. The Indian Office wanted to give the Cupeños their new homes to emphasize the fact that the government was now going to provide for their needs—and that it was now in charge. "[I]t is time they were taught that the Government has some voice in the affairs of the reservation," Superintendent Charles E. Shell wrote from his headquarters at Pala.[93]

By asserting its dominance, the government engaged in a massive blunder. Some official decided it would be best to purchase prefabricated buildings—the Ducker Patent Portable House. Designed for vacation use at summer resorts in the East, these portable homes had thin board and batten walls and a layer of tar paper over a wooden roof. Fully assembled, they were just twelve by twenty-two feet (264 square feet) and were meant to be divided into two or three rooms. Special Agent Charles E. Kelsey bordered on the sarcastic in his 1906 report when he wrote: "[T]hings were rather at a standstill until the brilliant idea was evolved of getting temporary houses for the Indians to live in permanently." He described the ordering of fifty Ducker Portable Houses by telegraph from New York, a distance of over four thousand miles. Six months passed before the houses arrived, at a cost "double what wooden cabins built on the spot would have been, and about four times the cost of adobes." The scheme "was hardly a success." He described the structures as little more than wooden tents—"as a permanent dwelling place for human beings they [were] far from satisfactory." They were hot in summertime and cold during the winter. The California sun not only "sprung the narrow strips composing the panels and made cracks in every panel" but "also warped the roof panels and injured the tarred paper which constitutes the rain-shedding part," continued Kelsey. They were "neither dust-proof, nor water-proof, and [were] far inferior to the despised adobes," he concluded.[94]

In his August 1904 report, Superintendent Shell notified Commissioner Jones that the first thirty houses began arriving in October 1903. When it was evident that this number would be insufficient, twenty more were ordered. But even fifty houses were not sufficient. In the spring of 1904 Shell reported that there were still six families without any home at all. Two years later there were only forty-nine houses standing; one had been destroyed in a wind storm. These flimsy structures were home to 236 people—156 of them over the age of eighteen! Most of the tiny homes had at least five residents; some had as many as nine.[95] Publically, Shell was noncommittal—"There was some grumbling about the size of these buildings and their airiness, but that has generally subsided."[96] In his private letters to the Indian Office, however, he bluntly described them as unsatisfactory. "I feel safe in saying that there is not a side section [of any] house that is not open admitting both light and wind when the wind blows which is most of the time here." He described a recent dust storm that left the floors covered with dust, blowing in through the cracks.[97]

Katherine Mojado was attending school at St. Boniface in Banning at the time of the removal, but came to Pala soon after. In a 1977 interview she explained that her entire family lived in a "two room wooden house." They added a kitchen, along with a tent on the side of the house, which made things sufficient for her family of four. "How people with large families lived in those houses I still wonder about," she told her interviewer. At first there were no pipes for water; there was a line of outhouses along what "we used to call 'toilet street.'" Her mother's refrigerator was a "screened-in box covered with burlap that she kept wet to cool the food."[98]

The other key issue on the new reservation was water. Soon after the Cupeños arrived, a shallow ditch was dug to irrigate some of the lands on the south side of the San Luis Rey River; however, most of the reservation farm lands lay to the north. This ditch washed out, and a replacement was completed in May 1913, at which time the Cupeños celebrated with a fiesta and a blessing of the work by the priests from San Luis Rey. An abundance of water had been one of the key factors in selecting Pala in the first place. However, as soon as Warner's Ranch was cleared of Indians, plans moved forward to dam the San Luis Rey River—thus depriving Pala, along with the other downstream reservations, of much of the water supply that had made the location attractive. It was William G. Henshaw who finally got the dam built in 1922. Once the dam's floodgates were closed, the flow of the San Luis Rey River was never the same—an issue still disputed to this day.[99]

With the arrival of the Cupeños, the old school building was taken over for the reservation day school, and a new schoolhouse was built downstream, off the reservation, for the local white children. Mrs. Babbitt, who had accompanied the Cupeños, held classes in a tent until the old building was available. She was soon reassigned—probably because of her long-standing opposition to the removal—and Ora Salmons was hired. She taught at Pala until her retirement in 1922, after a thirty-seven-year career teaching on various San Diego County reservations.[100] Some children were sent away to school, either to St. Boniface in Banning or to the new Sherman Institute in Riverside. Roscinda Nolasquez went to Sherman and lived there for several years. She spoke no English when she first arrived. As was the standard rule at government boarding schools, she was not allowed to speak her native language; for doing so, she could be subjected to a whipping. At times she left the table hungry because she was unable to even say "pass the bread" in English. A teenager at the time, she eventually learned English. It was far easier for the younger children than it had been for her. At first, Roscinda remembered, "all I did was just cry." Yet there were also good memories, especially from her years at Sherman—playing basketball in the park, sneaking out to steal oranges from local orchards, and learning to play the mandolin. "The first time [we played]," she recalled, "we were so proud of ourselves."[101]

The San Felipe Removal

The Kumeyaay villagers at San Felipe must have followed the events on Warner's Ranch with fear and apprehension. The lawsuit against them had followed the twin cases against their northern neighbors, and with the decision of the Supreme Court their fate was sealed.[102] Perhaps in anticipation of their impending removal, some families began to leave. Some years earlier Agent Estudillo had reported sixty-nine residents in the village; by 1901 their numbers had dropped to between thirty and forty.[103] Lummis described their village as a "pitiful and poverty-stricken place, with neither land nor water half-way adequate to their needs." Although they much preferred "their own old desert to any paradise," he truly believed they would be better off at Pala, with its fertile acres and irrigating system.[104]

At the beginning of September 1903, Agent Wright asked the village captain and some of his men to visit him at his office, where he "explained fully and comprehensively why their removal was required." Like the Agua Caliente Indians, they stubbornly refused to go.[105] In a last-minute attempt to hold onto their lands, they traveled to San Bernardino to consult with a lawyer (probably John Brown). Therefore on September 4 when Wright arrived at the village with eighteen wagons, these Indian representatives were away. Wright was accompanied by Norton Barnes, the agency farmer, as well as three Indian policemen and a group of teamsters.[106] Later Wright described the scene for Lummis—his arrival at the reservation with wagons, his explanation to them that "they had lost their land" and his "instructions to remove them to Pala," and their determination never to go there. Wright informed Lummis that "they still resisted removal and I gave them until noon to think it over." He then explained to them that he was under orders and "it would be much better for them to assist in packing up their goods so that they would be packed carefully and nothing forgotten" rather than letting the teamsters pack for them.[107]

Edward Davis, who followed the San Felipe removal closely, described the general scene: "After three hours of persuasion, with eighteen four-horse teams waiting outside, patience ceased to be a virtue, and the agent began operations by smashing in the locked door of the *Capitan's* house, with an axe, and ordering the contents to be loaded immediately onto the waiting wagons."[108] Wright, in a September letter to Lummis, provided more graphic details. "It is true that two or three of the women at the other end of the rancheria ran out into the brush, likely from fear, but they were soon brought back and assisted in packing their effects." After the removal was completed, with "goods from every house being taken as well as the animals, including chickens, cats and dogs," Wright concluded that "the San Felipe Indians are well behaved and did not show the rebellious spirit exhibited by the Agua Caliente Indians."[109]

As at Cupa, the villagers' possessions were loaded into a line of wagons, and the caravan set off on its seventy-five-mile trek late that same day. They spent three nights on the road, near Santa Ysabel, at Oak Grove, and on the Pauba Ranch, before reaching Pala on September 7, 1903, where they were taken to a campsite on the far side of the creek from the Cupeños. In a Sequoya League report, Lummis wrote that Wright had managed the removal "not only with tact and firmness, but with dignity."[110]

When Special Agent Kelsey visited Pala in 1906, he described the San Felipes as still "outraged in their feelings," adding that they would "never be satisfied at Pala," where they were "surrounded by an overwhelming number of their hereditary enemies" and felt "unwelcomed." Kelsey recommended that the San Felipe group be allowed to move to the Santa Ysabel Reservation, where many of their friends and relatives lived. More than half had already left Pala, he noted. In the end, only one or two families remained.[111] Most of the people from Mataguay and San José had left as well, joining relatives on other reservations. Part of the problem, Kelsey noted, was the mix of native peoples now shoved together. They represented people from six different villages—seven if we count the Luiseños already living at Pala—speaking three different languages. "The government seems to learn very slowly that Indians are not all alike, and that different stocks or races of Indians ordinarily cannot be put together."[112]

The End of the Mission Indian Agency

The removals to Pala marked a turning point in the government's administration of its Southern California reservations. A month after the Cupeños' removal, Indian Commissioner Jones recommended the division of the Mission-Tule River Consolidated Agency into two groups: one under the superintendent of the San Jacinto Training School and the second under the superintendent of the Pala Training School. The reason given was the "widely separated localities of these schools and reservations" made it "manifestly impossible for one agent properly to look after their respective interests."[113] The decision seems to have been a sudden one, though there had been signs of approaching trouble. In 1900, 1901, and 1902 Jones had recommended Agent Wright's dismissal and the elimination of the Mission Indian Agency. The *Los Angeles Times* described this as more of a personal matter, "conducted by a little band of men at Riverside, Cal., who are seeking to pay off some political grudge against Dr. Wright."[114]

Wright was convinced that the effort to eliminate the agency was driven by his own agency physician, Dr. Wainwright, and by Harwood Hall, the superintendent of the Perris school, along with some of the "Millerites" of Riverside. These were supporters of Frank Miller, who was in the midst of a campaign to have the Perris school moved to Riverside.[115] Wainwright and Hall, Wright asserted, expected to take over his job once the agency was closed. He also believed they were responsible for having Inspector Arthur Tinker investigate his conduct in August 1900. Tinker's report was negative, complaining that Wright seldom visited the reservations and knew little about the Indians' needs, and that the Indians, though largely self-supporting, were drunkards.

Wright fired back in a letter to Commissioner Jones, reporting that Tinker had only stayed one night, "spent most of his brief visit" conferring with Dr. Wainwright, and "did not talk 30 minutes with me concerning Agency matters." Instead the extent of Tinker's agency inspection was to glance at the cash book and walk through the wareroom. Wright had insisted the inspector accompany him to Soboba, just four miles distance, but he declined. Tinker's claim that he seldom visited the reservations was absurd, Wright said; in the past he had been censured for spending too much on his traveling expense. He did admit, however, that since losing his agency clerk, shortly before Tinker's arrival, he had been forced to do "double duty" and so had "not had as much time to devote to the Indians in the field as I would like." As for the assertion that the Indians were now self-supporting, he pointed out that much of their income came from working as farm hands and sheep shearers—seasonal and uncertain work.[116]

Wainwright remained the focus of most of Wright's attacks. The agent complained to Senator Bard: "[The doctor has] turned against me simply because I have tried to keep him honest." Wright remarked that on the first trip they had made together, in order to sound him out, Wainwright had said, "'You will never make half out of this business that your predecessor did.' I answered him that 'I know what my salary is, I will make that and no more.'"[117] Wright also accused the doctor of printing disparaging articles in the Democratic papers about him and under an assumed name. He "has made it a point for several months to do every thing in his power to discredit me and place me in a bad position. I will dismiss him with the statement that he is one of the most depraved individuals I ever met and he and his few friends will stoop to anything to carry out their schemes."[118]

Besides writing Senator Bard, Wright also complained to California Congressman James C. Needham. It seemed "useless for me to urge that this Agency be continued, the necessity is so apparent to every one save a few disgruntled individuals that it appears inexplicable that the Commissioner should take the position he does." It was not fair that an employee like himself who had "loyally, earnestly and honestly discharged his duties under adverse conditions should be ignored in a matter so important as this." Wright concluded that the continuation of the agency was "essential to the welfare of over 3000 people some of whom have not a place to lay their head." Dr. Wainwright, whom he called a "fraud" and who was "enjoying a sinecure," was a man "whose retention in the service is an insult to honest men."[119]

Dr. Wright's politicking seems to have helped extend his term despite calls from various quarters for his removal. With Bard's support, his position was protected for several more years. In fact, it was Wainwright who lost his job first, when the position of Mission Indian Agency physician was discontinued at the end of June 1901. The agency clerk was restored a year later, along with a second additional farmer. Wright was reconfirmed in his office as late as February 1903, but on July 17, 1903, the Mission-Tule River Consolidated Agency—on the recommendation of Inspector Jenkins—was dissolved and divided into two parts. From then on, the superintendents in charge were regular government employees, rather than political appointees. Dr. Wright retained the northern jurisdiction, headquartered at San Jacinto, while Superintendent Shell was placed in charge of the reservations in the western and southern parts of San Diego County, along with Pechanga in Riverside County, with headquarters at Pala. Both were designated as "superintendent" and "special disbursing agent." Reservations under Wright included Tule River, Palm Springs, Torres-Martinez, Cabazon, Morongo, San Jacinto, San Manuel, Santa Rosa, Santa Ynez, Twenty-Nine Palms, and Cahuilla. Reservations under Shell included Campo, Capitán Grande, Cuyapaipe, Inaja, Los Coyotes, Santa Ysabel (including Mesa Grande), Pala, Pauma, La Jolla, Rincon, Sycuan, La Posta, Manzanita and Pechanga.[120]

In his first annual report as superintendent of the San Jacinto Training School, Wright wrote that despite his change of title, he continued to discharge the same duties as an agent. "I feel that my work has been much more satisfactory and that much more permanent good has been effected on behalf of the Indians."[121] However, many of the same old problems remained in the new agencies. In September 1907 he and a group of white lawmen attempted to prevent the sale of liquor at the annual Soboba fiesta; they were overpowered by a group of Indians and Mexican visitors—one of the lawmen was even locked up in the reservation jail. "Mr. Wright did not consider it wise to attempt to quell the disturbance by ordering the officers to fire on the mob," reported the *Los Angeles Times*. Instead he held a council with the captain and, "by using diplomacy," secured the officer's release.[122]

Wright was criticized for his actions in the investigation that followed. Inspector Charles L. Davis faulted him for his weaknesses, citing his "maladministration" and his "do-nothing policy" that had earned him the Indians' contempt.[123] By then, Wright was clearly on the way out. He resigned in late 1907 when the superintendency was again divided, and Soboba school teacher Will Stanley was placed in charge.[124] Charles Shell, who seems to have been generally well liked during his tenure, did much to defuse the still-tense situation at Pala, and stood up for the Indians during the housing fiasco. He served until 1906.

The split of the Mission Indian Agency in 1903 and Dr. Wright's resignation four years later marked the end of an era. Gone were the days of a single government agent responsible for the many reservations scattered across Southern California. Gone were the days of political appointees and government patronage. The first decades of the twentieth century saw the slow rise of native political power, both on and off the reservations, changing government policies in Washington, and a continuing struggle for survival.

EPILOGUE

The seven men who served as Mission Indian agents were a varied lot. Each had his own strengths and weakness as an administrator and as a man. Each was influenced by his own view of American Indians, often formed long before he arrived in Southern California. They were also influenced by the general policies of the federal government, as well as the activities of the various reform associations that either helped or hindered their efforts. And finally, they were influenced by the pressing events of their time. These factors influenced their effectiveness and their accomplishments.

It has been suggested that federal concern about the Mission Indian Agency was limited because of the settled, peaceful nature of the local natives, especially in the 1870s and 1880s when the "Indian Wars" were still being fought elsewhere. The sheer distance from Washington added to delays and confusion. The agency, with its scattered reservations and villages, differed from the large, centralized reservations elsewhere, where government personnel could take direct charge of affairs—from medical care to distributing rations to dealing with the surrounding white communities and ranchers. The idea of severalty fared no better in Southern California, with the Dawes Act calling for the distribution of much more acreage (not to say livable acreage) than the region's reservations offered. Washington never seemed to quite know what to do with Southern California. As Agent McCallum observed in 1885, the Mission Indians "are not . . . 'agency' or 'reservation' Indians in the sense in which those terms are understood in most agencies." No Mission Indian agent, he explained, "has ever had control of their actions or movements as in [the] case of agency Indians elsewhere." Instead the Mission Indians made their own labor and sale contracts, "which are respected in the courts, the agent advising them only when necessary, so that they would not be defrauded."[1]

Another challenge was the political struggles between the various village and tribal leaders. It must be remembered that the Indian leaders of the time, especially with the waning power of the old hereditary tribal leaders, were *politicians*—with all that implies for good or ill. Some tried to cooperate with the agents; some tried to outmaneuver them; some saw them, as they sometimes were, as simply ineffective; and others, especially on the more isolated reservations, seldom saw them at all.

▼ ▼ ▼

Samuel Lawson certainly brought passion to his job. But passion and success—or even passion and praise—do not always go hand in hand. His successor, John Ward, suggested an interesting explanation for some of the criticism Lawson received from the white community. During his administration Lawson had "endeavored to hold the scales of Justice evenly between the Whites and the Indians," Ward wrote, whereas "I have not attempted to *pose* as the Indian's friend, *right* or *wrong*. This false sentimentalism was carried to such an extent by Mr. Lawson, that to-day he has neither the respect nor the confidence of the community in which he lives."[2]

Pioneer San Bernardino historian George W. Beattie considered Lawson "an able and conscientious executive" but one who had little previous experience with Indians and knew little of their characteristics.[3] Modern scholars Lowell Bean and Harry Lawton judged Lawson "a conscientious and capable executive."[4] A more recent scholar, Tanis Thorne, is far more harsh—"Like other Indian agents, he became infected with a case of paternalistic megalomania. . . . Though well-meaning, he was dangerous because of his power," she continues. "From the native perspective . . . he may well have been viewed as part of the problem, not a part of the solution." Yet she considers him more "sincere" in his efforts "as an advocate for Indian people" than McCallum, Ward, or Rust.[5]

Lawson has also suffered over the years because of his conflicts with Helen Hunt Jackson and her often negative opinion of him. It has thus been easy for later writers to simply mirror her views without looking more closely into his accomplishments, which include aiding in the creation of the Pechanga and Soboba Indian reservations. And his letters to Indian Office officials reflect a real interest and concern for the Mission Indians.

▼ ▼ ▼

Whatever good John McCallum may have accomplished as agent is tarnished by his other actions during and especially after his tenure. His lack of concern about how his business decisions—especially his attempts to control Southern California's most precious natural resource, water—impacted the Palm Springs Indians is disturbing. To take a specific instance, historian Van Garner notes that although McCallum "proclaimed himself a champion of Indian rights, he proved he was not when on September 29, 1884, he testified to the Senate Committee on Indian Affairs that whites who had squatted on desert lands should be awarded titles."[6] Taking into consideration the totality of McCallum's dealings with the Indians (not just as agent), we can conclude that although he may indeed have cared about them, there were other things he cared about even more. As Rachel Dayton Shaw explains in her detailed study of water affairs at Palm Springs, when McCallum began to devote more and more of his efforts to the Palm Valley Land & Water Company, "his ability to serve as an effective Indian Agent was compromised; he was forced to resign in the fall of 1885 because his actions had rewarded himself and his cronies at Indian expense."[7]

▼ ▼ ▼

John Ward's tenure was marred more by what he did not do than what he did. Consider his inability (or his unwillingness) to remove the trespassers at Capitán Grande and Morongo. Or his lack of attention to the construction of a major water project at Capitán Grande. Add to this the amazing rant in his final annual report in 1887, which surpasses anything in any of the published reports of the Mission Indian Agents—and perhaps any of their unpublished correspondence as well.[8] He sounds like an angry parent, frustrated with a disrespectful teen. The analogy seems apt, as Ward clearly viewed the Mission Indians as virtual children, lost without the firm hand of the government—a hand he wished was even firmer. More than once during his tenure, he boasted of his long experience with Southern California's Indians, yet even at the end of his term he sounded more like someone who had observed only the poor, downtrodden few, begging on the fringes of the larger cities, than like a public servant who had spent the better part of two years visiting distant villages and reservations where the Indians were as self-reliant and self-governing as their circumstances permitted.[9] It is difficult to know how else to explain his low opinion of the Indian people—and his continuing high opinion of himself and his ideas. Instead, it is his son, attorney Shirley Ward, who deserves real credit for helping the Mission Indians defend their homes, especially for his unprecedented victory in the Soboba case.

▼ ▼ ▼

With so many important issues decided by the courts or decreed from Washington, Joseph Preston's role was largely one of trying to enforce, negotiate, and adapt to the changing conditions. He does deserve respect, though, if only for his role in physically removing the trespassers at Capitán Grande and Morongo—though Thorne says he was "ambivalent" about his actions at Capitán Grande.[10]

Preston received high praise from several diverse sources. Boston Indian Citizenship Committee member Joshua W. Davis, during the September 1888 Lake Mohonk Conference, described the colonel as possessing a "vigorous grasp of his manifold new duties, reaching out as speedily as possible, inspiring the respect of all, and giving assurance of even-handed justice to white and red man alike." Several months earlier, William H. Waldby, a member of the Board of Indian Commissioners, praised Preston following his investigative tour of Indian schools.[11] Preston's professionalism also impressed Albert K. Smiley, who described him as "a most excellent man and good agent, firm and judicious. All of the conflicting parties [at Morongo] speak well of him."[12]

▼ ▼ ▼

Horatio Rust is a puzzle. How could someone who attracted the support of some of the leading Indian rights activists in the country sow so much discord and discontent? He comes across as the sort of person who aroused strong reactions from the people around him—either positive or negative. It is almost as if there was a disconnect between his academic interest in "Indians" and his demonstrated lack of concern for the people under his care. As agent, he pushed hard for schools, but in an article written soon after he left office, he decried the disappearance of the old traditional ceremonies in Southern California, complaining that "American schools" had made the younger generation "ashamed of the faith of their fathers." The eventual result, he feared, was a people who "will not be white men . . . but they will no longer be Indians." Compare this to his public statement in 1889, claiming that the government's policy was "to break up the tribal relations and give the Indian an industrial education." He admitted this policy was not popular, "but it should receive the support of good citizens."[13] Perhaps he was out of his depth as a government official; he clearly lacked the tact and diplomatic skills necessary.

"Compared to other Indian agents of the era," historian Donald Chaput writes, "Rust was probably as well qualified as any. . . . Yet, his years as agent were filled with bitterness." Among his "several failings" Chaput cites Rust's anti-Catholic bias and his "taking sides in reservation politics." These failings were only made worse with the increased attention Helen Hunt Jackson had brought to the Indians of Southern California; whatever Rust did, "for good or evil, was magnified and publicized widely." However, the "most damning evidence over Rust's abilities," according to Chaput, "came from Professor Charles C. Painter." In a late-April 1892 letter to Commissioner Morgan, Painter had condemned Will Pablo, noting that Rust had been correct in his moves—"however indiscreet [he] may be, and unguarded in his talk, and whatever animosities he has created against himself." Chaput concludes: "With friends of this sort, one doesn't need enemies."[14]

▼ ▼ ▼

Francisco Estudillo had many advantages in his role as agent and seems to have performed his duties well. One does sense in him a lack of urgency, a lack of determination. However, after the work of the 1891 California Mission Indian Commission he dealt well with the sudden increase in the number of reservations under his charge, some of which were very isolated and difficult to reach.

Charles C. Painter was initially skeptical about Estudillo's appointment, writing to President Cleveland that he feared it was an unfortunate selection.[15] But within a few months, he was singing Estudillo's praises to Herbert Welsh of the Indian Rights Association: "I hope and feel a degree of confidence, from all I learn, that he will make the best agent these Indians have had."[16]

In a memorial tribute, H. W. Patton remarked that Estudillo's "greatest sphere of usefulness was entered when he became agent of the Mission Indians in 1893." Patton, an allotting agent closely association with Estudillo for four years, believed that "no official ever treated the Government's wards with more fairness . . . and he was worshipped by all of them." Together they visited reservations repeatedly, and Patton "could see that [Estudillo's] whole thought was for the amelioration of the deplorable conditions which existed then."[17] It is also worth noting that Estudillo was virtually the only Mission Indian agent to mention the various village leaders by name in his annual reports, whereas his fellow agents only mentioned a few major tribal leaders—either to praise or condemn them. Will Pablo's attacks against him in the latter part of his term may well represent his own political maneuvering rather than any failings on Estudillo's part.

▼ ▼ ▼

Lucius A. Wright could lay claim to some practical achievements on the reservations, including wells and irrigation systems, and famine relief during the drought of the late 1890s. But his actions in the San Felipe removal are less praiseworthy. Perhaps because some of his private correspondence survives, we see more of him as a political appointee, soliciting support from elected officials and constantly maneuvering to hold on to his appointment. In the end, he perhaps stayed too long, as the incident at the 1907 Soboba fiesta shows. Yet he clearly believed he was capable of helping the Indians and tried to achieve that goal.

▼ ▼ ▼

Over the years, the Mission Indian agents all faced similar challenges. Charged with helping the Indians, they were dependent on Washington for approval and on a sometimes indifferent Congress for funding. Charged with carrying out government policies—usually designed for reservations utterly unlike their own—the agents found them a moving target, as attitudes, administrations, and approaches changed. Where most reservations across the country were home to a single tribe, the Mission Indian Agency at its peak was expected to serve a dozen different tribal groups, some with long-standing antagonisms against one another. Even more challenging was working with the various tribal and pantribal leaders as they competed for political power. Legally, the Indians were often in limbo, their exact status under the law unclear and inconsistent, while the agents had to navigate multiple layers of local, state, and federal jurisdictions. And all this had to be done in the public eye, where they were open to criticism from government inspectors, special agents, newspaper reporters, Indian rights advocates, and those who recognized no Indian rights at all—each with their own opinion on what should or should not be done. Locally, too many settlers perceived any support for the Indians as a loss to white ranchers and farmers. Conflicts also arose within pro-Indian groups and between individual reformers as they attempted to promote and carry out the programs they thought best. Meanwhile, the vast majority of Americans were largely indifferent—or worse. The Indians' problems were not their concern. That was something for the government (and its Indian agents) to solve. But none of this can absolve these individual Mission Indian agents from the fruits of their labors. Each of them, after all, willingly accepted his position; each of them had his own successes and failures, strengths and weaknesses, and each had an impact on the continuing story of the Indians of Southern California.

▼ ▼ ▼

NOTES

Introduction

1. The term "Mission Indians" was commonly used during the late nineteenth and early twentieth centuries as a generic term for Southern California's native peoples. It reflects the conditions the Americans found in villages and reservations at the time, where in many cases even the Indians who had never had direct contact with the Spanish missions had adopted at least some of the trappings of Spanish civilization: the Spanish language and Catholic beliefs (though both existed side by side with native languages and traditions), and European-style skills such as agriculture and adobe construction.
2. Katherine Ainsworth's book *The McCallum Saga: The Story of the Founding of Palm Springs* (Palm Springs: The Palm Springs Desert Museum, 1973) presents a one-sided view of John McCallum's dealings with the Indians. Tanis Thorne's view is clear from her title, "The Mixed Legacy of Mission Indian Agent S. S. Lawson, 1878–1883" (*Journal of California and Great Basin Anthropology*, vol. 25, no. 2 [2005]: 147–68). Jane Apostol's article "Horatio Nelson Rust: Abolitionist, Archaeologist, Indian Agent" (*California History*, vol. 58, no. 4 [Winter 1979/80]: 304–15) is generally positive, while Donald Chaput's "Horatio N. Rust and the Agent-as-Collector Dilemma" (*Southern California Quarterly*, vol. 64, no. 4 [Winter 1982]: 280–95) is more critical.

1. Superintendents and Special Agents, 1850–1877

Epigraph. Charles A. Wetmore, Report of Chas. A. Wetmore, Special U.S. Commissioner of Mission Indians of Southern California (Washington, D.C.: Government Printing Office [GPO], 1875), 1.

1. For Southern California's tribal groups, see Robert F. Heizer, ed., *Handbook of North American Indians*, vol. 8, *California* (Washington, D.C.: Smithsonian Institution, 1978). See also Lowell John Bean, *Mukat's People: The Cahuilla Indians of Southern California* (Berkeley: University of California Press, 1972); and William McCawley, *The First Angelinos: The Gabrielino Indians of Los Angeles* (Banning, Calif.: Malki Museum Press/Ballena Press, 1996). The importance of Indian labor is discussed by

George Harwood Phillips in *Vineyards and Vaqueros: Indian Labor and the Economic Expansion of Southern California, 1771–1877* (Norman, Okla.: Arthur H. Clark, 2010).

2. "Report of Special Agent John G. Ames, in Regard to the Conditions of the Mission Indians of California, with Recommendations, October 28, 1873," in "Mission Indians of Southern California," *Executive Documents Printed by Order of the House of Representatives*, 1873–74 [House of Representatives, 43d Cong., 1st sess., Ex. Doc. No. 91], vol. 9, p. 545 (Washington, D.C.: GPO, 1874), reprinted in Robert F. Heizer, ed., *Federal Concern about Conditions of California Indians 1853 to 1913: Eight Documents* (Socorro: Ballena Press, 1979), 51–73.
3. For an overview, see James Rawls, *Indians of California: The Changing Image* (Norman: University of Oklahoma Press, 1984); quote on 177.
4. The standard work on the Garra Uprising is George Harwood Phillips, *Chiefs and Challengers: Indian Resistance and Cooperation in Southern California, 1769–1906*, 2nd ed. (Norman: University of Oklahoma Press, 2014). See also William Edward Evans, "The Garra Uprising: Conflict between San Diego Indians and Settlers in 1851," *California Historical Society Quarterly*, vol. 45, no. 4 (December 1966): 339–51; Noel M. Loomis, "The Garra Uprising of 1851," in *Brand Book II* (San Diego: San Diego Corral of The Westerners, 1971), 2–26; and Leonard B. Waitman, "Chief Antonio Garra's Insurrection and the Confederation Myth of 1851," in *Brand Book Number 3* (San Diego: San Diego Corral of The Westerners, 1973), 97–103.
5. The Treaty of Temecula is reproduced in Horace Parker, *The Historic Valley of Temecula, The Treaty of Temecula* (Balboa Island, Calif.: Paisano Press, 1967). For the text of the Treaty of Santa Ysabel, see Michael Connolly Miskwish, *Kumeyaay, A History Textbook*, vol. 1, *Precontact to 1893* (El Cajon, Calif.: Sycuan Press, 2007), 147–51. Dana Ruth Hicks Dunn, in "Strategies for Survival: Indian Transitions in the Mountains of San Diego County, 1846–1907" (Ph.D. diss., University of California, Riverside, 2013), discusses a number of issues surrounding the treaties (127–67).
6. For more, see George Harwood Phillips, *Indians and Indian Agents: The Origins of the Reservation System in California, 1849–1852* (Norman: University of Oklahoma Press, 1997), 68–77, 92–154; and George Harwood Phillips, *"Bringing Them under Subjection": California's Tejón Indian Reservation and Beyond, 1852–1864* (Lincoln: University of Nebraska Press, 2004), 25–61. For the treaties, see Harry Kelsey, "The California Indian Treaty Myth," *Southern California Quarterly*, vol. 55, no. 3 (Fall 1973): 225–38; and Larisa K. Miller, "The Secret Treaties with California's Indians," *Prologue* (Fall/Winter 2013): 38–45.
7. Gerald Thompson, *Edward F. Beale and the American West* (Albuquerque: University of New Mexico Press, 1983). For more on Beale, see Phillips, *"Bringing Them under Subjection,"* 62–92.
8. Rawls, *Indians of California*, 150.
9. See Nat B. Read, *From Mountain Man to Mayor: Don Benito Wilson, Los Angeles 1841–1878* (Santa Monica, Calif.: Angel City Press, 2008).
10. B. D. Wilson, *The Indians of Southern California in 1852: The B. D. Wilson Report and a Selection of Contemporary Comment*, ed. by John Walton Caughey with introduction by Albert L. Hurtado (Lincoln: University of Nebraska Press, 1995), 22.

11. See Michael Magliari, "Free Soil, Unfree Labor: Cave Johnson Couts and the Binding of Indian Workers in California, 1850–1867," *Pacific Historical Review*, vol. 73, no. 3 (August, 2004): 349–89; Iris H. W. Engstrand and Mary F. Ward, "Rancho Guajome: An Architectural Legacy Preserved," *Journal of San Diego History*, vol. 41, no. 4 (Fall 1995): 250–83; and Richard Carrico, *Strangers in a Stolen Land: Indians of San Diego County from Prehistory to the New Deal* (San Diego: Sunbelt Publications, 2008), 96–100, 103.
12. Philips, *Chiefs and Challengers*, 160.
13. Burton to Major E. D. Townsend, January 27, 1856, quoted in Esther Boulton Black, *Rancho Cucamonga and Doña Merced* (Redlands, Calif.: San Bernardino County Museum, 1975), 13. As a result of this meeting, Burton recommended that soldiers visit Antonio's village every four to six weeks. It is interesting to note that Antonio was aware of Indian affairs upstate.

    For more on Antonio, see Louis Doody and Betty Kikumi Meltzer, *Losing Ground: The Displacement of San Gorgonio Pass Cahuilla People in the 19th Century* (Banning, Calif.: Malki-Ballena Press, 2007), 52–79. For a military report from the 1850s, see Robert F. Heizer, ed., "An Early Cahuilla Ethnographic Sketch," *The Masterkey*, vol. 4, no. 1 (January–March 1974): 14–21; and Robert W. Fraser, ed., "Lovell's Report on the Cahuilla Indians," *Journal of San Diego History*, vol. 22, no. 1 (Winter 1976): 4–10. Christopher S. Lovell, a U.S. Army captain, was assigned to report on the local Indians in 1854. Among those he visited were the Cahuillas, living in twenty-two *rancherias*, or villages, "totally unfit for cultivation."
14. Originally abolished in 1860, the California Superintendency was replaced by two superintending agencies, one for the north and the other for the south. In 1864 the agencies were replaced by a new California superintendency. Serving in succession were superintendents Austin Wiley (appointed April 14, 1864), Charles Maltby (March 22, 1865), Billington C. Whiting (October 12, 1866), Bvt. Maj. General John B. McIntosh (June 10, 1869), and Whiting again (June 20, 1870). See Edward E. Hill, *The Office of Indian Affairs, 1824–1880: Historical Sketches* (New York: Clearwater Publishing, 1974), 20–21, 25.
15. Born in Maine in 1881, Stanley came to California during the gold rush. He moved to Los Angeles, serving as county tax assessor from 1866 to 1867. He ran unsuccessfully for county treasurer in 1882. The 1880 census lists him as a farmer. He died sometime in the second half of the 1880s.
16. "Wiley to Indian Commissioner William P. Dole, April 12, 1865," 118–19; and "Stanley to Wiley, March 28, 1865"—both in *Annual Report of the Commissioner of Indian Affairs to the Secretary of the Interior for the Year 1865* (Washington: GPO, 1865) (hereafter cited as *Annual Report of the CIA*, with specific issue number, if present, and year), 119–20. See also Carrico, *Strangers in a Stolen Land*, 104, 106–7.
17. Lovett, who had been in Southern California since at least 1859, was appointed a special agent to investigate Indian affairs in Southern California in April 1865. See the *Los Angeles Tri-Weekly News*, April 22, May 9, July 8, and September 2, 1865.
18. In the early 1840s, Father José Maria Zalvidea, the last missionary at San Luis Rey, made a number of small, provisional land grants to former mission neophytes. These

grants, which took in existing village sites, were confirmed in 1845 by Governor Pío Pico. Including Apis's Little Temecula grant and ranchos at Guajome, Cuca, Buena Vista, and La Jolla, they appear to have been designed to preserve an Indian-owned land base in the face of expanding Mexican settlement. All but La Jolla were eventually confirmed by the U.S. Land Commission. Cave Couts, already the owner of Guajome and Buena Vista, bought out the Indians' claim at La Jolla, and his heirs later obtained a special act of Congress to pursue the claim. Ultimately they failed to secure title to La Jolla. See Phil Brigandi, "The Outposts of Mission San Luis Rey," *Journal of San Diego History*, vol. 45, no. 2 (Spring 1999): 106–112.

19. "Stanley to Wiley, May 19, 1865," 125–26; and "Lovett to Wiley (No. 18, n.d.)," 120–21—both in *Annual Report of the CIA, 1865*. See also Phillips, *Chiefs and Challengers*, 180–83, 189–91; Leland E. Bibb, "Pablo Apis and Temecula," *Journal of San Diego History*, vol. 37, no. 4 (Fall 1991): 256–71; and Anne J. Miller, "Maria Antonia Apis: A Young Luiseño Indian Woman," *Southern California Quarterly*, vol. 86, no. 2 (Summer 2004): 113–26.

20. "Stanley to Wiley, May 19, 1865," 126–27, *Annual Report of the CIA, 1865*.

21. Phillips (*Chiefs and Challengers*, 83) writes that Cota, whose father was José Manuel Cota, was born in 1818 at Mission San Luis Rey and baptized as Manuel Culijuat. He describes Cota as a "puppet" of the Americans, who "used his position to further his own ambitions" (336). Carrico (*Strangers in a Stolen Land*, 110) says Cota was a village captain at the time Couts first appointed him chief. Dunn (*Strategies for Survival*, 121) presents some alternative data on Cota and urges caution "before stating an absolute fact as to Cota's origin and family lineage." In his later years Cota lived at Pala, where he died in 1897. See *Oceanside Blade*, February 12, 1898.

22. Horace Parker, in *The Historic Valley of Temecula: The Temecula Massacre* (Balboa Island, Calif.: Paisano Press, 1971), summarizes the Pauma Massacre, suggesting several possible causes, including the Indians' desire to befriend Americans or simply to avenge long-standing grievances against Mexicans. "It seems to have been a frontier rule," Parker adds (10), "that when only whites were involved in a conflict it was called a *battle;* but when Indians were involved it became a *massacre.*"

23. "Stanley to Wiley, May 19, 1865," *Annual Report of the CIA, 1865*, 127. For a short biography, see Carrico, *Strangers in a Stolen Land*, 123–24, 127–30. See also Richard L. Carrico, "San Diego Indians and the Federal Government: Years of Neglect, 1850–1865," *Journal of San Diego History*, vol. 26, no. 3 (Summer 1980): 164–84; and Joel E. Hyer, *"We Are Not Savages": Native Americans in Southern California and the Pala Reservation, 1840–1920* (East Lansing: Michigan State University Press, 2001), 79–80.

Cota was often accused of being too energetic, and biased—trying to control "his" people and ordering floggings and other forms of corporal punishment. For a few examples see Phillips, *Chiefs and Challengers*, 169–70.

24. Rev. Francis J. Weber, ed., "Rumblings at Pala," *Journal of San Diego History*, vol. 21, no. 4 (Fall 1975): 38–42. Besides Maltby's support, a group of San Diego residents also petitioned for Cota's reinstatement.

25. Hyer, "*We Are Not Savages*," 79.
26. "Stanley to Wiley, May 19, 1865," 127; "Lovett to Wiley (No. 18)," 122, and for quote, 123—both in *Annual Report of the CIA, 1865*.
27. U.S. Congress, House of Representatives, "Stanley to Whiting, August 12, 1867," and "Stanley to Whiting, March 1867," *Message of the President of the United States and Accompanying Documents to the Two Houses of Congress*, 40th Cong., 2d sess., Ex. Doc. no. 1, 113–115. See also Phillips, *Chiefs and Challengers*, 183–84.
28. For the Peace Policy, see Francis Paul Prucha, *American Indian Policy in Crisis: Christian Reformers and the Indian, 1865–1900* (Norman: University of Oklahoma Press, 1976), 46–52, and for quote, 49.
29. "Greene to Parker, December 16, 1869," in "Indian Reservation in San Diego County, Cal.," *Executive Documents Printed by Order of the House, 1869–70*, 8–10 [1003–5]. For more on Greene, see Phillips, *Chiefs and Challengers*, 184–94.
30. See "Greene to Parker, December 16, 1869." Cota, Greene reported, had subsequently been appointed "chief" of the "San Luis Rey, San Bernardino, and Diegenes [Kumeyaay] Indians" by Special Agent Lovett on May 5, 1859, and as "general-in-chief" over all the "San Diego Indians" by Superintendent Charles Maltby on April 4, 1866. In truth Cota's authority never extended that far.
31. "Greene to Parker, December 16, 1869," 10–11. The Rancho Rincon del Diablo, carved out of former Mission San Diego de Alcalá lands, was originally granted to Juan Bautista Alvardo in 1843 and patented to his heirs. It was later sold off, first to Judge Oliver S. Witherby and later to Edward McGeary, and used for stock raising.
32. For Greene's report and supporting evidence, see *Executive Documents Printed by Order of the House, 1869–70*, 11–12. See also the *Daily Alta California*, April 9, 1870.

    Since only four days separated the sending of Greene's report and Grant's executive orders, it is obvious that Greene's report was simply the final confirmation of a policy the Indian Office had been recommending for several years.
33. "Greene to Parker, August 30, 1870," *Annual Report of the CIA, 1870*, quote on 90.
34. Ibid., 92–93. See also "The Indian Reservation Swindle," April 21, 1870; and "A Word for the Indians," May 26, 1870—both in the *San Diego Union*.
35. "Greene to Whiting, February 20, 1871," *Annual Report of the CIA, 1871*, 342.
36. "Greene to Parker, August 30, 1870," *Annual Report of the CIA, 1870*, quotes on 94.
37. "Greene to Whiting, February 20, 1871," *Annual Report of the CIA, 1871*, 341–45, quotes on 344.
38. Ibid., 344.

    Like Pala, Santa Ysabel had once been a mission outpost under the control of Mission San Diego. But the adobe chapel at Santa Ysabel had all but melted away by the 1880s, to be replaced by the current-day chapel, dedicated in 1924. See Charles Russell Quinn, *The Story of Mission Santa Ysabel* (Downey, Calif.: Elena Quinn, 1964).
39. For the list of village captain's names, including José Maria Moro and a representative of Manuel Largo, see Phillips, *Chiefs and Challengers*, 188–89; see also 195–203. The judge was careful to explain that he and the other officials were certifying only the statements the Indians had made to them.

For more on the Olegario / Cota rivalry, see Richard L. Carrico, "The Struggle for Native American Self-Determination in San Diego County," *Journal of California and Great Basin Anthropology* (1980): 199, 201, 203–4, 206–10; Carrico, *Strangers in a Stolen Land*, 111–12 (on the election), 120–23, and 130–31; and Hyer, *"We Are Not Savages,"* 82–86.

40. This quote is from a *San Francisco Evening Bulletin* interview with Olegario (October 27, 1871), originally in the *Los Angeles News.* Although he was sometimes called Olegario Sali or Olegario Calac, contemporary sources referred to Olegario as Manuel Olegario or simply Olegario. At the time of the interview, he was about forty years old and had spent much of the 1860s working in Los Angeles. He had returned to the area in 1869. Richard A. Hanks calls him a nephew of José Calac, a signer of the Treaty of Temecula. See *This War Is for a Whole Life: The Culture of Resistance among Southern California Indians, 1850–1966* (Banning, Calif.: Ushkana Press, 2012), 40.
41. "Greene to Whiting, February 20, 1871," *Annual Report of the CIA, 1871*, 342. Not long after Cota left Agua Tibia, the ranch passed to the Utt family, which would own it for many years.
42. Hyer, *"We Are Not Savages,"* 83–84. Trujillo is often described as Cota's sister, but the precise relationship in unclear. Helen Hunt Jackson attended her funeral in the spring of 1882 and afterward spent the night with her daughter on the Cuca ranch. See Mathes and Brigandi, *A Call for Reform: The Southern California Indian Writings of Helen Hunt Jackson* (Norman: University of Oklahoma Press, 2015), 24, 105–8.
43. "Part III. Executive Orders Relating to Indian Reserves," in *Indian Affairs: Laws and Treaties*, ed. Charles J. Kappler, vol. 1, *Law*, (Washington, D.C.: GPO, 1904), 819–20.
44. Just as the reservations were cancelled, the U.S. Army adopted a policy of prohibiting military officers from serving as agents, and in February 1871 Lt. Greene was replaced by John R. Tansey, whose appointment had been approved the previous December.
45. Phillips, *Chiefs and Challengers*, 200–1. See also "From Los Angeles—The Indian Council," *Sacramento Daily Union*, September 13, 1871. Warner was also on friendly terms with "Old" Chief Cabezon and his son.
46. In "Trouble among the Mission Indians," the *Sacramento Daily Union* (March 11, 1872) reported "open resistance" to the authority of José Antonio Sal by Olegario and his followers.
47. In "A New Indian Agent," the *Los Angeles Daily Star* (May 14, 1873) reported that Ames was a son-in-law of Secretary of the Interior Columbus Delano (1809–96) and expected to be made a special inspector for the department in June. In later years he lived in Washington, D.C., dying there in 1910.
48. "Report of Special Agent John G. Ames," in "Mission Indians of Southern California," *Executive Documents Printed by Order of the House*, 538.
49. Like Pablo Apis at Temecula, José Panto (ca. 1803–74), whom Sleigh called "Panto Lion," was not from San Pasqual but came in the mid-1830s after the secularization of the Mission San Diego. Unlike Apis, he was a signer of one of the 1852 treaties. The San Pasqual village had been organized as an Indian pueblo by the Mexican government, and until his death Panto did his best to preserve the Kumeyaays' rights.

See Glenn Farris, "Captain José Panto and the San Pascual Indian Pueblo in San Diego County, 1835–1878," *Journal of San Diego History*, vol. 43, no. 2 (Spring 1997): 116–31; David L. Toler Jr., *Band of Blood: An Ipai Family Story* (San Diego: Sunbelt Publications, 2015), 71–75, 78–79, 81, 83, 91, 96–97, 101, 114; and Carrico, *Strangers in a Stolen Land*, 118–20.

50. "Luther E. Sleigh, July 31, 1873," included in "Report of Special Agent John G. Ames," in "Mission Indians of Southern California," *Executive Documents Printed by Order of the House*, 6 [539].

51. Ibid.

52. This was the Rancho Cuca, not to be confused with the Potrero on today's Morongo Indian Reservation.

53. "Report of Special Agent John G. Ames," in "Mission Indians of Southern California," *Executive Documents Printed by Order of the House*, 7 [540].

54. Ibid., 7–8 [540–41]. See also "The Pala Indians," *San Diego Union*, August 7, 1873. Local American opinion also extolled the leadership of José Antonio Sal. The *Daily Alta California* (quoted in the *San Diego Union*, October 13, 1875) considered Sal a "prosperous and thrifty" farmer "who inclines to civilized life." Like Cota, the paper reported, he was of mixed heritage (presumably Mexican and Indian). On the other hand, the reporter claimed, Olegario was "still full of the savage instinct, and retires as much as possible from the neighborhood of the white man." Meanwhile, in "The Mission Indians," the *Sacramento Daily Union* (October 16, 1875) echoed Ames's defense of Olegario.

55. Ames was told that the Potrero was "regarded as a kind of retreat for the squaws and the aged of the tribe." Once thought to be well fortified, the canyon had recently been breached by a white man who had built a rude dwelling in the upper part. See Ames, "Report of Special Agent John G. Ames," in "Mission Indians of Southern California," *Executive Documents Printed by Order of the House*, 9 [542].

56. Ibid. In late 1823 a Mexican military expedition met a Cahuilla chief they called Chihachia. According to an elderly Cahuilla informant, this was the father of "Old" Chief Cabezon, mentioned as a tribal leader as early as 1845. See Lowell John Bean and William Marian Mason, *Diaries and Accounts of the Romero Expeditions in Arizona and California* (Palm Springs, Calif.: Palm Springs Desert Museum, 1962), 37, 102, 37n. According to Tom Hughes in *History of Banning and San Gorgonio Pass* (Banning, Calif.: Banning Record Print, 1938, p. 107), French Gilman, an early settler in the pass, remembered Cabezon as "a very tall, strongly built man, who carried his big head with ease and dignity." Anthropologist William Duncan Strong reported that Cabezon's village was near the mouth of Painted Canyon, about two miles northeast of Mecca, and that he was already the leader of several villages before the Mexicans recognized him as a chief. See Strong, *Aboriginal Society in Southern California* (Berkeley: University of California Publications in American Archaeology and Anthropology 26, 1929), 53–54. "Old" Chief Cabezon died in 1884. See "Death of Oldest Inhabitant," *Los Angeles Herald*, March 22, 1884. In the second half of the nineteenth century, the lower end of the Coachella Valley was sometimes called the Cabezon Valley.

57. "Report of Special Agent John G. Ames," in "Mission Indians of Southern California," *Executive Documents Printed by Order of the House*, 8–9 [541–42]. For more about the indigenous people in the San Gorgonio Pass, see Doody and Meltzer, *Losing Ground*.

58. Born about 1820, Largo was an important Cahuilla leader from the 1850s to the 1870s. After Juan Antonio's death, Largo moved to the Cahuilla area (modern-day Anza), where he was known for controlling his followers and for his resistance to encroaching white settlers. The *San Diego Union*, in "Our Indians" (July 3, 1873), wrote: "Largo is a remarkably intelligent Indian, and feels the dignity of his position fully. He is in fact a monarch in that part of the county, and his word is law among the Indians, and his mandates are executed without question. . . . [He] has driven off all who have attempted to locate there [at Cahuilla], and takes toll from all stock men whose cattle may graze upon those lands." In 1877, as age and failing vision hampered him, he passed his leadership to Fernando Lugo (*San Diego Union*, July 12, 1877). Yet Largo remained active, visiting with Agent Samuel S. Lawson at least twice in 1879 and meeting with Helen Hunt Jackson during her visit to Cahuilla in 1883. He died sometime in 1889 after wandering off into the hills alone. See "Old Chief's Death," *Los Angeles Times*, October 26, 1889.

For Antonio's death from smallpox, see "Correspondence," *Los Angeles Star*, February 21, 28, 1863.

59. "Report of Special Agent John G. Ames," in "Mission Indians of Southern California," *Executive Documents Printed by Order of the House*, 9–10 [542–43].

60. One of these was apparently Pedro Pablo, "who claims to be a chief of the Pala Indians" but had been working in Los Angeles for some time. With Christopher N. Wilson as his attorney, Pablo set out to challenge the state's voter registration laws. The *Los Angeles Daily Star*, however, believed Wilson's real goal was to prove that California's Indians were "denied political privileges and should therefore be protected in their lands by the Government." See the *Star*, "A Nice Question," June 15, 1873, and also "Gives Him Pause," June 20, 1873.

The Ohio-born Wilson (1830–1914) attended Alleghany College in Pennsylvania and received a law degree from Columbia University. Admitted to the bar in Washington, D.C., in 1869, he came to Southern California around 1870. For years he had a bee ranch near San Fernando (there is still a Wilson Canyon today) and a law practice in Los Angeles. His interest in Indians began while working on a survey crew in the Crow River country of Minnesota in the 1850s. Commissioned a major in the California State Guard, he was also active in the Historical Society of Southern California. See Oscar T. Shuck, ed., *History of the Bench and Bar of California* (Los Angeles: Commercial Printing House, 1901), 969. His descendants remained prominent in San Fernando Valley affairs for many years.

61. "Report of Special Agent John G. Ames," in "Mission Indians of Southern California," *Executive Documents Printed by Order of the House*, 10–11 [543–44].

62. Ibid., 12, 15 [545, 548].

63. Ibid., 14–15 [547–48].

64. Ibid., 15–16 [547–49].
65. "The Mission Indians," *San Diego Union*, September 11, 1873.
66. "The Mission Indians. What Should Be Done for Them," *San Diego Union*, January 23, 1874. (Italics in original. Unless noted otherwise, all italics in quotations appear in the original.) The *San Francisco Evening Bulletin*, January 28, 1874, scoffed at Ames's reservation proposal, dubbing it "a new Indian nursery."
67. Born in Maine, Wetmore (1847–1927) came to California with his parents. He lived briefly in San Diego. In 1870 he joined the staff of the *Alta California*, the oldest newspaper in San Francisco, and served as its Washington correspondent. He was a founding member of the State Viticultural Commission, and his former winery, Cresta Blanca in Livermore, California, is now a state historical landmark. See Theodore S. Van Dyke, *The City and County of San Diego: Illustrated and Containing Biographical Sketches of Prominent Men and Pioneers* (San Diego: Leberthon & Taylor, 1888), 114–17.
    The rival *San Francisco Chronicle* claimed that local Congressman S. O. Houghton had arranged for Wetmore's appointment so he could recommend the purchase of a new reservation, which would only profit the "Indian Ring" (which included Houghton). The *San Diego Union* denied all this. See "The Latest 'Chronicle' Sensation," *San Diego Daily Union*, October 29, 1875.
68. "Commissions under Indian Legislation by Congress: Mission Indians in California," *Annual Report of the CIA, 1874*, 18.
69. Wetmore, *Report of Chas. A. Wetmore*, 10–11. For Wetmore's arrival in San Diego, see "Visit of the Special Agent to the Southern Californian Missions," *Daily Alta California*, October 19, 1874.
70. Wetmore, *Report of Chas. A. Wetmore*, 11.
71. *Los Angeles Herald*, October 29, 1875. See also Wetmore, *Report of Chas. A. Wetmore*, 14–15.
72. *Report of Chas. A. Wetmore*, 13.
73. Jesuit scholar Francis Paul Prucha writes that American society "preached a 'pure' Americanism" that "eventually coalesced into the nativistic American Protective Association at the very time that Indian reform reached a climax." This association was strongly anti-Catholic, and Wetmore's policy would never have succeeded. Prucha, "Indian Policy Reform and American Protestantism, 1880–1900," in *Indian Policy in the United States*, 247.
74. Wetmore, *Report of Chas. A. Wetmore*, 5; see 15–17 for testimonials.
75. "The Temecula Indians. Rumors of Impending Trouble with Them," *San Diego Union*, September 30, 1875. The writer praised Wetmore as the only special agent to have "any comprehension" of his duties.
76. Dryden (ca. 1820–1894) came to California from Ohio in 1851 and held pastorates in Marysville, Stockton, San Jose, and Santa Cruz before becoming the first regularly appointed pastor of the First Methodist Episcopal Church in San Diego in 1869. Historian C. V. Anthony remembered him: "Genial, pleasant in speech, wielding an able pen, he soon [after his arrival] took rank among the strong men of the [California] Conference." See C. V. Anthony, *Fifty Years of Methodism: A History of the Methodist*

Episcopal Church within the Bounds of the California Annual Conference from 1847 to 1897 (San Francisco: Methodist Book Concern, 1901), 55–56. While the California Annual Conference of the Methodist Episcopal Church praised his work as Indian agent, it refused to return him to a church appointment after his term was over because of his unorthodox views on Christianity. See *Minutes of the Twenty-Fourth Session of the California Annual Conference of the Methodist Episcopal Church* (San Francisco: Methodist Book Depository, 1876), 26, 62. He was later affiliated with the New Jerusalem Church, a Swedenborgian denomination. He died in 1894 and is buried in Gilroy.

77. *San Diego Union*, October 14, 1875. The California senator in question was presumably Aaron A. Sargent.

78. "Dryden to Smith, June 30, 1875," *Annual Report of the CIA, 1875*, 223.

A graduate of Andover Theological Seminary, Smith (1827–76) initially served as a Congregational pastor in Pepperell, Massachusetts. His work with the American Missionary Association led to his appointment as Indian agent at the Chippewa Agency in Minnesota. He was appointed Indian commissioner in March 1873. See Richard C. Crawford, "Edward Parmelee Smith, 1873–75," in *The Commissioners of Indian Affairs, 1824–1977*, ed. Robert M. Kvasnicka and Herman J. Viola (Lincoln: University of Nebraska Press, 1979), 141–47.

79. "Dryden to Smith, June 30, 1875," *Annual Report of the CIA, 1875*, 224.

80. "The New Era," *San Diego Daily Union*, June 1, 1873. See also Hyer, *"We Are Not Savages,"* 87–90; and Carrico, *Strangers in a Stolen Land*, 137–38 (for an analysis of local newspaper coverage of the removal, see 138–42).

81. "From Temecula. The Indian Occupants Quietly Ejected by Sheriff Hunsaker," *San Diego Union*, September 30, 1875. For Jackson's account, see "The Temecula Exiles," *The Independent*, November 29, 1883, reprinted in Mathes and Brigandi, *A Call for Reform*, 113–23. See also Phillips, *Chiefs and Challengers*, 207–8.

The number of persons evicted varies; the *Union* says about one hundred, Olegario told a reporter about two hundred, and Agent Dryden estimated three hundred. The lower figure seems more reasonable.

82. "D. A. Dryden to Smith," undated short report following his letter of June 30, 1875, *Annual Report of the CIA, 1875*, 225.

83. "San Diego Indian Troubles," *Los Angeles Daily Star*, October 8, 1875. This account apparently came from Sheriff Hunsaker. A few days later (October 12, 1875), the *Star* complained that "Olegario is a bad Indian and has great influence with his people, and refuses to listen to mild counsels."

84. For Estudillo quote, see "The Temecula Indians. An Outbreak Imminent—Threatening Attitude of Olegario and His Band," October 7, 1875 (from daily of October 3); for final quote see "The Temecula Indian Troubles," October 7, 1875—both in the *San Diego Union*.

85. For first quote, see "The Temecula Case. Dispatch from General Schofield," *San Diego Weekly Union*, October 7, 1875. For the second, see "The Temecula Indians," *San Diego Union*, October 14, 1875. The *Union* later defended its coverage in "A Word with the 'Record-Union,'" *Daily Union*, October 30, 1875. For a pro-settler account, see "The

Mission Indians: The End of the Promised War," *Daily Alta California*, October 17, 1875.

86. "The Temecula Indians," *Los Angeles Herald*, October 16, 1875. For another sympathetic article, see "The Mission Indians," *Sacramento Daily Union*, October 16, 1875. For Dryden's reappointment, see "The M. E. State Conference," *Los Angeles Star*, September 25, 1875.
87. "Report of the Commissioner of Indian Affairs," *Annual Report of the CIA, 1875*, 10–11.
88. "That Olegario and his followers drew up petitions and hired an attorney is fascinating," notes Hyer in *"We Are Not Savages"* (85). "They were gradually learning that they had to address acts of injustice using methods that whites could comprehend. For this to have occurred during the nineteenth century is rather unique in Native American history." For an unsympathetic view, see "Olegario Again at Los Angeles," *Daily Alta California*, October 18, 1875, in which the reporter concluded, "The piteous howl which comes from Olegario is a bid for supplies from the Government, which shall not be given."
89. "A Pointed Letter. The Facts Relating to the Temecula Case," *San Diego Union*, November 11, 1875; "Olegario in Washington," November 16, 1875, and "Condensed Telegrams," November 18, 1875—both in the *Los Angeles Herald*. For Kalisher's support of Olegario, see Richard L. Carrico, "Wolf Kalisher: Immigrant, Pioneer Merchant and Indian Advocate," *Western States Jewish Historical Quarterly*, vol. 15, no. 2 (1983).
90. "The Temeculas at Washington," *Sacramento Daily Union*, November 19, 1875. The "Indian ring" was probably a reference to the activities of President U. S. Grant's secretary of war, William W. Belknap, who was impeached but acquitted of accepting bribes for lucrative trading post contracts on Indian reservations.
91. See "Mission Indian Reserves," *Annual Report of the CIA, 1882*, 253; and Carrico, "The Struggle for Native American Self-Determination," 209; Carrico, *Strangers in a Stolen Land*, 143, with map; Hyer, *"We Are Not Savages,"* 90–92, with map on 91; and "Settlement of the Mission Indian Question," *Los Angeles Express*, January 20, 1876.

    While congressional action on behalf of the Mission Indians took years to accomplish, executive order reservations setting aside public money often took only weeks.
92. Vandever (1811–93) was an attorney and Union Civil War veteran who served several terms as a congressman representing both Iowa and California. He served as an Indian inspector from 1873 to 1878 and then lost his appointment due to his increasing criticism of federal Indian policy. He moved to California in 1884 and spent the last years of his life in Ventura County. See Douglas Firth Anderson, "'More Conscience than Force': U.S. Indian Inspector William Vandever, Grant's Peace Policy, and Protestant Whiteness," *Journal of the Gilded Age and Progressive Era*, vol. 9, no. 2 (April 2010): 167–96.
93. William Vandever, *Mission Indians of California: Report of William Vandever, United States Indian Inspector* (Washington, D.C.: n.p., 1876). For quotes, see 4. The ranch owners were B. M. Hartsborn of San Francisco and A. H. Wilcox of San Diego.

    The Ohio-born Smith (1824–1901) served one term in the House of Representatives before becoming Grant's last Indian commissioner. See Edward E. Hill, "John Q. Smith, 1875–77," in Kvasnicka and Viola, *The Commissioners*, 149–53.

94. Vandever, *Mission Indians of California*, quotes on 6, 3.
95. Martinez is located northeast of Mecca. The modern community of Cabazon (note the misspelling) in the San Gorgonio Pass was named by the Southern Pacific railroad in Cabezon's honor.
96. For executive reservations, see "Mission Indian Reserves," *Annual Report of the CIA, 1882*, 253.
97. State school land was given to the state to be sold to provide funds for public schools. See W. W. Robinson, *Land in California* (Berkeley: University of California Press, 1948), 187.
98. "The Mission Indian Agency," *San Diego Union*, July 30, 1876 (quoting the *Los Angeles Express*) for first quote; and "Letter from Indian Agent Dryden," *San Diego Union*, August 3, 1876, for the second.
99. Commonly employed as sheep shearers, they also picked fruit, harvested grain, cut firewood, and at times were employed as cowboys on various ranches. A few years later, Agent Samuel S. Lawson complained that Indian workers faced problems with not getting paid or not getting paid as much as promised in cash, and were instead paid in goods or liquor. When one Indian complained, his employer shot him in the face with buckshot; Lawson had the man arrested. See "Lawson to Trowbridge, August 17, 1880," *Annual Report of the CIA, 1880*, 13.
100. "Colburn to Smith, August 15, 1877," *Annual Report of the CIA, 1877*, 36–37.
101. Morongo (ca. 1845–1898), a prominent Serrano tribal leader, later served as an interpreter for agents Lawson and Horatio Nelson Rust, and for Moravian cleric William Henry Weinland, assisting the latter in successfully establishing a Women's National Indian Association mission at the Potrero village. For more on his work with Weinland, see Valerie Sherer Mathes, *Divinely Guided: The California Work of the Women's National Indian Association* (Lubbock: Texas Tech University Press, 2012), 196–98, 225–26, 246–47. Morongo was often at odds with Cahuilla tribal leader Will Pablo.
102. In the late nineteenth century, white settlers generally called this area "the Potrero" (which is Spanish for "pasture land"); however, the original Cahuilla residents called it "Malki." In the mid-nineteenth century Serrano people began moving in, and the reservation eventually became known as "Morongo," "derived from the Serrano name for their people, Maringayam." See Lowell John Bean and Harry Lawton, *The Cahuilla Indians of Southern California* (Banning, Calif.: Malki Museum Press, 1965), 3. As early as 1887, Charles C. Painter, who represented the powerful Indian Rights Association as their agent in Washington, used "Morongo" to designate the reservation; gradually "Morongo" replaced "Potrero" in government documents. The name Malki was mostly used by Agent Clara True in the early 1900s and is best known today as the name of the museum on the reservation.
103. Colburn to Smith, August 3, 1877, Letter Received (LR) #1085–1877, Record Group 75, Special Case 31, Office of Indian Affairs, National Archives, Washington, D.C. (hereafter cited as RG 75, SC 31, OIA, NA).

The Desert Land Act, passed on March 3, 1877, enabled citizens to file a claim on 640 acres with a small initial payment in return for a promise to irrigate part of the property within three years. Once this requirement was met, the entire section could be purchased for one dollar per acre.

104. For a general overview, see W. W. Robinson, *Land in California* (Berkeley: University of California Press, 1948), 147–92.

105. For the executive orders, see "Mission Indian Reserves," *Annual Report of the CIA, 1882*, 253–54; for the August 25 order, see Doody and Meltzer, *Losing Ground*, 91.

106. "Colburn to Smith, August 15, 1877," *Annual Report of the CIA, 1875*, 38. This Rincon was a village in the lower Coachella Valley, not Olegario's home near the San Luis Rey River.

107. Ibid.

108. *Annual Report of the CIA, 1878*, xliv.

2. Setting the Stage: Samuel S. Lawson, 1878–1883

Epigraph. "Lawson to Price, August 20, 1881," Annual Report of the CIA, 1881, 13.

1. In May 1878, Frazee or his supporters had sent three letters to President Hayes in favor of endorse his candidacy—one signed by John Morongo as "chief of the Mission Indians of Southern California"; the second, signed by "Old" Chief Cabezon and others; and the third, which mentions a "Mr. Ubuck" of San Diego County who was also seeking the position—possibly a garbled reference to Father Anthony Ubach, the San Diego parish priest and defender of the Indians. How well these letters actually reflect the Indians' views is unknown. See Doody and Meltzer, *Losing Ground*, 95–96; and Phillips, *Chiefs and Challengers*, 231.

   Frazee (1822–1902) was an attorney, author, and editor of the *San Bernardino Argus*.

2. *Journal of the Executive Proceedings of the Senate of the United States of America, from March 5, 1877, to March 3, 1879, Inclusive*, vol. 21 (Washington, D.C.: GPO, 1901), 358. Riverside County was formed in 1893; and Imperial County, in 1907.

3. N. H. Hill, comp., *History of Coshocton County, Ohio: Its Past and Present, 1740–1881* (Newark, Ohio: A. A. Graham, 1881), 489; *The History of Henry County, Illinois, Its Tax-Payers and Voters* (Chicago: H. F. Kett, 1877), 471 and, for Lawson's pastorate and college education, 534–35. For his service record, see *Official Roster of the Soldiers of the State of Ohio in the War of the Rebellion, 1871–1866*, vol. 4 (Akron: Werner Printing, 1887), 601; William J. Bahmer, *Centennial History of Coshocton County Ohio*, vol. 1 (Chicago: S. J. Clarke, 1909), 128; U.S. Civil War Soldier Records and Profiles, 1861–1865, and U.S. Civil War Pension Index, General Index to Pension Files, 1861–1934, both available on Ancestry.com. It seems unlikely that Lawson became an officer, but like many public figures he was given the honorific title of colonel.

4. Thorne, "The Mixed Legacy of Mission Indian Agent S. S. Lawson," 147. For Grant's Peace Policy, see Prucha, *American Indian Policy in Crisis*, 30–102; and Robert H. Keller, *American Protestantism and United States Indian Policy, 1869–82* (Lincoln: University of Nebraska Press, 1983), 17–45 and, for the program's termination, 188–204. See also Francis Paul Prucha, "Assignment of Indian Agencies to Religious Societies," in *Documents of United States Indian Policy* (Lincoln: University of Nebraska Press, 1990), 143.

At the time of Lawson's appointment, the Peace Policy was a decade old, and the Republican Party that nominated Rutherford B. Hayes made no mention in its platform of continuing the policy. Furthermore, Hayes's selection of Carl Schurz as secretary of the interior in 1877 spelled its death knell. Therefore, there is some question whether Lawson was in fact a Peace Policy appointee.

5. "Lawson to Price, August 7, 1882," *Annual Report of the CIA, 1882*, 12.
6. Lawson to Hayt, December 27, 1878, LR #15–1879, RG 75, SC 31, OIA, NA.
7. Ibid.

   Born in New York State, Hayt (1823–1902) served as treasurer and later chairman of the Board of Foreign Missions of the Reformed Church's finance committee. He was a member of the Board of Indian Commissioners before being appointed as commissioner, serving during the Hayes presidency. See Roy W. Meyer, "Ezra A. Hayt, 1877–89," in Kvasnicka and Viola, *The Commissioners*, 155–66.
8. Where earlier statutes had made farmers responsible for protecting their fields from wandering livestock, the no fence laws of the 1870s made stock owners liable for any damage their animals caused.
9. Lawson to Hayt, December 27, 1878, LR #15–1879, RG 75, SC 31, OIA, NA.
10. This was probably the Verdugo family, who lived in the area until the 1950s. In the early 1920s, nearby rancher Henry Bergman (1863–1930) assisted them in securing a forty-acre homestead, located due south of the Aguanga Store at the foot of Palomar Mountain. In 1954 historian Horace Parker visited the two remaining brothers, Felix and Cayatan, and noted, "This clan or group at Aguanga, according to Felix were Temeculas, although their dialect was a little different." Even in the mid-twentieth century, one of the brothers always remained on their homestead when the other was away. Both men had died by 1958. See Horace Parker Research Notes (in a spiral notebook marked "New Temecula 80s"), Sherman Library and Gardens, Corona del Mar, California.
11. Lawson to Hayt, December 27, 1878, LR #15–1879, RG 75, SC 31, OIA, NA.
12. Ibid.
13. Lawson to Hayt, April 21, 1879, LR #413–1879, RG 75, SC 31, OIA, NA.
14. "Lawson to Hayt, August 28, 1879," *Annual Report of the CIA, 1879*, 15. G. Hazen Shinn, a local resident during the late 1880s, also praised Morongo, describing him as "the most intelligent and foremost Indian of Southern California in his time." An official interpreter, who was fluent in English and in the Cahuilla and Serrano dialects, as well as an adviser to Indian agents and manager of local Indian affairs, Morongo did not smoke or drink, "had an uncanny sense for detecting liquor violators, and was the bane of the low-lived white sellers of liquor to Indians." Shinn found him "to be courteous in speech and manner and an entertaining conversationalist," as well as "well versed in [American] manners and customs." Shinn strangely reports that Juan Morongo was Chief Cabezon's nephew (which has probably led some later writers astray). See G. Hazen Shinn, *Shoshonean Days* (Glendale, Calif.: Arthur H. Clark Co., 1941), 26, 28, 36, 90.
15. Lawson to Hayt, December 27, 1878, LR #15–1879, RG 75, SC 31, OIA, NA.

16. Doody and Meltzer, *Losing Ground*, 91.
17. In the early 1860s, the captain of the rancheria was named Torres (sometimes garbled as "Toros"), thus giving the village its modern name. See Jane Davies Gunther, *Riverside County, California, Place Names* (Riverside, Calif.: Rubidoux Printing, 1984), 546.
18. Lawson to Hayt, November 28, 1878, LR #826–1878, RG 75, SC 31, OIA, NA.
19. Ibid. Perhaps this was the area later set aside as the Mission Creek Reservation.

   "Mr. Hickman" was undoubtedly William Hickman, a Los Angeles businessman who intended to use a flume on the Potrero Creek as part of his plan to move lumber from the San Bernardino Mountains down to the Southern Pacific railroad. Because this would require control of the creek and all lands in Section 36 that it flowed through, he filed suit against the Indians, who desperately needed this water for their own needs. The case of *William Hickman v. Captain John Morongo et al.* was tried in San Bernardino in February 1878. The Indians won, and Hickman sold his interest to James H. Lawrence, who reminded government officials that the executive order had excluded Sections 16 and 36 and thus the land did not actually belong to the Indians. For more, see Doody and Meltzer, *Losing Ground*, 92–95, 99, 103, 125, 134.
20. Cecil C. Moyer, *Historic Ranchos of San Diego* (San Diego: Union-Tribune Publishing, 1969), 61–65; and Philip S. Rush, *Some Old Ranchos and Adobes* (San Diego: Neyenesch Printers, 1965), 72–74.
21. "Report of Special Agency John G. Ames," October 28, 1873, in "Mission Indians of Southern California," *Executive Documents Printed by Order of the House*, 7 [540]; and "A Visit to Smith's Mountain," *San Diego Union*, June 22, 1876.
22. *San Diego Daily Union*, June 27, 1877. See also Carrico, *Strangers in a Stolen Land*, 144–45.
23. Carrico, *Strangers in a Stolen Land*, 145, for initial quote; *San Diego Union*, July 19, 1877; for Olegario's death, see *San Diego Union*, August 9, 1887.
24. *San Diego Union*, August 18, 1877; and Phillips, *Chiefs and Challengers*, 212.
25. Scott to Lawson, December 7, 1878, included in Lawson to Hayt, December 17, 1878, LR #863–1878, RG 75, SC 31, OIA, NA.

   Scott's letter had been sent from the Couts family home at Guajome. Couts and his bride had received another of the small "Indian" ranchos at Buena Vista as a wedding present.
26. "Calendar. Eighteenth District Court," *San Diego Union*, August 5, 1877. Because both cases were heard in San Diego, Olegario and Calac were represented by the local firm of Jeff Gatewood and A. B. Hotchkiss, instead of by Christopher Wilson, who had served as Olegario's attorney in the past. Olegario visited San Diego to consult with the lawyers at least once in June–July 1877. For more, see Carrico, *Strangers in a Stolen Land*, 144–45.

   One wonders if the Calac suit was actually Trujillo's idea, as it would seem to pit her against her own relatives.
27. Scott to Lawson, December 17, 1878, LR #863–1878, RG 75, SC 31, OIA, NA. See also Lawson to Hayt, April 5, 1879, LR #348–1879, RG 75, SC 31, OIA, NA.

28. Lawson to Hayt, December 17, 1878, LR #863–1878, RG 75, SC 31, OIA, NA.
29. Lawson to Hayt, April 5, 1879, LR #348–1879, RG 75, SC 31, OIA, NA.
30. "Local News. Board of Supervisors," *San Diego Union*, January 9, 1880.
31. "Lawson to Trowbridge, August 17, 1880," *Annual Report of the CIA, 1880*, 12.

Trowbridge (1821–81) served in the Michigan state house and as a U.S. congressman. His appointment was due to his college friendship with President Hayes. See Michael A. Goldman, "Roland E. Trowbridge, 1880–81," in Kvasnicka and Viola, *The Commissioners*, 167–72.

Much of the rancho was acquired in the 1890s by the Mendenhalls, a pioneer Palomar cattle family, with the Trujillo heirs retaining just three hundred acres. See *Oceanside Blade*, January 22, 1898.

32. Lawson to Wiggington, December 21, 1878, LR #29–1879, RG 75, SC 31, OIA, NA.

Wigginton (1839–90) accompanied his family from Illinois to Wisconsin, where he attended the University in Madison, starting a law practice in 1859. He moved to California in 1862, serving as district attorney of Merced County before his 1875 election to Congress.

33. O. W. Giles to Interior Secretary Carl Schurz, October 12, 1878, LR #316–1879, RG 75, SC 31, OIA, NA. This package included a petition addressed to Secretary Schurz with 296 signatures, accompanied by a number of personal letters, several addressed to J. K. Luttrell, congressman from California's third district. Giles was a pastor of a San Diego Baptist Church.
34. Lawson to Wigginton, December 21, 1878, LR #29–1879, RG 75, SC 31, OIA, NA.
35. Lawson to Hayt, January 8, 1879, LR #66–1879; and Lawson to Hayt, February 8, 1879, LR #155–1879—both in RG 75, SC 31, OIA, NA.
36. For an eyewitness account of the council, see Doody and Meltzer, *Losing Ground*, 97–98.
37. "Petition to the Hon. S. S. Lawson," enclosed with Lawson to Hayt, March 26, 1879, LR #317–1879, RG 75, SC 31, OIA, NA.

The 1,055 Indians who signed were from Temecula (190), Aguanga (40), Soboba (173), Puerta Cruz (25), Puerta del Valle de San Jose (31), San Luis Rey (57), La Jolla (109), Pauma (96), Pala (112), Potrero and Rincon (162), and "Yapichi" (60).

38. Lawson to Hayt, March 1, 1879, LR #221–1879; and March 7, 1879, LR #151–1879—both in RG 75, SC 31, OIA, NA.

Page (1833–90) served in the House from 1873 to 1883; see C. C. Williams, *Congressional Career of the Hon. H. F. Page: A Sketch* (San Francisco: Francis, Valentine, 1880), 1–29.

39. Lawson to Hayt, April 22, 1879, LR #422–1879, RG 75, SC 31, OIA, NA.
40. Lawson to Hayt, December 19, 1879, LR #1124–1879, RG 75, SC 31, OIA, NA.

Lawson's visits were often in winter, giving him no chance to experience the summer heat or witness the lack of water for much of the year.

41. Ibid.; and Thorne, "The Mixed Legacy of Mission Indian Agent S. S. Lawson," 159–60, 166.

Page introduced a bill to authorize $100,000 for the purchase, but it failed. Commissioner Trowbridge opposed it, judging the ranch "wholly unfitted" for a reservation. See *Annual Report of the CIA, 1880*, xiii; and the *San Bernardino Daily Times*, February 6, 1880.

42. "Lawson to Trowbridge, August 17, 1880," *Annual Report of the CIA, 1880*, 12.

43. *San Diego Union*, February 26, 1880; and "Our Remarkable Agent," February 27, 1880. The *Union* did at least attribute to Lawson "an honest desire to do his duty."

44. S. S. Lawson, "A Card," *San Bernardino Daily Times*, February 14, 1880; and Lawson's letter to the editor, *Daily Times*, February 21, 1880. Lawson's threat was the catalyst for much of the venom in the *San Diego Union* in the coming weeks. The *Daily Times* supported him, pointing out on February 20, 1880, that there was no point petitioning Congress for his removal as he served at the pleasure of the president, who looked to the Evangelical Lutheran Church's Home Missions Secretary for nominations for the office.

45. The seventh governor of California, Downey (1827–94) was born in Ireland. He came to California in 1849, opened a drugstore in Los Angeles, engaged in ranching and real estate, established the town of Downey, and with a partner formed the Farmers and Merchants Bank. He was a founder of the University of Southern California and the Historical Society of Southern California. See H. Brett Melendy and Benjamin F. Gilbert, *The Governors of California: Peter H. Burnett to Edmund G. Brown* (Georgetown, Calif.: The Talisman Press, 1965), 100–113.

46. Lawson to Brooks, March 4, 1880, LR #382–1880, RG 75, SC 31, OIA, NA. See also Lawson to Trowbridge, May 11, 1880, LR #723–1880, RG 75, SC 31, OIA, NA, and "Part III: Executive Orders Relating to Indian Reserves," in Kappler, *Law*, 822.

47. "Lawson to Trowbridge, August 17, 1880," *Annual Report of the CIA, 1880*, 12–13.

48. Lawson to Trowbridge, January 10, 1881, LR #982 [4063]-1881, RG 75, SC 31, OIA, NA. See also Lawson to Trowbridge, February 4, 1881, LR #2710–1881, included with the January 10 letter. For the executive order, see Acting Commissioner to Lawson, March 8, 1881, Letters Sent–Land Division, vol. 39, LB 78, pp. 105–6, RG 75, OIA, NA; and for reservation, see "Mission Indian Reserves," *Annual Report of the CIA, 1882*, 254.

49. In her 1883 report, Helen Hunt Jackson described Magruder's relocation of the Indians; see "Report on the Condition and Needs of the Mission Indians of California, Made by Special Agents Helen Jackson and Abbot Kinney, to the Commissioner of Indian Affairs," in Helen Jackson, *A Century of Dishonor: A Sketch of the United States Government's Dealings with Some of the Indian Tribes* (Boston: Roberts Brothers, 1888) (hereafter cited as Jackson and Kinney, "Report"), 479–98.

50. Curo to Lawson, July 5, 1881, enclosed with Lawson to Price, July 12, 1881, LR #12362–1881, RG 75, SC 31, OIA, NA. See also Tanis C. Thorne, *El Capitan: Adaptation and Agency on a Southern California Indian Reservation, 1850 to 1937* (Banning, Calif.: Malki-Ballena Press, 2012), 48–49. Curo's letter was probably written by F. R. Sawday, who in the 1880s ran a store and post office at Witch Creek, between Ramona and Santa Ysabel.

51. The Indian Homestead Act, passed on March 3, 1875, granted Indian applicants the same benefits as the 1862 Homestead law, provided they give up their tribal affiliation. Homesteaded lands were inalienable for five years after the final patent was granted.

52. Lawson to Price, July 12, 1881, LR #12362–1881, RG 75, SC 31, OIA, NA.

Although born in Pennsylvania, Price (1814–1901) represented Iowa in Congress from 1863 to 1869. He returned to Congress in 1877, serving until 1881, and soon after was chosen as commissioner by fellow Iowan Samuel J. Kirkwood, newly appointed interior secretary. Price promoted land allotment in severalty and established policies that severely curtailed Indian religious customs. See Floyd A. O'Neil, "Hiram Price, 1881–85," in Kvasnicka and Viola, *The Commissioners*, 173–79.

53. Price to Lawson, March 7, 1883, from copy in Helen Hunt Jackson Papers, MS 0020, part 1, box 2, folder 7, Special Collections, Tutt Library, Colorado College, Colorado Springs, Colo. (hereafter cited as HHJ Papers).

54. For a defense of Hensley, see "Bowers Is Angry," *San Francisco Call*, January 15, 1893. California Congressman William W. Bowers, interested in returning Indian affairs to the War Department, informed the *Call* that Hensley "was deprived of his improved farm now included in the Capitan Grande reservation" by Rust's recommendation and under the direction of the Indian commissioner. Where there was "once a thriving orchard and vineyards," there was now only "an abandoned and desolate tract." Therefore Bowers had introduced a bill in the Senate for a $10,000 reimbursement to Hensley for lands taken. Although Bowers claimed he wanted "to see the Indians treated with justice and humanity," he still "did not want to see our own old settlers and pioneers deprived of their rights."

55. Lawson to Price, December 28, 1881, LR #198–1882, RG 75, SC 31, OIA, NA.

56. Ibid.

57. Lawson to Price, February 8, 1882, LR #3256–1882, RG 75, SC 31, OIA, NA.

58. "Lawson to Price, August 7, 1882," *Annual Report of the CIA, 1882*, 11–12. For the reservation, see "Mission Indian Reserves," *Annual Report of the CIA, 1882*, 255.

59. The initial government survey of the 35,500-acre rancho had not included the village, but the 1878 survey, approved on January 17, 1880, included not only the village but all of the Indians' farms and the nearby streams. See Jackson, *A Century of Dishonor*, 479, and Van H. Garner, *The Broken Ring: The Destruction of the California Indians* (Tucson, Ariz.: Westernlore Press, 1982), 75–95.

60. Stevens to Teller, April 24, 1883, LR #9541 [11342]-1883, RG 75, SC 31, OIA, NA. For Jackson's role, see Price to Teller, May 21, 1883, LR #9541 [11342]-1883. For the executive order, see "Part III: Executive Orders Relating to Indian Reserves," in Kappler, *Law*, 823.

In 1861 New Yorker Henry Moore Teller (1830–1914) went to Colorado, where he practiced law before becoming president of the Colorado Central Railroad in 1872. He was elected to the U.S. Senate in 1876, resigning in 1882 to become the first westerner to hold the position of interior secretary. He returned to the Senate in 1885, serving until 1909.

61. On the suit, see *San Diego Union*, December 13, 1883.

62. Elmer W. Holmes, *History of Riverside County, California* (Los Angeles: Historical Record Co., 1912), 245. See also "Teaching Indians," *Riverside Press*, May 29, 1903, and Mary Sheriff Fowler, "Early History of San Jacinto Valley," *Hemet News*, December 17, 1915.

Born in Pennsylvania, Sheriff (1841–1921) taught in the freedmen schools after the Civil War before coming to the San Jacinto Valley in 1879. She later married W. P. Fowler, and she lived in San Jacinto until her death. A memorial window in her honor was placed in the chapel at the Sherman Institute in 1925. For obituaries, see "Mrs. Mary Fowler Is Called Home" and "Mrs. Mary Fowler a Notable Woman," both in *Hemet News*, September 30, 1921; and "Noted Life Comes to Close," *San Jacinto Register*, September 29, 1921. Sheriff also became one of Helen Hunt Jackson's closest California friends. For Jackson's first impressions of her, see "Three Pennsylvania Women," *Christian Union*, December 28, 1882, and January 4, 1883, reprinted in Mathes and Brigandi, *A Call for Reform*, 149–60. (The other two Pennsylvania women were San Jacinto hotelkeeper Emmaline Jordan and Cahuilla schoolteacher Nancy Ticknor.)

63. C. Reasoner, "The San Jacinto Country," *San Diego Union*, April 23, 1885.

64. The reluctance of many parents to send their children to school forced Golsh to the "innocent ruse" of telling them that attendance reports were sent to Washington; thus, she told them, the fewer the students, the fewer farming supplies the government would send. See "An Indian School," *Los Angeles Times*, January 12, 1886.

65. "Lawson to Price, August 20, 1881," *Annual Report of the CIA, 1881*, 14; and "Lawson to Price, August 7, 1882," *Annual Report of the CIA, 1882*, 12.

66. "McCallum to Price, August 22, 1884," *Annual Report of the CIA, 1884*, 14; see also McCallum to Price, December 10, 1883, LR #23116–1883, RG 75, SC 31, OIA, NA; and "McCallum to Atkins, September 30, 1885," *Annual Report of the CIA, 1885*, 8.

67. "Ward to Atkins, August 17, 1887," *Annual Report of the CIA, 1887*, 11. Ward also used the school issue to argue for fewer, more centralized reservations. "If all the Mission Indians were collected on two large reservations, the question of their civilization could be accomplished within ten years," he wrote in his 1887 report (11). Agent Rust made a similar suggestion in 1889.

68. "Preston to Atkins, August 20, 1888," *Annual Report of the CIA, 1888*, 17.

69. "Rust to Thomas Jefferson Morgan, October 28, 1889," *Fifty-Eighth Annual Report of the CIA, 1889*, 125.

70. Rust, "Report on Condition of Mission Indian and the Perris School Buildings, etc. etc.," RU 487, box 9; and Rust, "Notes of an Address upon Mission Indians Delivered in Los Angeles," RU 497, box 10—both in Horatio Nelson Rust Papers, Huntington Library, San Marino, Calif. (hereafter cited as Rust Papers).

71. See Mathes, *Helen Hunt Jackson and Her Indian Reform Legacy*, 55–75; Valerie Sherer Mathes, ed., *The Indian Reform Letters of Helen Hunt Jackson, 1879–1885* (Norman: University of Oklahoma Press, 1989), esp. 203–352; and Mathes and Brigandi, *A Call for Reform*, 3–77.

72. New Jersey–born Abbot Kinney (1850–1920) was educated abroad before joining the family tobacco company as a buyer. Ill health brought him in 1880 to Southern California, where he established his ranch, Kinneloa, near Sierra Madre. He later founded the California cities of Venice and Ocean Park.

Jackson's husband, William Sharpless Jackson, was concerned about her safety while visiting isolated Indian villages. He consented to her plan to "undertake the investigation" if she was accompanied by Kinney. "Without Mr. Kinney's aid I could have done nothing," she wrote. See "A Letter from Mrs. Helen Jackson to Dr. T. A. Bland, November 13, 1884," *Council Fire and Arbitrator*, December 1884, reprinted in Mathes and Brigandi, *A Call for Reform*, 188–89.

73. For Stanley's letter reporting his visit, see Jackson and Kinney, "Report," 507–8.
74. Lawson to Jackson, March 2, 1883, HHJ Papers, part 1, box 12, folder 4.
75. In her diary, Jackson noted meeting with Lawson on March 15, 17, and 18; see HHJ Papers, part 1, box 5, diary 8.
76. Lawson to Price, June 1, 1883, LR #10808–1883, RG 75, SC 31, OIA, NA. Others shared Lawson's feelings. See "A Female Indian Agent," *San Luis Obispo Tribune* (April 20, 1883), a reprint from the *Idaho Avalanche*, which sarcastically surmised that the "gentle influence of a lady Indian agent will have a healthful and beneficial effect upon the sunburnt, copper-colored, breech-clouted savages, who use their squaws for pack animals," adding that she would not be in danger because the Mission Indians "have long since departed, or if alive, are wearing high healed [*sic*] shoes and carry parasols."
77. Lawson to Price, June 22, 1883, LR #11732–1883, RG 75, SC 31, OIA, NA, for the first serious of quotes, and Lawson to Jackson, June 6, 1883, HHJ Papers, part 1, box 2, folder 4, for the remainder.
78. For the best source on the history of the Golsh family, see Steve Williamson, "The Missing Link: The Source of the Golsh Nobility," *The High Country*, no. 77 (Spring 2010): 36–46. For an early description of Flora Golsh's work at Agua Caliente, see "The Nation's Wards," *Los Angeles Times*, September 3, 1882. The school had been open only about six months at that time.
79. Draft by Jackson to Lawson, May 8, 1883, and Lawson to Jackson, May 9, 1883, HHJ Papers, part 1, box 2, folders 4 and 6. See also Mathes, *Helen Hunt Jackson and Her Indian Reform Legacy*, 66–68.
80. Lawson to Jackson, May 13, and May 21, 1883, HHJ Papers, part 1, box 2, folder 4; and Lawson to Price, June 1, 1883, LR #10808–1883, RG 75, SC 31, OIA, NA.
81. Lawson to Jackson, March 2, 1883, HHJ Papers, part 1, box 2, folder 4.
82. Price to Jackson, May 16, 1883, HHJ Papers, part 1, box 2, folder 5. See also Thorne, *El Capitan*, 50–52.
83. "Lawson to Price, August 13, 1883," *Annual Report of the CIA, 1883*, 15–16; see also Lawson to Price, August 20, 1881, *Annual Report of the CIA, 1883*, 14.

    See also "Agent Lawson's Arrest: An Indian Prompted to Purchase Liquor," *San Francisco Chronicle*, September 6, 1882. This article describes a liquor case in the U.S. District Court "tending to show the questionable manner in which Indian Agent S. S. Lawson" forced arrests.
84. "San Bernardino Notes," *Los Angeles Times*, July 18, 1883 (quoting the *San Bernardino Index*). "Indian Agent Lawson informs us that he has sent in his resignation with the intention that it shall be accepted. He complains that Mrs. Helen Hunt Jackson had no right to meddle with his supervision of the Indians, and he does not care to divide his authority with her."

85. "The Indian Agency," *San Luis Rey Star*, August 4, 1883. Under "Local Brevities" in the *Los Angeles Herald* (July 17, 1883), the following was printed: "The *San Bernardino Times* reports the resignation of S. S. Lawson, United States Agent for the Mission Indians."
86. For the complete recommendations, see Jackson and Kinney, "Report," 464–73.
87. Jackson to Ephraim W. Morse, November 3, 1883, Document Files, Research Archives, San Diego Historical Society, San Diego, California, reprinted in Mathes, *The Indian Reform Letters of Helen Hunt Jackson*, 296; and "Mrs. Helen Jackson to Dr. T. A. Bland," reprinted in Mathes and Brigandi, *A Call for Reform*, 182. It is unclear what these "grave charges" were.
88. "A Suggestion from a Western Friend," August 25, 1884, *Council Fire*, October 1884, reprinted in Mathes and Brigandi, *A Call for Reform*, 185–87. The writer also complained of Jackson's "imperiousness and assumed superiority over an Indian agent."
89. "Suggestion from a Western Friend," 185–87 and "A Letter from Mrs. Helen Jackson," 189–92, both reprinted in Mathes and Brigandi, *A Call for Reform*.
90. "Lawson to Price, August 20, 1881," *Annual Report of the CIA, 1881*, 14.
91. Thorne, "The Mixed Legacy of Mission Indian Agent S. S. Lawson," 159–60, 165–66.
92. "Death Claims Pioneer Agent," *San Bernardino County Sun*, January 1, 1909. On January 17, 1891, Lawson had filed for a Civil War pension, and in 1904 he entered the Sawtelle Veterans Home, formerly the Pacific Branch of the National Home for Disabled Volunteer Soldiers, established in 1887 in what is today the metropolitan area of Los Angeles.

3. The Need for Water: John G. McCallum, 1883–1885

Epigraph. "McCallum to Price, August 22, 1884," Annual Report of the CIA, 1884, 13.

1. Miller to Teller, July 17, 1883, reproduced in Ainsworth, *The McCallum Saga*, 47–48.
   A lawyer and businessman, Miller (1831–76) served in the Indiana State Senate in 1860–61 before joining the Union Army. From 1865 to 1869 he was collector of the Port of San Francisco before his election to the Senate. He served from 1881 to 1886.
2. "Civilizing the Indians of California," *Overland Monthly* (December 1883), 581. See also Ainsworth, *The McCallum Saga*, 48–49; see 50 for a reprint of McCallum's certificate of appointment.
3. See Ainsworth, *The McCallum Saga*. While the factual material seems correct, the book's celebratory tone makes its assessments and conclusions questionable. See also Rachel Dayton Shaw, "Evolving Ecoscape: An Environmental and Cultural History of Palm Springs, California and the Agua Caliente Indian Reservation, 1877–1939" (PhD diss., University of California, San Diego, 1999), 28, 52, 66, 98, 154.
4. McCallum to Commissioner Price, December 10, 1883, LR #23116–1883, RG 75, SC 31, OIA, NA.
5. Ibid. The destruction of private property was common among most tribes, especially at funerals and mourning ceremonies. Food and gifts were also freely given to guests by the deceased's family. Some of these traditions have survived into the modern era in Southern California.

6. McCallum to Price, December 10, 1883, LR #23116–1883, RG 75, SC 31, OIA, NA.
7. Ibid.
8. Ibid.
9. McCallum to Price, January 12, 1884, LR #23116–1883, SC 31, OIA, NA. McCallum refers to the Byrne / Soboba case in his printed report, "McCallum to Price, August 22, 1884," *Annual Report of the CIA, 1884*, 13; for the boarding school, see 14.
10. "McCallum to Price, August 22, 1884," *Annual Report of the CIA, 1884*, 12, 15.
11. Ainsworth, *The McCallum Saga*, 52–53.

    Will Pablo, born William Pablo Gabriel (ca. 1860), had ties to both the Palm Springs area and Morongo. A tribal leader, shaman, and federal Indian policeman, he spoke Cahuilla, Diegueno, and Luiseño, as well as English and Spanish. See "Is Holding Out False Hopes to Lo," *San Bernardino Sun*, July 1, 1902. His daughter, Jane Pablo Penn, was one of the founders of the Malki Museum on the Morongo Reservation in 1963. For an obituary, see "Recall Active Leadership of Captain Pablo," *San Bernardino County Sun*, September 25, 1935. According to the *Sun*, "Bill Pablo" lived an interesting life. "A man of prominence at the reservation," he had traveled to Washington at one time as spokesman for his people." Indians from many neighboring reservations attended his funeral.
12. McCallum to Price, December 10, 1883, LR #23116–1883, RG 75, SC 31, OIA, NA.
13. Jackson and Kinney, "Report," 470–71; see 475–78 for the Brunson & Wells legal opinion of May 12, 1883. For the hiring of Anson Brunson and G. Wiley Wells, see Jackson to Mary Sheriff, May 13, 1883, Helen Hunt Jackson Manuscripts, HM14209, Huntington Library, San Marino, California (hereafter cited as HHJ Manuscripts); reprinted in Mathes, *The Indian Reform Letters of Helen Hunt Jackson*, 266–68.
14. Brunson & Wells to Hon. E. L. Stevens, acting Indian Commissioner, May 24, 1884, LR #10477–1884, RG 75, SC 31, OIA, NA.
15. McCallum to Price, June 9, 1884, LR #11434–1884, RG 75, SC 31, OIA, NA. McCallum reminded Price that there was no police presence connected with the agency. The nearest government employee was the female school teacher, whose school was too distant for her to keep watch on the activities of reservation intruders.
16. McCallum to Price, October 22, 1884, LR #20742–1884, RG 75, SC 31, OIA, NA.
17. "McCallum to Price, August 22, 1884," *Annual Report of the CIA, 1884*, 13.
18. See Jackson and Kinney, "Report," 467.
19. U.S. Congress, Senate, "Message from the President of the United States," S. Ex. Doc 49, 48th Cong., 1st sess., 1884, 1–7; Jackson and Kinney, "Report," 7–37; and "Mission Indians in California," *Annual Report of the CIA, 1884*, xxxvii.
20. United States Congress, Senate, "Message from the President of the United States," S. Ex. Doc. 15, 49th Cong., 1st sess., 1885, 1–4; Jackson and Kinney, "Report," 4–33. For Atkins's comment, see "The Mission Indians in California," *Annual Report of the CIA, 1885*, xlviii.
21. See Jessica Bird, "The San Gorgonio Pass," in Holmes, *History of Riverside County*, chapter 20, see p. 189.
22. McCallum to Price, March 28, 1885, LR #6898–1885; and McCallum to Price, April 30, 1885, LR #10090–1885—both in RG 75, SC 31, OIA, NA.

23. Moro to McCallum, May 5 and May 15, 1885, enclosed with Wells to Lamar, August 18, 1885, LR #19419–1885, RG 75, SC 31, OIA, NA. Moro's letters were probably written for him by Flora Golsh, the village schoolteacher, who had visited Lost Valley to verify the details and personally view the damage.
24. Wells to Lamar, August 18, 1885, LR #19419–1885, RG 75, SC 31, OIA, NA. McCallum's letters to Wells are dated May 14 and May 18, 1885.
25. See Phil Brigandi, "A Plea for Justice: Cupeño Indians versus Homesteaders in 1880s San Diego County," *Journal of San Diego History*, vol. 63, no. 1 (Winter 2017): 35–48.
26. Pablo to McCallum, February 18, 1885; and McCallum to Wells, Van Dyke & Lee, May 14, 1885—both included in Wells to Lamar, August 18, 1885, LR #19419–1885, RG 75, SC 31, OIA, NA.
27. Born in Virginia, Charles C. Painter (1833–95), was a Congregational clergyman who served as agent for the American Missionary Association before becoming an IRA official. See, for example, Valerie Sherer Mathes and Phil Brigandi, "Charles C. Painter, Helen Hunt Jackson and the Mission Indians of Southern California," *Journal of San Diego History*, vol. 55, no. 3 (Summer 2009): 89–118.

    Joshua William Davis (1828–1909) was a founding member of the Boston Indian Citizenship Committee, a corporate member of the American Board of Foreign Missions, and a director of the Congregational Sunday School and Publishing Society. For the Boston Committee, see Valerie Sherer Mathes, "Boston, the Boston Indian Citizenship Committee, and the Poncas," *Massachusetts Historical Review*, vol. 14 (2012): 119–48; see also "Mr. Davis Dead," March 26, 1909, and "Mr. Joshua W. Davis," *Newton Graphic*, April 2, 1909.
28. Painter, *A Visit to the Mission Indians of Southern California and Other Western Tribes* (Philadelphia: Office of the Indian Rights Association, 1886), 11; for his visit to the Mission Indians, see 11–18; see also William T. Hagan, *The Indian Rights Association: The Herbert Welsh Years 1882–1904* (Tucson: University of Arizona Press, 1985), 68–70; Mathes, *Helen Hunt Jackson and Her Indian Reform Legacy*, 90, 92, 95, 97–100, 104, 108, 110–19, 128, 148, 155–57; and Mathes, *Divinely Guided*, 179–84, 225, 234.
29. Jackson to the Coronels, June 27, 1885, Antonio F. Coronel Collection, Seaver Center for Western History Research, Los Angeles County Museum of Natural History, reprinted in Mathes, *The Indian Reform Letters of Helen Hunt Jackson*, 349.

    Born in Mexico, Antonio Franco Coronel (1817–94), moved to Los Angeles with his family. During the Mexican period of California history, he taught school and served as territorial deputy, street commissioner, justice of the peace, and inspector for the secularized missions. During the American period, he served as school superintendent, mayor of Los Angeles, and state treasurer. For some reminiscences, see Doyce B. Nunis Jr., ed., *Tales of Mexican California* (Santa Barbara, Calif.: Bellerophon Books, 1994).
30. Painter to Coronel, June 29, 1885, HHJ Manuscripts, HM 38231; and Painter to Rust, June 18, 1885, RU 462, box 8, Rust Papers. In both letters Painter noted that he had returned to Southern California at Jackson's request.
31. Ubach to Rosencrans [*sic*], September 4, 1885 (included with Rosecrans to Commissioner Atkins, September 10, 1885), LR #21068–1885, RG 75, SC 31, OIA, NA.

Anthony D. Ubach (1836–1907) came to San Diego from Spain in 1866 to take charge of the Catholic parish there. He met and assisted Jackson during her visits and was a strong advocate for Indian rights. See Edgar W. Hebert, "The Last of the Padres," *San Diego Historical Society Quarterly*, vol. 10, no. 2 (April 1964): 15–22. *Ramona* scholars believe that Ubach served as the model for Father Gaspara.

32. Ubach to Rosencrans [*sic*], September 4, 1885, LR #21068–1885, RG 75, SC 31, OIA, NA.

    William Starke Rosecrans (1819–98), a major general in the U.S. Army, represented California's First Congressional District in the House of Representatives from 1881 to 1885. At the time of this letter, he was the register of the U.S. Treasury.

33. Painter to Coronel, June 29, 1885, HHJ Manuscripts, HM 38231.

    Born in New York, Henry Harrison Markham (1840–1923) was at the time a member of the House of Representatives. He later became the eighteenth governor of California, serving from 1891 to 1895.

34. See Larry Burgess, "The Lake Mohonk Conference on the Indian, 1883–1916," PhD diss., Claremont Graduate School, 1972; and Valerie Sherer Mathes, ed., *The Women's National Indian Association: A History* (Albuquerque: University of New Mexico, 2015).
35. For WNIA missionary work among the Mission Indians, see Mathes, *Divinely Guided*, 177–261.
36. Jackson and Kinney, "Report," 470.
37. Ainsworth, *The McCallum Saga*, 89–90. Gardner also judged McCallum "a man of good moral character, energy and executive ability." Dr. Thompson later served as San Bernardino County physician in the 1890s.
38. S. S. Lawson, "The Mission Indians," *Los Angeles Times*, May 14, 1891.
39. "Ward to Atkins, August 14, 1886," *Annual Report of the CIA, 1886*, 45. Annual reports often included detailed statistics on Indian diseases, though for the Mission Indian Agency these tended to be incomplete.
40. "Ward to Atkins, August 17, 1887," *Annual Report of the CIA, 1887*, 11.
41. "Rust to Morgan, August 8, 1890," *Fifty-Ninth Annual Report of the CIA, 1890*, 17. At the time, the agency was spending about $6,000 a year for "relieving the sick and indigent." See *An Illustrated History of Southern California* (Chicago: The Lewis Publishing Co., 1890), 424.

    Every agent from Rust on argued for a government hospital. Not until 1923 was one established, in temporary quarters at Soboba. In 1928 it was replaced with a permanent building there, which operated until 1948. See Gordon Johnson, "A Healing Place," *Riverside Press-Enterprise*, August 23, 1998. For an unsuccessful effort to convince the government to reopen the hospital, see "Indians Make Final Plea for Reopening of Hospital," *San Jacinto Valley Register*, November 26, 1948.

42. Rust to Morgan, July 20, 1891, LR #27101–1891; and Rust to Morgan, October 1, 1891, LR #36334–1891—both in RG 75, OIA, NA.
43. "Estudillo to Browning, August 31, 1893," *Sixty-Second Annual Report of the CIA, 1893*, 129; and "Estudillo to Browning, August 31, 1894," *Annual Report of the CIA, 1894*, 122.
44. Born in Ohio in 1851, Wainwright first came to California around 1867. He taught school for three years before returning to Ohio to earn his medical degree in 1876.

Returning to California, he settled in San Bernardino in 1880, serving as county coroner for two terms (1885–90) and then as city health officer, even after he was appointed agency physician in February 1892. When the position was discontinued in 1901, he moved to Wyoming to practice medicine for several more years before moving to Los Angeles, where he died in 1926. For a biography, see *An Illustrated History of Southern California*, 528–29.

45. "Report of Physician, Mission-Tule River Agency, August 26, 1895," in "Wright to Browning, August 31, 1895," *Annual Report of the CIA, 1895*, 135; and "Wright to Jones, August 1897," *Annual Reports of the Department of the Interior for the Fiscal Year Ended June 30, 1897* (Washington, D.C.: GPO, 1897) (hereafter cited as *Annual Reports of the DOI*, with specific year), 119–20.
46. "Wright to Jones, September 20, 1902," *Annual Reports of the DOI, 1902* (GPO, 1903), 176. In his report for 1904, Wright, a pharmacist, added that he also sometimes put his own pharmacy skills to work preparing "simple remedies for the use of the schools and Indians throughout my territory." See "Wright to Jones, September 1, 1904," *Annual Reports of the DOI, 1904*, part 1 (GPO, 1905), 173.
47. "Shell to Jones, August 20, 1904," *Annual Reports of the DOI, 1904*, part 1, p. 167.
48. Ainsworth, *The McCallum Saga*, 90–92. See also p. 85 for more on the wood cutting incident.

    Welwood Murray (1832–1914), an early settler in the San Gorgonio Pass area, was brought in by McCallum in 1886 to run the first hotel in Palm Springs. The title "doctor" was complimentary. For a biography, see Hughes, *History of Banning*, 20–21. For more on Murray, his hotel, and his use of the Agua Caliente hot springs, see Shaw, "Evolving Ecoscape," 61, 248, 251, 253, 255, and 258–61.
49. Ubach to Rosencrans [*sic*], September 4, 1885, LR #21068–1885, RG 75, SC 31, OIA, NA. McCallum's letter of resignation is reproduced in Ainsworth, *The McCallum Saga*, 95.
50. "McCallum to Atkins, September 30, 1885," *Annual Report of the CIA, 1885*, 8–9. McCallum wrote (p. 8) that about two hundred fifty of the Mission Indians could read English, one hundred of them learning that past year, and one hundred or so who were proficient in English. Nearly all spoke Spanish.
51. Ibid. A collection of agency census rolls can be found at "Free US Indian Census Rolls 1885–1940," Access Genealogy, www.accessgenealogy.com/native/free-us-indian-census-rolls.htm.
52. "Wright to Jones, September 1, 1900," *Annual Reports of the DOI, 1900*, 208.
53. "McCallum to Atkins, September 30, 1885," *Annual Report of the CIA, 1885*, 8.
54. The purchase agreement is quoted in full in Ainsworth, *The McCallum Saga*, 68. McCallum eventually bought out all of Byrne's holdings.
55. Greg Niemann, in *Palm Springs Legends: Creation of a Desert Oasis* (San Diego: Sunbelt Publications, 2006, p. 38), describes Byrne and Slyke as the "first land speculators in Palm Springs." For McCallum's land purchase, see Van H. Garner, "Agua Caliente, a Fight for Survival," in his *The Broken Ring*, 122–23.
56. Ainsworth, *The McCallum Saga*, 94.

57. Charles C. Painter, *Visit to the Mission Indians of California* (Philadelphia: Indian Rights Association, 1887), 10.
58. Ward to Upshaw, November 4, 1885, LR #26498–1885, RG 75, SC 31, OIA, NA.
59. Ibid.
60. McCallum's denials are quoted in Ainsworth, *The McCallum Saga*, 95–97; for his acquittal, see 97, which quotes the *Banning Herald*, February 1, 1889.
61. Ainsworth, *The McCallum Saga*, 53. "As Lincoln felt toward the colored people my father felt toward the Indians," Pearl McManus later said in an interview. "He was both their benefactor and their champion." See the full quote on 97–98. For another overly celebratory article on the role of McCallum and others to make the Coachella Valley verdant, with little about the Indians, see Evelanne Heyman, "Sheer Pioneer Grit Overcame an Arid and Hostile Desert," *Desert Sun*, October 28, 1975.

4. A Brief, Bitter Tenure: John S. Ward, 1885–1887

Epigraph. "Ward to Atkins, August 17, 1887," Annual Report of the CIA, 1887, 9–10.

1. For more on Ward (1834–1904), see his obituary, "John Shirley Ward," *Confederate Veteran*, vol. 13, no. 1 (January 1905): 86; "John Shirley Ward: Death of a Prominent Resident of Southern California," *Los Angeles Herald*, January 5, 1905; and the biography of his son in Shuck, *History of the Bench and Bar of California*, 1084.
2. See "Native American Manifesto: John Morongo No Longer Chief of the Mission Indians," *Los Angeles Herald*, August 25, 1886; and "Chief Cabezon Publishes a Card to the Whites," *Los Angeles Times*, August 26, 1886.
3. Hughes, *History of Banning*, 119.
4. Ward to Upshaw, November 5, 1885, LR #26766–1885, RG 75, SC 31, OIA, NA.

   Christopher F. Jost (1846–1936) came to the pass in 1877. According to Hughes in *History of Banning* (134–35), "Mr. Jost described his relations with the Indians during his ten years in the Potrero as having been entirely pleasant. He said the few arguments he did have were with the Indian department officials." For more on the Josts, see Doody and Meltzer, *Losing Ground*, 90, 100, 102, 104, 106, 111, 117.
5. Ward to Atkins, February 1, 1886, LR #4136–1886, RG 75, SC 31, OIA, NA.

   A Tennessee native, John DeWitt Clinton Atkins (1825–1908) served in both houses of the state legislature before his election to the House of Representatives in 1857. During the war he served as a general in the Confederate Army, as well as a legislator in the Confederate Congress. See Gregory C. Thompson, "John D. C. Atkins, 1885–88," in Kvasnicka and Viola, *The Commissioners*, 181–88.

   Author Tom Hughes, who knew a number of the settler families in later years, described some of the uncertainties of the time in his 1938 *History of Banning* (28–29): "What of the settlers who took up the unsurveyed portions of the odd sections? Were they not justified in feeling secure in their tenure of railroad lands? They must have thought so; but here lay the joker that confused them. While it was true that Congress, tacitly at least, had promised to give title to the unsurveyed railroad lands on the odd sections whenever they should be surveyed, the President, before they had been surveyed, gave them over to the use of the Indians." He observed that "to discuss the ins and outs of the matter would be almost as big a job as digging into the issues that preceded the Civil War."

6. Ward to Upshaw, June 10, 1886, LR #16093–1886, RG 75, SC 31, OIA, NA.
7. "Ward to Atkins, August 14, 1886," *Annual Report of the CIA, 1886*, 43–46, quotes on 4. For ruling, see "A Banning Land Case Decided," *Riverside Daily Press*, August 14, 1886.
8. Ward to Atkins, November 16, 1886, LR #31024–1886, RG 75, SC 31, OIA, NA.
9. Shirley Ward to Pancoast, October 9, 1886, *Indian Rights Association Papers*, Glen Rock, N.J.: Microfilming Corporation of America, 1975 (hereafter cited as *IRA Papers*), reel 1.
10. "Something about Our Indians," *Riverside Daily Press*, November 10, 1886.
11. "Ward to Atkins, August 14, 1886," *Annual Report of the CIA, 1886*, 43–46, quote on 43.
12. Ibid., 46.
13. "Lawson to Price, August 13, 1883," *Annual Report of the CIA, 1883*, 16. For a summary of a year's worth of Lawson's liquor cases, see "Lawson to Price, August 7, 1882," *Annual Report of the CIA, 1882*, 13. See also the *Los Angeles Herald*, September 7, 1882.
14. "A Hard Gang. Brought Up for Selling Whisky to Indians," *Los Angeles Times*, July 23, 1887. Two of the other "saloonists" were identified in newspaper accounts as "McCord" and "Kislinger." There were actually five saloons on the reservation, one located in the former home of Ignacio Curo, which had been taken over by a white man. Presumably these saloons also did a lively business with the men at work building the San Diego flume across the reservation.
15. C. C. Painter, *The Condition of Affairs in Indian Territory and California* (Philadelphia: Office of the Indian Rights Association, 1888), 66; and Painter to Davis, July 17, 1887, *IRA Papers*, reel 2; see also Painter to Davis, July 12, 1887, *IRA Papers*, reel 2.
16. *Los Angeles Times*, August 14, 20, and 21, and September 28, 1888.
17. "Wants to Confiscate," *Los Angeles Times*, November 23, 1887.
18. "A Long Case," *Los Angeles Times*, February 27, 1889.
19. Castillo was a student of Mary Sheriff, the Soboba schoolteacher who befriended Helen Hunt Jackson and alerted her to the danger facing the Soboba village. See Mathes and Brigandi, *A Call for Reform*, 99; and Mathes, *The Indian Reform Letters of Helen Hunt Jackson*, 167, 228–31, 253–54.
20. Ward to Upshaw, November 5, 1885, LR #26570–1885; November 21, 1885, LR #28340–1885; and for quote, November 21, 1885, LR #28341–1885—all in RG 75, SC 31, OIA, NA.

    Castillo was not deterred. In 1888 he again made an attempt to secure title to his own lands. See *San Jacinto Register*, September 27, 1888. In September 1890 he received a homestead patent to 160 acres in what is still known as Castillo Canyon. See Gunther, *Riverside County*, 104.
21. See "Shirley C. Ward," *History of the Bench and Bar of California*, ed. J. C. Bates (San Francisco: Bench and Bar Publishing Company, 1912), 543–44. For an obituary, see "Pioneer's Obsequies Today," *Los Angeles Times*, November 26, 1929.

22. McKisick to Atkins, October 29, 1885, LR #26011–1885, RG 75, SC 31, OIA, NA. Garner (*The Broken Ring*, 79) says that C. C. Painter lobbied President Chester Arthur to help secure Ward's appointment.

The senior Ward seems to have viewed his son's appointment as a good political move. Thanking California Congressman Barclay Henley for mediating on behalf of his son regarding the appointment, Ward wrote: "It was my desire, in applying for this position for my son, to put him in the line of promotion, so that he would have some claims to the position of District Attorney in the event that a United States Court should be established for Southern California." See Ward to Henley, January 29, 1886, LR #4781–1886, RG 75, SC 31, OIA, NA.

23. Ward to Upshaw, November 11, 1885, LR #27366–1885, RG 75, SC 31, OIA, NA. Five days earlier the elder Ward had also written Upshaw, telling him that the uncertainty of Indian title created uneasiness among the Mission Indians. They were fearful to plant crops or even build a house. He urged the government "to bring suit to establish title, in all cases, when there is a conflict between the grantholders and the Indians." See Ward to Upshaw, November 6, 1885, LR #26767–1885, RG 75, SC 31, OIA, NA.

Shirley C. Ward, in an account before the U.S. Treasury, noted he had begun work on behalf of the Mission Indians as early as June 27, 1884. In October and November of 1884 he presented bills for filing and printing the *Byrne vs. Alas et al* case. See "Shirley C. Ward, Special Attorney for the Mission Indians," U.S. Congress, House of Representatives, 49th Cong., 2d sess., Ex. Doc. no. 161.

24. Garland to Interior Secretary Lamar, January 14, 1886, LR #1447–1886; and Shirley Ward to Garland, March 16, 1886, LR #8672–1886—both in RG 75, SC 31, OIA, NA.

25. Wells, Van Dyke, & Lee (successors to Brunson & Wells) to Hon. H. H. Markham, June 20, 1885 [enclosed with H. H. Markham to Interior Secretary Lucius Q. C. Lamar, June 30, 1885], LR #15095–1885, RG 75, SC 31, OIA, NA.

26. Wells to Markham, June 20, 1885, LR #15095–1885, RG 75, SC 31, OIA, NA. See also Indian Rights Association, *The Case of the Mission Indians in Southern California and the Action of the Indian Rights Association in Supporting the Defense of Their Legal Rights* (Philadelphia: Office of the IRA, 1886), 14. This pamphlet, which includes a history of the Soboba case, the legal roles of Brunson & Wells and Shirley Ward, was written to enlist the sympathies of the American public, to show obstacles faced by "friends of the Indians" in Washington, and to illustrate the need for a permanent organization to aid the Mission Indians.

27. Wells to Markham, June 20, 1885, LR #15095–1885, RG 75, SC 31, OIA, NA. Painter, however, stated that the court decided in favor of the plaintiff because of the failure of the Indians to make an appearance before a commission "appointed by act of Congress in 1851, which required all persons claiming title to land under old Spanish and Mexico laws to appear before them and establish their title." See Painter, *Visit to the Mission Indians of California*, 5.

28. Ward to Welsh, March 11, 1886, and Ward to Garland, July 10, 1886, *IRA Papers*, reel 1. For court decision, see "*M. Byrne vs. A. Alas*—Copy Findings" and "*M. Byrne vs. A. Alas et al.*—Copy Judgment," included with J. M. Dodge (court clerk) to Leland Stanford (U.S. senator), August 7, 1886, LR #6885–1886, RG 75, SC 31, OIA NA.

29. "John Ward to Atkins, August 14, 1886," *Annual Report of the CIA, 1886*, 45.
30. For Welsh's payment, see Ward to Pancoast, October 9, 1886, *IRA Papers*, reel 2; and "Proceedings of the Mohonk Lake Conference," in *Eighteenth Annual Report of the Board of Indian Commissioners, 1886* (Washington; GPO, 1887) (hereafter cited as *BIC*, with date of publication), 46. For repayment, see Ward to Welsh, May 6, 1888, *IRA Papers*, reel 3.

    Philadelphia-born Herbert Welsh (1851–1941) was the nephew of William Welsh, the first chairman of the Board of Indian Commissioners. In 1882 Welsh and his friend Henry Pancoast visited the Rosebud Sioux Reservation, after which, joined by Welsh's father and others, they founded the IRA. Welsh initially assumed the key position of corresponding secretary, then serving the organization as executive secretary and president until 1927. For more, see Hagan, *The Indian Rights Association*, 1–19.
31. Dodge to Leland Stanford, August 7, 1886, LR #6885–1886, RG 75, SC 31, OIA NA.
32. "Third Day: Morning Session," in "Proceedings of the LMC," *Eighteenth Annual Report of the BIC, 1886*, 83.
33. "The Mission Indians of California" (presentation by Hiles), in "Proceedings of the LMC," *Eighteenth Annual Report of the BIC, 1886*, 79–81 and 83. For more, see Francis Paul Prucha, "A 'Friend of the Indian' in Milwaukee: Mrs. O. J. Hiles and the Wisconsin Indian Association," in *Indian Policy in the United States: Historical Essays* (Lincoln: University of Nebraska Press, 1981), 214–28; and Mathes, *Helen Hunt Jackson and Her Indian Reform Legacy*, 100–106. The Wisconsin Indian Association was an auxiliary of the WNIA. In January 1888 Hiles again returned to California, visiting fourteen reservations and Mexican grants along with several government schools during a three-month tour. She returned again to Lake Mohonk to report on her findings. Poor health prevented her continued work on the Indians' behalf.
34. "Third Day: Closing Session," "Proceedings of the Mohonk Lake Conference" (1886), 88–89.

    Quinton (1833–1926) was born in Jamesville, New York, educated at Cortland Academy in Homer, New York, and lived in Madison, Georgia, with her husband, James Franklin Swanson, a Baptist minister, whom she wed in 1854. When he died, she moved north, married Richard Linton Quinton, and in 1879 with Mary Lucinda Bonney founded the WNIA. She served as the association's secretary from 1881 to 1887, and president from 1887 to 1905. She was the WNIA's major organizer and chair of its Missionary Department. See Valerie Sherer Mathes, "Mary Lucinda Bonney and Amelia Stone Quinton, Founders of the Women's National Indian Association," *American Baptist Quarterly*, vol. 28, no. 4 (Winter 2009): 421–40; and Mathes, "Mary Bonney, Amelia Quinton, and the Formative Years," in Mathes, *The Women's National Indian Association*, 25–45.
35. Upshaw to Quinton, November 10, 1885, LS: Education Division, vol. 2, LB, pages 177–79, RG 75, OIA, NA. For Round Valley, see Mathes, *Divinely Guided*, 51–71; and Valerie Sherer Mathes, "Baptist Missionary Work at Round Valley, California," *American Baptist Quarterly* (Fall 2010): 172–86.
36. Indian Rights Association, *The Case of the Mission Indians*, 15. See also a February 25, 1886, letter from Painter to Welsh, also in *The Case of the Mission Indians*, 16.

Earlier Albert B. Weiner, IRA secretary, had addressed Ward's inadequate salary in Weiner to Lamar, February 15, 1886, LR #5194–1886, RG 75, SC 31, OIA, NA.

37. "Proceedings of the LMC," *Eighteenth Annual Report of the BIC, 1886*, 45–46.
38. Painter, *Visit to the Mission Indians of California*, 5; and Herbert Welsh to Horatio N. Rust, January 26, 1886, RU 522, box 8, Rust Papers. For Ward's brief, see Ward to Painter, May 20, 1886, *IRA Papers*, reel 1.
39. In a letter to Atkins on June 10, 1886 (LR #15947–1886, RG 75, SC 31, OIA, NA), Ward noted he had written Dawes about adequate compensation. See also Ward to Garland, March 16, 1886, LR #8672–1886; here Ward requested that the terms of his appointment be changed to allow him "such compensation as would in some degree be commensurate with the labor to be performed." See also Welsh to Atkins, March 27, 1886, LR #8794–1886, RG 75, SC 31, OIA, NA.
40. F. Orleans Brackett to Ward, February 13, 1886; and Ward to Atkins, February 17, 1886—both in LR #5870–1886, RG 75, SC 31, OIA, NA.
41. Ward to Atkins, February 20, 1886, LR #5935–1886; and Ward to Atkins, March 12, 1886, LR #8013–1886—both in, RG 75, SC 31, OIA, NA.
42. Lippitt to Lamar, August 12, 1886, LR #22378–1886, RG 75, SC 31, OIA, NA.
43. Ibid.
44. Ward to Atkins, October 1, 1886, LR #27577–1886, RG 75, SC 31, OIA, NA.
45. For the verdict, see "Indians Who Will Vote," *San Francisco Chronicle*, September 26, 1888; and "Indian Voters: San Diego County to Cast 500 Indian Votes This Fall," *San Jacinto Register*, September 27, 1888. Charles F. Seymour, in "Relations between the United States Government and the Mission Indians of Southern California" (master's thesis, UC Berkeley, May 1906), gives a lengthy discussion of the citizenship status of the Mission Indians (14–23).

    For more on Calac, see Painter, *Visit to the Mission Indians of California*, 12–13; and Mathes and Brigandi, "Charles C. Painter," 105. Painter claimed Calac was "the first Indian in California who has been allowed to purchase State [school] land as a citizen, whose right to do so was recently affirmed by the Superior Court" (64).

    For Morgan's views on Indians' citizenship status under the Treaty of Guadalupe Hidalgo, see "Report of Commissioner Thomas Jefferson Morgan, October 1, 1891," *Sixtieth Annual Report of the CIA, 1891*, part 1, 26–30.
46. For Painter's meeting with tribal leaders at Pala in the summer of 1887, see "Land in Severalty. The Mission Indians Confer about It," *Los Angeles Times*, June 30, 1887.
47. Painter to Joshua W. Davis, June 30, 1887, *IRA Papers*, reel 1, reprinted in Mathes and Brigandi, "Charles C. Painter," 95.

    Officials demanded a school attendance of at least twenty; schools were closed at Soboba, Cahuilla, Rincon, and La Jolla.
48. Painter to Joshua W. Davis, June 30, 1887. See also Painter, *Affairs in Indian Territory and California*, 51. In his 1887 annual report Ward notes that the school was only in operation a few months before closing "for reasons not necessary to mention."
49. "Mr. Ward Resigns," *Los Angeles Times*, July 3, 1887. In "Democratic Officials Resigning," August 18, 1887, the *Los Angeles Herald* reported that Ward resigned because he could "earn a much larger amount of money in any other kind of business."

50. "Ward to Atkins, August 17, 1887," *Annual Report of the CIA, 1887*, 12, 9–10.
After an 1877 visit to the school at Mesa Grande, the last one built during Ward's tenure, Painter described one of these "heroic" teachers. A Miss Hood of Mississippi, she was "a very bright nice young woman" who was also doing good service as a doctor, noted Painter. See Painter to Davis, June 30, 1887, *IRA Papers*, reel 2.
51. "Ward to Atkins, August 17, 1887," *Annual Report of the CIA, 1887*, 9–10.
For details and the failure of this legislation, see D. S. Otis, *The Dawes Act and the Allotment of Indian Lands* (Norman: University of Oklahoma Press, 2014); and Leonard A. Carlson, *Indians, Bureaucrats and Land: The Dawes Act and the Decline of Indian Farming* (Westport, Conn.: Greenwood Press, 1981).
52. Painter, *Affairs in Indian Territory and California*, 72.
Ward's entire report was printed as "Mission Indians, Hon. J. Shirley Ward's Final Report on Them" in the *Los Angeles Herald* on September 14, 1887.
53. "John Shirley Ward: Death of a Prominent Resident of Southern California," *Los Angeles Herald*, January 5, 1905; and "John Shirley Ward," *Confederate Veteran* (Nashville), February 1905, 86.

5. A Show of Force: Joseph W. Preston, 1887–1889

Epigraph. "Preston to Atkins, August 20, 1888," Fifty-Seventh Annual Report of the CIA, 1888, 11–12.

1. See Lucian Lamar Knight, *A Standard History of Georgia and Georgians* (Chicago: Lewis Publishing, 1917), 3110–12. For Preston's appointment, see *Journal of the Executive Proceedings of the Senate of the United States of America from December 5, 1887 to March 3, 1889*, vol. 26 (Washington, D.C.: GPO, 1901), 339; and "Appointments: Officers Whose Names Are to Go Before the Senate," *Daily Alta California*, November 30, 1887.
In later government records the word "Consolidated" in the agency name was often quoted and abbreviated as "Cons."
2. In "Report of the Commissioner John D. C. Atkins, September 21, 1887" (*Annual Report of the CIA, 1887*, xlix–1), Atkins noted that because the Tule River agency had a population of only 140 Indians, who were "fairly advanced in civilization," the government abolished the agency, placing the Indians in the care of the Mission Indian agent—at a savings of $700 in salaries.
The Tule River Reservation had been established by executive order in 1877 and was home mostly to Southern Yokut people. The villagers at Santa Ynez were Chumash. The Fort Yuma Indians were primarily Quechans. The reservation was mostly in what is now southeastern Imperial County but included some territory across the Colorado River near Yuma, where the bulk of the residents lived. It was separated from the Mission-Tule Agency in 1900. For a detailed study of the Tule River Reservation, see Gelya Frank and Carole Goldberg, *Defying the Odds: The Tule River Tribe's Struggle for Sovereignty in Three Centuries* (New Haven, Conn.: Yale University Press, 2010).
3. "Report of the Commissioner John D. C. Atkins, September 21, 1887," *Annual Report of the CIA, 1887*, li–lii; Thorne, *El Capitan*, 53–55.

4. "Ward to Atkins, August 17, 1887," *Annual Report of the CIA, 1887*, 10; and "Our Sentiments Exactly," *Redlands Citrograph*, October 13, 1888. The *Citrograph* article noted that some of the evicted "settlers," given until October 1, 1888, to vacate, were now "penniless as well as homeless."
5. North, who was born in Minnesota in 1885, was superintendent of the Riverside Water Company. His father was a county judge in Riverside. Gird, originally from New York, had come to California during the gold rush and became wealthy prospecting in Arizona. For more, see *Illustrated History of Southern California*, 483, 489; and also Doody and Meltzer, *Losing Ground*, 109–10.
6. "Preston to Atkins, August 20, 1888," *Fifty-Seventh Annual Report of the CIA, 1888*, 12–13; and Doody and Meltzer, *Losing Ground*, 104, 109. See also "They Must Vacate. Forcible Ejection by Government Authorities," *Los Angeles Herald*, September 30, 1887; and the *Alta California*, September 30, 1887. For antiremoval sentiment, see "The Indian Reservation," *Riverside Press*, November 5, 1887, quoting the *Los Angeles Porcupine*.
7. "The Mission Indians. Their Lands to Be Cleared of Squatters by Troops," *Los Angeles Times*, September 30, 1887.
8. Hughes, *History of Banning*, 30; and Doody and Meltzer, *Losing Ground*, 104. For an angry letter opposing the removal, see "Government Eviction. An Old Man Driven from his Home to Make Room for Indians," *Los Angeles Times*, October 12, 1887.
9. Shirley Ward to Preston, May 5, 1888, LR #12991–1888, RG 75, SC 31, OIA, NA; and Ward to W. H. H. Miller, U.S. Attorney General, April 1890, "Mission Indians of California," U.S. Congress, Senate, 51st Cong., 1st sess., report no. 1510, in *Reports of Committees of the Senate of the United States for the First Session of the Fifty-First Congress, 1889–1890* (Washington, D.C.: GPO, 1890), 13–14.
10. Ward to W. H. H. Miller, U.S. Attorney General, April 1890, 13. For some *Herald* articles on *Morongo v. North*, see Doody and Meltzer, *Losing Ground*, 136–46. The *Banning Herald* was unsympathetic, stating that if the Indians lost their homes it would be "because of their ignorance" of the laws and their failure to "perform such requirements as are prescribed for perfecting titles." See "Ten Tons of Bear Meat," *San Francisco Chronicle* (reprinted from the *Banning Herald*), April 24, 1889. For an article on five of the government's Indian witnesses, reputedly between the ages of 75 and 120, who attracted "a good deal of attention, and [were] curiosities in themselves," see "Ancient Indians. They Are Brought Here to Testify in a Case," *Los Angeles Herald*, June 1, 1889.
11. "Veteran Indians. They Come to Claim Their Reservation Rights," *Los Angeles Times*, June 1, 1889.
12. "Evicted Settlers. White Men Driven Out for Indians," *San Francisco Chronicle*, March 23, 1889.
13. Letter to the editor, published April 13, 1889, and quoted in Doody and Meltzer, *Losing Ground*, 137.
14. "Rust to Morgan," September 10, 1891, *Sixtieth Annual Report of the CIA, 1891*, 223.
15. Doody and Meltzer, *Losing Ground*, 126, 150.

16. Painter, *Affairs in Indian Territory and California*, 66; "Prof. Painter's Work at Washington and Elsewhere," *The Fifth Annual Report of the Executive Committee of the IRA* (Philadelphia: Office of the IRA), 1888, 14–15; and Thorne, *El Capitan*, 54–55.
17. See Thorne, *El Capitan*, 59, 179–80. At least one of the settlers continued to press for reparations from the government into the 1890s.
18. Painter, *Affairs in Indian Territory and California*, 66; "Prof. Painter's Work at Washington and Elsewhere," 14–15; and Thorne, *El Capitan*, 55.
19. "Preston to Atkins, August 20, 1888," *Fifty-Seventh Annual Report of the CIA, 1888*, 13–14; Thorne, *El Capitan*, 56–59.
20. "Report of William H. Waldby, March 27, 1888," *Twentieth Annual Report of the BIC, 1888* (Washington, D.C.: GPO, 1889), 10.
21. "Preston to Atkins, August 20, 1888," *Annual Report of the CIA, 1888*, 14; and Thorne, *El Capitan*, 55–60, 65, for quote, see 58, and for the text of the 1888 agreement, 181–82. See also Lewis to Rust, August 26, 1889, RU 443, box 9, Rust Papers; and "Indian Lands. Trespassers on the Mission Reservation," *San Francisco Call*, May 14, 1890.

    San Diego's water needs continued to plague the reservation; in the mid-1930s almost all the arable land on the reservation was flooded under the city's new Capitán Grande Reservoir. Most of the remaining residents were moved to two new reservations at that time—Barona and Viejas. For details see Thorne, *El Capitan*.
22. Shaw, "Evolving Ecoscape," 98–99.
23. Preston to Atkins, February 20, 1888, LR #5497–1888, RG 75, SC 31, OIA, NA.
24. Ibid.
25. Ainsworth, *The McCallum Saga*, 78–80. Ainsworth cites a "lengthy report" submitted by Preston on May 10, 1888.
26. Shaw, "Evolving Ecoscape," 99–100, 156–57.
27. Preston to Atkins, February 20, 1888, LR #5497–1888, RG 75, SC 31, OIA, NA.
28. Ibid. For the hot springs and its value to the Cahuilla, see Shaw, "Evolving Ecoscape," 244–67, 273–76.
29. Ferguson, Shannan, and Smith to Preston, n.d., with approval by Preston on March 31, 1888, RG 75, SC 31, box 24, OIA, NA. For more detail see also Preston to Atkins, February 20, 1888, LR #5497–1888, RG 75, SC 31, OIA, NA.
30. "Indian Title Confirmed," *Riverside Press & Horticulturalist*, May 12, 1888, quoting the *San Diego Sun*, which notes that this was a "test case to determine and establish the legal status and rights of all Indians on Mexican grants in California."
31. Shirley Ward to Atkins, February 21, 1888, LR #5713–1888, RG 75, SC 31, OIA, NA; for date of argument, see Ward to Welsh, December 17, 1887; see also Ward to Welsh, February 11, 1888—both in reel 3, *IRA Papers*. For the decision in *M. Byrne v. Antonio Alas, et al.* [No. 11,855], see "Commissioner John H. Oberly, December 3, 1888," *Fifty-Seventh Annual Report of the CIA*, lxiv–lxx. For a summary of the legal issues involved, see Donald G. Shanahan Jr., "Compensation for the Loss of the Aboriginal Lands of the California Indians," *Southern California Quarterly*, vol. 57, no. 3 (Fall 1975): 306–8.

32. "C. R. Moody Explains Suit against Indians," November 17, 1916; see also, "Will Fight to Hold Soboba for Indians," November 3, 1916—both in *Hemet News.*
33. *Indian Claims Commission, Soboba Band of Mission Indians vs. the United States of America*, "Findings of Fact Regarding Liability of Defendant for Plaintiff's Loss of Water" (1976), available at www.digital.library.okstate.edu/icc/v37/iccv37p416.pdf. For more on Soboba's water woes, see Garner, *The Broken Ring*, 75–76, 81–95.
34. Shirley Ward to Preston, May 5, 1888, LR #12991–1888; and Preston to Atkins, May 9, 1888, LR #12991–1888—both in RG 75, SC 31, OIA, NA.
35. "Proceedings of the LMC: First Session," *Twentieth Annual Report of the BIC, 1888* (GPO, 1889), 85.

    Born in Milwaukee in 1863, Lewis moved frequently with his parents during his formative years. In 1885 he was living in Washington, D.C., where he worked for the War Department and attended law school at the National University. He was later appointed as a U.S. special Indian agent with inspection duties. He then served the U.S. Justice Department as a special attorney for the Mission Indians. In 1892 he moved to Riverside, where he practiced law before turning to raising oranges and other fruit and developing West Riverside. In 1903 he served as assemblyman for the seventy-eighth State Assembly district. For more, see Holmes, *History of Riverside County*, 575–76.
36. "Proceedings of the LMC," *Twenty-First Annual Report of the BIC, 1889* (GPO, 1890), 94. For Davis's treasury report and Lewis's compensation from September 1, 1888, to August 13, 1889, see 95.

    Jacob Bergman (1832–94) served on the San Diego County Board of Supervisors from 1873 to 1875. See Coral R. Bergman, *Jacob Bergman of Aguanga: The Real Story* (Warner Springs, Calif.: Coral R. Bergman, 1996).
37. For Davis, see "Proceedings of the LMC," 86; and for Waldby, see "Report of William H. Waldby, March 27, 1888," 10—both in *Twentieth Annual Report of the BIC, 1888* (GPO: 1889).
38. Albert Keith Smiley (1828–1912) and his twin brother, Alfred Homans Smiley, were born in Maine and educated at Haverford College. The brothers purchased property at Lake Mohonk, where they eventually built a major resort. In 1883 Albert inaugurated the first Lake Mohonk Conference of Friends of the Indians. See Larry E. Burgess, *The Smileys: A Commemorative Edition* (Redlands, Calif.: Moore Historical Foundation, 1991).
39. "Report of Albert K. Smiley to Whittlesey, March 1, 1889," in "Report of the BIC," Report of the Secretary of the Interior for the Fiscal Year Ending June 30, 1889, vol. 2 (Washington, D.C.: GPO, 1890), 805.

    Eliphalet Whittlesey (1821–1909) was born in Connecticut. A prominent reformer, he was a clergyman, college professor, judge advocate general of the United States Volunteers during the Civil War, the first assistant commissioner of the Freedmen's Bureau, and secretary of the BIC. He joined Smiley on investigative tours to California.
40. Lewis to Davis, December 26, 1888, reel 4, *IRA Papers.* For Preston's politics, see "Preston, Joseph W., Sir," Georgia Genealogy Trails website, http://genealogytrails.com/geo/glynn/bios.htm, accessed on October 4, 2014.

41. The Weinlands formerly worked in Alaska. See "The Moravian Mission in Alaska," *New York Times*, November 29, 1884. Quinton to Oberly, February 18 1889, LR #4927–1889, RG 75, OIA, NA; and Oberly to Quinton, February 28, 1889, LS: Education Division, vol. 16, LB, pages 32 and 33, RG 75, OIA, NA. See also Quinton to Oberly, March 1, 1889, LR #19602 [5839]-1889, RG 75, SC 143, OIA, NA. On April 8 Oberly agreed to grant five acres; see Quinton to Oberly, April 12, 1889, LR #9615–1889, RG 75, OIA, NA.
42. *Ramona Mission, 1889–1899*, box 15; *Report of Ramona Mission for Decade 1889–1899*, box 18; and Sarah M. Taylor to Weinland, August 13, 1889, box 8—all in Papers of William Henry Weinland, Huntington Library, San Marino, Calif. (hereafter cited as Weinland Papers), For Preston, see Quinton to Weinland, July 1889, box 7, Weinland Papers. For Weinland at Potrero, see H. J. Bachman to the Board of Commissioners on Appropriations of Indian lands, February 12, 1891, LR #46165–1891, RG 75, SC 31, OIA, NA.

For Weinland's missionary work, see Mathes, *Helen Hunt Jackson and Her Indian Reform Legacy*, 121–27, 131–35, 138–40, 142, 146–50, 152, 154; Mathes, *Divinely Guided*, numerous pages; and Edmund de Schweinitz Brunner, *History of the Moravian Mission to the Indians of Southern California*, reprinted from *Proceedings of the Society for Propagating the Gospel among the Heathen* (Bethlehem, Penn.: The Society, 1914), 7–34.

Quinton and Weinland believed that Catholics were behind the Cahuillas' refusal to grant the land. Upon the death of Mrs. N. J. Ticknor, the beloved school teacher in the village, her replacement was a Mrs. Thayer of Baltimore, a Catholic, who according to Weinland "through underhanded work" prejudiced the Indians against the Protestant missionary work. See "Report of Ramona Mission for Decade 1889–1899," Weinland Papers. Mission Indians were the descendants of people missionized by Catholic Franciscans, and therefore often Catholic.
43. Lewis to Davis, December 26, 1888, reel 4, *IRA Papers*.

6. A Controversial Collector: Horatio Nelson Rust, 1889–1893

Epigraph. "Rust to Morgan, September 10, 1891," Sixtieth Annual Report of the CIA, 1891, 222.

1. For Rust's appointment, see *Journal of the Executive Proceedings of the Senate of the United States of America*, vol. 27 (Washington, D.C.: GPO, 1901), 284. For his salary, see "Report of Commissioner Thomas Jefferson Morgan, September 5, 1890," *Fifty-Ninth Annual Report of the CIA, 1890*, cxix.

Years later, Rust claimed that he had been appointed "without [his] knowledge and consent." See Chaput, "Horatio N. Rust," 281, citing a letter from Rust to the commissioner of Indian Affairs in 1905.
2. Jackson to Price, November 25, 1883, LR #22018–1883, RG 75, SC 31, OIA, NA.
3. Apostol, "Horatio Nelson Rust," 304–15.
4. Rust to Morgan, July 4, 1889; and Morgan to Rust, July 13, 1889—both in RU 474, box 9, Rust Papers.

Born in Indiana, Morgan (1839–1902) commanded African-American troops during the Civil War and afterward attended Rochester Theological Seminary and was ordained a Baptist minister. After a brief pastorate, he began a career as a secular educator, becoming a strong advocate for allotment and the Dawes Act as well as Indian education. See Francis Paul Prucha, "Thomas Jefferson Morgan, 1889–93," in Kvasnicka and Viola, *The Commissioners*, 193–203.

5. Noble to Rust, July 29, 1889, RU 461, box 9, Rust Papers.

Noble (1831–1912) was an attorney and a brevet general during the Civil War. Born in Ohio, a graduate of Yale, he studied law at Columbia, opening a practice in Keokuk, Iowa. He served as interior secretary from 1889 to 1893.

6. "Reduction in the Number of Agencies," *Fifty-Eighth Annual Report of the CIA, 1889*, 47–48. Morgan condemned the consolidation, as well as the ridiculous trek from the Mission Agency at Colton to the Hoopa Valley—540 miles by rail to San Francisco, 230 miles to Eureka by sea, a 12-mile ferry ride to Arcata, a 10-mile rail trip to the north fork of Mad River, and the final 30-mile horseback trip over a pack trail to the agency. The subagents at Hoopa continued to file their own annual reports during the brief period they were connected to the Mission Agency.

7. Rust to Markham (ca. late 1889 or early 1890), RU 475, box 9, Rust Papers.

8. The average agent's salary was $1,533; therefore Rust's pay was not the lowest. See "Report of Commissioner Thomas Jefferson Morgan, September 5, 1890," *Fifty-Ninth Annual Report of the CIA, 1890*, cxix. His successors, Estudillo and Wright, also got $1,600 a year.

Government farmers were a regular position at Indian agencies, hired to teach and encourage better agricultural practices. The Mission Indian Agency had two by the mid-1880s. William L. Anderson, at the Morongo (now Potrero) Reservation, supported himself and distributed crops he raised among the Indians. Even greater responsibility was given the farmers on the more outlying reservations, such as Andrew Stice, who served at the far-off Tule River Reservation under Agent Estudillo. Agent Ward complained about "court house or political farmers" being appointed instead of real farmers, believing they should be able to "compel" the Indians to work. See "Ward to Atkins, August 17, 1887," *Annual Report of the CIA*, 10.

9. At an IRA meeting, Rust read a history of the Mission Indians, asking "every citizen of Southern California to see that justice is rendered to the few left." See "Indian Rights: The Association Addressed by Several Eloquent Speakers," *Los Angeles Herald*, March 7, 1887.

10. For selling artifacts, see Chaput, "Horatio N. Rust," 293; also Apostol, "Horatio Nelson Rust," 304–15; and A. L. Kroeber, "Horatio Nelson Rust," *Journal of American Folklore* (April–June 1907), 153. For an autobiographical sketch, see Rust to Prof. Beardsley, May 24, 1894, RU 1125, box 10, Rust Papers; and Hiram A. Reid, *History of Pasadena* (Pasadena: Pasadena History Company, 1896), 130–31.

11. "Diary of Reservation Visits—1889," RU 510, Rust Papers.

Born in Illinois on June 11, 1858, Sarah Elizabeth Morris traveled with her parents by covered wagon to Missouri, where she taught school. In March 1888 she moved to

Banning, teaching initially in a "miserable dilapidated box building" on the Morongo Reservation. Within a year the Indians had built her a comfortable school house with two small living quarters. She remained at her post for seventeen years. On August 16, 1899, she married Marshall French Gilman. The family ranch at Banning is now a Riverside County historical park. See "A Retrospection," Gilman Family Papers, box 24, in Weinland Papers.

12. See "In Quaint Saboba [*sic*]. A Village Made Famous in 'Ramona'—Where Indian Life Is Seen at Its Best," *San Jacinto Register*, April 5, 1893, reprinted from the *San Francisco Chronicle*, February 19, 1893; and "An Indian Newspaper. Something Unique and Interesting in Indian Journalism," *San Jacinto Register*, May 25, 1893, which quotes extracts from the *Soboba News*, a manuscript newspaper published by Noble's students.
13. "Diary of Reservation Visits—1889," RU 510, Rust Papers. The population figures given in this source differed from those in Rust's published 1890 annual report.
14. Ibid.
15. Ibid.
16. For more on Alexander and Salmons, see WNIA, *The Indian's Friend*, December 1903, 11. During her first visit to Salmons at Rincon in 1891, WNIA president Amelia Stone Quinton described the schoolteacher as exerting "a strong influence for industry and morality, while also doing good educational work we were told." See WNIA, "Through Southern California: Letter Number Seven," *The Indian's Friend*, October 1891, 6. In "Our Policy toward the Mission Indians" (in *Proceedings of the Tenth Annual Meeting of the LMC, 1892*, 115), Joseph B. Moore, who visited Rincon in 1892, noted that after Salmons and her mother had moved to California from Atlanta, Georgia, they purchased a small ranch from a local Mexican, using the house and its flower gardens and fruit orchard as an "object-lesson" for the children and adults in the village.
17. "Diary of Reservation Visits—1889," RU 510, Rust Papers; and "Rust to Morgan, August 8, 1890," *Fifty-Ninth Annual Report of the CIA, 1890*, 19.
18. "Diary of Reservation Visits—1889," RU 510, Rust Papers.

    In the 1930s, Margaret Boynton wrote down some of Patencio's memories; they were published in 1943 as *Stories and Legends of the Palm Springs Indians* and republished by the Palm Springs Desert Museum in 1969.
19. Rust, "Report on Conditions of Mission Indians and the Perris School Buildings, etc. etc.," RU 487, box 9, Rust Papers.

    A third Catholic boarding school had been established in 1884 at old Fort Yuma, on the California side of the Colorado River. Teresa Baksh McNeil, in "Catholic Indian Schools of the Southwest Frontier: Curriculum and Management" (*Southern California Quarterly*, vol. 72, no. 4 [Winter 1990]: 321–38), notes that because Commissioner Morgan was opposed to teaching religion in government-sponsored schools, Washington began imposing stricter rules during his tenure, prompting the Sisters of St. Joseph of Carondelet to give up their educational work at Yuma in 1900.
20. Teresa Baksh McNeil, "St. Anthony's Indian School in San Diego, 1886–1907," *Journal of San Diego History*, vol. 34, no. 3 (Summer 1988): 186–200. In 1893 the school

apparently received about $160 per student from the government, with a maximum of seventy-five boys and girls. Additional students' tuition was paid for through contributions from other sources.

21. Tanya L. Rathbun, "Hail Mary: The Catholic Experience at St. Boniface Indian School," in *Boarding School Blues: Revisiting American Indian Educational Experiences* (Lincoln: University of Nebraska Press, 2006), 155–73; and R. Bruce Harley, "The Founding of St. Boniface Indian School, 1888–1890," *Southern California Quarterly*, vol. 81, no. 4 (Winter 1999): 449–66. For a contemporary description, see "Padres Teaching Indians Farming," *Hemet News*, November 4, 1927. See also Hughes, *History of Banning*, 180–82. The school later moved, and it survived until 1978; the old buildings were torn down in 1974.

Born in Germany, Hahn (1849–1916) was ordained to the priesthood in Ohio and served churches in the Midwest before coming to California to take charge of St. Boniface in 1890. He also served parishes in Banning, Beaumont, and Palm Springs and Indian chapels as far away as Warner Hot Springs. Heart trouble forced him to move to St. Francis de Sales Parish in Riverside in 1913. "Father Hahn did noble work among the people of Banning for more than twenty-three years," the *Banning Record* noted on his leaving. "Kind, diplomatic and firm he succeeded admirably in the work among the Indians here." See "Father Hahn Says Goodbye," *Banning Record*, September 18, 1913. He returned to St. Boniface to be buried with some of his students and staff. For obituaries, see "Rev. Father Hahn Called Home," *Banning Record*, August 10, 1916; and "Rev. Father Hahn Passes On," *Beaumont Leader*, August 11, 1916.

22. Rust to Morgan, December 1, 1891, and December 2, 1891, "Letter from the Secretary of the Interior," *The Executive Documents of the Senate of the United States, 1891–92* (Congress, Senate, 52d Cong., 1st sess., Ex. Doc. no. 108), vol. 16 (Washington, D.C.: GPO, 1892), 8–9. Chaput, in "Horatio N. Rust," remarked that rather than allowing the Catholic priests to enroll more Indian students, Rust "plowed ahead" with his plans for the school at Perris. This "anti-Catholic attitude" did not serve him well (282, 284). For more on Rust's anti-Catholic bias, see Phillips, *Chiefs and Challengers*, 304–5.

Following an interview with John Morongo, who criticized St. Boniface, Father Hahn explained that Morongo had not been elected by his people but appointed by Rust, and that neither man, the agent nor the captain, had ever been friendly to the presence of St. Boniface because they were not Catholic. Furthermore, Hahn pointed out, the average school attendance during 1891–92 was 115 students, higher than Morongo had claimed. Girls were taught more than merely how to sew, as Morongo had stated. They learned to cook, bake, wash and iron, knit, and do needlework. See "The Banning Indians: How They Are Instructed at St. Boniface's School," *Los Angeles Herald*, January 25, 1893.

23. Morongo visited the school before allowing his daughter and other girls from his village to attend. See "The Anaheim Indian School," *Anaheim Gazette*, February 21, 1885; "An Indian School," *Los Angeles Times*, January 4, 1885; and "Anaheim," *Los Angeles Times*, January 17, 1885.

24. Thomas J. Morgan, "Supplemental Report on Indian Education," in *Americanizing the American Indians*, ed. Francis Paul Prucha (Cambridge: Harvard University

Press, 1973), 222–23. For Morgan's suggested curriculum for Indian day schools, see "Commissioner Thomas Jefferson Morgan, December 8, 1890," *Fifty-Ninth Annual Report of the CIA*, clvi–clx.

25. "McCallum to Atkins, September 30, 1885," *Annual Report of the CIA, 1885*, 8; and "Ward to Atkins, August 14, 1886," *Annual Report of the CIA, 1886*, 44. "While the Indian's head needs training, his hand needs it the more," he wrote (43). But in his typically bitter way, Ward also complained that Indian parents did not appreciate the schools the government provided.
26. Rust, "Report on Condition of Mission Indian and the Perris School Buildings, etc. etc.;" RU 487, box 9, pp. 4–5, Rust Papers.
27. "The Second Institute: Interesting Exercises at Wilson School. Sup. Monroe, Mrs. Rice and Indian Agent Rust Speak," *Los Angeles Times*, November 2, 1890.
28. Rust, "Notes of an Address upon Mission Indians Delivered in Los Angeles," RU 497, box 10, Rust Papers.
29. "Rust to Morgan, September 10, 1891," *Sixtieth Annual Report of the CIA, 1891*, 224. See also "Lo, The Poor Indian: Has Many Friends in Pasadena," *Los Angeles Times*, August 27, 1891. See "Pasadena: Friends of the Indians," *Los Angeles Times*, May 10, 1892, for another Rust address before the WNIA. Members across the country were soon supporting Fleming's sewing classes and other activities.
30. Rust, "Report on Condition of Mission Indian and the Perris School Buildings, etc. etc.;" RU 487, box 9, p. 6, Rust Papers.

    Carlisle was founded in Pennsylvania in 1879 by Richard Henry Pratt, a former army officer, who felt the school's five-year academic and vocational training period, sprinkled with military and Christian training, "would sever Indian children's attachment to family, community, and all aspects of their past and teach them to dress, talk, behave, and think like white Americans." See Jacqueline Fear-Segal, "The Man on the Bandstand at Carlisle Indian Industrial School," in *Boarding School Blues: Revisiting American Indian Educational Experiences*, 101.
31. In Rust to Morgan, February 3, 1891 (LR #5190–1891, RG 75, OIA, NA), Rust wrote that the same party giving the eighty acres "will execute a deed for one hundred within ten days." See also "Rust to Morgan, September 10, 1891," *Sixtieth Annual Report of the CIA, 1891*, 224–25.
32. Morgan to Assistant Commissioner R. V. Belt, November 17, 1890, LR #35960–1890, RG 75, OIA, NA. Morgan visited the site while on a tour of government schools. See "An Indian Training School: A Big Institution That Is to Be Located in Perris Valley," *San Francisco Chronicle*, August 2, 1891. The *Chronicle* erroneously reported that both Rust and Morgan intended to gather all Indian children then attending the eight reservation day schools there.
33. Rust, "Report on Condition of Mission Indians and the Perris School Buildings, etc. etc.," RU 487, box 9, Rust Papers. Ella Morongo, the second daughter of Rust's interpreter, John Morongo, attended during the last year or so of the school's existence. Years later she addressed a meeting of the Redlands Indian Association, a WNIA auxiliary, where she read extracts from papers written by Perris students about their home life. See WNIA, "Redlands Association," *The Indian's Friend*, June 1901, 9–10.

Savage was later charged with fraud and embezzlement. See "Fraud and Rascality: The Perris Indian School Management," *San Francisco Chronicle*, August 5, 1894.

34. "Edgar A. Allen, Report of School at Perris, Cal., August 14, 1895," *Annual Report of the Secretary of the Interior, 1895*, vol. 2 (Washington, D.C.: GPO, 1896), 362. See also Clifford E. Trafzer, Matthew Sakiestewa Gilbert, and Lorene Sisquoc, eds., *The Indian School on Magnolia Avenue: Voices and Images from Sherman Institute* (Corvallis: Oregon State University Press, 2012).

35. Lewis to Rust, August 26, 1889, RU 443, box 9, Rust Papers.

G. S. Bailey, editor of the *Southern California Baptist*, had recommended to Commissioner Oberly and President Cleveland that the California Indians be removed to Indian Territory for their allotments. See Bailey to Oberly, June 22, 1887, LR #16712–1887; and Bailey to Cleveland, June 22, 1887, LR #17306–1887—both in RG 75, SC 31, OIA, NA.

36. Although the General Land Office had suspended his original filing on May 24, 1885, Walsh filed a second claim, stating that he had occupied the land since March 1, 1888. This prompted Agent Preston to file a protest on April 25 that "the Indians were then occupying said tract" and had done so for years. Walsh's claims were finally cancelled on May 16, 1891. See "Pre-emption Claim—Indian Lands: Mission Indians v. Walsh," *Decisions of the Department of the Interior and General Land Office in Cases Relating to Public Lands*, vol. 12, ed. S. V. Proudfit (Washington, D.C.: GPO, 1891), 516–18.

37. Lewis to Rust, August 26, 1889, RU 443, box 9, Rust Papers.

38. Ibid.

Under instructions of August 13 and October 7, 1890, Lewis began serving as a special Indian agent assigned to oversee the allotting of lands under the Dawes legislation to Indians living near Redding, California. See "November 12, 1890, Semi-Weekly Report of Frank D. Lewis," LR #35796–1890; and Lewis to Morgan, November 12, 1890, LR #35876–1890—both in RG 75, OIA, NA. A *San Francisco Call* article dated December 13, 1890, noted that the Justice Department had recently appointed Lewis as a special attorney for the Mission Indians.

39. Garrett to Morgan, February 17, 1890, LR #5723–1890, RG 75, SC 31, OIA, NA.

Charles O. Barker (1858–1935) came to Banning in June 1884 and taught school for two years before becoming manager of the Banning Land & Water Co. In 1892 he was elected an assemblyman and in 1893 introduced the bill to create Riverside County. He was also involved in fruit farming, cattle ranching, and real estate. For a biography, see Hughes, *History of Banning*, 115–16.

40. Garrett, Rust, Smiley, and Ward to Morgan, February 21, 1890, LR #7188–1890, RG 75, SC 31, OIA, NA. See also Garrett to Morgan, February 17, 1890, LR #5723–1890, RG 75, SC 31, OIA, NA

41. Garrett, Rust, Smiley, and Ward to Morgan, February 21, 1890, LR # 7188–1890.

42. Rust to Morgan, November 16, 1890, LR #36284–1890, RG 75, OIA, NA.

At the bottom of this letter, U.S. Indian Inspector William N. Jenkins wrote that such a delegation "would do much toward securing the justice to which these people are entitled."

43. Preston to Atkins, August 31, 1887, LR #23676–1887, RG 75, SC 31, OIA, NA.
44. Rust to Weinland, December 11, 1889, box 6, Weinland Papers. See also Rust, October 31, 1889, LR #31742–1889, OIA, RG 75, SC 143, NA; "Rust to Commissioner Morgan," October 28, 1889," *Fifty-Eighth Annual Report of the CIA, 1889*, 125; and Rust to Morgan, August 8, 1890," *Fifty-Ninth Annual Report of the CIA, 1890*, 18–19. A Catholic chapel was built on the reservation in 1898; visiting priests had been holding services there for many years.
45. "Indian Justice," *San Francisco Chronicle*, July 24, 1892, reprinted in Robert F. Heizer, ed., *Some Last Century Accounts of the Indians of Southern California* (Ramona, Calif.: Ballena Press, 1976), 21–25. Reports of flogging as a punishment for crimes such as theft were still reported from other reservations in the mid-1890s.
46. As early as 1874 the BIC had raised the issue of an Indian police force, but not until May of 1878 did Congress authorize such an expenditure. Indian judges had to wait until the Court of Indian Offenses was established in 1883, and then the agent often served as judge. See Prucha, *American Indian Policy in Crisis*, 201–11.
47. "Preston to Atkins, August 20, 1888," *Fifty-Seventh Annual Report of the CIA, 1888*, 20; and "Rust to Morgan, August 8, 1890," *Fifty-Ninth Annual Report of the CIA, 1890*, 17. Rust also noted that since he did not issue rations, he could not use withholding them as a punishment.
48. An undated list of Indian policemen in the Coachella Valley area (seemingly from the early 1890s) lists Francisco Patencio at Agua Caliente, H[enry?] Pablo and Segundo Chino at Potrero, Will James at Indio, and Anastascio Chapula at Martinez. See box 5, folder 1, John Brown Papers, Sherman Library and Gardens, Corona del Mar, Calif. Beginning in 1893 the Indian commissioner's annual reports list the agency police force under the statistics for agency employees; the names of a number of well-known Indian leaders are included.
49. "Estudillo to Browning, August 31, 1894," *Annual Report of the CIA, 1894* (GPO, 1895), 123; and "Wright to Jones, August 21, 1899," *Annual Reports of the DOI, 1899*, part 1, 173. For more on the Indian police force, see Seymour, "Relations between the United States and the Mission Indians," 86–87.
50. "Rust to Morgan, August 8, 1890," *Fifty-Ninth Annual Report of the CIA, 1890*, 18.
51. Rust to Morgan, June 25, 1890, LR #20466–1890, RG 75, SC 31, OIA, NA.
52. Hiles to Noble, May 13, 1890, LR #15352–1890, RG 75, OIA, NA.
53. *Redlands Citrograph*, May 3, 1890. See also "The Banning Lynching. What Indian Agent Rust Says about the Man," *Los Angeles Times*, May 1, 1890.

Hughes, in his *History of Banning and San Gorgonio Pass* (33–34), writes: "Banning's only public lynching, to date, was celebrated the evening of May 5th [*sic*], when Tacho Razon, who seems to have been a very young brother of Fig Tree John's, escaped from the Carpenter & Hamilton livery stable, where he was tied to a stall, under arrest for horse stealing. He had been captured in the desert. The Oregon boot he wore in his retreat from the stable made travelling so slow that when the boy Ben de Crevecoeur spread the news that Tacho was legging it through the orchards east of town, capture was quick.

"Next sunrise found him hanging from a telegraph pole about where the railroad begins to make the bend. He was officially pronounced dead, but no official sequel is recorded."

54. U.S. Congress, Senate, "Message from the President of the United States," S. Ex. Doc 49, 48th Cong., 1st sess., 1884, 1–7; and "Mission Indians in California," *Annual Report of the CIA, 1884*, xxxvii. For the Jackson/Kinney recommendations, see Jackson and Kinney, "Report," 464–73.
55. When passage seemed assured, the *Redlands Citrograph* groused that the Indians already "had set apart for them in San Bernardino and San Diego counties more than 500 acres for every buck, squaw and papoose they have, of the choicest lands to be found." The Indians had government schools, and rations, plus an agent "at a luxurious salary." "What wonder they are lazy?" the paper asked. "Why should they receive any better treatment than white men? Why should they be pampered by the Government when white men must work, beg, steal or starve?" The paper advocated full allotment instead. See "The Mission Indians," *Redlands Citrograph*, December 20, 1890.
56. Born in Commerce, Michigan, Moore (1845–1930) attended Hillsdale College and the University of Michigan. He opened a law practice in Lapeer in 1868 and pursued a political career, serving as prosecuting attorney for two terms and in the state senate for one year, 1878. In 1888 he was elected a circuit judge, and beginning in 1896 he served as a justice in the Michigan State Supreme Court for the next thirty years. See http://www.micourthistory.org/special-sessions/in-memoriam-joseph-b-moore/, accessed on July 2, 2017. Painter wrote that while Moore was simply a political appointee and knew nothing about the California Indians, the Indian Office could not have made a better choice for the third member of the commission. See Indian Rights Association, "Report of Mr. C. C. Painter, Washington Agent of the Association," *in Ninth Annual Report of the IRA EC* (hereafter cited as "Painter Report"), 12.
57. For Painter and Moore's arrival, see "Mission Lands. The Commissioners Appointed Arrive in San Diego," *Los Angeles Herald*, November 4, 1891.
58. A cover letter by Noble to Morgan, dated January 24, 1891, was included with the lengthy letter from Morgan to Smiley, Moore, and Painter, dated January 31, 1891 (LR #3101–1891, RG 75, SC 31, OIA, NA). A printed copy of this January 31 letter was included in George Chandler to Morgan, February 9, 1891, LR #5319–1891, RG 75, SC 31, OIA, NA.

    For a summary of the commission's work, including a listing of the new reservations established, see "Painter Report," 11–23. Before the commission began its work, the Mission Indians lived on nineteen reservations embracing nearly 270,000 acres. See also Mathes, "The California Mission Indian Commission of 1891: The Legacy of Helen Hunt Jackson," *California History*, vol. 72, no. 4 (Winter 1993–94): 339–59; and Larry E. Burgess, "Commission to the Mission Indians, 1891," *San Bernardino County Museum Association Quarterly*, vol. 35, no.1 (Spring 1988): 1–46.
59. See "Painter Report," 15–16.

60. Morgan to Smiley, Moore, and Painter, January 31, 1891, LR #3101–1891, RG 75, SC 31, OIA, NA. On March 13, 1891, Lewis wrote Morgan asking that the Indian Office request the attorney general to instruct him "to accompany the Commission." Since Lewis had just forwarded his oath of office to the Department of Justice, he was not authorized to work with the commission until after April 1. See Lewis to Morgan, March 13, 1891, LR #10899–1891, RG 75, SC 31, OIA, NA.
61. Rust to Morgan, March 27, 1891, LR #12233–1891, RG 75, SC 31, OIA, NA. For Lewis's appointment, see George Chandler, Acting Interior Secretary, to Lewis, May 20, 1891, LR #18465–1891, RG 75, OIA, NA. For Lewis's oath of office, see Lewis to Morgan, June 1, 1891, LR #20356–1891, RG 75, OIA, NA.
62. Unaware of the "continuous" work required to serve, Smiley requested a temporary release, suggesting that Painter, Lewis, and a surveyor continue the work. He described Lewis as "a most competent and valuable assistant" who was "ready to devote his time to C. C. Painter during the ensuring summer." See Smiley to Noble, April 1, 1891, LR #13939–1891. Moore was also granted a leave of absence because of a family illness, see Noble to Moore, April 9, 1891, LR #13695–1891—both in RG 75, SC 31, OIA, NA.
63. Rust to Morgan, February 3, 1891, LR #5190–1891, RG 75, SC 31, OIA, NA; and "Rust to Morgan, September 10, 1891," *Sixtieth Annual Report of the CIA, 1891*, 221.
64. For more on Laguna and the Lucas family, see Lora L. Cline, *Just before Sunset* (Tombstone, Ariz.: LC Enterprises, 1984). Tom Lucas secured title to 320 acres of the former reservation in the 1940s. Cuyapaipe is today known as the Ewiiaapaayp Reservation.
65. The Augustine Reservation took in the La Mesa village, south of Coachella. The Cabazon Reservation included the two small "village" reservations near Indian Wells, which were by then deserted. See Robert Perez, *The History of the Cabazon Band of Mission Indians, 1776–1876* (Indio, Calif.: Cabazon Band of Mission Indians, 1999).
66. For the complete report, see Albert Smiley et al., "Smiley Commission Report: Mission Indians," *Report of Indian Commissioners*, December 7, 1891, Smiley Collection, A. K. Smiley Library, Redlands, California; also available at Stand Up for California! website, http://www.standupca.org/gaming-law/unique-federal-indian-law-california-specific/Smiley%20Commission%20Report.pdf/view, accessed on June 15, 2017. See also Acting Commissioner Belt to Noble, December 19, 1891, LR #9299–1891, RG 75, OIA, NA. Painter's summary is found in *Ninth Annual Report of the IRA EC*, 11–23.

A reservation was also recommended for some of the former residents of San Pasqual, but the area had not yet been officially surveyed and so no patent could be issued. It has been suggested that the proposed 1891 reservation was accidentally mislocated six miles north of its intended location. The first Indian family did not move there until 1909. By then, a number of squatters occupied the land and had to be bought out or evicted by the government. A patent to the reservation was finally issued in 1910. For more on the reservation and the San Pasqual people, see Toler, *Band of Blood* (especially 123–55). For suggestions that the 1891 location was an error, see C. E. Kelsey, *Report of the Special Agent for California Indians to the*

Commissioner of Indian Affairs, March 21, 1906 (San Jose: Cleveland Printing, 1907), 32; and Wayland H. Smith, "In Re. California Indians to Date," *Out West*, vol. 30, no. 2 (February–March 1909): 138–39.

67. "Estudillo to Browning, August 31, 1894," *Annual Report of the CIA, 1894* (GPO, 1895), quotes on 119–21. For final quote, see "Estudillo to Browning, August 1, 1896," *Annual Report of the CIA, 1896*, 129. Except for his descriptions of one or two reservations, Estudillo was generally more complimentary in his descriptions than most of his predecessors. Seymour, in "Relations between the United States and the Mission Indians" (101), reports that the Ramona Reservation was unoccupied by 1906.

68. "Painter Report," 18.

69. Ibid., 20; and Acting Commissioner Belt to Noble, December 19, 1891, LR #9299–1891, RG 75, OIA, NA, 23–24.

In 1883 Bishop Mora had offered to sell the rancho to the government to use for a reservation. Helen Hunt Jackson recommended his offer be accepted, but the funds were not forthcoming.

70. Smiley to Whittlesey, December 4, 1891, LR #46165–1891, RG 75, OIA, NA. See also Smiley's notes, quoted in Doody and Meltzer, *Losing Ground*, 117; and Lewis to Morgan, December 7, 1891, LR #44547–1891, RG 75, SC 31, OIA, NA.

71. Hathaway (1861–1938) was born in Milwaukee, Wisconsin, and came to Banning in 1883, serving as the city's first mayor when Banning incorporated in 1913. There is still a Hathaway Canyon, marking the site of his former ranch on the reservation. For a biography, see Hughes, *History of Banning*, 110–11.

72. Acting Commissioner Belt to Noble, December 19, 1891, LR #9299–1891, RG 75, OIA, NA, 27–35.

73. For more details and a map, see "Morongo Reservation. Status of Lands in and about Banning," *Los Angeles Times*, July 21, 1892. Unmentioned is that Attorney Barker carefully preserved the Banning Land & Water Company's water rights in Banning Water Canyon, succeeding in having that area removed from the reservation. See also Doody and Meltzer, *Losing Ground*, 115.

The commission's success with the Southern Pacific should not be overlooked, especially considering the vast political power the railroad wielded in the state at that time.

74. See Doody and Meltzer, *Losing Ground*, 104–19, and especially 147–53 for a detailed timeline.

75. "Estudillo to Browning, August 31, 1894," *Annual Report of the CIA, 1894*, 120; and Smith, "In Re California Indians to Date," 137. Mrs. Toutain apparently still held her claim when she died in 1912. For more of the history of the Morongo Reservation in later decades, see Harlan Lanas Hoffman III, "In the Shadow of the Mountain, The Cahuilla, Serrano, and Cupeño People of the Morongo Indian Reservation, 1885–1934" (2006).

76. "The Torros [*sic*] Reservation," *Sacramento Record-Union*, January 3, 1897. The Torres (now Torres-Martinez) Reservation still retains its dispersed, checkerboard boundaries. Much of the reservation was flooded in the formation of the Salton Sea in the early 1900s.

77. "Estudillo to Browning, August 1, 1896," *Annual Report of the CIA, 1896*, 127.

In 1903 Congress approved a land swap with the state for Section 16, where the Martinez village relocated. See Seymour, "Relations between the United States and the Mission Indians," 81.

78. "Estudillo to Browning, August 31, 1894," *Annual Report of the CIA, 1894*, 119–20.

George Washington McCain (1810–82) brought his family to the area in 1868, but just which of his many sons and grandsons, most of them cattlemen, had land at Cosmit is unclear. As late as 1907 the Interior Department was still trying to settle the matter with Peter McCain, either a son or a grandson. See "Report of Indian Commissioner Francis E. Leupp, September 30, 1907," *Annual Report of the CIA, 1907*, 92.

79. "Estudillo to Browning, August 31, 1894," *Annual Report of the CIA, 1894*, 119; and "Painter Report," 14.

In his "Report of the Special Agent for California Indians" (36), C. E. Kelsey noted that a white man claimed to have purchased Cosmit from one of the old Indians for a cattle ranch, an illegal transaction, even if true, and that the actual village was off the reservation.

80. "Estudillo to Browning," August 31, 1895, *Annual Report of the Secretary of the Interior, 1895*, vol. 2, 132; and "Wright to Jones, August 1897," *Annual Reports of the DOI, 1897*, 117–18.

81. Babbitt (1852–1940) was born in Illinois, the daughter of a prominent attorney and the wife of Henry W. Babbitt, a clerk in the Department of the Interior. By 1884 she was already teaching at a government school on the Omaha and Winnebago Agency in Nebraska. She accompanied the Warner Ranch Indians when they were removed to Pala and continued teaching there before transferring to the Santo Domingo Pueblo as a field matron, eventually working at Algondones, New Mexico. She died at age ninety in the Panama Canal Zone, where she lived for a number of years on an island in Gatun Lake with Woodford Babbitt, her son. See "Mrs. Josephine Babbitt," *New York Times*, July 14, 1940; Valerie Sherer Mathes and Phil Brigandi, "The Mischief Record of 'La Gobernadora' Amelia Stone Quinton, Charles Fletcher Lummis, and the Warner Ranch Indian Removal," *Journal of San Diego History*, vol. 57, no. 1–2 (Winter/Spring 2011): 84–86, 91n3.

82. "Rust to Morgan, September 10, 1891," *Sixtieth Annual Report of the CIA, 1891*, 224–25.

83. For Quinton's views, see her "Woman's Work in Solving the Indian Problem," in *Christian Educators in Council: Sixty Addresses by American Educators* (New York: Phillips & Hunt, 1884), 103. For her work in California, see Mathes, *Divinely Guided*.

84. This program, reflective of the nineteenth-century attitude toward the role of women, expected field matrons to care for the home, hearth, and child. They were unmarried or widowed white women imparting this knowledge of domesticity to Indian women as part of the assimilation process. Because field matron responsibilities were similar to those of WNIA-sponsored missionaries, the WNIA wholeheartedly lent its support. See "Field Matrons," *Sixty-First Annual Report of the CIA, 1892*, 100–2; and "Field Matrons," *Sixty-Second Annual Report of the CIA, 1893*, 54–57. See especially Lisa E. Emmerich, "Promoting Homemaking on the Reservations: WNIA Field Matrons," in Mathes, *The Women's National Indian Association*, 84–101.

For Morgan's appointment of Fleming as a government "assistant teacher," see Quinton to Morgan, August 4, 1891, LR #29440–1891.

85. Quinton to Morgan, June 28, 1891, LR #24101–1891, RG 75, SC 31, OIA, NA. For the building of a hospital at Agua Caliente, see Quinton to Morgan, December 18, 1891; Morgan to Quinton, January 14, 1892; and Morgan to Quinton, January 28, 1892—all in LR #14976–1891, RG 75, OIA, NA. Because the village was not on a reservation, Morgan could not grant any land.
86. "Rust to Morgan, October 28, 1889," *Fifty-Eighth Annual Report of the CIA, 1889*, 125; and "Rust to Morgan, September 10, 1891," *Sixtieth Annual Report of the CIA, 1891*, 223. See also Rust to Morgan, July 20, 1891, LR #27101–1891, and Rust to Morgan, October 2, 1891, LR #36334–1891—both in RG 75, OIA, NA.
87. Quinton to Weinland, May 15, 1892, and May 16, 1892—both in box 7, Weinland Papers. In a May 22 letter, Quinton accused Rust of wanting to build the hospital himself; "I do hope we can circumvent his machinations," she wrote to Weinland on May 22, 1892 (box 7, Weinland Papers). See also Quinton to Rust, May 23, 1892; and Quinton to Weinland, May 30, 1892—both in box 7, Weinland Papers; and "Association News and Notes," *The Indian's Friend*, August 1892, 2.
88. Quinton to Morgan, February 29, 1892, till March 8th, LR #8669–1892, RG 75, OIA, NA; Morgan to Rust, March 5, 1892, box 8; and Rust to Quinton, March 22 and May 5, 1892, box 6—both in Weinland Papers.
89. Morgan to Rust, June 11, 1892, box 8, Weinland Papers.
90. Rust to Morgan, May 6, 1892, box 6, Weinland Papers.
91. Quinton to Rust, May 23, 1892; and Quinton to Weinland, May 30, 1892—both in box 7, Weinland Papers; and "Association News and Notes," *The Indian's Friend*, August 1892, 2.
92. Rust to Morgan, August 19, 1892, LR #30911–1892, RG 75, OIA, NA; and Lewis to Morgan, September 10, 1892, LR #3396–1892, SC 31, RG 75, OIA, NA.
93. For more, see Quinton to Morgan, November 24, 1892, LR #42167–1892, RG 75, OIA, NA; Quinton to Weinland, December 19, 1892; and Quinton to Weinland, January 30, 1893—both in box 7, Weinland Papers; and Mathes, "A Hospital at Warner Ranch," *Divinely Guided*, 231–61.
94. See "Mischief Record of 'La Gobernadora.' Former Indian Agent Tells of Devil She Raised," *Los Angeles Times*, May 26, 1902.

    Rust was hardly alone in squabbling with female reformers. While sexism (and dueling egos) no doubt played a part, the agents may have also envied the reformers' independence and their ability to sometimes act without waiting for policy or permission from Washington.
95. WNIA, "Agua Caliente," *Sunshine Work* (Philadelphia: December 1894); see 18–19 for Hallowell and 15 for French.
96. Quinton to Morgan, January 11, 1893, LR #1404–1903, RG 75, SC 143, OIA, NA. See also Quinton to Morgan, November 1, 1892, LR #39462–1892, RG 75, OIA, NA; and Weinland to Rust, January 23, 1893, box 10, Weinland Papers, for selection of the five-acre parcel.
97. Born in New York City in February 1855, Johnson had her earliest schooling in

Orange, New Jersey. She opened a medical practice there before becoming a WNIA medical missionary. Following her resignation, she opened up a practice in Redlands, California. See *Woman's Who's Who of America: A Biographical Dictionary of Contemporary Women of the United States and Canada, 1914–1915* (New York: American Commonwealth Company, 1914), 433; and *History of Essex and Hudson Counties, New Jersey*, vol. 1 (Philadelphia: Everts & Peck, 1884), 345. Her medical college thesis, completed in March 1881, was published in *Philadelphia Medical Times* five months later. The topic was neurasthenia, viewed as a female nervous system disease. See Anna Hayward Johnson, "Neurasthenia," *Philadelphia Medical Times, a Bi-Weekly Journal of Medical and Surgical Science, 1880–1881*, vol. 11, August 27, 1881 (Philadelphia: J. B. Lippincott, 1881), 737–44.

98. "Copy of Letter Sent the Commissioner Replying to Mrs. Quinton's Charge," RU 1–1231, box 9, Rust Papers.

99. Rust to Morgan, February 20, 1893, LR #7381–1893, RG 75, OIA, NA. For Quinton's reply to Rust's response, see Quinton to Morgan, February 4, 1893, LR #4665–1893, RG 75, SC 143, OIA, NA. For additional details, see Mathes, "WNIA among the Cahuillas and at Martinez," in *Divinely Guided*, 205–30.

In "Mischief Record of 'La Gobernadora.' Former Indian Agent Tells of Devil She Raised" (*Los Angeles Times*, May 26, 1902), Rust vehemently expressed his displeasure with Quinton, calling her an "old arch enemy." He claimed he invited her to come to Southern California to organize. "In my simplicity," he wrote, "I had no thought but she would cooperate with me as a friend to the Indian." Although warned she "would surely make trouble," he resolved to "meet her as friend" and "treated her as generously." He complained "she was constantly at work misrepresenting him." This is highly unlikely; as president and chair of the WNIA Missionary Committee, Quinton needed no invitation or assistance in her WNIA organizing.

100. "Agent Rust: The Curio Collector Causing Discord. Report of Trouble with the Cahuillas Indians," *Los Angeles Herald*, March 22, 1892, originally printed in the *San Francisco Chronicle*, March 14, and later reprinted as "Causing Discord. Agent Rust Distasteful to the Cahuilla Indians," *Los Angeles Times*, March 23, 1892.

Gilmour was a self-proclaimed expert on the Cahuillas. Born in Allahabad, British India, on June 17, 1858, and educated in England, he wrote for Indian newspapers before coming to California, where he was a regular contributor to the *Sunday Chronicle* and served as editor of the *Evening Post*. See Ella Sterling Cummins Mighels, *The Story of the Files: A Review of California Writers and Literature* (San Francisco: World's Fair Commission of California, Columbian Exposition, 1893), 432–33. Seven of Gilmour's Cahuilla articles are reprinted in Heizer, *Some Last Century Accounts*.

101. "Agent Rust: The Curio Collector Causing Discord." See also Phillips, *Chiefs and Challengers*, 298–300 and 305–6, for a reprinting of some of these same articles.

102. Frémont to Dawes, March 23, 1892, in Dawes to Morgan, April 2, 1892, LR #12447–1892, RG 75, OIA, NA. Frémont and her husband had first met Rust in Chicago fourteen years earlier. Now that she resided in Los Angeles, she occasionally visited him in Pasadena.

103. Ibid.

104. J. H. Gilmour, "An Indian Election. Prospect of Trouble with the Cahuillas," *San Francisco Chronicle*, March 20, 1892; see also "Desert Indians. They Elect a New Chief in Place of Cabezon," *Los Angeles Times*, June 17, 1891.

Williams's election over Cabezon had taken place in 1891. "I will always be glad to see you and do anything I can properly for you," Rust wrote to Cabezon in June, but then changed his tone, adding: "I am sorry that you should join hands against me with Will Pablo and John Brown as they are not good friends to me." (Rust to Chief Cabezon, June 10, 1891, box 5, folder 1, John Brown Papers, Sherman Library and Gardens, Corona del Mar, Calif.) A vote tally in the same folder apparently dates from that election. Seven supported Cabezon while only four backed Williams, who was listed as the captain at Alamo Bonita.

105. "Rust and Gilmour. The Newspaper Correspondent Comes Back at the Agent," *Los Angeles Times*, May 8, 1892. For the initial closing of this ditch, see "Closing a Ditch. Indian Agent Rust Making Trouble at Palm Springs," *San Francisco Chronicle*, April 14, 1892.

106. For the election, see "Desert Indians. They Elect a New Chief in Place of Cabezon," *Los Angeles Times*, June 17, 1891. Williams personally reported the election results to Rust at Colton.

107. Rust to Morgan, March 30, 1892, LR #12570–1892, RG 75, OIA, NA. Three months earlier, in a December 1891 letter, Rust informed Morgan that he had conferred with Inspector William W. Junkin, who subsequently "signified to Pablo and the other Indians his approval of my course." Both letters were printed in "Letter from the Secretary of the Interior," Ex. Doc. no. 108, 6 and 7. For more on the Rust/Cabezon/Pablo power struggles, see Phillips, *Chiefs and Challengers*, 303–10.

108. Rust to Morgan, March 30, 1892, LR #12570–1892, RG 75, OIA, NA.

A year later Williams and four of his captains (Joaquin Torres, Jose Ramon, Augustin Messes, and José Rafael) from the villages of Martinez, Torres, Messes, and Agua Caliente wrote to the *Los Angeles Times* objecting to a recent news item describing Cabezon as chief of the Cahuilla and Serrano Indians (and Will Pablo as his "assistant chief" and interpreter). "Cabazon [*sic*] has no right to the office or title of chief, he having forfeited the same by neglecting the interests of his people, and by neglecting to carry out the orders of Government officials," wrote the five Indians. They explained that Cabezon had more followers among the white residents of San Bernardino than he did among the Cahuilla and Serrano Indians. The letter accused Will Pablo of "bad character" as well. See "'Injuns,'" *Los Angeles Times*, March 25, 1893.

Williams died soon after his election/appointment. In 1894 Agent Estudillo ordered a new election among the captains of "all the reservations from Palm Springs eastward," and they selected Joaquin Torres, Chief Cabezon "being for a second time compelled to step back." Estudillo then gave Torres a government commission for the year 1894–95, all this on the word of John Morongo in a letter to the *Los Angeles Times*. See "Salvage Indian Unity," *Los Angeles Times*, November 9, 1894. For more on the Cabezon/Torres rivalry, see "An Indian Habeas Corpus Case Dismissed," *Los*

Angeles Times, March 7, 1895, which describes a case involving Juan Antonio Razon ("Fig Tree John"), a Cabezon ally.

109. "Agent Rust: The Curio Collector Causing Discord," *Los Angeles Herald*, March 22, 1892.

110. Gilmour, "Indian Politicians. Bossism Has a Firm Hold on Them," *San Francisco Chronicle*, May 15, 1892, reprinted in Heizer, *Some Last Century Accounts*, 8–11.

For more on Rust and his struggles with Morongo, Will Pablo, and Cabezon, see Hanks, *This War*, 65–79. Hanks speaks of Pablo's "defiant character" (121). "Will Pablo was clearly a man of cunning and charisma," he notes, "along with certain manipulative qualities. He also changed and adapted his positions over time."

111. "Agent Rust. The Curio Collector Causing Discord," *Los Angeles Herald*, March 22, 1892.

112. Ibid. Also see Gilmour, "Thrifty Agent Rust. Collecting Valuable Curios from Indians. Selling What He Gets for Nothing," *San Francisco Chronicle*, August 27, 1892, reprinted in Heizer, *Some Last Century Accounts*, 26–29.

113. Rust to Prof. Beardsley, May 24, 1894, RU 1125, box 10, Rust Papers.

114. Lawson to Morongo, November 22, 1890, RU 439, box 9, Rust Papers. How this letter ended up in Rust's possession is unclear. Hanks, in *This War Is for a Whole Life* (82n36), speculates that either Morongo turned it over to Rust, or Rust discovered it while engaged in a "bit of political intrigue" to protect his position as agent.

115. Rust to Morgan, December 2, 1891, "Letter from the Secretary of the Interior," Ex. Doc. no. 108, 7. Rust, too, claimed that Pablo had killed a man, in Redlands in a "drunken row." See also "Chief Morongo and His People. The Ruler of the Potrero Reservation in Town," *Los Angeles Herald*, January 19, 1893. Weinland had baptized Morongo on April 20, 1890; see Weinland, "Report of Ramona Mission for Decade 1889–1899," box 18, Weinland Papers.

116. "Ought to Go," *San Bernardino Daily Courier*, March 24, 1891. Pablo, the reporter added, "is a bright, intelligent and well-posted Indian," who could both read and write in English and Spanish. Furthermore, "he converses intelligently and keenly. He is, in fact, the brightest Indian the writer has met in Southern California."

117. Rust to Morgan, December 20, 1890; and Morgan to Rust, January 12, 1891—both in "Letter from the Secretary of the Interior," Ex. Doc. no. 108, 14–15.

In R. V. Belt to Noble, June 2, 1892, the acting commissioner pointed out that "the general policy of the Government" for a number of years had been "to ignore and disregard the claims and pretentions of chiefs among tribes, and to deal directly with the heads of families and individuals." See "Letter from the Secretary of the Interior," Ex. Doc. no. 109, 2. Rust supported this policy to break up "tribal relations" and end the role of captaincy.

118. The Potrero "Messiah craze" appears to have been based on the teachings of Wovoka, or Jack Wilson, a Northern Paiute who, following a vision in 1889, began to teach his followers that performing a traditional round dance in a specific way, called the Ghost Dance, would result in a renewed world—all whites would disappear and the buffalo and deceased Indians would return. Although Wovoka's message was a

peaceful one, the emissaries sent to him by the Sioux returned to their reservation with a more militant message, ultimately resulting in the death of Sitting Bull and the massacre of more than one hundred Sioux at Wounded Knee in December of 1890. For more, see Jeffrey Ostler, *The Plains Sioux and U.S. Colonialism from Lewis and Clark to Wounded Knee* (Cambridge: Cambridge University Press, 2004), 243–369.

119. Rust to Morgan, February 4, 1891; and Rust to Morgan, July 4, 1891—both in "Letter from the Secretary of the Interior," Ex. Doc. no. 108, 14 and 13.

120. Rust to Morgan, September 10, 1891, *Sixtieth Annual Report of the CIA, 1891*, 223. Rust failed to add that "even so intelligent a man as Chief Morongo" had also fled to the mountains as the water rose. See "A Strange Phenomenon," *Redlands Citrograph*, July 4, 1891.

See also J. H. Gilmour, "An Indian Prophet. A Banning Witch Doctor's Forebodings," *San Francisco Chronicle*, April 1892, reprinted in Heizer, *Some Last Century Accounts*, 5–7; and Hanks, *This War Is for a Whole Life*, 74–75.

121. Rust wrote to Morgan that Brown had "been accustomed to advise these Indians for several years (his wife being part Indian), collecting fees and only making the Indians and the agent trouble." Rust to Morgan, February 4, 1891; see also Rust to Morgan, July 4, 1891—both in "Letter from the Secretary of the Interior," Ex. Doc. no. 108, 14, and 13.

Brown was born on the frontier in what is now Colorado in 1847 and came to California with his family in 1849. They settled in San Bernardino three years later. He remained in the area for the rest of his life, as a teacher initially and later as an attorney. He died in 1932. For a biography (which he may have written himself) and portrait, see John Brown Jr. and James Boyd, *History of San Bernardino and Riverside Counties* (Chicago: Lewis Publishing, 1922), 1130–32. His wife, the former Miss Mattie Ellen Hinman, was from Grand Rapids, Michigan. A collection of Brown's correspondence is held by the Sherman Library and Gardens in Corona del Mar, California.

122. Rust to Morgan, February 4, 1891, and July 4, 1891; for the school, see Rust to Morgan, December 2, 1891—all in "Letter from the Secretary of the Interior," Ex. Doc. no. 108, 14, 13, and 8. For Rust's anti-Catholic bias, see Phillips, *Chiefs and Challengers*, 304–5. According to Hanks (*This War Is for a Whole Life*, 77), Pablo had created a pantribal network of Southern California Indians that stretched from the Potrero to as far south as Rincon in the hopes of resisting "attacks on the traditional ways of the Cahuilla." His network included friendly whites such as Brown and Gilmour.

123. "Too Much Bric-A-Brac," *Los Angeles Herald*, April 17, 1891.

124. S. S. Lawson, "The Mission Indians," *Los Angeles Times*, May 14, 1891. The issue at Potrero seems to have been Rust's rental of reservation lands to white cattlemen—and how the profits were distributed. The Indian Office was also not completely satisfied with Rust's handling of the funds—but only complained that he held them, hoping to spend them on an irrigation ditch, instead of forwarding them to Washington, so officials there could decide when and how to spend the money. See Belt to Rust, September 16, 1891; and Rust to Morgan, July 4, 1891—both in "Letter from the Secretary of the Interior," Ex. Doc. no. 108, 3, 11, 13.

125. "The Indian Question," *Los Angeles Times*, May 20, 1891.

126. "Indian Affairs," *San Bernardino Daily Courier*, March 14, 1891. Two days earlier, in "The Indian Commission," the *Courier* had noted: "The Indians complain bitterly of their treatment by Agent Rusk [*sic*]. They accuse him of gross partiality, bitter prejudice—in fact they charge that he is tyrannical in secular and bigoted in 'spiritual' affairs."

127. Belt to Noble, May 24, 1892, and May 26, 1892, in "Letter from the Secretary of the Interior," Ex. Doc. no. 108, 4, 3.

128. In Belt to Noble, June 2, 1892 ("Letter from the Secretary of the Interior," Ex. Doc no. 108, 2), the acting commissioner informed the interior secretary that he found no instructions from the department that authorized the removal of Cabezon; instead, based on Rust's correspondence, it was clear that the chief had been deposed by his own followers.

129. Noble to the President of the U.S. Senate, June 3, 1892, "Letter from the Secretary of the Interior," Ex. Doc. no. 108, 1.

130. "No Billy Williams in Theirs. Indian Agent Rust and the Coahuillas. The Senate Wants Information on the Affair," *Los Angeles Herald*, June 10, 1892.

131. J. H. G. [John Hamilton Gilmour], "The Indian Question: Cahuillas to Have Lands in Severalty," *San Francisco Chronicle*, July 23, 1892, reprinted in Heizer, *Some Last Century Accounts*, 17–20. For Tinker's appointment, see "The Appointment Mill," *Daly Alta California*, July 2, 1889; see also Phillips, *Chiefs and Challengers*, 310–12; for Tinker's visit, see Shaw, "Evolving Ecoscape," 253–54.

132. "Rust to Morgan, September 7, 1892," *Sixty-First Annual Report of the CIA, 1892*, 225–26. For a description of the buildings and a list of the staff, see "The Red Man's Child. School at Perris to Teach Him the Ways of Civilization," *Los Angeles Herald*, January 29, 1893.

133. Garesché to Noble, November 14, 1892, reprinted in Alex. J. [John] P. [Peter] Garesché, *Coahuila or Mission Indians of California: Letters to Secretary of the Interior in Their Behalf by Alex. J. P. Garesché of St. Louis, Mo.* (St. Louis: R. & T. A. Ennis, 1892), quotes on 5, 18, and 19.

Born in Cuba to French refugees from San Domingo, Garesché was educated at Georgetown College in Washington, D.C., and later at St. Louis University. He began the study of law in 1842 and was admitted to the bar three years later. From 1846 to 1847 he served as city attorney. During the Civil War he fought on the Confederate side, returning to Saint Louis at the war's end. See "Bench and Bar," *History of Saint Louis City and County*, vol. 2 (Philadelphia: Louis H. Everts, 1883), 1495–96. According to Chaput's "Horatio N. Rust" (284), Garesché, after a visit to Cahuilla, concluded that Rust was "doing a disastrous job."

134. Garesché, *Coahuila or Mission Indians of California*, quotes on 17, 3, and 18.

135. See Chaput, "Horatio N. Rust," 284.

136. Ibid., 290.

137. "At Outs with Themselves. Insurrection Threatened on an Indian Reservation. Strange State of Affairs for Which the Agent Is Blamed," *Los Angeles Herald*, February 23, 1895.

138. Chaput, "Horatio N. Rust," 293; for a more neutral assessment, see Apostol, "Horatio Nelson Rust."

7. A Troubled Tenure: Francisco Estudillo, 1893–1897

Epigraph. "Estudillo to Browning, August 1, 1896," Annual Report of the CIA, 1896, 129.

1. Cadwallader to Cleveland, March 4, 1893, box 1; Weinland to Smith, March 15, 1893, box 10—both in Weinland Papers.
2. Julia M. French to Smith, March 16, 1893, box 1; R. C. Hallowell, M.D., to Smith, March 16, 1893, box 1; Mary E. (Sheriff) Fowler to Smith, March 16, 1893, box 1; Salmons to Smith, March 18, 1893, box 6; Johnson to Smith, March 18, 1893, box 4; and Salsberry to Smith, March 18, 1893, box 6—all in Weinland Papers.
3. For an account of Morongo's close working relationship with Weinland, see Ida Goepp, "A Visit to the Ramona Mission at Potraro [*sic*]," *Periodical Accounts Relating to the Foreign Missions of the Church of the United Brethren*, vol. 1 (London: Printed for the Brethren's Society, 1890), 171 and 173. The author described Morongo as Weinland's "right hand man and neighbour."
4. For Estudillo's appointment, see *Journal of the Executive Proceedings of the Senate of the United States of America*, vol. 28 (Washington, D.C.: GPO, 1909), 461. Estudillo's name had been presented by the vice president on April 12 before the Fifty-Third Congress in special session. See also WNIA, "Association News and Notes," *The Indian's Friend*, April 1893, 3.
5. "Morongo in Riverside. The Chief of the Banning Indians on a Tour," *Los Angeles Herald*, June 2, 1893. See also "Chief of the Indians," *Riverside Enterprise*, May 30, 1893.
6. Quinton to Weinland, April 15, 1863, and April 16, 1893, box 7, Weinland Papers. There is no evidence that Quinton and Estudillo ever met.
7. For biographies of Estudillo, see *An Illustrated History of Southern California*, 170–71; and the *San Jacinto Register*, February 9, 1893.
8. "He Received a Warm Welcome," *Los Angeles Herald*, June 11, 1893. See also "Indian Jubilee," *San Bernardino Weekly Courier*, June 17, 1893. The fiesta may have also served "to celebrate the departure" of Agent Rust, Phillips wryly adds in *Chiefs and Challengers* (see 313–14).

   Chief Gervasio Cabezon remained a prominent figure until his death in 1906. His obituary ("Aged Chief Cabezon Dies," *Los Angeles Times*, December 6, 1906) described him as "one of the most progressive chiefs in the country."
9. Browning (1846–1903) was born in Illinois, serving his home state as both a country judge and a circuit judge. Originally interested in an appointment as commissioner of the General Land Office, he came to his position as Indian commissioner with little interest in or knowledge of Indians. See William T. Hagan, "Daniel M. Browning, 1893–97," in Kvasnicka and Viola, *The Commissioners*, 205–9.
10. WNIA, "Association News and Notes," March 1893, 3; and "Progress at Coahuilla," April 1893, 1 and 3—both in *The Indian's Friend*. See also WNIA, "Cahuilla Again," May 1893, 2; and "News and Notes," June 1894, 3—both in *The Indian's Friend*.

11. Estudillo to Browning, July 12, 1893, LR #26444–1893; and Quinton to Browning, June 2, 1893, LR #20529–1893—both in RG 75, SC 143, OIA, NA. Johnson rented the land as a pasture for her horse and a place to plant a garden to demonstrate to the Indians the proper method of gardening; see "Progress at Coahuilla [*sic*]," *The Indian's Friend*, April 1893, 1.
12. Estudillo to Browning, July 28, 1893 (with enclosures including a copy of the petition in Quinton to Browning, July 13, 1893, LR #25849–1893); and Browning to Quinton, August 14, 1893—both in LR #28670–1893, RG 75, SC 143, OIA, NA.

    In Quinton to Weinland, August 5, 1893 (box 7, Weinland Papers), Quinton wrote that the association did not want the Indians' springs, "only *use* of water for the lot." She asked Weinland to assure Estudillo of this.
13. Estudillo to Quinton, July 25, 1893, LR #34301–1893, RG75, OIA, NA.
14. Quinton to Estudillo, August 9, 1893, LR #34301–1893, RG 75, OIA, NA; see also Quinton to Browning, August 17, 1893, LR #31665–1893, RG 75, SC 31, OIA, NA.
15. Quinton to Browning, August 17, 1893, LR #31665–1893, RG 75, SC 31, OIA, NA. For evidence of Johnson's good works, Quinton quoted from a March 24, 1893, letter written by former village captain Leonicio Lugo, who declared that "all the people are very thankful" for her. "She helps us [a] great deal." Quinton also noted that Reverend Weinland had checked on the water situation and reported that the Cahuilla's main water source was not on that tract of land.
16. Quinton to Estudillo, August 9, 1893, LR #34301–1893, RG 75, OIA, NA.
17. Estudillo to Quinton, August 18, 1893, LR #34301–1893, RG 75, OIA, NA.
18. Quinton to Estudillo, August 24, 1893, LR #34301–1893, RG 75, OIA, NA.
19. Estudillo to Browning, September 11, 1893, LR #34928–1893, RG 75, SC 31, OIA, NA; see also Quinton to Browning, February 27, 1894, LR #9206–1894, RG 75, OIA, NA. For Johnson's departure, see WNIA, *The Indian's Friend*, February 1895, 9. Her last duties had been to supervise the repairs and the addition of a new room to her WNIA cottage. For more, see Mathes, *Divinely Guided*, 217–21.
20. F. M. C., "A Letter from Cahuilla Valley. An Old Time Resident Expresses Himself as Satisfied with the Management of the Indian School at Cahuilla," *San Jacinto Register*, May 4, 1893.
21. Tripp Bros. [probably Will and Shasta Tripp], "The Cahuilla Indians," *San Jacinto Register*, July 6, 1893. Martin Costo was anthropologist David Prescott Barrow's guide and friend in the 1890s; he was also the uncle of Rupert Costo, founder of the American Indian Historical Society in San Francisco.
22. "Rust to Morgan, September 7, 1892," *Sixty-First Annual Report of the CIA*, 225.
23. Seymour, in "Relations between the United States Government and the Mission Indians" (53), writes: "The fact is that the government is in a hurry to unload itself of its wards, and this policy is encouraged by unintelligent philanthropy away from the actual scene, and which consequently cannot appreciate the conditions [in Southern California]."

    William Collier was appointed a special attorney for the Mission Indians in the late 1890s.

24. "Estudillo to Smith, August 31, 1893," *Sixty-Second Annual Report of the CIA, 1893*, 128.
25. "Estudillo to Browning, August 1, 1896," *Annual Report of the CIA, 1896*, 127.
26. "Estudillo to Browning, August 31, 1893," 128. Describing the land at Rincon as extremely rough and "absolutely impossible to subdivide . . . into regular shapes for allotment," Foote had written Morgan that to "do justice to the Indians," she needed permission to divide the land into irregular lots. Morgan passed the letter on to Acting Interior Secretary Cyrus Bussez, who gave permission to have the surveyor "subdivide the lands into such irregular lots as may be necessary" to ensure the Indians received "arable lands with the best water privileges." See Bussez to Morgan, November 5, 1892, LR #40040–1892, RG 75, SC 31, OIA, NA.
27. "Estudillo to Browning, August 31, 1895," *Annual Report of the Secretary of the Interior, 1895*, vol. 2, 133.
28. "Wright to Jones, August 1898," and "Wright to Whittlesey, Secretary of the BIC, May 12, 1898," *Annual Reports of the DOI, 1898*, 135 and 1101–2. Most of the Southern California allotments seem to have been just ten or twenty acres.
29. "Wright to Merrill Gates, Secretary of the BIC, January 15, 1900," in *Annual Reports of the DOI, 1899*, part 2, 265. About four-fifths of the allottees were living on their allotments, Wright added, but not all of them farmed. In his report of July 20, 1906, Superintendent Charles E. Shell mentioned that many of the 1890s allotments were never "approved." See "Report of Superintendent in Charge of Mission Indians," *Annual Report of the DOI, 1906*, 204.
30. "Wright to Jones, September 1, 1900," *Annual Reports of the DOI, 1900*, 210.

    In his 1894 annual report, Estudillo wrote that the allotting of the Morongo Reservation "will accomplish very much in the way of destroying the two factions that there exist." "Estudillo to Browning, August 31, 1894," *Annual Report of the CIA, 1894* (GPO, 1895), 120.
31. C. E. Kelsey, *Report of the Special Agent*, 14–15, quotes on 15 and 17, reprinted in Heizer, *Federal Concern*, 123–50. See also Mathes, *Divinely Guided*, 129–40; and Larisa K. Miller, "Counting Context: C. E. Kelsey's 1906 Census of Nonreservation Indians in Northern California," *American Indian Culture and Research Journal*, vol. 38, no. 2 (2014): 41–66.
32. "Estudillo to Browning, August 31, 1893," *Annual Report of the Secretary of the Interior, 1895*, vol. 2, 126.
33. "Buried the Hatchet. Morongo and Pablo Heap Good Indians Now," *Los Angeles Herald*, December 30, 1893.
34. "Wright to Commissioner Jones, August 1898," *Report of the CIA, 1898*, in *Annual Reports of the DOI*, 136.

    In "'Captain John.' One of Southern California's Most Notable Characters," July 24, 1898, the *Los Angeles Times* wrote that Morongo died at his home on the Morongo Reservation of lung infection and other complications. The lengthy obituary reported that he was born about 1846 and had worked in San Bernardino in the mid-1860s, later supervising a work crew when the Southern Pacific railroad was built across the desert in the mid-1870s. When the Mission Indian Agency was established, he was appointed interpreter, a position he held for twelve years. He spoke all the "dialects" of the Mission Indians, along with Spanish, English, and French. "In religious matters he was a man of independent opinions, which inclined him toward Protestantism." In 1890 he became a member and "a staunch supporter" of the Moravian Mission on the Potrero, encouraging temperance and helping catch whisky sellers. "To his own people his word was law, and he was looked up to by his brown brethren from Yuma to Tule River as a man of sound judgment, impartial disinterestedness, and as having an eye single on the welfare of all Indians."

35. "Estudillo to Commissioner Browning, August 31, 1893," *Annual Report of the Secretary of the Interior, 1895*, vol. 2, 127.
36. Quinton to Browning, August 22, 1893, LR #31667–1893, RG 75, OIA, NA.
37. Estudillo to Quinton, August 29, 1893, LR #34301–1893, RG 75, OIA, NA; and Quinton to Browning, September 4, 1893, LR #34301–1893, RG 75, OIA, NA. (The latter contains the copies of the following letters: Estudillo to Quinton, July 25, 1893; Quinton to Estudillo, August 9, 1893; Estudillo to Quinton, August 18, 1893; Quinton to Estudillo, August 24, 1893; Estudillo to Quinton, August 29, 1893; Quinton to Browning, September 4, 1893; and Quinton to Estudillo, September 6, 1893.)
38. Quinton to Estudillo, September 6, 1893, LR #34301–1893, RG 75, OIA, NA; see also Quinton to Weinland, September 4, 1893, box 7, Weinland Papers.

    To acquaint the larger reform community of the work of French and Hallowell, Quinton addressed the October 1895 LMC. See "Mrs. A. S. Quinton," *Proceedings of the Thirteenth Annual Meeting of the LMC of Friends of the Indian, 1895* (LMC, 1896), 89.
39. Quinton to Browning, November 23, 1893, LR #43864–1893, RG 75, OIA, NA; and Quinton to Weinland, December 23, 1893, box 7, Weinland Papers. Johnson stayed on at Cahuilla until resigning early in 1895. See *San Jacinto Register*, February 7, 1895.
40. Quinton to Weinland, May 31, 1894, box 7, Weinland Papers.
41. "Estudillo to Commissioner Browning, August 31, 1893, *Annual Report of the Secretary of the Interior, 1895*, vol. 2, 127.

    The Rancho Vallé de San Felipe, granted by the Mexican government in 1846 to Felipe Castillo, was the easternmost rancho in Mexican California. Beginning around 1900, Thomas Duque became the majority stockholder in the San Felipe Land & Water Company, which then owned the ranch. See Phil Brigandi, "Historical San Felipe Ranchero [*sic*] Still in Operation," *Borrego Sun*, July 28, 1994.
42. Davis, "The Last Eviction" (manuscript dated September 14, 1903), reproduced in Charles Russell Quinn and Elena Quinn, eds., *Edward H. Davis and the Indians of the Southwest United States and Northwest Mexico* (Downey, Calif.: Elena Quinn,1965), 84–89. Davis (1862–1951) was born in New York. He studied art and worked as an accountant in his family's shipping company before moving to California in 1885 for his health. Originally employed as a surveyor and draftsman, he purchased acreage in Mesa Grande two years later, developing his property into a working ranch. Fascinated by the local Indian culture, he began collecting artifacts, which he eventually sold to George G. Heye's Museum of the American Indian in New York City (now part of the Smithsonian). From 1917 to 1930 he served as the museum's field collector.

The second observation is from Constance Goddard Du Bois, "The Mission Indian Exiles," *The Land of Sunshine*, vol. 15, no. 4 (October 1901): 250. Du Bois (ca. 1869–1934), a member of the Connecticut Indian Association, a WNIA affiliate, wrote compelling essays on the miserable treatment of the Mission Indians for *The Indian's Friend* and for IRA pamphlets. A novelist and pioneering ethnographer, she spent summers in the San Diego area, studying Luiseño religion and Kumeyaay mythology. For more, see Mathes, *Divinely Guided*, 251–54.

43. "Wants to Eject Indians," *Los Angeles Times*, March 27, 1892. See also the *San Diego Union*, "Wants to Eject the Indians," March 19, 1892. The same lawsuit also sought the eviction of several white settlers on the ranch and was thus filed as the *San Felipe Land & Water Company v. Paul Sentenac, et al.*

44. Indian Rights Association, "What the Indian Rights Association Is," *The Fourth Annual Report of the Executive Committee of the IRA, for 1886* (Philadelphia: Office of the IRA, 1887), 3–4; and WNIA, "The Resolutions," *Annual Report of the WNIA* (Philadelphia: WNIA, 1892), 33.

45. Lewis to Morgan, September 10, 1892, LR #33961–1892, RG 75, SC 31, OIA, NA.

46. Phillips, *Chiefs and Challengers*, 257.

47. As early as 1851, Moro was said to command the Cupeños when Antonio Garra was away. He seems to have served as captain until his death in 1885; see *San Diego Union*, July 31, 1885. Machola Moro was born a Chutnicut and died at Pala around 1910. She was apparently Moro's second wife.

48. *Supreme Court of the State of California . . . J. Downey Harvey . . . vs. Allejandro Barker, et al. . . . Transcript on Appeal* [Los Angeles?]: Charles W. Palm Co. [1897?], copies available at the California State Law Library and in the microfilm edition of the IRA Papers. For a detailed discussion of the trial, including depositions and Indian testimony, see Phillips, *Chiefs and Challengers*, 256–71. For contemporary news articles from the *San Diego Union*, see "Must They Leave?" July 18, 1893; "Their Birthplace," July 19, 1893; and "Their Case Closed," July 20, 1893. See also "Anxious Indian Squatters," *San Francisco Call*, July 17, 1893; and "Fighting for Homes: Mission Indians in the Courts. Their Claims to Warner's Ranch," *San Francisco Chronicle*, July 29, 1893.

49. "Indians Beaten in the Courts. Decision in a Noted Case," *San Francisco Chronicle*, December 30, 1896; and "Their Birthplace," *San Diego Union*, July 19, 1893. A prominent Cupeño leader and owner of some of the tourist bathhouses at the springs, Barker had a white father, which accounts for his Anglo surname. He died on September 11, 1896, before the case was resolved; see "San Diego Brevities," *Los Angeles Times*, September 15, 1896.

50. "Indians Must Go," *San Diego Union*, December 30, 1896. Downey's health and state of mind had deteriorated following an 1883 railroad accident in which he was severely injured and his first wife was killed. It is interesting that most of his erratic behavior was reported in the *Union* only after his death in 1894.

51. Phil Brigandi, "Law but Not Fact, Land Tenure and Legal Fiction on the Warner Ranch," *The Branding Iron*, no. 260 (Fall 2010): 11–12.

52. Downey had no children; Harvey was the son of one of his sisters. Born around 1860, Harvey lived most of his life in San Francisco and was active in real estate development. In his later years he suffered various financial reverses. He died in 1947; see *San Francisco Chronicle*, December 19, 1947.

53. "Between about 1888 and 1892 Judge George Puterbaugh and his associates . . . made an earnest and sustained effort to develop the north coastal region of San Diego County by the construction of a dam at Warner's Ranch itself, on the San Luis Rey River," writes Joseph J. Hill in *The History of Warner's Ranch and Its Environs* (Los Angeles: privately published, 1927, p. 170). A year after the case was heard, the judge was still boosting the reservoir plan at public meetings. See "Municipal Water Supply," *San Diego Union*, July 10, 1894. Pioneer San Diego County developer Ed Fletcher claimed that Puterbaugh lost "a large amount of money" trying to get the project off the ground. See *Memoirs of Ed Fletcher* (San Diego: n.p., 1952), 53.

54. *Supreme Court of the State of California, J. Downey Harvey, Administrator, et al., vs. Allejandro* [*sic*] *Barker et al., Brief of Defendants and Appellants.* [Los Angeles?]: Charles W. Palm Co., 1898, 6 (italics in original). For contemporary news coverage, see "Harvey Wins His Suit," *Sacramento Daily Union*, December 30, 1896; and "Indians Beaten in the Courts. Decision in a Noted Case" and "Indian Changes," both in *San Francisco Chronicle*, December 31, 1896.

55. Ward to Herbert Welsh, June 19, 1897, reel 13, *IRA Papers.*

56. "Estudillo to Commissioner Browning, August 31, 1893," *Annual Report of the Secretary of the Interior, 1895*, vol. 2, 125. In "Indian Depravity. Yuma Girls Sold for Sin by an Ex-Chief," *San Francisco Chronicle*, July 31, 1893, Estudillo was interviewed about the sale of "innocent and comely children" by the "vile old chief."

57. "Arizona News," *Los Angeles Times*, July 27, 1893, for the first quote; for the second, see "A Horrible Case of Depravity. Yuma Indian Girls Sold to White Men," *Los Angeles Herald*, July 15, 1893.

58. "Bad Indians. Miguel Creates More Trouble at Yuma," *Los Angeles Times*, September 29, 1893. Later (October 5, 1893) the *Times* noted that Miguel lost the next election.

59. "Dying Out. The Mission Indians Rapidly Decreasing," *Los Angeles Herald*, July 23, 1893.

60. "The Yuma Indians," and "An Outbreak Imminent," *Los Angeles Times*, September 30, 1893. See also "Redskins Riled. Yuma Indians Are Still Wrangling," *San Francisco Call*, October 1, 1893.

Miguel was still causing problems six years later. In April 1899 Agent Wright accompanied a U.S. marshal with an armed posse to Yuma to arrest him for arson. He was taken to San Bernardino for arraignment. See "Yuma Indians Excited Over the Arrest of Ex-Chief Patrick Miguel," *Los Angeles Herald*, April 6, 1899.

61. Estudillo to Browning, April 12, 1897; and Acting Commissioner Thomas P. Smith to Cornelius Bliss, Interior Secretary, May 12, 1897—both in *Papers Relating to the Foreign Relations of the United States with the Annual Message of the President, December 6, 1897* (Washington, D.C.: GPO, 1898), 394 and 391–93.

62. W. O. Hendricks, "On an Attempt to Expel Some Yuma Indians from Baja California," *Pacific Coast Archaeological Society Quarterly*, vol. 4, no. 1 (January 1968): 55–66; and Hendricks, "On an Attempt to Expel Some Yuma Indians from Baja California, Part II," *Pacific Coast Archaeological Society Quarterly*, vol. 6, no. 1 (January 1970): 47–57.
63. Smith to Bliss, May 12, 1897, *Papers Relating to the Foreign Relations of the United States*, 392.
64. Father Zephyrin Engelhardt, *Mission Santa Inés* (Santa Barbara: Mission Santa Barbara, 1932), 47–54, 101–2; "Painter Report," 21. While the mission uses the spelling "Inés," the Indian Office used "Ynez" in official documents from the time. Today it is commonly known as the Chumash Reservation.
65. "Painter Report," 21–22.
66. Frank D. Lewis, "Report of Special Attorney in Charge of Matters Relating to the Mission Indians," *Annual Report of the Attorney-General of the United States for the Year 1896* (Washington, D.C.: GPO, 1896), 215 for quote.
67. "Estudillo to Browning, August 1, 1896," *Annual Report of the CIA, 1896*, 128.
68. Lewis, "Report of Special Attorney in Charge of Matters Relating to the Mission Indians," *Annual Report of the Attorney-General of the United States for the Year 1898* (GPO, 1898), 215. See also, in the same report, Lewis to the Attorney General, October 30, 1897 (219).
69. "Wright to Jones, August 21, 1899," *Annual Reports of the DOI, 1899*, part 1, 174; Wright to Jones, September 20, 1901, *Annual Reports of the DOI, 1901*, part 1 (GPO, 1902), 197; and "Wright to Jones, September 25, 1903," *Annual Reports of the DOI, 1903*, part 1 (GPO, 1904), 149. The reservation totaled 120 acres. For Collier, see Collier to Philander C. Knox, U.S. Attorney General, October 27, 1902, "Report of the Special Attorney for the Mission Indians," *Annual Report of the Attorney-General of the United States for the Year 1902*, 272–73.
70. Seymour, "Relations between the United States Government and the Mission Indians," 104. See also C. E. Kelsey, *Report of the Special Agent*, 6.
71. "Estudillo to Browning, August 31, 1894," *Annual Report of the CIA, 1894* (GPO, 1895), 121.
72. "Estudillo to Browning, August 31, 1893," *Sixty-Second Annual Report of the CIA, 1893*, 128.
73. "Estudillo to Browning, August 31, 1894," *Annual Report of the CIA, 1894* (GPO, 1895).

    Like Torres, five miles to the west, the Martinez village (and subsequent reservation) was named for an 1860s Cahuilla captain known as "Martinez" to the Mexicans and "Martin" to the Americans. See Gunther, *Riverside County*, 312. On November 27, 1869, the *Los Angeles Star* ("San Bernardino Correspondence") reported that "Old Martinez," captain of the Indians "occupying a *rancheria* of his own name," died suddenly. A December 10 news item added that he had died of smallpox, like so many Southern California Indians in the 1860s.
74. "Programme of the Teacher's Institute," in Estudillo to Browning, August 31, 1894, *Annual Report of the CIA, 1894* (GPO, 1895), 124. See also "Colton Brevities," April 24, 1894; "Educate the Indian. Teachers of the Mission Schools at Colton," April 25, 1894; "The Indian's Future. Is Discussed by the Teachers Institute at Colton," April

26, 1894; and "Indian Education. Close of the Teacher's Institute at Colton," April 27, 1894—all in the *Los Angeles Times*.

Estudillo continued the institutes for several more years. In 1896, Morongo was reported to have made a "dignified little speech which would have done credit to any assemblage." See "Captain John Morongo, Who Addressed the Teachers," *San Francisco Chronicle*, August 7, 1896.

75. "Estudillo to Browning, August 1, 1896," *Annual Report of the CIA, 1896*, 126–30, for schools, see 127–29.

Burton was later put in charge of the Moqui (Hopi) Indians in Arizona. His strict enforcement of government regulations and harsh punishments eventually drew the ire of Charles Lummis, who attacked him repeatedly in a blistering series of articles entitled "Bullying the 'Quaker Indians'" (as he liked to call the "peaceful" Hopi) in his *Out West* magazine from June to October 1903. James Jenkins, an inspector from the Interior Department, was eventually sent out to investigate; Burton was reprimanded by the Indian Office.

76. Newton H. Chittenden, "Among the Mission Indian Schools of Southern California," *San Francisco Chronicle*, August 1, 1897.

77. Ibid.

78. "It was Murder. The Indians Undoubtedly Killed Mrs. Platt," *Los Angeles Times*, September 24, 1894; and "Indian Missionary Killed. Teacher of a School Murdered at Pechanga, Cal.," *New York Times*, December 12, 1894. See also "Murdered by Indians," *San Diego Union*, September 27, 1894; "The Gentle Savage," *San Francisco Chronicle*, September 26, 1894; and "Mrs. Platt's Death. Murdered within a Few Feet of Her Sleeping Niece," *San Francisco Call*, January 15, 1896. See also Hanks, *This War Is for a Whole Life*, 88–93; and Mathes, *Divinely Guided*, 221–23.

The Pechanga School was rebuilt, reopening in February 1896, but the new teacher, Belle Dean, did not live on the reservation.

79. Edward B. Howell, "A Tragic Sequel to 'Ramona,'" *Review of Reviews*, November 1894, quote on 509, see also 511–13, reprinted in Heizer, *Some Last Century Accounts*, 85–92. See also Edward B. Howell, "The Pachanga [*sic*] Indians," *Los Angeles Times*, December 26, 1892; and C. C. Pierce, "The Pachangos [*sic*]. The Indians Immortalized by Helen Hunt Jackson," *Los Angeles Times*, October 7, 1894. For the burning of the school, see "Rust to Morgan, September 10, 1891," *Sixtieth Annual Report of the CIA, 1891*, 224. Rust described Platt as changing "the habits of the people and [making] the school one of the best."

80. "It Was Murder. The Indians Undoubtedly Killed Mrs. Platt," *Los Angeles Times*, September 24, 1894; and "Indian Missionary Killed. Teacher of a School Murdered at Pechanga, Cal.," *New York Times*, December 12, 1894.

81. "Estudillo to Browning, August 31, 1895," *Annual Report of the Secretary of the Interior, 1895*, vol. 2, 131; "The Murder of a Missionary," November 1894, 1, and "Martyred Mrs. Platt," March 1895, 6—both in *The Indian's Friend*.

82. C. C. Pierce, "The Pachangos [*sic*]," *Los Angeles Times*. Shortly after Platt's murder, Sarah Morris, the government teacher at Morongo, bought a revolver and learned how to use it. See Hughes, *History of Banning*, 165.

83. "Mateo Pa's Trial. Life Is Short and Time Is Long. So Said the Indian Who Is Charged with Killing the School Teacher," March 24, 1895; and "Mateo Pa on Trial for the Murder of Mrs. Platt," March 23, 1895—both in the *Los Angeles Times*. For Lewis's investigation of the murder, see "Lewis to U.S. Attorney General Judson Harmon, November 13, 1895," *Annual Report of the Attorney-General of the United States for the Year 1895*, 243.
84. "Mateo Pa's Trial," March 24, 1895; and "Mateo Pa Acquitted of the Murder of Mrs. Platt," March 26, 1895—both in the *Los Angeles Times*. See also "The Murder of Mrs. Platt," *Redlands Daily Facts*, August 14, 1895.
85. "Mrs. Platt's Slayer. An Imprisoned Cowthief Said to be a Murderer," *Los Angeles Times*, January 15, 1896. For Martin Aguirre, see "Murderers Discovered: Mystery Clearing about Mrs. Platt's Murder," *Los Angeles Times*, February 14, 1896.
86. For the *Los Angeles Times* coverage, see "Murderers Discovered. Mystery Clearing about Mrs. Platt's Murder," February 14, 1896; "A Full Confession. Details of the Murder of Mrs. Platt," February 15, 1896; "Riverside County. Ventura [*sic*] Molido Tells of His Horrible Crime," March 27, 1896; "Riverside County. End of the Mrs. Platt Murder Trial," May 10, 1896; and "Riverside County. An Alleged Murderer Displeased with the Jail Accommodations," June 10, 1896. For Estudillo's comment, see "Estudillo to Browning, August 1, 1896," *Annual Report of the CIA, 1896*, 127.

    Hanks (*This War Is for a Whole Life*, 88–93) admits that the cause of Platt's murder "cannot be easily determined" but suggests that fear over the Perris rumors played a part, as did her insistence on haircuts for her students in violation of a "tribal taboo." He writes: "[T]he people of Pechanga turned to the only option left to them—violent resistance," claiming that they "reacted as any concerned parents would react, white or Indian, when confronted with fear for their children and lack of respect for their way of life." However, he never shows that any of the men accused were parents of school children.
87. "Estudillo to Browning, August 1, 1896," *Annual Report of the CIA, 1896*, see 127 for Morongo and 128 for Martinez.
88. WNIA, "A New Desert Mission," *Missions of the Women's National Indian Association for 1895*, 17–18; WNIA, "The Mission of the Brooklyn Indian Association," *Our Missionary Report for 1897*, 35–38; and Amelia S. Quinton, "From California No. 3: Into the Desert," *The Indian's Friend*, July 1895, 6–8. For the setting aside of ten acres of reservation land for the WNIA mission, see William H. Sims, Acting Interior Secretary, to Browning, June 20, 1896, box 8, Weinland Papers. For more details see Mathes, *Divinely Guided*, 224–29.
89. Browning to Quinton, June 17, 1896, box 8, Weinland Papers.
90. "Wright to Jones, September 25, 1903," *Annual Reports of the DOI, 1903*, part 1 (GPO, 1904), 149. Seymour reports that there were twenty-two government wells on the Torres Reservation by 1903.
91. "Will Develop Water. Government's Relief for Destitute Mission Indians," *Los Angeles Times*, March 21, 1899.
92. Shaw, "Evolving Ecoscape," 160.

93. "Palm Springs. Trouble Being Caused by the Indians Over Water," *Los Angeles Times*, December 27, 1893 (quoting the *Banning Herald*). The *Herald* claimed that a new ditch to serve the village would cost about $3,000, "for the purpose of giving a few worthless Indians water."
94. "Indians Claim Water Rights. A Singular Demand at Palm Valley," *San Francisco Chronicle*, December 13, 1895. See also Ainsworth, *The McCallum Saga*, 138–39; and Shaw, "Evolving Ecoscape," 160–62.
95. For the agreement, see Lewis, "Report of Special Attorney for Mission Indians," *Annual Report of the Attorney-General of the United States for the Year 1896*, 213–16. For McCallum's death, see Ainsworth, *The McCallum Saga*, 142.

    It was not until 1911 that the Indian Irrigation Service began work on developing and delivering more water from Tahquitz Canyon. See Shaw, "Evolving Ecoscape,"167–77, for later developments and conflicts.
96. "Don't Like Him. Mission Indians Petition President McKinley to Remove Agent Estudillo," *Los Angeles Herald*, April 17, 1897. See also Phillips, *Chiefs and Challengers*, 316–17.

    "My commission," Pablo noted, "comes from the Mission Indians at Santa Ysabel, Mesa Grande, Los Coyotes, Incapa, Lagona [*sic*], Long Canyon, Campo, Manzanita, La Posta, San Jose, San Felipe, Puerta Cruz, Matahua [*sic*], reservations and villages numbering about 700 mission Indians." Plus, of course, his own village at Potrero—a rather far-flung and diverse area including at least four different tribal groups.
97. "Don't Like Him. Mission Indians Petition President McKinley." John Morongo, as cited in "He's After Chief Pablo" (*San Bernardino Weekly Sun*, April 10, 1897), attacked Will Pablo, supporting Estudillo's efforts against him. Estudillo's son did in fact work on allotment surveys; see the *San Jacinto Register*, August 29, 1895.
98. "Irregularities Alleged. Claims that the Law Is Violated on the San Jacinto Reservation," *San Francisco Call*, October 12, 1895.
99. *San Jacinto Register*, December 26, 1901. "Subdivision of the Estudillo Ranch Only Half Mile from Town" (*Hemet News*, January 22, 1909) reported that Estudillo had lost his land due to the financial troubles and the drought of the 1890s.

8. The Continuing Struggle: Dr. Lucius A. Wright, 1897–1903

Epigraph. "Wright to William A. Jones, September 20, 1902," Annual Reports of the DOI, 1902, part 1 (GPO, 1903), 176.

1. For an account of one "distribution day," see "Big Day for Mission Reds. Farm Tools Allotted to the Cahuilla Indians," *Los Angeles Times*, February 26, 1905.
2. John Hamilton Gilmour, "Indians and Indian Agents," *Los Angeles Times*, January 14, 1897.
3. "Nominations Confirmed," *San Francisco Call*, May 30, 1897. A resident of San Jacinto, Wright may well have known his predecessor, Francisco Estudillo.
4. Quinton to Bliss, June 15, 1897, box 8, Weinland Papers. In Bliss to Welsh, July 1, 1897 (reel 13, *IRA Papers*), Bliss informed Herbert Welsh of Quinton's accusation.

5. See J. M. Guinn, ed., *Historical and Biographical Record of Southern California* (Chicago: Chapman Publishing, 1902), 995–96; E. Polk Johnson, *A History of Kentucky and Kentuckians: The Leaders and Representative Men in Commerce, Industry and Modern Activities* (Chicago: Lewis Publishing, 1912), 1482–83; and "Dr. L. A. Wright. The Newly-Appointed Indian Agent at Tule River Reservation," *Los Angeles Times*, August 21, 1897.

   Wright's wife, Namaah, also a licensed pharmacist, joined her husband in running the drug store throughout his tenure as agent.
6. A former teacher and county superintendent of schools, Jones (1844–1912) served in the Wisconsin state assembly before his appointment. During his eight years in office he worked harmoniously with Indian reformers and Congress. See W. David Baird, "William A. Jones, 1897–1904," in Kvasnicka and Viola, *The Commissioners*, 211–20.
7. "Wright to Jones, August 1897," *Annual Reports of the DOI, 1897: Report of the CIA*, 117–18. See also Phillips, *Chiefs and Challengers*, 317–20.
8. "Wright to Jones, August 1897," *Annual Reports of the Department of the Interior, 1897*, 117.
9. Wright to Thomas Bard, October 8, 1901, box 2, folder 23, Lucius Wright Collection, Seaver Center for Western History Research, Natural History Museum of Los Angeles County, Los Angeles, Calif. (hereafter cited as Wright Collection).
10. "Indians Alarmed at Inroads of White Settlers," *Riverside Enterprise*, January 1, 1903. The petition was drawn up for them, perhaps by Rev. R. M. Stavely, the Christian missionary at Martinez, or attorney John Brown Jr., both of whom signed as witnesses. The site Wright had in mind was northwest of the Martinez school, in Section 8.

    It is curious that Chief Cabezon was not involved in this protest, for he still played an active leadership role at other times in 1903.
11. Wright to Jones, June 23, 1903, box 3, folder 20, Wright Collection.
12. Leupp (commissioner from 1905 to 1909) graduated from Columbia Law School to pursue a career in journalism, eventually purchasing the *Syracuse Herald*. He later moved to Washington, D.C., to become a correspondent for the *Evening Post*. When his friend Charles C. Painter died, he became the IRA's agent, gaining the experience he would use effectively as Indian commissioner. See Donald L. Parman, "Francis Ellington Leupp, 1905–1909," in Kvasnicka and Viola, *The Commissioners*, 221–32.
13. Wright to Leupp, January 21, 1907, box 3, folder 81, Wright Collection.
14. "Wright to Jones, August 21, 1899," *Annual Reports of the DOI, 1899*, part 1, quotes on 171, 173, and 174; and "Wright to Jones, September 25, 1903," *Annual Reports of the DOI, 1903*, part 1, 148.
15. "Wright to Jones, September 20, 1901," *Annual Reports of the DOI, 1901*, part 1 (GPO, 1902), 197–98.
16. "Wright to Jones, September 25, 1903," *Annual Reports of the DOI, 1903*, 148.
17. Seymour, "Relations between the United States Government and the Mission Indians," 81.
18. "Wright to Jones, September 20, 1901," *Annual Reports of the DOI, 1901*, part 1 (GPO, 1902), 198.

19. In "Report of C. C. Wainwright" (included in "Wright to Jones, August 21, 1899," *Annual Reports of the DOI, 1899*, 175), the doctor reported that the death rate among the Indians was worse than at any time during his eight years on the job.
20. "Indians Destitute. Chief Agent Wright in a Quandary," *Los Angeles Times*, March 3, 1899; see also "Southern California Indians," *Los Angeles Herald*, March 22, 1899; and "News and Notes," *The Indian's Friend*, May 1899, 10, quoting an unidentified Southern California newspaper.
21. Weinland, "Mission Indians of California. Present Condition of a Race That Is Rapidly Growing Extinct," *Los Angeles Times*, April 16, 1899. Reprinted as "The Indians of Southern California," December 1899, 2; "Indians of Southern California, No. 2. Indian Industries," February 1900, 2; and "The Indians of Southern California. No. 3. Indian Festivals," April 1900, 1—all in *The Indian's Friend*.
22. "Wright to Jones, August 21, 1899," *Annual Reports of the DOI, 1899*, 171; and *Hemet News*, March 3, 1899; see also the *San Jacinto Register*, March 9, 1899.
23. George Hamlin Fitch, "Where the Date Palm Grows," *Land of Sunshine*, vol. 13, no. 3 (August 1900): 142. Fitch was literary editor of the *San Francisco Chronicle*.
24. "Wright to Jones, September 2, 1900," *Annual Reports of the DOI for 1900*, 208–11, quote on 209.
25. Wright to Thomas Bard, October 8, 1901, box 2, folder 23, Wright Collection.
26. "Wright to Jones, September 1, 1900," *Annual Reports of the DOI, 1900: Report of the CIA*, 209.
27. See "Earthquake's Horrors. Scenes at San Jacinto and Hemet after the Shake-up," *Los Angeles Herald*, December 28, 1899. Rumors were circulating that the hilly country about Cahuilla had been "rolled out flat by the earthquake."
28. "Wright to Jones, September 20, 1902," *Annual Reports of the DOI, 1902*, part 1 (GPO, 1903), 176.
29. Wright to Bard, December 29, 1900, box 2, folder 16, Wright Collection.
30. "Wright to Jones, August 1897," *Annual Reports of the DOI, 1897*, quotes on 118. For motion to set aside and denial of a new trial, see Phillips, *Chiefs and Challengers*, 266–67; and "Lands Where Their Fathers Were Born. Indians May Lose Homes," *San Francisco Chronicle*, June 27, 1897.
31. Indian Rights Association, "The Warner Ranch Case," *The Fifteenth Annual Report of the Executive Committee of the IRA* (Philadelphia: Office of the IRA, 1898), 3–5, quotes on 4 and 5; and WNIA, *The Indian's Friend*, August 1897, 6. See also LMC, "Joshua W. Davis's Report on the Mission Indian Committee," in *Proceedings of the Fifteenth Annual Meeting of the LMC* (1896), 50–52. In Quinton to Sniffen, July 8 and July 10, 1897 (Herbert Welsh Collection, #702, box 41, Historical Society of Pennsylvania, Philadelphia), Quinton described Welsh's contribution on behalf of the IRA as "a splendid deed."
32. *The Pacific Reporter*, vol. 56, *Containing all the Decisions of the Supreme Court of California* (St. Paul: West Publishing, 1899), 692–99. See also Phillips, *Chiefs and Challengers*, 267–70; "The Indians Lose. Supreme Court Shuts Them Out of Their Old Homes," October 6, 1899, and "Mission Indians Lose," October 10, 1899—both

in the *San Francisco Call;* and "Carried to Highest Court. Warner Land Decisions Will Be Reviewed at Washington," *San Francisco Chronicle*, October 27, 1899.

33. "The Facts in the Case," *San Diego Union*, November 3, 1899.

After the removal, Withington felt free to speak his mind. Any sympathy for the Cupeños was "misplaced" and irrational. He scoffed at their "morality," claiming that "their chief diversion is gambling" and insisting that they had "held these springs and lived there without working" for more than half a century, living "like princes among their fellows" from the income they received from the hot springs. See "Other Side of Indian Eviction," *San Diego Union*, July 13, 1903.

Charles Shell, the first superintendent at Pala, had a different observation about Indian morality: "I may be very unobservant and easily deceived, but my belief is that these women are as virtuous as white women in general"—then, knowing the stereotypes of his day, he added—"and this is not intended as a reflection upon white women." See "Shell to Jones, August 20, 1904," *Annual Reports of the DOI, 1904*, part 1, 167.

34. WNIA, "Good News for Agua Caliente Indians," *The Indian's Friend*, January 1900, 11.

35. Hoyt to Welsh, July 31, 1901, reel 15, *IRA Papers*. For a summary, see Indian Rights Association, "The Warner Ranch Case," *The Nineteenth Annual Report of the Executive Committee of the IRA, for 1901* (Philadelphia: Office of the IRA, 1902), 8–11; an extract of Hoyt's letter appears on 9. For the conjoining of the cases, see Charles Fletcher Lummis, "The Sequoya League," *Out West*, October 1903, 421. In "Redmen Must Pack Up and Go. Southern Reservation Indians in a Sad Predicament" (*San Francisco Call*, December 9, 1901), the reporter noted that although the San Felipe case was "practically the same . . . a decision of the court has not yet been written." See also Phillips, *Chiefs and Challengers*, 256–71. For the decision that the Indians "had no standing in view of the recognition by the Government of the validity of the Mexican grant," see "Mexican Grant Titles Are Held to Be Valid," *San Francisco Call*, May 14, 1901.

36. *Annual Report of the Attorney-General of the United States for the Year 1901.* The full text of the decision is reprinted in Commissioner's Jones's report dated October 15, 1901, *Annual Reports of the DOI, 1901*, part 1 (GPO, 1902), 115–23.

37. Quinton to Weinland, July 5, 1901, box 7, Weinland Papers.

38. "Wright to Jones, September 20, 1901," *Annual Reports of the DOI, 1901*, 196.

39. "Wright to Jones, September 20, 1902," *Annual Reports of the DOI, 1902*, 177. See also "Pro-Indian Advocates," *Los Angeles Times*, December 21, 1901.

40. Bard (1841–1915) was a prominent pioneer in the California oil industry and founder of the city of Port Hueneme. Appointed to the Senate in 1901, he served until 1905. See Amy E. Smith, "Thomas Robert Bard, Pioneer of Ventura County," master's thesis, University of Southern California, 1930.

Collier (1845–1928) was appointed special attorney in May 1899. The *Los Angeles Times* claimed that "among the Mission Indians, Mr. Collier is one of the most trusted white men in the State. 'El Abogado' (the lawyer) is a household name among them. Gentle and sympathetic, his advent among the tribes is ever a matter of importance, and an occasion for the presentation of some wrong which it is believed El Abogado may have the power to right." See "'El Abogado' Confers with 'El Senador,'" *Los Angeles Times*, November 23, 1902. For an obituary, see the *Elsinore Leader-Press*, March 15, 1928.

41. "National and Local Affairs. Interview with United States Senator Bard at Hotel Coronado," *San Diego Union*, October 31, 1901; and "Bard Interviews the Indians of San Diego County," *Elsinore Press*, November 1, 1901, for quote. A young man from Mataguay later told Wright, "Yes, I can go up on Volcan [Mountain] if I have to . . . but there is my mother in the house. Everything that she loves, everything that she knows is buried here. She has lain down; move her if you can." See "Indians Object to Proposed Eviction," *Los Angeles Times*, September 6, 1903.
42. Joseph Hill, *The History of Warner's Ranch and Its Environs*, 161.
43. "Redmen Must Pack Up and Go," *San Francisco Call*, December 19, 1901.
44. McLaughlin (1841–1923) may have been a good inspector, but he was a poor judge of California real estate. He spent a total of fifty-two years working for the Indian Office, twenty-four of them as an agent in South Dakota and twenty-eight as a special inspector. See his book, *My Friend the Indian* (Boston: Houghton Mifflin, 1910), and Louis Pfaller's biography, *John McLaughlin: The Man with an Indian Heart* (New York: Vantage Press, 1978).
45. For McLaughlin's report and choice, see E. A. Hitchcock, "Letter from the Secretary of the Interior with a Copy of a Report of the Commission of Indian Affairs, a Draft of a Bill for the Relief of Certain Mission Indians in California," 57th Cong., 1st sess., House Document #319 (1902); "Providing Home for Warner Ranch Indians. Proposition to Locate the Red Men on a Tract Near Oceanside," *San Francisco Chronicle*, January 28, 1902; "An Agent's Mission, to Find a New Reservation," December 9, 1901, and "Government Investigating Indian Affairs," December 10, 1901—both in the *San Diego Union*.
46. "Wright to Jones, September 20, 1902," *Annual Reports of the DOI, 1902: Report of the CIA*, 177. See also "Redmen Must Pack Up and Go," *San Francisco Call*, December 19, 1901; and "To Care for the Indians," *Imperial Valley Press*, December 17, 1901.
47. Lummis (1859–1928) was born in Lynn, Massachusetts, and attended Harvard, where he met Theodore Roosevelt. He began his career as a newspaper editor in Ohio, then journeyed across the country on foot to become the city editor for the *Los Angeles Times*. A decade later he became editor of *Land of Sunshine*, eventually resigning to become head of the Los Angeles Public Library. He helped found the Landmarks Club, which began the restoration of California missions; established the Sequoyah League; and aided in the founding of the Southwest Museum. See Turbesé Lummis Fiske and Keith Lummis, *Charles F. Lummis: The Man and His West* (Norman: University of Oklahoma Press, 1975); and Mark Thompson, *American Character: The Curious Life of Charles Fletcher Lummis and the Rediscovery of the Southwest* (New York: Arcade Publishing, 2001), especially 213–43.
48. "A New Indian Policy," *Land of Sunshine* (December 1901): 457–64. According to "Founding a National Movement" (*Out West*, January 1902, 66), the organization was established "to forward and assist a more tolerable policy toward the Indians of California." See Francis Watkins, "C. F. Lummis and the Sequoya League," *Quarterly*

Publication of the Historical Society of Southern California, vol. 26, no. 2–3 (June/September 1944): 99–114. The league issued its last bulletin in 1911. Of all people, J. Harvey Downey was listed as a member in 1906.

49. Lummis, "The Sequoya League," *Out West*, vol. 17, no. 1 (July 1902): 81–83.

50. For Allen, see Guinn, *Historical and Biographical Record of Southern California*, 958. Born in 1859, he graduated from Harvard in 1880 and moved to California two years later. In 1890 he became the manager of the Sweetwater Fruit Company, which grew lemons at Bonita in San Diego County. See also *San Diego County Pioneer Families* (San Diego: San Diego Historical Society, 1977).

Partridge was killed in a railroad accident in June 1908; his papers are now at the Bancroft Library, University of California, Berkeley, California. He made investigative tours of local Mission Indian villages and was closely associated with the Redlands Indian Association, a WNIA affiliate. For a short time he took over the association's presidency. See his article, "A Brief Sketch of the Mission Indians," in the *Redlands Citrograph*, June 14, 1902.

51. Commission members were listed in "Wright to Jones, September 20, 1902," *Annual Reports of the DOI, 1902*, 177; and Lummis, "The Sequoya League," *Out West*, vol. 17, no. 1 (July 1902): 81. See also "To Choose New Home for Warner's Ranch Indians. Charles F. Lummis Heads the Commission That Will Select the Lands," June 7, 1902; and "Glimpses of the Starving Warner's Ranch Indians," June 9, 1902—both in the *San Francisco Chronicle*.

Richard Egan (1842–1923) was born in Ireland but came to America as a child, moving to San Juan Capistrano in 1868, where he remained the rest of his life. He served as a justice of the peace, a county supervisor, and a school trustee. He had worked with Lummis earlier, during the Landmarks Club's efforts to restore the old mission there. "[T]hough not a licensed surveyor," his biographer notes, he "was regarded as an authority on old Mexican and Spanish land grant boundaries." See E. M. Herstory [Marah Ryan], "The Alcalde of San Juan Capistrano," *Los Angeles Times*, June 10, 1923; and Ellen K. Lee, "The Irish Alcalde," *Orange Countiana*, vol. 1 (1973): 30–37.

52. "The Public Pulse. Horatio N. Rust, The Indian Commission," *Los Angeles Herald*, June 22, 1902.

53. Quotes from Charles Fletcher Lummis, "The Exiles of Cupa," 472; and Lummis, "The Sequoya League," 409—both in *Out West*, vol. 16, no. 5 (May 1902).

José Cecilio Blacktooth, the hereditary leader of the Blacktooth clan, held the office of village captain in 1892 and again in 1902. Born around 1840, he was the son of Pío and Marcelina Blacktooth; his mother had testified at the 1893 trial. He apparently died at Pala around 1918. "Blacktooth" was originally a nickname for the family, originating in the effect that drinking the highly fluorinated water of the hot springs had on their teeth as children.

54. Salvador Nolasquez (1861–1933) served as captain at Agua Caliente in 1899 and again at Pala in 1908. His daughter, Roscinda, was a respected tribal elder.

Ambrosio Ortega (1869–1922) was a step-brother of Salvador's mother, Mercedes. He was both a leader in traditional Cupeño rituals and also the lay reader for the Catholic chapel at Agua Caliente. He served as captain at Pala in 1906. John Steven McGroarty published a memorial to him in the *Los Angeles Times Illustrated Magazine* (May 21, 1922), which was later reprinted and expanded in *The Indian Sentinel* (a publication of the Bureau of Catholic Indian Missions), vol. 2, no 11 (July 1922): 527–28.

55. For Lummis's description of their travels, see "The Sequoya League," July 1902, 81–83, and August 1902, 214–16—both in *Out West;* and "Removal of Warner's Ranch Indians," *San Francisco Chronicle*, April 22, 1903.

56. For their visit, see "Warner's Ranch Indians Anxious. Force May Have to Be Used to Remove Them," *San Francisco Chronicle*, July 26, 1902. For the petition text, see Phillips, *Chiefs and Challengers*, 275–76.

57. "Indians' Last Hope Is Gone. President Will Not Interfere in Removal of Warner Ranch Tribes," *San Francisco Chronicle*, December 24, 1902; and Ortega and Nolasquez to Theodore Roosevelt, n.d. [July 1902?], copy in Charles Fletcher Lummis Manuscript Collection, Braun Research Library (Southwest Museum), Autry National Center of the American West, Los Angeles, California.

58. Jones to Ortega and Nolasquez, July 28, 1902, Charles Partridge Papers Concerning Resettlement of Warner's Ranch Indians, 1901–1924, Bancroft Library, University of California, Berkeley, Calif. See also "Warner Ranch Indians Will Go. Partridge of Redlands Says They Will Make No Resistance," *San Francisco Chronicle*, August 3, 1902; and "The Commissioner Went in Hiding," *Los Angeles Times*, July 27, 1902.

59. The "Final Report of the Warner's Ranch Indian Advisory Commission," August 26, 1902, and "Account of Expenses of the Commission with Vouchers, Certificates, Receipts, etc." are in the Lummis Manuscript Collection. The report was quoted extensively in *Out West*, in April (440–55) and May (589–602), 1903, under the title "Turning a New Leaf."

60. "Removal of Warner's Ranch Indians," *San Francisco Chronicle*, April 22, 1903. For Lummis's justification of the Pala valley location, see "The Sequoya League," March 1903, 355–56; and "Turning a New Leaf," April 1903, 441–55—both in *Out West.* For purchase of the land from Salmons, see "Warner's Ranch Indians on Pala Reservation, Cal.," *Annual Reports of the DOI, 1903: Report of the CIA* (GPO, 1904), 75–76. The deed was approved by the government on January 22, 1903.

Salmons, who ran a small store in the Pala valley, was the brother of teacher Ora Salmons. His discovery of tourmaline mines brought him wealth, enabling him to later restore the Pala Mission. See Francis J. Biermann, "The Gem of Prophecy," *Sunset: The Pacific Monthly*, October 1916: 27, 67–68.

61. WNIA, A.S.Q, "At Agua Caliente," *The Indian's Friend*, July 1902, 2. For a detailed history and reprinting of letters by Quinton, Lummis, Babbitt, and Wright, see Mathes and Brigandi, "The Mischief Record of 'La Gobernadora,'" 69–96.

62. "Fight till Last Ditch. Trouble Is Brewing at Warner's Ranch," *Los Angeles Times*, July 26, 1902.

63. "Poor Indians Victimized. Female False Pretender among Them," *Los Angeles Times*, May 23, 1902.

64. Wright to Lummis, May 26, 1902, L.A. Wright MS1.1.4763A, Lummis Manuscript Collection. See also Wright to William Collier, May 26, 1902, box 2, folder 78, Wright Collection.

65. Lummis, "The Sequoya League," vol. 17, no. 6 (December 9, 1902): 732–34; Lummis, "The Sequoya League," vol. 17, no. 6 (August 1902), 218—both in *Out West*.

Lummis was not Brown's only detractor. Several newspapers criticized him for posing as a "friend of the Indian" while making good money off them as an attorney. See especially "An Indian Moses," *Riverside Press & Horticulturalist*, March 28, 1891, quoting an article from the *Banning Herald*.

66. "The Indians Will Be Removed Today," *San Diego Union*, May 11, 1903.

67. *Riverside Daily Press*, April 22, 1903. Conser later served as superintendent of Sherman Institute (1909–1930).

68. Edward H. Davis, "Agua Caliente Ind. Removal," manuscript notes, April 19, 1903 (microfilm), San Diego Historical Society Research Archives, San Diego, California.

69. "So far as is known," Lummis boasted, "never before in our history as a nation were Indians moved to better lands than those from which they were dispossessed." See Lummis, "Turning a New Leaf," *Out West*, vol. 18, no. 4 (April 1903): 442. For an interview with Lummis, see "Expect No Trouble. Warner Indians to Be Moved Quietly," *Los Angeles Herald*, April 20, 1903.

70. "The Indians Will Be Removed Today," *San Diego Union*, May 11, 1903.

71. Edward Davis, who got an account of the meeting from Mrs. Babbitt a few days later, described Lummis as showing "an amazing lack of tact in attempting to pacify the Indians." See "Agua Caliente Ind. Removal," manuscript notes, April 19, 1903 (microfilm), San Diego Historical Society Research Archives, San Diego, California.

72. Lummis to Wright, April 28, 1903, Lummis Manuscript Collection.

The *San Francisco Chronicle*, on April 19, 1903, reported that Lummis had warned the Cupeños "that if they did not go they would be compelled to do so." The *New York Times*, on June 14, 1903, reported that Lummis, Wright, and the others had "wired to Washington, reporting that it would be impossible to evict the Indians without the presence of United States troops."

73. Jenkins had visited Agent Wright in 1898 in his role as a special agent. According to the local paper, he "was a newspaper man in Iowa and during the campaign was a red hot advocate of McKinley and republicanism. His reward was a good fat plum." *San Jacinto Register*, February 3, 1898. Jenkins later returned to California and served as agent at the Morongo Reservation near Banning from 1918 to 1919.

74. Matthews to Conser, May 7, 1903, from a manuscript note in the Horace Parker Papers, Sherman Library and Gardens, Corona del Mar, Calif.

75. "Indians Face Pala Homes," *Los Angeles Times*, May 12, 1903; Joseph J. Schirmer, "Graphic Story Is Told of Indians' Removal," *Riverside Daily Press*, May 14, 1903. See also "Wagons Start for Reservation. Warner Ranch Indians Will Begin Moving Saturday," *San Francisco Call*, May 8, 1903.

Despite a ban on reporters, Schirmer slipped in with the teamsters, writing his dispatches while hidden beneath a blanket in the back of a wagon. His diary-like descriptions provide a valuable first-hand account of the removal.

76. *San Diego Union*, May 13, 1903.

77. Schirmer, "Graphic Story Is Told of Indians' Removal," *Riverside Daily Press*, May 14, 1903.

78. Ibid.
79. "Eviction Left a Trail of Tears from Village of Kupa to Pala," *Riverside Press-Enterprise*, May 21, 1985. Nolasquez died in 1987 at age 94; see Phil Brigandi, "Roscinda Nolasquez Remembered," *Journal of California and Great Basin Anthropology*, vol. 9, no. 1 (1987): 2–3.
80. Grant Wallace, "The Exiles of Cupa," *Out West*, vol. 19, no. 1 (July 1903): 25–42, quote on 37.
81. *Los Angeles Times*, May 14, 1903.
82. *New York Times*, June 14, 1903.
83. *Los Angeles Times*, May 14, 1903. The San José villagers arrived at Pala around May 23. Most of the people from San José and Mataguay eventually moved to Santa Ysabel.
84. Wallace, "The Exiles of Cupa," 37.
85. Interview by Phil Brigandi, July 27, 1980.
86. Interview by Phil Brigandi, July 12, 1978.
87. Interview by Phil Brigandi, February 17, 1986.
88. *Los Angeles Herald*, May 15, 1903.
89. Interview by Phil Brigandi, July 12, 1978.
90. Interviews by Phil Brigandi, July 27, 1980, and December 5, 1981.
91. For first quote, see Lummis to James Jenkins, September 16, 1903; and for second, Lummis to Theodore Roosevelt, June 3, 1903—both in Lummis Manuscript Collection, MS.1SL.1.1.24C.
92. Wallace, "The Exiles of Cupa," 39.

    See also Phil Brigandi, "In the Name of the Law—The Cupeño Removal of 1903," www.socialhistoryland.mysite.com/article_12.html, accessed June 19, 2017; Phillips, *Chiefs and Challengers*, 256–71; Carrico, *Strangers in a Stolen Land*, 155–63; Hyer, "*We Are Not Savages*," 111–28; and Steven M. Karr, "The Warner's Ranch Indian Removal: Cultural Adaptation, Accommodation, and Continuity," *California History*, vol. 86, no. 4 (2009): 24–43.
93. Shell to Indian Commissioner Jones, September 24, 1903, Records of the Pala Superintendency, Letters Sent, 1903–1908, National Archives Pacific Region Branch, Perris, Calif. (hereafter cited as Pala Agency Records).
94. C. E. Kelsey, *Report of the Special Agent*, 30–31; also quoted in *Federal Concern*, 144. See also "Injun House Fierce Joke," *Los Angeles Times*, October 10, 1903. The *Times*, in its April 10, 1927, issue, reported that the Cupeños called these portable houses "coffin houses."
95. Holland to Leupp, August 9, 1906, Pala Agency Records.
96. "Shell to Jones, August 20, 1904," *Annual Reports of the DOI, 1904*, part 1, 165.
97. Shell to Jones, December 26, 1903, Pala Agency Records.
98. Gordon Johnson, "Sharing Memories with Katherine Mojado," *Nock-Ma Quarterly*, vol. 1, no. 1 (December 1977): 14–15.

    Mojado (1895–1982) was the daughter of Salvadora Valenzuela (1874–1953) and the granddaughter of Manuela Griffith (1852–1927), who worked closely with some of the earliest anthropologists studying the Cupeños.

99. Henshaw (1860–1924) was involved in numerous San Diego County water development projects. He acquired Warner's Ranch in 1911, but World War I delayed dam construction until 1922. As Lake Henshaw began to fill, the company agreed to relocate the San José village graveyard, which was about to be inundated by the rising waters. A one-acre site east of the lake was donated, and fifty-six bodies were moved—some of them thought to be as much as two hundred years old, while others dated to shortly before the 1903 removal. See *Hemet News*, October 26, 1923. In 1923 the Vista Irrigation District was formed to buy water from Lake Henshaw, delivered via the canal of the Escondido Mutual Water Company from La Jolla. Today Vista Irrigation controls much of the ranch. For Henshaw's involvement, see Joseph Hill, *The History of Warner's Ranch*, 167–82. See also the *Memoirs of Ed Fletcher* (Fletcher was associated with Henshaw). In 1969, five reservations filed suit against the Escondido and Vista companies for loss of water from the San Luis Rey River. See *Escondido Times-Advocate*, June 25, 1969; and *San Diego Union*, July 6, 1982. See also Steven M. Karr, "Water We Believed Could Never Belong to Anyone: The San Luis Rey River and the Pala Indians of Southern California," *American Indian Quarterly*, vol. 24, no. 3 (Summer 2000): 381–99.
100. Salmons was the sister of Pala storekeeper Frank Salmons. She died in 1923 at the age of seventy; see *Hemet News*, February 16, 1923. Roscinda Nolasquez recalled that Mrs. Babbitt "came here [to Pala] . . . with the people and she stayed with us. But then she went back—I guess to Los Angeles. She was a good friend." Interview by Phil Brigandi, August 7, 1985.
101. Interview by Phil Brigandi, November 28, 1980. See Jane Hill and Roscinda Nolasquez, *Mulu'Wetam: The First People* (Banning, Calif.: Malki Museum Press, 1973), 22–23a.
102. In "Redmen Must Pack Up and Go. Southern Reservation Indians in a Sad Predicament" (*San Francisco Call*, December 9, 1901), the reporter noted that although the San Felipe case was "practically the same . . . a decision of the court has not yet been written."
103. "Wright to Jones," September 20, 1901," *Annual Reports of the DOI, 1901*, 196.
104. Lummis, "The Sequoyah League," *Out West*, vol. 19, no. 5 (October 1903): 421. See also "San Felipe Indians Must Also Move. Occupy Coveted Lands and Must Go," *Los Angeles Herald*, September 5, 1903.
105. Wright to Lummis, September 27, 1903, GC1309, Wright Collection.
106. "San Felipe Indians Object to Removal. Anxious Redskins Consult Lawyers about the Chance of Holding Lands," *San Francisco Call*, September 6, 1903. See also [Lummis?], "The Last Eviction," *Out West*, vol. 19, no. 5 (November 1903): 485–91.
107. [Lummis?], "The Last Eviction," 485–91.
108. Edward Davis, "The Last Eviction" (manuscript dated September 14, 1903), reproduced in Quinn and Quinn, *Edward H. Davis*, 84–89. Davis sent his account for Agent Wright to look over. The agent made a few corrections and admitted to Lummis that he "had broken in a door or two and showed them that I meant to carry out my orders."
109. Wright to Lummis, September 27, 1903, Wright Collection.

110. Lummis, "The Sequoya League," *Out West*, vol. 19, no. 4 (October 1903): 421. For some *San Diego Union* coverage, see "White Man Greedy, Red Must Move On. San Felipe Indians Captured and Sent to the Reservation at Pala," September 7, 1903; "San Felipe Indians Have Reached Pala," September 8, 1903; and "No Sentiment in Indian Exodus. Removal of San Felipe Tribe to Pala Accomplished in Matter-of-Fact Way," September 15, 1903. See also "Removal of San Felipe Indians. Have Joined Contingent at Pala Reservation," *Los Angeles Herald*, September 8, 1903.

111. C. E. Kelsey, *Report of the Special Agent*, 31.

Smeaton Chase met a few of the remaining San Felipes near their old home at San Felipe when he passed through the area around 1915. He described the "cluster of decaying adobes at the foot of the mountain" as all that remained of their deserted village. On the road he met a small procession of three wagons, one of which held a small, roughly made, unpainted coffin. "It was the funeral of a San Felipe boy on its way to the old burying-ground," he wrote. See J. Smeaton Chase, *California Desert Trails* (Boston: Houghton Mifflin, 1919), 241–42.

112. C. E. Kelsey, *Report of the Special Agent*, 31. For more on the San Felipe removal, see Phillips, *Chiefs and Challengers*, 269–92; and Hyer, *"We Are Not Savages,"* 133–36.

113. "Report of the Commissioner of Indian Affairs," *Annual Reports of the DOI, 1903*, 28.

114. See "The Perris Indian School," March 10, 1900; "Dr. L. A. Wright's Place," January 16, 1901; "Wright's Salary," January 17, 1901; and "Mission Tule Agency. Fight against Dr. Wright," January 10, 1902—all in the *Los Angeles Times*. Lummis defended Wright, claiming he "seems to be doing his duty as well as one can whose hands are tied." See Charles Fletcher Lummis, "To Make Better Indians," *Out West*, vol. 16, no. 2 (February 1902): 178–79.

Wright's salary at the time was $1,500 a year, which Jones attempted to have stricken from the Indian Office's annual appropriations bill.

115. For Mission Inn founder Frank Miller's efforts to locate the school, see Nathan Gonzales, "Riverside Tourism, and the Indian: Frank A. Miller and the Creation of Sherman Institute," *Southern California Quarterly*, vol. 84, no. 3–4 (Fall/Winter 2002): 193–222.

116. Wright to Jones, February 4, 1901, box 3, folder 66, Wright Collection.

117. Wright's predecessor, Agent Estudillo, had been criticized by the *Los Angeles Record* for improprieties, having one of his sons on the payroll and moving the agency offices to his property in San Jacinto. See "Alleged Fraud of Indian Agent," *Riverside Daily Press*, October 12, 1895.

118. Wright to Bard, January 28, 1901, box 2, folder 17, Wright Collection. Pointing out that Wainwright printed his attacks in Democratic papers was surely meant to score a point with the Republican Senator, though Wainwright—at least in the 1880s when he first ran for San Bernardino County coroner—was himself a Republican. Wright repeatedly pointed out that Superintendent Hall was a Democrat.

119. Wright to Needham, December 29, 1900, box 2, folder 15, Wright Collection. The *San Bernardino County Sun*, in "Resigned His Office" (July 24, 1901), seemed to agree with Wright about Wainwright's "sinecure" when it wrote, "[T]hough there is not

much honor in the office it is considered one of the best governmental plums in this part of the State. The work is easy and the salary is good."

120. "Shell to Jones, August 20, 1904," and "Wright to Jones, September 1, 1904," *Annual Reports of the DOI, 1904*, part 1 (GPO, 1905), 165, 169. See also "Mission Indian Agency Divided," *San Francisco Chronicle*, July 18, 1903.

121. "Wright to Jones, September 1, 1904," *Annual Reports of the DOI, 1904*, part 1, 170.

122. "Indians Catch Peace Officer," *Los Angeles Times*, September 17, 1907; and "Indians Made Mad by Liquor Attack Officers at Fiesta," *Riverside Enterprise*, September 17, 1907. Wright later had ten Indians arrested, but the court dismissed the charges; see *Riverside Enterprise*, October 31, 1907.

In his 1903 annual report Wright described the fiesta as a "breeder of immorality, seriously interfering with the good conduct of the Indians." He continued, "The Indians have numerous feast days and enjoy them. They seem, indeed, to be a part of their very existence, and it would be a heroic task and require considerable force to prevent them." See "Wright to Jones, September 25, 1903," *Annual Reports of the DOI, 1903*, 148.

123. Tanis Thorne, "The Death of Superintendent Stanley and the Cahuilla Uprising of 1907–12," *Journal of California and Great Basin Anthropology*, vol. 24, no. 2 (2004): 240–41.

124. Stanley was later murdered by a group of Indians at Cahuilla in a notorious incident in 1912. See Thorne, "The Death of Superintendent Stanley," 233–58.

In 1909 Wright moved across the valley to Hemet, where he ran a drug store. He sold out in 1913 and moved to Los Angeles (see *Hemet News*, July 11, 1913), where he again operated a drug store, in Boyle Heights. He died in Los Angeles in 1933 at the age of eighty-two; see *Hemet News*, April 14, 1933.

Epilogue

1. "McCallum to Atkins," September 30, 1885," *Annual Report of the CIA, 1885*, 10.
2. John Ward to Atkins, September 2, 1887, LR #24151–1887, RG 75, SC 31, OIA, NA.
3. See Helen Pruitt Beattie, "Indians of San Bernardino Valley and Vicinity," *Historical Society of Southern California Quarterly*, vol. 35, no. 3 (September 1953): 246.
4. Bean and Lawton, in *The Cahuilla Indians* (4), further write: "Over the years, the Indian agents responsible for Morongo Reservation varied in abilities, ranging from those who were hard-working and altruistic to a few who bordered on the unscrupulous. The work of one Indian agent was often undone by the agent who followed."
5. Thorne, "The Mixed Legacy of Mission Indian Agent S. S. Lawson," 166.

   Hanks (*This War Is for a Whole Life*, 65) claims that Lawson "viewed Native Americans as unruly children in need of discipline and constant oversight to wean them from their pagan and unchristian ways"—though he seems to overestimate Lawson's "Christian zealotry," which he never openly expressed, either during or after his tenure.

6. Garner, *The Broken Ring*, 122.
7. Shaw, "Evolving Ecoscape," 66.
8. Ward to Atkins, August 17, 1887, *Annual Report of the CIA*, 12.
9. Carrico, in *Strangers in a Stolen Land* (74), describes Indian settlements near the San Diego area: "Indian villages or rancherias near white settlements . . . became hodgepodge collections of tattered huts, evil odors, and barking dogs. Within these squalid confines lived the destitute and forgotten elders, Indian outlaws, and tribal members who were forced to eke out a tenuous, parasitic life similar to that of the age-old camp followers." For an even more poignant description from Monterey, see H. H. [Helen Hunt Jackson], "Queen Eumesia," *Christian Union*, vol. 28, no. 25 (December 20, 1883): 541–42.
10. Thorne, *El Capitan*, 59.
11. "The Mission Indians of California," in "Proceedings of the LMC," *Twentieth Annual Report of the BIC, 1888*, 86; and "Report of William H. Waldby, March 27, 1888," *Twentieth Annual Report of the BIC, 1888*, 10.
12. "Report of Albert K. Smiley to Whittlesey, March 1, 1889," in "Report of the BIC," *Report of the Secretary of the Interior for the Fiscal Year Ending June 30, 1889*, vol. 2 (Washington, D.C.: GPO, 1890), 805.
13. H. N. Rust, "A Fiesta at Warner's Ranch," *Land of Sunshine*, vol. 10, no. 5 (April 1899): 237, for the first quote; and "The Indian. Agent Rust Discusses Him and Illustrates Him," *Pasadena Daily Star*, November 30, 1889, for the second.
14. Donald Chaput, "Horatio N. Rust," 282–84 and 289, citing a letter from Painter to Morgan, April 4, 1892.
15. Painter went even further, writing that the whole Agency "should be abolished. There is no need of an agent for those people. They have been injured and not helped by having an Agency established." Copy enclosed with letter from Painter to Herbert Welsh, April 26, 1893, IRA Papers, reel 10.
16. Painter to Welsh, September 1, 1893. IRA Papers, reel 10.
17. H. W. Patton, "Don Francisco Estudillo Dead," 1921 clipping from unidentified Los Angeles newspaper, Phil Brigandi collection.

BIBLIOGRAPHY

Manuscript Collections

Brown, John. Papers. Sherman Library and Gardens Corona del Mar, Calif.

Coronel, Antonio F. Coronel. Collection. Seaver Center for Western History Research, Los Angeles County Museum of Natural History, Los Angeles, Calif.

Davis, Edward H. Collection (microfilm). San Diego Historical Society Research Archives, San Diego, Calif.

Gilman Family Papers. (In Weinland Papers). Huntington Library, San Marino, Calif.

Jackson, Helen Hunt. Manuscripts. Huntington Library, San Marino, Calif.

Jackson, Helen Hunt. Papers. Tutt Library, Colorado College, Colorado Springs, Colo.

Lummis, Charles Fletcher. Manuscript Collection, Braun Research Library (Southwest Museum). Autry National Center of the American West, Los Angeles, Calif.

National Archives. Bureau of Indian Affairs, Record Group 75, Washington, D.C.

National Archives. Records of the Pala Superintendency. Letters Sent, 1903–1908. Pacific Region Branch, Perris, Calif.

Parker, Horace. Papers, Research Notes (in a spiral notebook marked "New Temecula 80s"), Sherman Library and Gardens, Corona del Mar, Calif.

Partridge, Charles L. Papers Concerning Resettlement of Warner's Ranch Indians, 1901–1924. Bancroft Library, University of California, Berkeley, Calif.

Quinton, Amelia Stone Quinton. MS1.1.3648, Charles Fletcher Lummis Manuscript Collection Braun Research Library. Autry National Center of the American West, Los Angeles, Calif.

Rust, Horatio Nelson. Papers. Huntington Library, San Marino, Calif.

Smiley, Albert et al. "Smiley Commission Report: Mission Indians," *Report of Indian Commissioners,* December 7, 1891. Smiley Collection, A. K. Smiley Library, Redlands, Calif.

Weinland, William Henry. Papers. Huntington Library, San Marino, Calif.

Welsh, Herbert. Collection. Historical Society of Pennsylvania, Philadelphia, Penn.

Wright, Lucius. Collection. Seaver Center for Western History Research, Natural History Museum of Los Angeles County, Los Angeles, Calif.

Government Documents

"An Act to Provide for the Better Organization of Indian Affairs in California." 38th Cong., sess. 1, ch. 46–48, 1864, pp. 39–41 (addendum 1, The California Indian Reservation Act of April 8, 1864–13 Stat. 39).

*Annual Report of the Attorney-General of the United States for the Year 1895.*Washington, D.C.: Government Printing Office, 1895 (various years, from 1895 to 1902).

Annual Report of the Commissioner of Indian Affairs to the Secretary of the Interior for the Year 1865. Washington, D.C.: Government Printing Office, 1865.

Annual Report of the Secretary of the Interior, 1895. Vol. 2. Washington, D.C.: Government Printing Office, 1896.

Annual Reports of the Department of the Interior for the Fiscal Year Ended June 30, 1897. Report of the Commissioner of Indian Affairs. Washington, D.C.: Government Printing Office, 1897 (various years from 1897 to 1906).

Board of Indian Commissioners. *Eighteenth Annual Report of the Board of Indian Commissioners, 1886.* Washington, D.C.: Government Printing Office, 1887.

———. *Sixteenth Annual Report of the Board of Indian Commissioners, 1884.* Washington, D.C.: Government Printing Office, 1885.

———. *Twentieth Annual Report of the Board of Indian Commissioners, 1888.*Washington, D.C.: Government Printing Office, 1889.

———. *Twenty-First Annual Report of the Board of Indian Commissioners.* Washington, D.C.: Government Printing Office, 1890.

*Papers Relating to the Foreign Relations of the United States with the Annual Message of the President, December 6, 1897.*Washington, D.C.: Government Printing Office, 1898.

"Pre-emption Claim—Indian Lands: *Mission Indians v. Walsh.*" *Decisions of the Department of the Interior and General Land Office in Cases Relating to Public Lands.* Vol. 12. Edited by S. V. Proudfit. Washington, D.C.: Government Printing Office, 1891.

U.S. Congress, House of Representatives. 43rd Cong., 1st sess., Ex. Doc. No. 91. *Executive Documents Printed by Order of the House of Representatives, 1873–74.* Vol. 9. Washington, D.C.: Government Printing Office.

———. *Executive Documents Printed by Order of the House of Representatives during the Second Session of the Forty-First Congress, 1869–70.* Washington, D.C.: Government Printing Office, 1870.

———. *Executive Documents Printed by Order of the House of Representatives, 1873–74.* Washington, D.C.: Government Printing Office, 1874.

———. *Message of the President of the United States and Accompanying Documents to the Two Houses of Congress,* 40th Cong., 2d session, Ex. Doc. No. 1, 113–15.

———. "Report of Special Agent John G. Ames, in Regard to the Conditions of the Mission Indians of California, with Recommendations, October 28, 1873." In "Mission Indians of Southern California." *Executive Documents Printed by Order of the House of Representatives, 1873–74.* Vol. 9. Washington: Government Printing Office, 1874.

———. "Restoration of Capitan Grande Mission Lands in California." *House Documents,* 59th Cong., 1st sess. (December 4, 1905–June 30, 1906). Vol. 19. Washington, D.C.: Government Printing Office, 1906.

U.S. Congress, Senate. 52d Cong. 1st sess., Ex. Doc. No. 108. *Executive Documents of the Senate of the United States, 1891–92*. Vol. 16. Washington, D.C.: Government Printing Office, 1892.

———. *Journal of the Executive Proceedings of the Senate of the United States of America, from March 5, 1877, to March 3, 1879, Inclusive*. Vol. 21. Washington, D.C.: Government Printing Office, 1901.

———. *Journal of the Executive Proceedings of the Senate of the United States of America from December 5, 1887 to March 3, 1889*. Vol. 26. Washington, D.C.: Government Printing Office, 1901.

———. *Journal of the Executive Proceedings of the Senate of the United States of America. from March 5, 1889, to March 3, 1991, Inclusive*. Vol. 27. Washington, D.C.: Government Printing Office, 1901.

———. *Journal of the Executive Proceedings of the Senate of the United States of America*. Vol. 28. Washington, D.C.: Government Printing Office, 1909.

———. "Message from the President of the United States." S. Ex. Doc. 49, 48th Cong., 1st Sess., 1884.

———. "Message from the President of the United States." S. Ex. Doc. 15, 49th Cong., 1st Sess., 1885.

———. *Reports of Committees of the Senate of the United States for the First Session of the Fifty-First Congress, 1889–1890*. Washington, D.C.: Government Printing Office, 1890.

Books, Articles, Reports, Proceedings, Theses, and Dissertations

Ainsworth, Katherine. *The McCallum Saga, The Story of the Founding of Palm Springs*. Palm Springs: The Palm Springs Desert Museum, 1973.

Ames, John G. "Report of Special Agent John G. Ames, in Regard to the Conditions of the Mission Indians of California, with Recommendations, October 28, 1873." Reprinted in Robert F. Heizer, ed., *Federal Concern about Conditions of California Indians 1853 to 1913: Eight Documents* (Socorro: Ballena Press, 1979), 51–73.

Anderson, Douglas Firth. "'More Conscience than Force': U.S. Indian Inspector William Vandever, Grant's Peace Policy, and Protestant Whiteness." *Journal of the Gilded Age and Progressive Era*, vol. 9, no. 2 (April 2010): 167–96.

Anthony, C. V. *Fifty Years of Methodism. A History of the Methodist Episcopal Church within the Bounds of the California Annual Conference from 1847 to 1897*. San Francisco: Methodist Book Concern, 1901.

Apostol, Jane Apostol. "Horatio Nelson Rust: Abolitionist, Archaeologist, Indian Agent." *California History*, vol. 58, no. 4 (Winter 1979/80): 304–15.

Bahmer, William J. *Centennial History of Coshocton County Ohio*. Vol. 1. Chicago: S. J. Clarke, 1909.

Bates, J. C., ed. *History of the Bench and Bar of California*. San Francisco: Bench and Bar Publishing, 1912.

Bean, Lowell John. *Mukat's People: The Cahuilla Indians of Southern California*. Berkeley: University of California Press, 1972.

Bean, Lowell John, and Harry Lawton. *The Cahuilla Indians of Southern California.* Banning, Calif.: Malki Museum Press, 1965.

Bean, Lowell John, and William Marian Mason. *Diaries and Accounts of the Romero Expeditions in Arizona and California.* Palm Springs, Calif.: Palm Springs Desert Museum, 1962.

Beattie, Helen Pruitt. "Indians of San Bernardino Valley and Vicinity." *Historical Society of Southern California Quarterly,* vol. 35, no. 3 (September 1953): 239–64.

Bergman, Coral R. *Jacob Bergman of Aguanga: The Real Story.* Warner Springs, Calif.: Coral R. Bergman, 1996.

Bibb, Leland E. "Pablo Apis and Temecula." *Journal of San Diego History,* vol. 37, no. 4 (Fall 1991): 256–71.

Biermann, Francis J. "The Gem of Prophecy." *Sunset: The Pacific Monthly,* October 1916: 67–68.

Bingham, Edwin R. *Charles F. Lummis, Editor of the Southwest.* San Marino: The Huntington Library, 1955.

Black, Esther Boulton. *Rancho Cucamonga and Doña Merced.* Redlands: San Bernardino County Museum, 1975.

Boynton, Margaret. *Stories and Legends of the Palm Springs Indians.* Palm Springs: Palm Springs Desert Museum, 1969.

Brigandi, Phil. "Backcountry Badman." *The High Country,* no. 65 (Fall 2003): 18–22.

———. "Law but Not Fact: Land Tenure and Legal Fiction on the Warner Ranch." *The Branding Iron,* no. 260 (Fall 2010): 11–12.

———. "The Outposts of Mission San Luis Rey." *Journal of San Diego History,* vol. 45, no. 2 (Spring 1999): 106–12.

———. "Roscinda Nolasquez Remembered." *Journal of California and Great Basin Anthropology,* vol. 9, no. 1 (1987): 2–3.

Brown Jr., John, and James Boyd. *History of San Bernardino and Riverside Counties.* Chicago: Lewis Publishing, 1922.

Brunner, Edmund de Schweinitz. *History of the Moravian Mission to the Indians of Southern California.* Bethlehem, Penn.: Times Pub. Co, 1923. Reprinted from *Proceedings of the Society for Propagating the Gospel among the Heathen.* Bethlehem, Penn.: Published by the Society, 1914.

Burgess, Larry E. "Commission to the Mission Indians, 1891." *San Bernardino County Museum Association Quarterly,* vol. 35, no.1 (Spring 1988): 1–46.

Burgess, Larry. "The Lake Mohonk Conference on the Indian, 1883–1916." Ph.D. diss., Claremont Graduate School, 1972.

———. *The Smileys: A Commemorative Edition.* Redlands: Moore Historical Foundation, 1991.

Carlson, Leonard A. *Indians, Bureaucrats and Land: The Dawes Act and the Decline of Indian Farming.* Westport, Conn.: Greenwood Press, 1981.

Carrico, Richard L. "San Diego Indians and the Federal Government: Years of Neglect, 1850–1865." *Journal of San Diego History,* vol. 26, no. 3 (Summer 1980): 164–84.

———. *Strangers in a Stolen Land: Indians of San Diego County from Prehistory to the New Deal.* San Diego: Sunbelt Publications, 2008.

———. "The Struggle for Native American Self-Determination in San Diego County." *Journal of California and Great Basin Anthropology* (1980).

———. "Wolf Kalisher: Immigrant, Pioneer Merchant and Indian Advocate." *Western States Jewish Historical Quarterly*, vol. 15, no. 2 (1983).

Chaput, Donald. "Horatio N. Rust and the Agent-as-Collector Dilemma." *Southern California Quarterly*, vol. 64, no. 4 (Winter 1982): 280–95.

Chase, J. Smeaton. *California Desert Trails*. Boston: Houghton Mifflin, 1919.

Cline, Lora L. *Just before Sunset*. Tombstone, Ariz.: LC Enterprises, 1984.

Dobyns, Henry F. *Hepah, California! The Journal of Cave Johnson Couts from Monterey, Nuevo Leon Mexico to Los Angeles, California, during the years 1848–1849*. Tucson: Arizona Pioneers' Historical Society, 1961.

Doody, Louis, and Betty Kikumi Meltzer. *Losing Ground: The Displacement of San Gorgonio Pass Cahuilla People in the 19th Century*. Banning, Calif.: Malki-Ballena Press, 2007.

DuBois, Constance Goddard. "The Mission Indian Exiles." *The Land of Sunshine*, vol. 15, no. 4 (October 1901): 248–52.

Dunn, Dana Ruth Hicks. "Strategies for Survival: Indian Transitions in the Mountains of San Diego County, 1846–1907." Ph.D. diss., University of California, Riverside, 2013.

Ellis, Elmer. *Henry Moore Teller: Defender of the West*. Caldwell, Idaho: Caxton Printers, 1941.

Elliott, Wallace W. *History of San Bernardino and San Diego Counties* (reprint). Riverside, Calif.: Riverside Museum Press, 1965.

Engelhard, Father Zephyrin, *Mission Santa Ines*. Santa Barbara: Mission Santa Barbara, 1932.

Engstrand, Iris H. W., and Mary F. Ward. "Rancho Guajome: An Architectural Legacy Preserved." *Journal of San Diego History*, vol. 41, no. 4 (Fall 1995): 250–83.

Evans, William Edward. "The Garra Uprising: Conflict between San Diego Indians and Settlers in 1851." *California Historical Society Quarterly*, vol. 45, no. 4 (December 1966): 339–51.

Farris, Glenn. "Captain José Panto and the San Pascual Indian Pueblo in San Diego County, 1835–1878." *Journal of San Diego History*, vol. 43, no. 2 (Spring 1997): 116–31.

Fear-Segal, Jacqueline. "The Man on the Bandstand at Carlisle Indian Industrial School." In *Boarding School Blues: Revisiting American Indian Educational Experiences*, 99–122. Lincoln: University of Nebraska Press, 2006.

Fiske, Turbesé Lummis, and Keith Lummis. *Charles F. Lummis: The Man and His West*. Norman: University of Oklahoma Press, 1975.

Fitch, George Hamlin. "Where the Date Palm Grows." *Land of Sunshine*, vol. 13, no. 3 (August 1900): 135–42.

Fletcher, Ed. *Memoirs of Ed Fletcher*. San Diego: n.p., 1952.

Frank, Gelya, and Carole Goldberg. *Defying the Odds: The Tule River Tribe's Struggle for Sovereignty in Three Centuries*. New Haven, Conn.: Yale University Press, 2010.

Fraser, Robert W. Fraser, ed. "Lovell's Report on the Cahuilla Indian." *Journal of San Diego History*, vol. 22, no. 1 (Winter 1976): 4–10.

Garesché, Alex. J. [John] P. [Peter]. *Coahuila or Mission Indians of California: Letters to Secretary of the Interior in Their Behalf by Alex. J. P. Garesché of St. Louis, Mo.* St. Louis: R. & T. A. Ennis, 1892.

Garner, Van H. *The Broken Ring: The Destruction of the California Indians.* Tucson: Westernlore Press, 1982.

Goepp, Ida. "A Visit to the Ramona Mission at Potraro [*sic*]." *Periodical Accounts Relating to the Foreign Missions of the Church of the United Brethren.* Vol. 1. London: Printed for the Brethren's Society, 1890: 171–73.

Gonzales, Nathan. "Riverside Tourism, and the Indian: Frank A. Miller and the Creation of Sherman Institute." *Southern California Quarterly*, vol. 84, no. 3–4 (Fall/Winter 2002): 193–222.

Guinn, J. M., ed. *Historical and Biographical Record of Southern California.* Chicago: Chapman Publishing, 1902.

Gunther, Jane Davies. *Riverside County, California, Place Names.* Riverside: Rubidoux Printing, 1984.

Hagan, William T. *The Indian Rights Association: The Herbert Welsh Years, 1882–1904.* Tucson: University of Arizona Press, 1985.

Hanks, Richard A. *This War Is for a Whole Life: The Culture of Resistance among Southern California Indians, 1850–1966.* Banning, Calif.: Ushkana Press, 2012.

Harley, R. Bruce. "The Founding of St. Boniface Indian School, 1888–1890." *Southern California Quarterly*, vol. 81, no. 4 (Winter 1999): 449–66.

Herbert, Edgar W. "The Last of the Padres." *San Diego Historical Society Quarterly*, vol. 10, no. 2 (April 1964): 15–22.

Heizer, Robert F., ed. "An Early Cahuilla Ethnographic Sketch." *The Masterkey*, vol. 4, no. 1 (January–March 1974): 14–21.

———, ed. *Federal Concern about Conditions of California Indians 1853 to 1913: Eight Documents.* Socorro, N.Mex.: Ballena Press, 1979.

———, ed. *Handbook of North American Indians.* Vol. 8, *California.* Washington, D.C.: Smithsonian Institution, 1978.

———, ed. *Some Last Century Accounts of the Indians of Southern California.* Ramona, Calif.: Ballena Press, 1976.

Heizer, Robert F., and Alan J. Almquist. *The Other Californians: Prejudice and Discrimination under Spain, Mexico, and the United States to 1920.* Berkeley: University of California Press, 1971.

Hendricks, W. O. "On an Attempt to Expel Some Yuma Indians from Baja California." *Pacific Coast Archaeological Society Quarterly*, vol. 4, no. 1 (January 1968): 55–66.

———. "On an Attempt to Expel Some Yuma Indians from Baja California, Part II." *Pacific Coast Archaeological Society Quarterly*, vol. 6, no. 1 (January 1970): 47–57.

Hill, Edward E. *The Office of Indian Affairs, 1824–1880: Historical Sketches.* New York: Clearwater Publishing, 1974.

Hill, Jane, and Roscinda Nolasquez. *Mulu'Wetam: The First People.* Banning, Calif.: Malki Museum Press, 1973.

Hill, Joseph John. *The History of Warner's Ranch and Its Environs.* Los Angeles: privately published, 1927.

Hill, N. H., comp., *History of Coshocton County, Ohio: Its Past and Present, 1740–1881.* Newark, Ohio: A. A. Graham, 1881.

History of Essex and Hudson Counties, New Jersey. Vol. 1. Philadelphia: Everts & Peck, 1884.

The History of Henry County, Illinois, Its Tax-Payers and Voters. Chicago: H. F. Kett, 1877.

History of Saint Louis City and County. Vol. 2. Philadelphia: Louis H. Everts, 1883.

Holmes, Elmer W. *History of Riverside County, California.* Los Angeles: Historical Record Company, 1912.

Howell, Edward B. "A Tragic Sequel to 'Ramona.'" *Review of Reviews*, 10 (November 1894): 507–13.

Hughes, Tom. *History of Banning and San Gorgonio Pass.* Banning, Calif.: Banning Record Print, [1938].

Hyer, Joel E. *"We Are Not Savages": Native Americans in Southern California and the Pala Reservation, 1840–1920.* East Lansing: Michigan State University Press, 2001.

An Illustrated History of Southern California Embracing the Counties of San Diego, San Bernardino, Los Angeles and Orange. Chicago: The Lewis Publishing Company, 1890.

Indian Rights Association. *The Case of the Mission Indians in Southern California and the Action of the Indian Rights Association in Supporting the Defense of Their Legal Rights.* Philadelphia: Office of the Indian Rights Association, 1886.

———. *The Fifteenth Annual Report of the Executive Committee of the Indian Rights Association, for the Year Ending December 13, 1897.* Philadelphia: Office of the Indian Rights Association, 1898.

———. *The Fifth Annual Report of the Executive Committee of the Indian Rights Association, for the Year Ending December 20, 1887.* Philadelphia: Office of the Indian Rights Association, 1888.

———. *The Fourth Annual Report of the Executive Committee of the Indian Rights Association, for the Year Ending December 14, 1886.* Philadelphia: Office of the Indian Rights Association, 1887.

———. *The Nineteenth Annual Report of the Executive Committee of the Indian Rights Association, for the Year Ending December 6, 1901.* Philadelphia: Office of the Indian Rights Association, 1902.

———. *The Ninth Annual Report of the Executive Committee of the Indian Rights Association for the Year Ending December 15th, 1891.* Philadelphia: Office of the Indian Rights Association, 1892.

———. *Papers.* Glen Rock, N.J.: Microfilming Corporation of America, 1975.

———. *The Seventeenth Annual Report of the Executive Committee of the Indian Rights Association, for the Year Ending December 15, 1899.* Philadelphia: Office of the Indian Rights Association, 1900.

———. *The Twentieth Annual Report of the Executive Committee of the Indian Rights Association, for the Year Ending December 10, 1902.* Philadelphia: Office of the Indian Rights Association, 1903.

Jackson, Helen Hunt. *A Century of Dishonor: A Sketch of the United States Government's Dealings with Some of the Indian Tribes.* Boston: Roberts Brothers, 1888. See especially "Report on the Condition and Needs of the Mission Indians of California, Made by

Special Agents Helen Jackson and Abbot Kinney, to the Commissioner of Indian Affairs," 458–514.

———. "The Temecula Exiles." *The Independent*, November 29, 1883: 3.

James, George Wharton. *In and Out of the Old Missions of California*. Boston: Little, Brown, 1905.

Johnson, Anna Hayward. "Neurasthenia." *Philadelphia Medical Times, a Bi-Weekly Journal of Medical and Surgical Science, 1880–1881*. Vol. 11. Philadelphia: J. B. Lippincott, 1881: 737–44.

Johnson, E. Polk. *A History of Kentucky and Kentuckians: The Leaders and Representative Men in Commerce, Industry and Modern Activities*. Chicago: Lewis Publishing, 1912.

Johnson, Gordon. "Sharing Memories with Katherine Mojado." *Nock-Ma Quarterly*, vol. 1, no. 1 (December 1977): 14–15.

Kappler, Charles J., ed. *Indian Affairs: Laws and Treaties*. Vol. 1, *Laws*. Washington, D.C.: Government Printing Office, 1904.

Karr, Steven M. "The Warner's Ranch Indian Removal: Cultural Adaptation, Accommodation, and Continuity." *California History*, vol. 86, no. 4 (2009): 24–43.

———. "Water We Believed Could Never Belong to Anyone: The San Luis Rey River and the Pala Indians of Southern California." *American Indian Quarterly*, vol. 24, no. 3 (Summer 2000): 381–99.

Keller, Robert H. *American Protestantism and United States Indian Policy, 1869–82*. Lincoln: University of Nebraska Press, 1983.

Kelsey, C. E. *Report of the Special Agent for California Indians to the Commissioner of Indian Affairs, March 21, 1906*. San Jose: Cleveland Printing, 1907.

Kelsey, Harry. "The California Indian Treaty Myth." *Southern California Quarterly*, vol. 55, no. 3 (Fall 1973): 225–38.

Knight, Lucian Lamar. *A Standard History of Georgia and Georgians*. Chicago: Lewis Publishing, 1917.

Kroeber, A. L. Kroeber. "Horatio Nelson Rust." *Journal of American Folklore* (April–June 1907): 153.

Kvasnicka, Robert M., and Herman J. Viola, eds. *The Commissioners of Indian Affairs, 1824–1977*. Lincoln: University of Nebraska Press, 1979.

Lake Mohonk Conference. *Proceedings of the Fifteenth Annual Meeting of the Lake Mohonk Conference of the Friends of the Indian, 1897*. N.p.: Lake Mohonk Conference, 1897.

———. "Proceedings of the Mohonk Lake Conference." In *Eighteenth Annual Report of the BIC. 1886*, Washington, D.C.: Government Printing Office, 1887.

———. *Proceedings of the Tenth Annual Meeting of the Lake Mohonk Conference of the Friends of the Indian, 1892*. N.p.: Lake Mohonk Conference, 1892.

———. *Proceedings of the Third Annual Meeting of the Lake Mohonk Conference of Friends of the Indian*. Philadelphia: Sherman & Co., Printers, 1886.

———. *Proceedings of the Thirteenth Annual Meeting of the Lake Mohonk Conference of Friends of the Indian, 1895*. N.p.: Lake Mohonk Conference, 1896.

———. *Proceedings of the Twentieth Annual Meeting of the Lake Mohonk Conference of Friends of the Indian, 1902*. N.p.: Lake Mohonk Conference, 1903.

Lee, Ellen K. "The Irish Alcalde." *Orange Countiana*, vol. 1 (1973): 30–37.

Lewis, Frank D. "The Warner Ranch Indians and Why They Were Removed to Pala." *Overland Monthly* (August 1903): 171–73.

Loomis, Noel M. "The Garra Uprising of 1851." In *Brand Book II*, 2–26. San Diego: San Diego Corral of The Westerners, 1971.

Lovett, W. E. "Report of W. E. Lovett, Special Indian Agent, to Austin Wiley, Superintendent of Indians Affairs in California." *Appendix to Journals of Senate and Assembly of the Sixteen Session of the Legislature of the State of California*. Vol. 3. Sacramento: O. M. Clayes, State Printer, 1866.

Lummis, Charles Fletcher. "A New Indian Policy." *Land of Sunshine* (December 1901): 457–64.

———. "The Exiles of Cupa." *Out West*, vol. 16, no. 5 (May 1902):465–79.

———. "Founding a National Movement." *Out West*, vol. 16, no. 1 (January 1902): 66.

———[?]. "The Last Eviction." *Out West*, vol. 19, no. 5 (November 1903): 485–91.

———. "To Make Better Indians." *Out West*, vol. 16, no. 2 (February 1902): 178–79.

———. "The Sequoya League." *Out West*, vol. 17, no. 1 (July 1902): 81–83.

———. "The Sequoya League." *Out West*, vol. 17, no. 2 (August 1902): 214–20.

———. "The Sequoya League." *Out West*, vol. 17, no. 6 (December 9, 1902): 731–34.

———. "The Sequoya League." *Out West*, vol. 19, no. 4 (October 1903): 419–23.

———. "Turning a New Leaf." *Out West*, vol. 18, no. 4 (April 1903): 441–55.

———. "Turning a New Leaf." *Out West*, vol. 18, no. 5 (May 1903): 589–602.

Magliari, Michael. "Free Soil, Unfree Labor: Cave Johnson Couts and the Binding of Indian Workers in California, 1850–1867." *Pacific Historical Review*, vol. 73, no. 3 (August 2004): 349–89.

Mathes, Valerie Sherer. "Baptist Missionary Work at Round Valley, California." *American Baptist Quarterly* (Fall 2010): 172–86.

———. "Boston, the Boston Indian Citizenship Committee, and the Poncas." *Massachusetts Historical Review*, vol. 14 (2012): 119–48.

———. "The California Mission Indian Commission of 1891: The Legacy of Helen Hunt Jackson." *California History*, vol. 72, no. 4 (Winter 1993–94): 339–58, notes 390–95.

———. *Divinely Guided: The California Work of the Women's National Indian Association*. Lubbock: Texas Tech University Press, 2012.

———. *Helen Hunt Jackson and Her Indian Reform Legacy*. Austin: University of Texas Press, 1990.

———, ed. *The Indian Reform Letters of Helen Hunt Jackson, 1879–1885*. Norman: University of Oklahoma Press, 1998.

———. "Mary Lucinda Bonney and Amelia Stone Quinton, Founders of the Women's National Indian Association." *American Baptist Quarterly*, vol. 28, no. 4 (Winter 2009): 421–40.

———, ed. *The Women's National Indian Association: A History*. Albuquerque: University of New Mexico, 2015.

Mathes, Valerie Sherer, and Phil Brigandi. *A Call for Reform: The Southern California Indian Writings of Helen Hunt Jackson*. Norman: University of Oklahoma Press, 2015.

———. "Charles C. Painter, Helen Hunt Jackson and the Mission Indians of Southern California." *Journal of San Diego History*, vol. 55, no. 3 (Summer 2009): 89–118.

———. "The Mischief Record of 'La Gobernadora' Amelia Stone Quinton, Charles Fletcher Lummis, and the Warner Ranch Indian Removal." *Journal of San Diego History*, vol. 57, no. 1–2 (Winter/Spring 2011): 69–96.

McCawley, William. *The First Angelinos: The Gabrielino Indians of Los Angeles*. Banning, Calif.: Malki Museum Press/Ballena Press, 1996.

McLaughlin, John. *My Friend the Indian*. Boston: Houghton Mifflin, 1910.

McNeil, Teresa Baksh. "Catholic Indian Schools of the Southwest Frontier: Curriculum and Management." *Southern California Quarterly*, vol. 72, no. 4 (Winter 1990): 321–38.

———. "St. Anthony's Indian School in San Diego, 1886–1907." *Journal of San Diego History*, vol. 34, no. 3 (Summer 1988): 186–200.

Melendy, H. Brett, and Benjamin F. Gilbert. *The Governors of California: Peter H. Burnett to Edmund G. Brown*. Georgetown, Calif.: The Talisman Press, 1965.

Mighels, Ella Sterling Cummins. *The Story of the Files: A Review of California Writers and Literature*. San Francisco: World's Fair Commission of California, Columbian Exposition, 1893.

Miller, Anne J. "Maria Antonia Apis: A Young Luiseño Indian Woman." *Southern California Quarterly*, vol. 86, no. 2 (Summer 2004): 113–26.

Miller, Larisa K. "Counting Context: C. E. Kelsey's 1906 Census of Nonreservation Indians in Northern California." *American Indian Culture and Research Journal*, vol. 38, no. 2 (2014): 41–66.

———. "Primary Sources on C. E. Kelsey and the Northern California Indian Association." *Journal of Western Archives*, vol. 4, issue 1, article 8 (2013). Available at: http://digitalcommons.usu.edu/westernarchives/vol14/iss1/8.

———. "The Secret Treaties with California's Indians." *Prologue* (Fall/Winter 2013): 38–45.

Minutes of the Twenty-Fourth Session of the California Annual Conference of the Methodist Episcopal Church. San Francisco: Methodist Book Depository, 1876.

Miskwish, Michael Connolly. *Kumeyaay, A History Textbook*. Vol. 1, *Precontact to 1893*. El Cajon, Calif.: Sycuan Press, 2007.

Morgan, Thomas. "Supplemental Report on Indian Education." In *Americanizing the American Indians*, edited by Francis Paul Prucha, 221–38. Cambridge: Harvard University Press, 1973.

Moyer, Cecil C. *Historic Ranchos of San Diego*. San Diego: Union-Tribune Publishing, 1969.

Niemann, Greg. *Palm Springs Legends: Creation of a Desert Oasis*. San Diego: Sunbelt Publications, 2006.

Nolasquez, Roscinda. *Mulu'Wetam: The First People*. Banning, Calif.: Malki Museum Press, 1973.

Nunis Jr., Doyce B., ed. *Tales of Mexican California*. Santa Barbara: Bellerophon Books, 1994.

Official Roster of the Soldiers of the State of Ohio in the War of the Rebellion, 1871–1866. Vol. 4. Akron, Ohio: Werner Printing, 1887.

O'Neil, Floyd A. "John H. Oberly 1888–89." In *The Commissioners of Indian Affairs, 1824–1977*, edited by Robert M. Kvasnicka and Herman J. Viola, 189–91. Lincoln: University of Nebraska Press, 1979.

Ostler, Jeffrey. *The Plains Sioux and U.S. Colonialism from Lewis and Clark to Wounded Knee*. Cambridge: Cambridge University Press, 2004.

Otis, D. S. *The Dawes Act and the Allotment of Indian Lands*. Norman: University of Oklahoma Press, 2014.

The Pacific Reporter. Vol. 56, *Containing All the Decisions of the Supreme Court of California*. St. Paul: West Publishing, 1899: 692–99.

Painter, Charles C. *The Condition of Affairs in Indian Territory and California*. Philadelphia: Office of the Indian Rights Association, 1888.

———. "Report of Mr. C. C. Painter, Washington Agent of the Association." *The Ninth Annual Report of the Executive Committee of the Indian Rights Association for the Year Ending December 15th, 1891*. Philadelphia: Office of the IRA, 1892.

———. *A Visit to the Mission Indians of California*. Philadelphia: Indian Rights Association, 1887.

———. *A Visit to the Mission Indians of Southern California and Other Western Tribes*. Philadelphia: Office of the Indian Rights Association, 1886.

Parker, Horace. *The Historic Valley of Temecula: The Temecula Massacre*. Balboa Island, Calif.: Paisano Press, 1971.

———. *The Historic Valley of Temecula: The Treaty of Temecula*. Balboa Island, Calif.: Paisano Press, 1967.

Perez, Robert. *The History of the Cabazon Band of Mission Indians, 1776–1876*. Indio, Calif.: Cabazon Band of Mission Indians, 1999.

Pfaller, Louis. *John McLaughlin: The Man with an Indian Heart*. New York: Vantage Press, 1978.

Philadelphia Medical Times: A Bi-Weekly Journal of Medical and Surgical Science, 1880–1881. Vol. 9. Philadelphia: J. B. Lippincott, 1881.

Phillips, George Harwood. *"Bringing Them under Subjection": California's Tejón Indian Reservation and Beyond, 1852–1864*. Lincoln: University of Nebraska Press, 2004.

———. *Chiefs and Challengers: Indian Resistance and Cooperation in Southern California, 1769–1906*. 2nd ed. Norman: University of Oklahoma Press, 2014.

———. *Indians and Indian Agents: The Origins of the Reservation System in California, 1849–1852*. Norman: University of Oklahoma Press, 1997.

———. *Vineyards and Vaqueros: Indian Labor and the Economic Expansion of Southern California, 1771–1877*. Norman: Arthur H. Clark, 2010.

Prucha, Francis Paul. *American Indian Policy in Crisis: Christian Reformers and the Indian, 1865–1900*. Norman: University of Oklahoma Press, 1976.

———. *Documents of United States Indian Policy: Historical Essays*. Lincoln: University of Nebraska Press, 1990.

———. "A 'Friend of the Indian' in Milwaukee: Mrs. O. J. Hiles and the Wisconsin Indian Association." In *Indian Policy in the United* States, 214–28. Lincoln: University of Nebraska Press, 1981.

———. "Indian Policy Reform and American Protestantism, 1880–1900." In *Indian Policy in the United States: Historical Essays*, 229–51. Lincoln: University of Nebraska Press, 1981.

Quinn, Charles Russell. *The Story of Mission Santa Ysabel*. Downey, Calif.: Elena Quinn, 1964.

Quinn, Charles Russell, and Elena Quinn. *Edward H. Davis and the Indians of the Southwest United States and Northwest Mexico*. Downey, Calif.: Elena Quinn, 1965.

Quinton, Amelia S. "Woman's Work in Solving the Indian Problem." In *Christian Educators in Council: Sixty Addresses by American* Educators, 102–5. New York: Phillips & Hunt, 1884.

Rathbun, Tanya L. "Hail Mary: The Catholic Experience at St. Boniface Indian School." In *Boarding School Blues: Revisiting American Indian Educational Experiences*, 155–73. Lincoln: University of Nebraska Press, 2006.

Rawls, James. *Indians of California: The Changing Image*. Norman: University of Oklahoma Press, 1984.

Read, Nat B. *From Mountain Man to Mayor: Don Benito Wilson, Los Angeles 1841–1878*. Santa Monica, Calif.: Angel City Press, 2008.

Reid, Hiram A. *History of Pasadena*. Pasadena, Calif.: Pasadena History Company, 1896.

Robinson, W. W. *Land in California*. Berkeley: University of California Press, 1948.

Rush, Philip S. *Some Old Ranchos and Adobes*. San Diego: Neyenesch Printers, 1965.

Rust, H. N. "A Fiesta at Warner's Ranch." *Land of Sunshine*, vol. 10, no. 5 (April 1899).

San Diego County Pioneer Families. San Diego: San Diego Historical Society, 1977.

Seymour, Charles F. "Relations between the United States Government and the Mission Indians of Southern California." Master's thesis, University of California, Berkeley, 1906.

Shanahan Jr., Donald G. "Compensation for the Loss of the Aboriginal Lands of the California Indians." *Southern California Quarterly*, vol. 57, no. 3 (Fall 1975): 306–8.

Shaw, Rachel Dayton Shaw. "Evolving Ecoscape: An Environmental and Cultural History of Palm Springs, California and the Agua Caliente Indian Reservation, 1877–1939." PhD diss., University of California, San Diego, 1999.

Shinn, G. Hazen. *Shoshonean Days*. Glendale, Calif.: Arthur H. Clark, 1941.

Shuck, Oscar T., ed. *History of the Bench and Bar of California*. Los Angeles: Commercial Printing, 1901.

Smith, Amy E. "Thomas Robert Bard: Pioneer of Ventura County." Master's thesis, University of Southern California, 1930.

Smith, Wayland H. "In Re. California Indians to Date." *Out West*, vol. 30, no. 2 (February–March 1909): 138–39.

Strong, W. D. *Aboriginal Society in Southern California*. Berkeley: University of California Publications in American Archaeology and Anthropology 26, 1929.

Thompson, Gerald. *Edward F. Beale and the American West*. Albuquerque: University of New Mexico Press, 1983.

Thompson, Mark. *American Character: The Curious Life of Charles Fletcher Lummis and the Rediscovery of the Southwest*. New York: Arcade Publishing, 2001.

Thorne, Tanis C. "The Death of Superintendent Stanley and the Cahuilla Uprising of 1907–12," *Journal of California and Great Basin Anthropology*, vol. 24, no. 2 (2004): 233–58.

———. *El Capitan: Adaptation and Agency on a Southern California Indian Reservation, 1850 to 1937*. Banning, Calif.: Malki-Ballena Press, 2012.

———. "The Mixed Legacy of Mission Indian Agent S. S. Lawson, 1878–1883." *Journal of California and Great Basis Anthropology*, vol. 25, no. 2 (2005): 147–68.

Toler Jr., David L. *Band of Blood: An Ipai Family Story*. San Diego: Sunbelt Publications, 2015.

Trafzer, Clifford E., Matthew Sakiestewa Gilbert, and Lorene Sisquoc, eds. *The Indian School on Magnolia Avenue: Voices and Images from Sherman Institute*. Corvallis: Oregon State University Press, 2012.

Vandever, William. *Mission Indians of California: Report of William Vandever, United States Indian Inspector*. Washington, D.C.: n.p., 1876.

Van Dyke, Theodore S. *The City and County of San Diego. Illustrated and Containing Biographical Sketches of Prominent Men and Pioneers*. San Diego: Leberthon & Taylor, 1888.

Waitman, Leonard B. "Chief Antonio Garra's Insurrection and the Confederation Myth of 1851." In *Brand Book Number 3*, 97–103. San Diego: San Diego Corral of The Westerners, 1973.

Wallace, Grant. "The Exiles of Cupa." *Out West*, vol. 19, no. 1 (July 1903): 25–42.

Wanken, Helen. "'Woman's Sphere' and Indian Reform: The Women's National Indian Association, 1879–1901." PhD diss., Marquette University, 1981.

Watkins, Francis. "C. F. Lummis and the Sequoya League." *Quarterly Publication of the Historical Society of Southern California*, vol. 26, no. 2–3 (June/September 1944): 99–114.

Weber, Rev. Francis J., ed. "Rumblings at Pala." *Journal of San Diego History*, vol. 21, no. 4 (Fall 1975): 38–42.

Wetmore, Charles. *Report of Chas. A. Wetmore, Special U.S. Commissioner of Mission Indians of Southern California*. Washington, D.C.: Government Printing Office, 1875.

Williams, C. C. *Congressional Career of the Hon. H. F. Page: A Sketch*. San Francisco: Francis, Valentine, 1880.

Williamson, Steve. "The Missing Link: The Source of the Golsh Nobility." *The High Country*, no. 77 (Spring 2010): 36–46.

Wilson, B. D. *The Indians of Southern California in 1852: The B. D. Wilson Report and a Selection of Contemporary Comment*. Edited by John Walton Caughey with introduction by Albert L. Hurtado. Lincoln: University of Nebraska Press, 1995.

Woman's Who's Who of America: A Biographical Dictionary of Contemporary Women of the United States and Canada, 1914–1915. New York: The American Commonwealth Company, 1914.

Women's National Indian Association. *Annual Report of the WNIA*. Philadelphia: WNIA, December 1892 (various reports cited).

———. *The Indian's Friend*. Philadelphia: WNIA (various issues cited).

——. *Missions of the Women's National Indian Association for 1895*. Philadelphia: WNIA, 1895.

——. *Our Missionary Report for 1897*. Philadelphia: WNIA, 1897.

——. *Sunshine Work*. Philadelphia: WNIA, December 1894.

Interviews

Nolasquez, Roscinda, interviewed by Phil Brigandi. July 12, 1978–Feb. 17, 1986, Pala, California.

INDEX